CHANGING CHRISTIAN PARADIGMS

AND THEIR IMPLICATIONS FOR MODERN THOUGHT

BY

CRAWFORD KNOX

E.J. BRILL

LEIDEN • NEW YORK • KÖLN

1993

The paper in this book meets the guidelines for permanence and durability of the Committee on Production Guidelines for Book Longevity of the Council on Library Resources.

BT
22
.K66
1993

Library of Congress Cataloging-in-Publication Data

Knox, Crawford.
    Changing Christian paradigms and their implications for modern thought / by Crawford Knox.
        p.   cm.—(Studies in the history of religions, ISSN 0169-8834; v. 57)
    Includes bibliographical references and index.
    ISBN 9004096701 (alk. paper)
    1. Theology, Doctrinal—History.   I. Title.   II. Series.
BT22.K66   1993
231.7—dc20
                                                                    92-39189
                                                                        CIP

ISSN   0169-8834
ISBN   90 04 09670 1

PRINTED IN THE NETHERLANDS

CHANGING CHRISTIAN PARADIGMS

STUDIES

IN THE HISTORY OF RELIGIONS

(*NUMEN* BOOKSERIES)

EDITED BY

H.G. KIPPENBERG • E.T. LAWSON

VOLUME LVII

To the memory of Amanda

I am the Alpha and the Omega, the beginning and the end.
I will give unto him that is athirst of the fountain of the water of life freely.
He that overcometh shall inherit all things;
and I will be his God , and he shall be my son.

Rev. 21 6-7

CONTENTS

PART II

GOD AND THE WORLD: SOME IMPLICATIONS OF THE CHANGES BETWEEN BIBLICAL AND EARLY CHURCH IDEAS AND THOSE OF THE WEST

PART III

GOD AND THE WORLD: CONFIRMATION OF BIBLICAL AND EARLY CHURCH IDEAS IN MODERN SCIENCE AND THEIR RELEVANCE TO SURVIVAL OF DEATH AND JESUS CHRIST

PREFACE

That this is a book about theology, religion and God will be obvious even to the most cursory browser. But any such description of it at once imports the Western understanding that separates theology from science; the religious from the secular; supernatural from natural; faith from reason; and physical from mental and spiritual. We shall find good reasons to question such separation which was not a feature of the Old and New Testaments and the early Church. What is more, for reasons that we shall explore, Western Christianity has been deeply concerned to keep our understanding of God separated from our understanding of the world. So while God has been seen as creating, sustaining and in some circumstances intervening in the world, his life has been regarded as essentially separate from the world. Even when it is accepted that in some sense God must be present in the world, any suggestion that the world is an intrinsic feature of his life; that in some sense the world can be viewed as the 'body' of God; that the energy that constitutes the physical world is in some sense an intrinsic feature of the nature of God: any such ideas have been shunned with the deepest abhorrence as 'pantheistic', and as compromising the inherent freedom of God. As for the nature of that freedom, since mediaeval times this has been seen as freedom to *choose* and, in particular, to choose whether, and in what form, to create the world and intervene in it. Yet these, too, were not the understandings of the early Church for which belief in the mutual indwelling of God and the world and in growth 'in' Christ — the order and reason of God — was fundamental. In contrast to the Western understandings, which we shall find open to serious question, these early understandings prove, not only to be remarkably coherent, but, as we shall show, to be in line with modern science, so forming a largely empirically falsifiable whole.

How these Western understandings came to take a form so different from those of the early Church, we shall explore, and in so doing, we shall find the role of Augustine was fundamental. Not surprisingly, we shall find, also, that these Western understandings have carried through into our current understanding of God. And, as belief in God has faded, such understandings have also shaped the framework of thought, the paradigm, out of which has grown, and which still underlies, the materialist understanding of what was left of the world when God was evacuated from it. Any examination of these understandings therefore raises very far-reaching issues. In particular, it raises the question whether the very form and nature of this world can be understood as in some sense flowing from the creative but entirely free nature of God, or whether, if God plays any role at all, the world needs to be seen, as in current understandings, as the product of his free *choice*, in some way distinguished from his nature. As we shall find also, that the character of the world in some way flows from the nature of God, entails that fundamental features of modern science flow also from his nature.

Thus we shall find grounds for suggesting that, given the nature of God as conceived by the early Church, this world *had* to be an evolutionary world grounded in quantum physics, that necessity flowing not from any external constraint on God but from the constraints of self-consistency on his entirely free nature. What is more, we shall find that the very purpose of religion as seen in such a context, was not so much to foster the morality of man as to foster his personal development towards wholeness and maturity as the form taken by the higher reaches of the evolutionary process of growth into the life of God. To describe this book as concerned with theology, religion and God is, therefore, true; but its implications extend, not only into areas which are now the autonomous preserves of philosophy and the sciences, but into areas beyond even their reach, including psychic phenomena and survival of death which have virtually no place in current thought.

Despite the radical nature of these claims, the understanding of the Christian faith that emerges in this book proves to be profoundly traditional, finding strong support from empirical evidence for doctrinal claims that many modern theologians have abandoned. As it seeks to show, any problems with such doctrines, at any rate as understood by the early Church, have lain less with the doctrines themselves than with the changing frameworks of thought — the paradigms — within which they have subsequently been viewed.

Not surprisingly, in view of its scope, this book has been developed over a number of years. Some of its ideas were presented in rudimentary form as long ago as 1956 in *The Idiom of Contemporary Thought* which was subsequently republished in the USA but has long since been lost to sight.

The argument of the present book was fundamentally advanced by the research that I was able to undertake over some years at Oxford University in the Department of Theology. I owe a deep debt to the University, the Department of Theology and, in particular, to Professor Basil Mitchell, then Nolloth Professor of the Philosophy of the Christian Religion in the University of Oxford, for guidance that he gave me. I also had much help, especially in Patristics, from Professor Maurice Wiles, then the Regius Professor of Divinity. It is doubtful whether this book could have seen the light of day but for their assistance and encouragment: though in no way can they be held responsible for its claims. I owe much to many others, too, especially Margaret Yee and Caroline Franks Davis.

I have learned much from a long series of Consultations on Science and Religion held at St George's House, Windsor Castle, under the guidance of Canon Derek Stanesby, to which I was first invited by the then Dean,

Bishop Michael Mann.   My debt, however, is not just for what I have learned at them, but for the friendship and encouragment that I found there.

Not surprisingly, there have been many others to whom my debt is great, Thus I owed much to Professor Sir Alister Hardy and was privileged at one time to be able to make some contribution to his work by serving as a member of the Council, a Trustee and hon Treasurer of the Religious Experience Research Unit which he founded in Oxford.   My own experiences have been enriched and informed by my membership of the Council of the Society for Psychical Research.   In earlier years, I owed much to the London Library; and, over much of my life, to *The Times Literary Supplement* which has helped me to keep abreast in the many disciplines in which I was not expert but on which my work impinged. Above all, I owe a deep debt to my family and, in particular, to my wife, Amanda, who sadly did not live to see this book published.

Naturally, the book raises far more questions than it answers and the most that I can hope is that it will encourage others to pursue them.   I retain the hope that I may be able to write a version of it more accessible to everyman, and that I may be able to develop further the deep implications that it holds in the areas of ethics and the social sciences.

Burrow Wood
East Hill
Ottery St Mary
Devon

CHAPTER ONE

THE PROBLEM THAT WE FACE

That major features of Western Civilisation are becoming established in all parts of the world and are changing or displacing traditional cultures, is obvious: that Western Civilisation is itself changing rapidly and has in many respects lost its sense of direction, is hardly less obvious. The fact that informed observers can reach radically different conclusions about the nature of that loss of direction and about what might be done about it, is itself a sign, not only of the complexity of Western Civilisation but also of the increasingly fragmented judgements and values embedded in it. In the absence of a deeper, more coherent view, more comprehensive, longer term aims are largely lacking. As for the question whether this world is all there is or whether it is some form of preparation for another that lies beyond the grave, notwithstanding that it confronts each of us when we face our own or others' deaths, it is seemingly hardly open to debate and even the responses of the Churches are embarrassedly muted.

These uncertainties and confusions are reflected in many other aspects of Western religions whose uncertainties and confusions have themselves contributed to and underlie the wider scene. Not surprisingly, therefore, institutional religion has become increasingly irrelevant to Western culture, despite its continuing importance in many areas and to many groups of people.

It is, therefore, desirable to set out, but not to seek to justify at this point, one central theme of this study. Both within and without the Western Churches today, men and women, if and when they think of God, tend to think of him as in some sense 'a person' 'outside' the world; of God being quite other than the world; and of God's main concern with the world being essentially moral. In contrast, the early Church thought of the world as in a sense embedded in and as an integral feature of the life of God which, though veiled from it, none the less embraced and was present in and structured it; of the world having to grow and develop (evolve) to participate in the Divine life; and of man doing so by becoming a more ordered, whole, mature person who thereby became more rational, caring and holy. Though to grow in this way, man had to become morally purer, for this was seen both as a prerequisite and a consequence of such development, this was not an end in itself. The process towards attaining such a state of wholeness, at any rate in its higher reaches, was *gnosis* (which must not be confused with the amalgam of beliefs and superstition which threatened the early Church and is known as Gnosticism).

Gnosis is, of course, 'knowledge', but what was entailed here was not adding facts or skills but deepening insights which could not be commanded or learned but which, in a long sequence of conceptual leaps extending throughout life, 'came to' a person. The essential points to appreciate on this are that such deepening insights into the nature of this life are found in all aspects of creative work and thought and have themselves an ordering, deepening, widening and integrating effect upon the very structure of the mind, so leading towards wholeness and maturity; and in the early Church, this process was seen in terms of increasing participation in, and so manifestation of, the order and reason of the Divine life which was the realm of the divine Word, Logos, the Son or Divine Christ. This process was seen also as inseparable from openness to the love and guidance of the Holy Spirit and the holiness of God the Father and their manifestation in men's lives. This participation in the life of God, which is central to the teaching of Paul, was regarded as what really mattered in the eyes of God — not morals as such — though morality was seen as of great importance as a precondition and consequence of such growth, and was emphasised accordingly.

Even at this point, it needs to be stressed that such a view of growth and development of the personality, and, indeed, of creation as a whole, by participation in the order and reason of the life of God, is not pantheistic; and we shall find that it has large implications for psychology, for science generally, for education, for ethics and for politics, as well as entailing a quite different view of the scope and purpose of religion from that prevalent today. What is more, as we shall see, it implies that the sharp division that prevails in current thought between God and the world, religion and science, faith and reason, is a 'conceptual artefact', a product of the way in which we have come to see God and the world, which has developed as an implication of changes in our understanding which have taken place over the centuries.

Though many more people than is generally realised not only still believe in God but have a deep sense of his guiding presence in their lives, the widespread tendency of our current Western secular culture to regard God as an optional extra to its life has developed from an earlier step by which devout men, in an effort to exalt God, came to see the world as an optional extra for God. This in turn was but one step in the much longer process of conceptual change from the highly integrated understanding of God and the world which took form in the New Testament and in the thinking of the early Church. One of the purposes of this book is to trace, albeit in a very incomplete way, some of the salient features of this process of change and so how we have attained our present state; and what we have lost in the process.

As we shall see, therefore, perhaps the most remarkable, and perhaps the most startling feature in all this has been the way in which theological understanding of the relationship of God to the world, with all that this entails, has gradually but steadily drifted away from that of the Old and New Testaments and early Church, while still claiming the closest adherence to and dependence on them. A sketch of these developments forms the first main part of this book and necessarily raises large questions about how far the Western churches can still claim to speak with the authentic voice of Christ.

More specifically, we shall see something of how, as this conceptual separation proceeded, the implications of the changing picture at each stage led to changes of understanding and perspective to keep the framework of thought — or succession of frameworks — broadly coherent. But we shall also find evidences of incoherence and conflict within these changing theological understandings that have been widely disregarded. The exploration of some specific areas of change forms the second part of this book.

Perhaps the most important issue raised in these two parts is, therefore, whether, in keeping with the thinking of the New Testament and the early Church, we should understand the world as in some sense 'within' the life of God — of God enclosing, not enclosed — while still recognising his transcendence: or whether, with the Western Church since that time, we need to think of the world as 'outside' God — of creation *ad extra*. We shall find that this change was far from just a change of words: it entailed changes in the framework of men's thought, of paradigms, which carried profound implications which now lie at the very heart of our current way of thinking. In particular, it opened the way for the gradual conceptual separation of ideas of God in heaven from the world below and for the rejection of the strong New Testament theme of the mutual indwelling of man in God and God in man — the idea of participation in the life of God — which is still a feature of Eastern Orthodox belief.

This separation is greatly stressed by many Western theologians who are anxious to emphasise the difference between God and the world; yet, as we shall see, such difference does not require separation. Obviously, it is easier to think of God as a 'person' if we think of him as 'outside' the world than if we think of the world as in some sense evolving 'within' his life. Also, if we think of God as 'a person', it is a lot easier to think of him as having power to 'choose' to do anything whatever: yet this was not the earlier understanding in which the freedom of God was freedom to express his own unchanging nature. Of course, in no understanding of the Christian God can he be thought of as impersonal. Any Christian must think of God as having such attributes as love, reason and power and as in some sense personally seeking to create, develop, sustain and redeem the world as a whole and each individual person within it. Suffice at this point to say, however, that a distinction needs to be drawn between thinking of God as 'personal' and thinking of him as 'a person'.

This is a distinction that has not been recognised by many theologians in recent times. Austin Farrer commented that: 'One of the silliest of all discussions is whether God is personal — it would be as useful to enquire whether ice is frozen. The theological question is ... whether the world depends on a supreme creative will; and that is the same thing as supreme person.'[1] And Richard Swinburne sets out as a premiss of his book 'The Existence of God, one of his three volumes on the philosophy of religion, the following definition: 'I take the proposition "God exists" (and the equivalent proposition "there is a God") to be logically equivalent to "there exists a person without a body (ie a spirit) who is eternal, is perfectly free, omnipotent, omniscient, perfectly good and the creator of all things." I use "God" as the name of the person picked out by this description.'[2]

On the other hand, Paul Tillich remarks that 'Personal God' does not mean that God is a person and he adds that 'God became a person only in the nineteenth century, in connection with the Kantian separation of nature ruled by physical law from personality ruled by moral law. Ordinary theism has made God a heavenly, completely perfect person who resides above the world and mankind. The protest of atheism against such a highest person is correct. There is no evidence for his existence, nor is he a matter of ultimate concern. God is not God without universal participation. "Personal God" is a confusing symbol.'[3] And elsewhere Tillich says: 'We can say it was the nineteenth century that made God into a person, with the result that the greatness of the classical idea of God was destroyed by this way of speaking.[4] None the less, as we have seen, many recent theologians and philosophers of religion as well as many others have built their understanding of and reasoning about God and his relation to the world around this picture of God as 'a person'.

The conceptual separation of God and the world had, of course, many other implications. Thus it led to the loss of the understanding of the early Church that the ultimate concern of God was to enable man to develop into the order and reason of his life to share it with him. For this was substituted the idea that God had created man perfect, that man had sinned morally and

---

[1] *Saving Belief* (1964) p 30

[2] *The Existence of God* (1979) p 8

[3] *Systematic Theology* (1953) vol 1   p 271

[4] *A History of Christian Thought* (1968) p 190

that the ultimate purpose of God was to restore man to that state of full morality. This emphasis on morality in the Western Churches is well brought out in one contribution to *Cosmology and Theology*.[5] This is an essay by Bishop Tshishiku, where he summarises by reference to Denzinger, the authoritative statement of such teachings, the beliefs of the Roman Catholic Church about what is ultimately important in the eyes of God — the basis of his judgement of each person on death. 'Once death has occurred, the person appears before God's judgement, which takes place immediately. The recompense due for the total of a person's deeds, reward or punishment, is then declared. In theory, the soul of the person found pure and perfect is admitted immediately to the presence of God in heaven. ... In fact, in most cases souls, being stained by at least minor impurities, by what are called venial sins, are not allowed to enter heaven immediately. They pass through a preliminary stage of purification known as "purgatory". On the other hand, when the dead person's soul is found to be stained with serious moral faults, mortal sin, "a radical rejection of God", it is punished by hell.'[6]

A quotation from Cardinal Newman shows how far these beliefs have been pressed: 'The Church holds that it were better for the sun and the moon to drop from Heaven, for the earth to fail, and for all the millions who are upon it to die of starvation in extremest agony ... than that one soul ... should commit one single venial sin, should tell one wilful untruth though it harmed no one, or steal one poor farthing without excuse.'[7]

It is important and relevant to contrast these Western views with findings of psychotherapists, whatever their persuasion. These findings bear a close relationship to those of the early Church, though what is seen by psychotherapists as a realisation of man's innate potentialities would have been seen by the early Fathers as deriving from and manifesting the attributes of life in God. Anthony Storr comments that psychotherapists concur in valuing the human personality highly, and, however much they differ about the process of development, they also agree *that the personality is an achievement, not simply a datum of ethics*. 'To be oneself, to realise one's own personality to its fullest extent, *is to develop from childhood to maturity;* and every psychotherapeutic system is concerned with this development.' He calls this final achievement self-realisation, by which he means *the fullest possible expression in life of the innate potentialities of the individual*, the realisation of his own uniqueness as a personality: and he

---

[5] D Tracy and N Lash eds (1983) pp 27-34

[6] *op cit*   (1983) p 28

[7] *Difficulties felt by Anglicans*   (1850)   p 199

also puts forward the hypothesis that, consciously or unconsciously, every man is seeking this goal. (My italics)[8] Storr emphasises both that *such self-realisation entails the attainment of a mature relationship with others, and that subjectively, 'it seems to be attended by a sense of being fully adapted to, rather than attempting entirely to direct, the course of one's own development'*. This latter attitude, he notes, is, in the wide sense in which Jung uses the term, religious: 'for it implies that the individual is acknowledging his ultimate dependence upon forces which may be depicted as either inside or outside himself, but which are nevertheless *not of his making.'* (my italics) And Storr quotes Hamlet v 2 'There's a divinity that shapes our ends, rough-hew them how we will.'[9]

It was the conceptual separation of God and the world, and which came to imply the evacuation of God from the world, that opened the way for the world to be understood as primarily physical, governed by physical laws, and so for mind to be seen as an anomalous by-product of it, strictly localised in human heads. In contrast, the earlier view implied that the entire processes of the physical world are but one feature of some dynamic spiritual realm that we may for convenience call the mind of God. That, for most professional philosophers, for many scientists, and even, it seems, for most theologians, is not now seen as a viable option: it is literally inconceiveable. It will be revealing in the course of this study to see how changes in the framework of Western thought have made this so: for current Western philosophy and science have developed within this changing framework of thought — the framework is not primarily the product of these disciplines, though there has, of course, been constant feedback.

The critical question to which this gives rise, and which is mainly the concern of the third part of the book, is whether such later knowledge, and in particular, the evidence of science, can find a coherent place within the earlier perspective and in a form that would lay even theological claims open to falsification if empirical evidence so demanded. As we shall see, any such idea is likely to be rejected out of hand by most modern theologians, some of whom take great satisfaction from the fact that their understanding of God is not open to such falsification. They see this as happy evidence of the conceptual gulf that they find between God and the world and of its utter dependence on his unfettered choice. As one distinguished modern theologian, Eric Mascall, says: 'Interesting as they undoubtedly are in themselves, cosmological theories as such are of no ultimate theological importance. ... Whether the universe had an infinite past or not, the theist will insist that its existence is due to an extra temporal act freely exercised

---

[8] *The Integrity of the Personality* (1963) pp 26-7

[9] *op cit* pp 174-5

by a transcendent God.'[10] — a view which will lead us into some fundamental issues in theology.

Directly related to this view, but as seen from the other side of the conceptual gap, is the dismissal of all religious claims as 'metaphysical'. This separation of religion and science and of our understanding of God and the world was crystallised as long ago as 1936 by A J Ayer in his significant and influential book, *Language, Truth and Logic*. He there defined a metaphysical sentence as a sentence which purports to express a genuine proposition, but does, in fact, express neither a tautology nor an empirical hypothesis. Ayer concluded that all such metaphysical assertions are nonsensical and he included religious knowledge as metaphysical.[11] Intensive discussion and considerable changes in the prevailing philosophical ethos since then have significantly modified that claim. Metaphysics is no longer a pejorative term in many circles, not least because it has been found in the heart of philosophy, including in Ayer's claim itself; and the recognition of the contextual and cultural dependence of scientific understanding, notably as a result of the work of Thomas Kuhn, has done much to soften the contrast seen by Ayer. Current analyses of the status of religious belief, such as that of Basil Mitchell,[12] now have an elegance and subtlety that make such simple distinctions between religion and science seem very dated. Yet the broad distinction pointed to by Ayer appears still to be recognised and, indeed, to be taken for granted by most modern philosophers and theologians: and the difficulty of pointing to any unambigous empirical implications of theological statements seems to be widely accepted. Thus K Nielsen, writing as a philosopher of religion, records Ayer's remark that it is now generally agreed that what Jews and Christians call 'God' can neither be demonstratively proved to exist nor do we have good inductive arguments which would justify our asserting that there probably is such a reality: and Nielsen adds: 'Here, along with .... nearly everyone ... who has examined the subject closely, he is on safe and rather uncontroversial ground.'[13] Just how theology itself prepared the way for such a view, thereby drifting far from earlier understandings, will emerge in due course, for, as G R Evans noted, 'No technical terminology changes more subtly and elusively in meaning from generation to generation than that of the theologian.'[14] As we shall see, many of these changes have been

---

[10] *Christian Theology and Natural Science* (1956) pp 161-2

[11] *Language Truth and Logic* 2nd edn (1950) pp 41 and 116

[12] B Mitchell *The Justification of Religious Belief* (1973)

[13] *Contemporary Critiques of Religion* (1971) p 19

[14] *Augustine on Evil* (1982) p ix

cumulative. And, naturally, squeezed between the pejorative view of metaphysics and the spreading empirical fields of science, the role of philosophy has itself been greatly restricted.

It is true that in the last few years philosophy has gradually again become rather more ambitious. But in many academic minds the view still prevails that metaphysical studies should be much more modest than they have been in the past: a view epitomised by Rom Harré when he said that 'No one of any discretion writes about the universe, man and God.'[15] However, in a concern to be modest and limit our conceptual commitments, we formulate our ideas within a largely unconscious conceptual framework that might not bear open scrutiny. As will emerge in the course of this study, we do not avoid metaphysical commitments by ignoring them. Similarly, because current understandings of science include a large element of interpretation, such interpretations themselves reflect the materialist framework of thought within which they have been formulated. Yet our current materialist paradigm is not a necessary way of viewing the world; for all such paradigms — like scientific hypotheses, as Mary Hesse has pointed out — are underdetermined by the evidence;[16] and, as we have already noted, that materialist paradigm came about as what was left when, for reasons at least as much theological as secular, God was conceptually evacuated from the world. In the third part of this study, we shall find some of the ways in which fundamental empirical findings of science corroborate the earlier theological understandings.

Our materialist view of the world has a direct bearing also on another basic feature of current thought. That there is a one-to-one correlation between mental and physical events in the brain, with brain having priority, is simply taken for granted by those working in the relevant fields of science. D O Hebb, in his classic book *The Organisation of Behaviour*, noted that 'Modern science takes completely for granted that behaviour and neural function are perfectly correlated, that one is completely caused by the other. There is no separate soul or life-force to stick a finger into the brain now and then to make the neural cells do what they would not otherwise.' Though he added that this was a working assumption only.[17] This reservation is, however, often not observed and strong movements in philosophy in recent years have sought to explain mind in entirely physical terms. Such a view was starkly put by D M Armstrong in his influential book *A Materialist Theory of Mind*, where he said that 'There are no good philosophical reasons for denying that mental processes are purely physical

---

[15] *The Philosophies of Science* (1972) p 8

[16] *The Structure of Scientific Inference* (1974) e g p 393

[17] *op cit* (1949) p xiii

processes in the central nervous system and so, by implication, that there are no good philosophical reasons for denying that man is nothing but a material object.'[18]

This understanding is reflected in the impoverished view of mind held by many modern philosophers and psychologists. Iris Murdoch describes it thus: '"Reality" is potentially open to different observers. What is "inward", what lies between overt actions, is either impersonal thought, or "shadows" of acts, or else substanceless dream. Mental life is, and logically must be, a shadow of life in public. Our personal being is the movement of our overtly choosing will. Immense care is taken to picture the will as isolated. It is isolated from belief, from reason, from feeling, and yet is the essential centre of the self. "I identify myself with my will"'[19] Not surprisingly, this view of mind finds parallels in the current view of God, in which great emphasis is placed on his autonomous will and the omnipotent power seen as associated with it. We shall see in this study a very different view which better allows for the ordered plenitude of God and the potential depth and wholeness of men's minds, their creativity and richness — views which, as we shall see, have much in common with those of a respected and original modern philosopher, Thomas Nagel.

That this current framework of thought did not spring forth ready-made, like Athena from the head of Zeus, is, of course, obvious. It is the outcome of a long process of development in which, as we trace it back, we find men's present deeply separated understandings of God and the world becoming more and more completely integrated, with greater emphasis being given to his immediate presence and immanence without in any way detracting from his transcendence. As long ago as 1883 Ernst Mach pointed out that an undue preoccupation with the conflict between science and theology could be extremely misleading because, in his considered opinion, many of the conceptions 'which completely dominate modern physics' actually arose under the influence of theological ideas.[20] This is a claim for which we shall find strong substantiation.

What was involved, we shall find, was changes in the framework of thought, with the conceptual consequences which flowed from them. Within the perspective of current understandings of God and the world, it is, therefore, perhaps not surprising that earlier understandings have become incomprehensible even to many theologians. This will emerge clearly when we come to consider their bafflement when faced with the very important

---

[18] *A Materialist Theory of Mind*   (1968)   p 2

[19] *The Sovereignty of the Good*   (1970)   pp 7-8

[20] see F Oakley Christian Theology and the Newtonian Science in *Creation: the Impact of an Idea*   ed D O'Connor and F Oakley   (1969)   p 81

New Testament theme of life 'in' Christ. As E P Sanders, a New Testament scholar on whose work we shall rely heavily in some later pages, exclaims: 'But what does it mean? How are we to understand it? We seem to lack a category of "reality" — real participation in Christ, real possession of the Spirit — which lies between naive cosmological speculation and belief in magical transference on the one hand and a revised self-understanding on the other.' But he adds: 'The realism of Paul's view indicates that he had one.'[21]

If we are to give full weight to these differences in conceptual framework, we need to understand their power of conditioning not just what we think but even what we notice in the world around us. In his book *Witchcraft, Oracles and Magic amongst the Azande,* Sir Edward Evans-Pritchard showed how the Azande understood the world in terms of a mesh, a lattice or framework of ideas or concepts, each of which was linked with others and which together formed a conceptual system or, to use a term employed by Thomas Kuhn, a paradigm.[22] Thus as Evans-Pritchard said, 'They reason excellently in the idiom of their beliefs but they cannot reason outside or against their beliefs because they have no other idiom in which to express their thoughts.'[23] And in similar vein he said, 'In this web of belief every strand depends on every other strand, and the Zande cannot get out of its meshes because it is the only world he knows. The web is not an external structure in which he is enclosed. It is the texture of his thought and he cannot think his thought is wrong.'[24] The Azande were not, of course, in this respect unique. Though the ideas that make up these webs and frameworks vary greatly from culture to culture and in detail from person to person, every person in every culture has such a web or conceptual framework — a model — in terms of which he sees the world. Because, however, it is so basic to his every thought, providing it with meaning, it is largely unrecognised as such and is accepted for the most part uncritically: yet, as we shall see, it moulds his thoughts and determines not only what he sees as important and unimportant but what he notices and fails to notice. Of course, men have always from time to time noticed new aspects of the world in which they live and have questioned their beliefs, but no man can question all his beliefs at once. We all need such an unquestioned base from which to question. As von Neurath said in another context, we seek to repair the ship at sea, one plank at a time.

---

[21] *Paul and Palestinian Judaism* (1977) p 522-3

[22] *The Structure of Scientific Revolutions* 2nd edn (1970)

[23] *Witchcraft, Oracles and Magic among the Azande* (1937) p 338

[24] *op cit* pp 194-5

These conceptual frameworks have their counterparts in the structure of the minds — and more specifically, the memories — of those who hold them. This was noted by Erich Neumann when he said that 'The integration of the personality is equivalent to an integration of the world. Just as an uncentred psyche which is dispersed in participations sees only a diffuse and chaotic world, so the world constellates in a hierarchical order about the integrated personality. This correspondence between one's view of the world and the formation of the personality extends from the lowest level to the highest.'[25] In other words, whole, mature minds tend to discern the unified order underlying the world, its wonder and its beauty: divided minds tend to have a more limited view and to find in the'wider scene a more or less meaningless disorder. And similarly, in so far as a culture or church offers a more rational and unified view of the world, it tends to produce more mature minds within it, whereas a culture or church which has a fragmented view of the world tends to produce divided minds which, whether they recognise it or not, have a deep spiritual hunger. We shall find later in this study the profound significance of these claims for the mental and spiritual health of individuals and society. We shall also find how the work of Jean Piaget has cast light on the manner in which such conceptual frameworks or models develop to form both our ways of looking at the world and our personalities. In particular, we shall find that great importance attaches to the openness of mind necessary for the leaps of conceptual insight which lie at the heart of all creative thinking, of spiritual growth and of psychological development of the personality at all stages from infancy to its potential culmination in maturity, wholeness and integrity. This was the developmental process that lay at the heart of the faith of earlier Christians and their predecessors.

As one feature of our current paradigm and underlying the consensus that exists about the 'metaphysical' status of belief in God, we shall find that there is seemingly a consensus about the kind of 'picture' of reality in terms of which it is appropriate to think about God and his relationship to the world. This 'picture' of God as a 'person' outside the world and of the world as primarily physical, underlies and in many ways determines the relationship and the logic of the concepts. The importance of such 'pictures' has, perhaps, not yet been fully appreciated. It arises because many, perhaps most, of our concepts, particularly very abstract concepts, carry a range of meanings. The meaning appropriate to any particular application tends to be determined by the context in which it is being used and the context tends to be structured by 'pictures' in our minds, albeit hazy. Iris Murdoch comments that 'Plato is right to exclaim (Timaeus 47b) that sight (vision)

---

[25] *The Origin and History of Consciousness* (1954) p 359

is our greatest blessing, without which we would not reach philosophy. Our ability to use visual structures to understand non-visual structures (as well as other different visual ones) is fundamental to explanation in any field.'[26] In 1945 Jacques Hadamard inquired among American mathematicians about their working methods and produced the striking conclusion that, with only two exceptions, they tackled their problems neither in words nor in mathematical symbols but in vague, rather hazy visual imagery.[27] More recently Richard Rorty has claimed that 'It is pictures rather than propositions, metaphors rather than statements, which determine most of our philosophical convictions.'[28] He has sought to show how one such picture has dominated philosophy since the time of Descartes: a picture that is only now coming into serious question. That there should be a particular and influential picture of the relationship of God to the world that pervades current thinking on these issues and holds it in thrall and that it is not the only possible, or even the most appropriate way of viewing it, may thus become conceivable.

Today, so firmly is our thought embedded in materialist preconceptions, that this is a change the implications of which can hardly even be sensed by most people, many of whom find it almost inconceiveable that wise and learned men and women of other ages and cultures should not share this way of viewing the world. Yet such people were no more stupid or irrational than we are. To use Evans-Pritchard's words, 'they reasoned excellently in the idiom of their beliefs.' They saw broadly the same world as we do but, in a different conceptual context, different aspects of experience had different significance. It was partly a question of 'handling the same bundle of data as before, but placing them in a new system of relations with one another by giving them a different framework.'[29] But more is entailed, for, as will emerge more clearly in due course, our own framework of thought has moved so far that whole areas — whole depths — of experience have no rational place within its materialist perspective: indeed, an issue so central as the relationship of body to mind has found no widely accepted place within it. Thus though mind is usually seen as a by-product of the physical, yet, as will emerge presently, this idea, however obvious it may seem, is paradoxical and is, indeed, itself 'metaphysical' in that we can seek to verify or falsify it only by the further use of mind: and, of course, if there is survival of death, a belief that is fundamental to the Christian faith

---

[26] *The Fire and the Sun*   (1977)   pp 67-8

[27] *The Psychology of Invention in the Mathematical Field*   (1949)

[28] *Philosophy and the Mirror of Nature*   (1980)   p 12

[29] H Butterfield   *The Origins of Modern Science 1300-1800*   (1949) p 1

and which has been accepted as obvious by most people in most cultures throughout history, not only must the assumption that mind is entirely the by-product of the physical be wrong, but the lack of any natural conceptual home within our framework of thought for such an idea will in the course of this study become a conspicuous lacuna.

Among theologians, the problems that they face are clear. The tensions are graphically and poignantly described by Frances Young: 'So I find myself driven to tell two stories, to think in terms of two models, which cannot be fitted together in a literal way or spelled out in relation to one another, but in some sense reflect both the "scientific" model of the world which my culture forces upon me and the "mythological" model from which my religious faith cannot escape.'[30] For all but a few, like Frances Young herself, the separation of the world, and, in particular, the mind from the plenitude of the divine represents a profound impoverishment.

In these circumstances, it is hardly surprising that under the influence of modern theological liberalism, there has been a determined effort to dilute what, for earlier generations, had been radical Christian claims — 'a stumbling block to the Jews and folly to the Gentiles' (1 Cor. 1 23) — to make them acceptable to as many people as possible, regardless of their preconceptions, education or culture. As the Doctrine Commission of the Church of England said in 1987, the Church should not attempt 'a doctrinal definition to which all can consent, for some would always be unable to assent and would then risk being "unchurched".' Not surprisingly, in this process, in much religious as in secular life, any belief in absolute truths and values has become deeply unfashionable. As D E Nineham said in 1976, the task of doctrinal theology 'means removing all unnecessary obstacles to the acceptance of faith, which have arisen simply as a result of cultural change, and relieving us of any necessity to "believe what we know cannot possibly be true".... It will be evident that doctrinal theologians ... cannot expect to find direct or definitive answers to their twentieth century questions in the beliefs and formularies of earlier generations, even the Biblical generations.' And he goes on to note that the story the Christian tells 'will have to be compatible with the rest of his knowledge of reality and appropriate to his cultural situation.'[31] Earlier generations had sought to understand their cultural situation in terms of their religious beliefs: modern relativism turns this on its head. But as Dean Inge once commented 'the Church that is married to the Spirit of the Age will be a widow in the next'.

---

[30] A Cloud of Witnesses in *The Myth of God Incarnate* ed J Hick (1977) p 37

[31] *Christian Believing: a Report by the Doctrine Commission of the Church of England* (1976) pp 87-8

This disinheritance of the Western mind has carried through into virtually all aspects of Western thinking and so into education. Allan Bloom seeks to show in his thought-provoking book, *The Closing of the American Mind*, how many American students and their academic mentors have lost their belief in objective values and how this has led in America to a superficiality and parochialism in much university teaching in the Humanities and Social Sciences. Whereas Greek philosophers related the good to the fulfilment of the whole natural human potential, he shows that the modern approach is to discount the idea that there are great wise men in other places and times who can cast light upon this quest. Instead it tends to see all kinds of men, all life-styles and all ideologies as equally acceptable and has lost faith in its own. Yet the attack on the exclusiveness of particular cultures itself entails an unconscious assertion of the superiority of modern scientific understandings of them. The openness that invites a quest for knowledge and new insights has thus been replaced by the openness of indifference, and what is seen as a great opening of American minds has become a great closing. Indeed, he claims that contempt for the heroic is only an extension of the perversion of the democratic principle that denies greatness and wants everyone to feel comfortable in his skin without having to suffer unpleasant comparisons. The dangers facing Western culture are thus not just fragmentation and evil but triviality. Western man has become a value-creating, not a good-discovering being: and love and striving for truth has been supplanted by emphasis on commitment, intellectual honesty and authenticity; but since they are largely void of content there is little awareness of the cost of achieving these in terms of effort. Bloom sums up his view of the crisis of liberal education as being a reflection of a crisis at the peaks of learning, an incoherence and an incompatibility among the first principles with which we interpret the world, an intellectual crisis of the greatest magnitude, which constitutes the crisis of our civilisation.

Bloom has analysed the form and origins of that crisis as it faces American universities. His account is controversial and is doubtless selective: but it is uncomfortably recognisable. What is more, universities, perhaps particularly in America, are not isolated from society as a whole and America is not isolated from the Western world: their crisis is our crisis. However we view it — as the loss of an awareness of an objective good; that values are to be found, not chosen; that ways of life are not of equal value and are to be lived and developed into, and for that reason not easily chosen; that life is an arduous pilgrimage, not a free bazaar — however we view it, we shall find its roots in the working out of ideas which started far back in history and in the spiritual depths of religion. To understand the crisis that we face, our initial guides must therefore be men and women of earlier times who gained insights that we today have lost.

In a much-quoted saying, Hegel noted that the owl of Minerva flies at dusk — that only when a culture is in decline can we understand it. But the owl returns to Minerva with the dawn. In this book we chart its journey and the wisdom that it bears, starting, not as does Bloom, with the Greeks, but with Israel, as revealed in the Wisdom literature of the Old Testament: for important as the Greeks were, as we shall see, it is primarily from the rise and development of Christianity, channelled above all through St Augustine, that the Western understanding of the world has come. By tracing that rise and development, we shall hope to cast light upon its strengths and on its failings. But our main concern will be to show the case for considering afresh the earlier understanding of the relationship of God to the world and to point to some of its implications.

It is worth at this point listing some of these though any substantiation of them will have to await later pages.

(a) It is a dynamic developmental view entailing, as order evolves and develops in creation as a whole and, in particular, in the human personality, the progressive and cumulative manifestation of life, consciousness, understanding, love and holiness, culminating in the full mystical experience. These are normally seen as in some mysterious way inherent in, or as by-products of, the physical world. Within the picture being presented here, however, they manifest themselves as a result of progressive participation in the plenitude, including the order and reason, of the life of God. This view offers, therefore, one unified conceptual framework for the evolutionary aspects of the physical, biological and social sciences, psychology and theology and has also strong pastoral implications.

(b) On a wider scale it sees the divine process in terms of the evolution of ordered systems: it thus has wide scientific implications.

(c) This developmental process entails learning from the collective wisdom of the groups of which the individual is part; it sees Christianity as *paideia*, the education of man, into the order and reason of God, the Divine Christ, the Way. It has, therefore, strong implications for education, particularly its creative role, and so for society as a whole.

(d) This process of growth and development entails a less egocentric, more outward-looking, objective, rational and caring attitude of concern for others. It has, therefore strong implications for morality and ethics.

(e) It implies an ultimately pre-determined path of development for creation as a whole, for society and for each individual, though one which has constantly to readjust itself to respond to deviations from it. This developmental process entails the spontaneous emergence of self-regulating systems at many levels, including social. To follow this path requires both order and freedom. This requirement of freedom to follow this path entails also freedom to deviate and so to distort the entire process, but always with ultimately self-defeating and often catastrophic results, so that at any one time, creation is the outcome of these constructive and warping forces. This has, *inter alia*, large political implications for it implies that man needs liberty to grow and develop his potentialities yet that only in a very qualified sense can man plan his own destiny.

(f) As a whole, it has large philosophical and religious implications. It implies the intimate and dynamic presence of the divine and so conflicts with materialism and reductionism. It emphasises the potential creative depths of human experience and the need to open the personality to the enlightenment and guidance that these depths offer — a Jungian as well as religious theme which finds empirical support in the findings of the Oxford-based Alister Hardy Religious Experience Research Centre. It thus entails a world in which objective order and value are discovered and realised in it, not created by it.

Because these issues carry such far-reaching implications, the scope of this study is therefore very wide and far-ranging. It attempts to open or re-open a debate rather than determine it. Whether it will succeed in doing so depends upon its readers.

PART I

GOD AND THE WORLD

HOW BIBLICAL AND EARLY CHURCH IDEAS
CHANGED IN THE WEST

CHAPTER TWO

THE OLD TESTAMENT UNDERSTANDING OF THE RELATIONSHIP OF GOD AND THE WORLD

We shall seek in this chapter to sketch the framework of thought which underlay much Old Testament thinking and which, we shall find, remains of profound importance for an understanding of the modern world. It was shared also by the New Testament writers and, in large measure, by the early Church, but was lost to the Western Churches and is far removed from that commonly attributed to the Old Testament in recent years.

The Old Testament is a collection of writings by many different hands and embodying community traditions of very different times and circumstances. As James Barr comments, though the Books are deeply theological in concern and significance, they are not books of theology as such, and this is one reason why they can accommodate inconsistencies and variability that would not be acceptable in a theological treatise.[1] In some parts of the Bible, therefore, 'God is treated rather "anthropomorphically", rather like a human being but of much greater size, power and lastingness.'[2] However, though Israel conceived even Jahweh himself as having human form, according to Old Testament ideas of Jahwism, it cannot be said that Israel regarded God anthropomorphically; she considered man as theomorphic.[3] Indeed, G von Rad speaks of the impressive demonstration by H Gollwitzer that Israel so conceived the encounter between God and man that the use of anthropomorphic language was quite inevitable.[4]

The very fact that Israel was so insistent that no image should be made of God spoke against any simple anthropomorphism, for, as will become clear presently, God was seen, not as manifested in varying degrees in a quasi-autonomous world, but as its creator who was present in its every facet in the most intimate and personal way possible — in a way that totally excluded any dualism between God and the world and, indeed, required an explanation of that dualism within God himself.[5] And because of the very plenitude of God, his ability to spring surprises as events unfolded, did not necessarily imply inconsistencies.

---

[1] *Escaping from Fundamentalism* (1984) p 117

[2] *op cit* p 34

[3] G von Rad *Old Testament Theology* vol 1 (1975) p 145

[4] *The Problem of the Hexateuch and other Essays* (1966) p 149

[5] G von Rad *op cit* p 151

None the less, Barr notes that the interpreter is likely at some point to feel a need for a more final and consistent view of God and that this has been done, as far as it could be done, within all currents of Christianity. Moreover, within the Bible itself this was already being done. 'Already in ancient times it was being felt that the consistency of God demanded that he did not change his mind over his own decisions as so many of the texts say that he did.'[6]

It is necessary, therefore, to stress from the outset that, despite the passages in the Old Testament that suggest otherwise and contrary to widespread Christian misunderstandings, the God of Israel was not generally seen as a distant, arbitrary and forbidding 'person' in his work of creating, ordering, sustaining and guiding the world, but as intimately present and accessible in every aspect of it and as consistent, reasonable, just and caring. For Old Testament man, therefore, the idea of the world as the creation of a God who, though transcendentally mysterious, was always present in it, was fundamental. As Claus Westermann says, the workings of the Creator 'reach into every generation, independent of all people, of race, nation or religion. As long as and wherever there is life, the creator is at work. At the creation, the creator acknowledges that "it was good". Because the word *tōb* means good *and* beautiful, beauty belongs to the creation and is reflected back in praise of the creator.'[7]

There was thus no question of belief in creation. It was a presupposition that there was no reality other than that established by God in which he was personally present and accessible; and since reality without the working of God did not exist for the Old Testament people, what the Old Testament says about God, it says about reality.[8]

In the Western Churches, however, belief in creation has faded into the background of the preaching and theology. As we shall see, God is no longer thought of as personally present in the world but as a distant figure who has somehow materialised a largely physical world outside himself. The prestige of science has led to the dismissal of creation 'myths' and, as we have seen, the Churches have reacted by maintaining that the creation accounts in the Bible have nothing whatever to do with scientific knowledge — that they deal only with religion and belief, and that in any event religion is concerned primarily with 'salvation'.[9] In keeping with this, emphasis has been placed increasingly on man, and the context of God as Creator of the

---

[6] J Barr *op cit* p 36

[7] *What Does the Old Testament say about God?* (1979) p 40

[8] *op cit* p 14

[9] C Westermann *Creation* (1974) p 2

whole of Heaven and earth has lost its meaning. Not surprisingly, therefore, because, following mediaeval thinkers, God has often come to be thought of as infinitely distant from the world and as in some sense having to reach out to intervene in it; because the world has come to be thought of as primarily physical and as largely autonomous; and because the theology and preaching of the Churches have become concerned primarily with salvation of man in this otherwise largely autonomous physical world, the world view of Israel has come to be seen as antiquated and superseded, and the relationship of God to the real everyday world has come increasingly into question. It is, therefore, Israel's concern with its history that has come to be seen as all-important: yet Israel drew no such distinction between nature and history, for it regarded them as one single area of reality under the control of God in which he was present.[10]

Not surprisingly, therefore, the doctrine of creation, namely the belief that God has created and is sustaining the order of the world in all its complexities, is not a peripheral theme of biblical theology but is plainly the fundamental theme. What is more, what Israel experienced in her history and what the early Christian community experienced in relation to Jesus is understood and interpreted in terms of this one basic theme.[11]

The process of creation was seen in the belief of Israel and other early peoples, not as in current thought, in terms of some form of materialisation in a void outside God, but as the struggle between the development and maintenance of order and the omnipresent tendency of order to collapse into chaos. And for Israel and the early Church alike, that chaos was not some quasi-autonomous primordial matter but, as we shall see later, was a feature of the process of creation and so occurred within the life of God. Whereas, however, other Middle Eastern peoples had seen this struggle to establish order in terms of its recurring, cyclic, re-enactment, Israel came to see this activity of God as a long process of historical change as events continuously unfolded: of God creating the world by a process of creating order out of chaos, his choosing of Israel, and his leading of his people through to the final culmination of this ordering process when God's order would reign supreme as his Kingdom. Virtually everything that happened to Israel was interpreted in terms of these fundamental dimensions. There was thus no ultimate dualism of order and chaos, good and evil: chaos and evil came with creation and did not precede it. Evil was the fruit of the freedom that was inherent in the ordering process of creation and so was seen in terms of deviation from and opposition to the ordering process that manifested God's

---

[10] G von Rad *op cit* (1966) p 155

[11] H D Schmid 'Creation, Righteousness and Salvation' in *Creation in the Old Testament* ed B W Anderson (1984) p 111

purpose. Evil had no existence apart from the creation process, and it was destined finally to be overcome when the perfect order of the Kingdom of God prevailed. It is not coincidence that the first and last books of the Bible are concerned with the beginning and end and both are concerned with the establishment of order out of chaos.

As we shall see, this process of building order, yet allowing creation to frustrate and deviate from it, though always with disastrous consequences, has to be seen in the context of a world that is continuously coming into existence and passing out of existence as future becomes present and present becomes past. We today tend to picture the world as in some sense historically as well as spatially present — a picture that takes scientific form in the idea of the 'block universe'. For the Israelites, however, it was the transitoriness of the world that was salient and it was the openness of the future as events unfolded, often unpredictably, that allowed God to work his creative will in mysterious ways and allowed creation to frustrate his intentions. For us the world is largely a physical state, an entity; for the Israelites it was primarily an ordering *process* in which God was personally present.

This emphasis on the ordering by God implies an emphasis on the activity of God and this is basic to an understanding of the Old Testament. We shall find later its widespread relevance, not least in science. The Old Testament is overwhelmingly dominated by verbs. Thinking about God means primarily trying to understand what he has done. As Westermann says: 'In the Old Testament the entirety of the universe is something which happens and only in a secondary sense something which exists'[12] And he comments that the Old Testament does not emphasise the state caused by the saving, i e the "salvation" (*das Heil*), but rather the process of saving. The Old Testament narrates, not a history of salvation, but a history of the saving acts of God.[13]

Yet the working of God in history does not only consist of specific acts. The Old Testament knows at the same time of an equally important continuous working of God, which cannot be comprehended in individual acts and which is called blessing. The whole realm of nature belongs to the working of God as much as does his specific working in history. The blessing of the creator is effective in the movement of the generations of the human race through space and time: it is effective in the ever-constant rhythm of conception, birth and death.[14]

---

[12] *What does the Old Testament say about God?*   (1979) p 42

[13] *op cit*   p 29

[14] *What Does the Old Testament say about God?*   pp 33 and 40

Westermann shows that whereas Genesis 1-11 is meant to be a unity, the Church isolated the first three chapters of Genesis and neglected those following. As a result, it came to be believed that God had created a perfect world and put man in it; that man had been disobedient and fallen; and that he now lives in a different state, the state of fallen man in a fallen creation. The next most important event in the history of mankind was therefore seen to be the decisive act to restore that situation: hence the 'sending' of Jesus Christ and his suffering, death and resurrection. The remainder of history was thus to be seen as being played out between the poles of Fall and Redemption.

Westermann argues that this very narrow view leaves out of consideration everything else which the Biblical account of the origins sets out as basic for the world and man. The correct understanding of the Old Testament account is thus not of God creating man in a perfect state and man, as a matter of history, falling to a lower state: but of creation and the Fall seen together as part of the primeval scene — a setting from which man and indeed the whole of creation has to emerge in an ordering process: in effect, evolution. It is just such an interpretation that prevailed in the early Church and which accords well with the modern scientific evolutionary picture. Thus man appears from his very beginning as a social being who must work and know problems arising from this emerging state. Man's painful striving after knowledge is his from the very beginning, and so is the drive to improve his achievements in art and technology. The history of man is prefigured by two lines, always interacting with each other, namely, the blessing which brings increase, and the natural and personal catastrophes and the divisions of the peoples which are the source of personal and political history. In the Biblical account of the origins, sin is thus not the narrow individualistic moral notion which it has become in Church tradition.[15]

The Old Testament does not know an abstract concept of sin: sinfulness is not an abject state of man: sins are mentioned only when they threaten human existence, the human community, or the communion between God and man. This threat varies depending on the historic, economic, cultural, and religious circumstances.[16] What is more, the statement that God created man in his image, after his likeness, refers to no specific quality of man but simply to his being man — something which cuts through all the differences between men — of belief, of religion and of race. On this basis, therefore, sin shows itself in many forms in all areas of human life and not merely in personal confrontation of man and God. It is to be reckoned with in all

---

[15] C Westermann *Creation*   p 19

[16] C Westermann *What does the Old Testament say about God?*   p 57

aspects of the human community where man is at work. The man whom God had created (Genesis 2) was a man perverse and limited as much in his relation to God (Genesis 3) as in his relationship to his brother (Genesis 4).[17] Man's responsibility to God and his responsibility in community were thus not to be separated.

Westermann goes on to note how the broad lines of the beginnings of human civilisation are traced in a genealogy in the second part of Genesis 4, and the development of civilisation is seen as a command of God. The outcome of the Flood is God's promise never again to destroy the life which he had created 'as long as earth remains'.[18] God is thus much more than first cause for he is also sustainer of the universe and will bring it to fruition: to speak of the Creator is thus to speak, not just of beginnings but of the entire world process from origin to end. 'He who speaks of God, speaks of the whole; where God acts, his activity must embrace all.'[19]

This understanding is of prime importance, as we shall see, for whereas it takes form in the New Testament in the idea of the mutual indwelling of God and the world, and, in the early Church, in the idea of God enclosing, not enclosed, in the West, God came to be seen as creating *ad extra*, outside himself, something fundamentally different from himself. Perforce, much of this work will be concerned with tracing some of the momentous implications of this change.

Westermann notes how, for early man, the world in its incomprehensible complexity and variety was grasped as a totality by reflection on Creation: which, as we shall see, resulted in deepening insights through *gnosis*. Reflection on creation offers an approach that is both unified and concrete.[20] It is unified in the sense that the world as a whole and in its every facet is on this basis to be seen as the activity, however limited and warped, of God; and it is concrete in the sense that this activity is to be seen, not as the indirect outcome of a causal process or of the fiat of a distant God but, despite its warping and finitude, as the direct activity of a God who is himself present in it.

The Wisdom Literature of Israel

When we look to see how these understandings were made specific in the Old Testament, we can best, for the purposes of this study, turn primarily,

---

[17] C Westermann *Creation*   p 19

[18] *op cit*   p 22ff

[19] *op cit*   p 31

[20] *op cit*   p 37

not to the narrative parts, including those in which the Prophets were seen as channels for specific messages between God and man, but to the Wisdom books. Though earlier scholarship assigned the Wisdom literature to the post-exilic period and it has been treated even as a foreign element in the Old Testament world, it has now become clear that it had very early roots throughout the ancient east, and that Israel put her own specific stamp on her versions of it. This literature records the form in which man sought to establish his bearings within the sphere allotted to him by God[21] and reveals a total attitude that underlies the Old Testament writings.

If the Wisdom literature is to be understood, the first point that needs to be noted is that for Israel there was only one world of experience and within this, rational and religious perceptions were not differentiated.[22] Contrary to the widely prevailing Christian view of a legalistic religion worshipping a remote and inaccessible God, 'the experiences of the world were for her always divine experiences as well, and the experiences of God were for her experiences of the world. ... It was precisely because this knowledge of Yahweh was so strong, so unassailable, that Israel was able to speak of the orders of this world in quite secular terms.'[23]

Von Rad illustrates the implications of these Israelite presuppositions in ways which, at later stages of this study, will find constant echoes and will prove to have profound significance. He shows that effective knowledge about God was seen by Israel as the only thing that puts man into a right relationship with his environment and his fellow creatures. The knowledge which ultimately matters is, therefore, not so much discursive, factual knowledge but the deeper insights of *gnosis*. Wisdom stands or falls according to the right attitude of man to God.[24]

That attitude, as we shall see, is that associated with righteousness, which is not just a matter of morality but of the wholeness or maturity to which we have already referred. In the process of attaining that attitude, the underlying order of the world becomes incorporated into the structure of the mind of man, and it is this that ensures, as far as possible, insight and harmony not only between man and nature, but, in that nature itself manifests the Word and so the order of God, insight and harmony between man and God.

This profoundly important perception finds its counterpart in the thought of Plato. Iris Murdoch notes that he suggests that we work with the idea of

---

[21] G von Rad *Wisdom in Israel* (1975) p 309

[22] *op cit* p 61

[23] *op cit* pp 62-3

[24] *op cit* pp 67-9

a hierarchy of forms in so far as we introduce order into our conceptions of the world through our apprehension of the Good; and she adds that this seems to her to be true. Plato's image implies that complete unity is not seen until one has reached the summit, but moral advance carries with it intimations of unity that are increasingly less misleading.[25] The Israelite understanding offered, therefore, in a sense, a profoundly empirical way of viewing a much wider and deeper range of experiences and of reality than modern science-based man is normally open to, for it involved openness to the Wisdom of Yahweh expressed in all fields of experience and a recognition that, however profound those insights were, they were always embedded in the even more profound Divine mystery.

This way of viewing the world entailed a wide range of value judgements and moral obligations, drawing, contrary to modern presuppositions, as we shall see, from the existing order of the world. Explicitly or implicitly, evaluations were continually being made against a background of basic knowledge which also entailed moral obligations. A man was considered to be wise only when he allowed his whole way of life to be modelled on these insights which put their emphasis on values. 'The wise man is also a "righteous man". One has to "walk" in wisdom (Prov 28.26), wisdom is "knowing the way" in which one, of course, must also walk. (Prov 14.8)'[26] In contrast, folly is lack of order in one's inmost being which can be observed taking many different forms but always involves lack of knowledge, almost lack of realism. (Prov 17.24)[27] And this has always to be thought of in dynamic terms — in terms of response to changing situations. When truth is offered to a man through an emerging situation, therefore, there is no longer free decision: a refusal to accept it puts man under moral judgement and indeed involves misjudging God himself.[28] Von Rad notes that 'fear of Yahweh' has a wide range of meaning but seems to have been understood by the Wisdom teachers as simply obedience to the divine will: the modern reader has, therefore, to eliminate the idea of something emotional: and von Rad refers to ideas of 'commitment to', 'knowledge about' Yahweh, even tending to 'confidence in' Yahweh as possible meanings.[29]

In keeping with this all-embracing understanding of the divine which was achieved through this empirical attitude towards emerging reality, was the

---

[25] *The Sovereignty of the Good*   (1970)   p 95

[26] G von Rad   *op cit*   p 64

[27] *op cit*   pp 64-5

[28] *op cit*   p 65

[29] *op cit*   p 66

view that the good was not just something internal but public: being good and prospering were closely related, for such 'goodness' was a sign of righteousness and righteousness involved being 'right' not just with God but with the community and indeed the natural world. There was no room here for ethical exclusivism, or 'for lofty ethical demands to which only a circle of like-minded men are capable of submitting; there is no place for any form of moral heroism nor for fanatics for virtue nor for ethical individualists.'[30] Man faced forces of order in the world to which the wise man conformed for not to conform was not just in practice folly but also involved a self-destructive rebellion against God: and rebellion against God normally took the form of an offence against one's fellow men.[31] In no way, therefore, did Yahweh exercise some sort of judicial function, exercised after the event, of reward and retribution in accordance with pre-established moral norms. It is rather that, throughout the Old Testament, actions have built-in consequences which flow directly from them.

The relation between doing good and salvation and between sin and calamity is, therefore, less a feature of ethics than a feature of the laws of the natural world: yet the natural world is not apart from Yahweh for he is present in it and acting through it and the correspondence between actions and consequences is a result of his faithfulness.

The prevalence of the idea of a judicial or ethical God who stands apart from his creation is the product of the reading into the Old Testament of the Western separation of God and the world. In contrast, in the Old Testament, human behaviour is determined, not by general ethical norms but by the experience of inherent natural laws.[32] In this sense, von Rad suggests, the book of Proverbs lacks a clear-cut religious quality. 'According to the convictions of wise men, Yahweh obviously delegated to creation so much truth, indeed he was present in it in such a way, that man reaches ethical *terra firma* when he learns to read these orders and adjusts his behaviour to the experiences gained. ... The expression "inherent laws", which is sometimes used, can be employed only in a restricted sense. In the long run it was always Yahweh himself with whom man saw himself confronted, and in him the indirectness of the apparently neutral event was again superseded.'[33] Thus the exhortation not to requite evil done to one (Prov

---

[30] *op cit* p 81
[31] *op cit* p 88
[32] *op cit* p 90
[33] *op cit* p 92

20.22) lay not so much in lofty ethical principle as in faith in the order of
Yahweh which is good and life-promoting.[34]

What is more, because that good and life-promoting order could be
discerned by the man who stood right with God by having attained
wholeness and maturity, so could he perceive deviations from it: deviations
that led to evil and suffering. As we have already suggested, therefore,
contrary to a shibboleth entrenched in modern understanding, at least since
the time of Hume, which has separated what *is* from what *ought to be*, what
ought to be done by man to order his life and to bring blessing and
fruitfulness of God upon him and his fellows, was to be discerned, not so
much by the application of abstract ethical principles, but from man's
harmonious interactions within the unfolding natural order which was itself
the order of God: harmonious interactions summed up in the great Jewish
word *shalom*.

Man could not, therefore, depend on his own planning for it was always
subject to God's concurrence and God could protect man even from his own
plans.[35] Man had, therefore, always to keep himself open to the unfolding
activity of God, 'an activity which completely escapes all calculation, for
between putting into practice of the most reliable wisdom and that which
actually takes place, there always lies the great unknown.'[36] Although,
therefore, the characteristic feature of the sages was their pursuit of insight,
gnosis, their search for the unknown, this entailed awareness that wisdom
could not be found but had to come as an insight — 'the awareness that
Wisdom eludes those who search for her and the conviction she gives herself
freely to those who love her.'[37]

Faith and trust in God were thus essential for 'victory comes from the
Lord'. Self-confidence and self-glorification could not be combined with
trust in Yahweh.[38] Rather (and we shall find reference to this attitude of
mind in quite other fields of modern life) the fear of God (in the sense
referred to above) 'not only enabled a man to acquire knowledge, but also
had a predominantly critical function in that it kept awake in the person
acquiring the knowledge the awareness that his intellect was directed
towards a world in which mystery predominated.' This fear of God trained
him to openness, the readiness for an encounter even with the inscrutable
and the imponderable. It taught him, therefore, that the sphere in which

---

[34] *op cit*   p 95

[35] *op cit*   p 100

[36] *op cit*   p 101

[37] J L Crenshaw   *Old Testament Wisdom*   (1982)   pp 58-9

[38] G von Rad   *Wisdom in Israel*   p 102

definite, verifiable orders can be discerned is a very limited one. The mysteries of the unfolding world have, however, no independent existence. In them man directly confronts the mystery of God. 'This is, indeed, the fascinating thing about this investigation of life, the fact that men dared to address themselves to a world in which they had to reckon at every step with the possibility of encountering the totally incommensurable God. Fascinating, too, is the calm, unperturbed way in which this investigation is pursued on such a terrain and faced with such a partner.'[39]

Linked with this understanding of the world as a direct manifestation of the divine was a strong awareness that all ability to act successfully is tied to specific times which a man has to recognise but cannot change. But if the right time comes, then one has to make the most of it. Yet Wisdom was not thereby seen as impersonal. Von Rad comments that the most interesting feature of what is new in the didactic poem in Prov. 8 is that 'this world order turns, as a person, towards men, wooing them and encouraging them in direct address. What is objectified here, then, is not an attribute of God but an attribute of the world, namely that mysterious attribute, by virtue of which she turns towards men to give order to their lives.' What is more, this personal element was no stylistic device: it was 'completely indispensable.' 'This world reason was there before all the works of creation, playing in the world like a child; like a "favourite", she was the delight of God and, even from the very beginning, she was turned towards men in cheerful playful disposition' — a point which is particularly important for the understanding of the whole poem. 'In contrast to Job 28, this Wisdom which is immanent in the world is considered less from the point of view of the economic order than from an aesthetic point of view. As "favourite", she is God's "delight", and she "sports" with and "takes delight" in men.' In so speaking, however, both texts speak of a reality which is surrounded by the most profound mystery.[40]

'The facts are clear. Wisdom .... calls to men. ... In this call we are dealing with the very opposite of something private and personal or even esoteric, which would be accessible only to initiates. She stands, not in a hidden place but "on the heights", "by the roadside", where "the paths cross" (Prov 8 2). She speaks not from the sacral sphere of the sanctuary, but in the most profane public place. And what she says is clear and precise, that men should learn from her and listen to her. (Prov 8.5f, 10.32); she will lead men out of stupidity and idle gossip (Prov 1.22); she teaches intelligence and truth (Prov 8.5,7); finally, she promises wealth and honour as well as righteousness (Prov 8.18,21). She even promises life, divine favour and

---

[39] G von Rad *op cit* p 109

[40] *op cit* pp 156- 157

security: "For he who finds me has found life and obtains Yahweh's favour. (Prov 8.35) He who listens to me dwells secure and is safe from the terrors of disaster. (Prov 1.33)"[41]

Though Wisdom is so readily available and indeed seeks out those who are open to her, she can also withdraw from anyone who does not heed her or who disobeys her — with resulting frustration and sometimes catastrophe. Wisdom offers an invitation to let man be guided by her in all the decisions of life.[42] Thus God can reach men not only by priests and prophets but also by a voice which comes from creation itself. Creation as it unfolds discharges truth: and in so doing, to those who are responsive, 'it promises cleverness, understanding, righteousness, reliability, wisdom, counsel, success, strength, wealth, honour.'[43] Thus Wisdom sought a dwelling amongst men and was directed by God to the people of Israel. 'Only here could she develop, for only here were men open to her, only here did they serve her aright, for in Israel the primeval order had revealed herself in the form of the Torah.'[44]

Von Rad goes on to show that Wisdom not only addresses man: she also loves him and the tone of man's relationship with her can verge on the mystical.[45] As Crenshaw says: 'considerable emphasis falls on Wisdom's initiative. Not only does she meet her lover half-way, but she also actively invites people to search for her. Those who love her are loved in return, and whoever finds her discovers life.'[46] It is thus by means of wisdom that man finds favour with God. And Von Rad notes that there thus developed in Israel a doctrine of revelatory experience which happens to men, 'not through a specific, irreversible sign of salvation in history, but which, rather, emanates from the power of order which is held to be self-sufficient. It is this power and not, therefore, priests, prophets or actualised traditions of the saving history, that is the great mediator.'[47] It was for this reason that Israel did not have a general concept of revelation. Apart from special acts and occurrences of his speaking, God spoke through the ways in which the natural order unfolded.

We may, perhaps, crystallise the ways in which this view of the world and its relationship to God manifests itself by noting first that the order of

---

[41] *op cit*   p 158

[42] *op cit*   pp 161-3

[43] *op cit*   p 165

[44] *op cit*   p 166

[45] *op cit*   p 169

[46] *Old Testament Wisdom*   p 60

[47] *op cit*   p 175

God was seen as taking form in the order of the world and, as we shall see, that order is itself the basis of the ordering of the human personality, as Piaget has shown. Personally to develop in that order was thus to respond to the creative will of God; to participate in that order was to respond to the Word of God; and in so developing towards wholeness and maturity, one manifested more fully the reason and love of God. Thus whereas Western man views himself as a detached observer of a largely impersonal world around him which proceeds in accordance with impersonal laws continuously mediated by blind chance, the world of men and women of Israel compelled commitment and complete trust and if they attained a right attitude towards it, this world was expected to respond with intelligence and insight to their personal needs, for it was God they met in it.

That most people respond with warmth if they meet in another person's attitude, openness, sincerity, integrity, confidence and trust, will hardly be controversial. That many animals tend similarly to respond to people who are open towards them may also seem fairly obvious to many people. Some will even accept that some people seem to establish some kind of rapport with their plants — that they have 'green fingers'. But that the environment as a whole, down to the very stones, has some sort of personal attitude to man as it unfolds, takes us right outside Western understanding and credence — though there are, perhaps, even in our Western society, many more people than is generally recognised, who have a strong sense, not only of being personally guided and that God will bring about what is needed at the appropriate time, but of his presence. This is precisely what the Wisdom Books of the Old Testament testify to.

Having noted that Israel's search for knowledge was directed at the objects of her environment, for these were revealing of God, von Rad reiterates that this was only one side of the matter. 'Man was, at the same time, always the object of movements which reached him from men and also from things. But these movements of the environment — and this is the most important factor — did not disappear into an unrelated outer sphere in accordance with some strange law; they were, rather, turned quite personally and in unending mobility towards man; indeed, they corresponded to his behaviour even in areas which we would call "natural"'. In all the endlessly varied forms which they could assume, they were ready to accept man. Everything that happens to man is appropriate to him. 'The man who has brought his relationship with God into order is himself in league with the stones of the field and is befriended by the beasts of the field. (Job 5.20ff) The environment is not only the object of man's search for knowledge. In so far as it is turned towards him, man is the object of its advance on him.'

As Paul says: '"We know that to those who love God everything works together for good." (*sunergei*, Rom 8.28)'[48]

'The ancients also knew that this attitude, this working together of "everything", could take on for man very complicated forms. ... To the man who entrusts himself to this order, it is not only that the movements of his environment appear different to him (this we could still understand), but it is actually different things that happen to him. ... Anyone who fails to be aware of the constitutive idea of this reciprocally determined sphere of action between man and his environment and who appraises the sentences by means of the modern understanding of reality, will, of necessity, misunderstand from the outset much of what the wise men say, will indeed feel that their sentences are foolish and capricious postulates. But they were not postulates; they were statements of experiences' — experiences of the ways in which the future unfolded into the present.[49]

We shall see later in this study how this might be understood in modern terms and can indeed be true. Yet, all this is seen as coming from Yahweh and depends on an attitude in men of trust. 'All that the wise men say, especially also what they have to say about the beneficient turning of the world towards men, only has meaning if one places one's trust in the orders, and that means, in the last resort, in Yahweh.'[50] Wisdom, therefore, was seen, not as separate from God but as an aspect, a function, of God who expressed herself in and through creation including man himself. The intimacy that this implies between creation and Wisdom and Wisdom and Yahweh and so between creation and Yahweh thus becomes clear and, as we have noted, this intimacy carried forward into the New Testament in the idea of the mutual indwelling: it was clearly manifested in the life and attitude of Jesus to the Father and carried thence into the understanding of the early Church Fathers: whence in the West it was gradually lost.

As for the form which instruction in Wisdom took, von Rad remarks that a certain liberality has long been noted. 'It is directed towards the understanding of the person being instructed; it cannot and will not take away from him the power of decision. Even when man was being urgently addressed, an area was always left which the teacher never entered but which he left free for the pupil to use as he wished; one could in fact say that it was left for a kind of intuition which helped the pupil to transfer correctly the general instruction to his particular situation, for here it was man who intervened, whether he was endeavouring to hold his forces together, to utilize his opportunities or to cultivate relations with his fellow

---

[48] *op cit*   p 302
[49] *op cit*   pp 302-3
[50] *op cit*   p 307

men.' In other words, the insight had to come to him: it could not be forced upon him; he had himself to make the conceptual leap: something that applies in all creative learning, as we shall see. 'But this humanity could not be protected by a handful of clever rules. Again and again it had to be established anew from the very heart of Yahwism. More and more we saw the wise men involved in a struggle with fundamental problems which threatened to darken their relationship with God and which called for fairly decisive theological reflection. And finally we even saw them — bordering on hubris — summoned and wooed by the mystery of the world itself and responding to that wooing with an intellectual love. Thus wide, then, was the theological framework stretched, within which the wise men in Israel believed they could begin to understand themselves correctly. To live intellectually in such spheres, to be able to handle such knowledge, really required a *rōhab lēb*, a 'width', a 'breadth' of heart and mind (1 Kings 4.29)'[51]: something which, as we have already suggested and will see further, we may perhaps translate as wholeness and maturity.

As for man's use of this 'breadth' of mind, whatever help and urging he was offered, in the last resort, he had to be left free to gain his own insights and translate them into action; but if he was not constantly 'listening' to the unfolding order established by God, then he was lost. 'The man who listens, who reflects and who then entrusts himself to his perceptions; that is the highest form of human existence in the eyes of the wise men.'[52] Basically, therefore, the orders of the world turned benevolently towards men who took refuge in it for 'salvation is not brought about by Yahweh descending into history or by any kind of human agency such as Moses or David or one of the patriarchs, but by the specific factors inherent in creation itself.'[53]

Modern Understandings of the Old Testament

It may be claimed by some theologians and Churchmen that in the Old Testament these insights are peripheral and, in particular, that what is central is the evidence of the working out of the will of God in history. John Collins notes the widely held view that the Old Testament attaches little importance to cosmology and locates revelation in history; but, as he says: 'The theology of the Psalms and Wisdom books is based in creation rather than history and cosmic imagery abounds in the prophets'. And he remarks

---

[51] *op cit* pp 309-310

[52] *op cit* p 310

[53] *op cit* p 314

that the Jewish Apocalypses 'share the conviction that salvation depends on a proper understanding of the workings of the cosmos.'[54]

Indeed, Collins goes on to note that from the perspective of the Gospel of John, Jesus of Nazareth is the supreme expression of a cosmic principle which was present in the world long before Jesus was born; that Christian life is an attunement to this cosmic principle and that these insights shaped the development of Christian eschatology and Christology.[55] Yet, as we shall see, these insights were lost to Western theology as gradually the concepts of God and the world separated and the Old and New Testaments, as well as the Early Fathers, were read selectively in the light of later preconceptions. As a result, the underlying insights enshrined in the Wisdom Books dropped out of sight, natural theology played a decreasing role, and it is the narrative parts of the Old Testament, separated from their context and woven into a context of a very different character that have been most influential in recent times in wider theological and Church thinking.

Clearly, however, there is no necessary conflict between the idea, as set out in the Wisdom literature, of the essential underlying features of a relationship with Yahweh revealed through and in the events facing man in creation, and the idea of creation not just constantly changing but as itself developing progressively in response to the guidance of Yahweh; guidance more specifically revealed in the historical process in which Israel was led forward by the constant emergence of new religious ideas as a nation in pilgrimage. That pilgrimage involved repeated breaks, with new insights emerging and with God inaugurating new starts with new eras of tradition and new institutions in the light of which both past and future had to be reappraised. This process, manifested in the history of Israel, finds its counterpart in new conceptual insights which come to individuals and lead them to reappraise their understandings of their own pasts and futures. What is more, in the history of Israel, these progressive developments entailed not progressive insights into some form of static reality, but the change and development of that reality as itself a progressive revelation of the plenitude of Yahweh. This led to new and greater expectations of yet fuller initiatives by God and these were passed down to succeeding generations and augmented in the process.[56] In this way, Israel stood out from other peoples around her, for whereas she looked forward to new and fuller revelations of the ways of Yahweh, they tended to look back in times of crisis to a revival of primeval beliefs and rites.

---

[54] New Testament Cosmology in *Cosmology and Theology* Concilium 166 (1983) pp 3 & 4

[55] *op cit* p 7

[56] see G von Rad *Old Testament Theology* vol II (1965) pp 319-21

The events of the New Testament tended, therefore, to be interpreted in terms of the Old Testament but an Old Testament itself reinterpreted in the light of later events. As we shall see, Jesus was seen by his believing contemporaries and those who followed, as the Christ, the Messiah. At this point, however, we do not need to pursue the implications of the understanding of Jesus as Messiah save to indicate it as one, but a very important, example of the way in which the events recorded in the New Testament were seen in terms of new insights and their embodiment in events which flowed out of and fulfilled ideas developed in the Old Testament.

These insights were taken even further when the Risen Christ came to be identified with Wisdom itself and then with the Word, the Son of God, the Lord. As von Rad says, 'even a cursory glance at the New Testament reveals that right down to its latest writings it is absolutely permeated with a sense of wonder at the advent of a tremendous new event, an overwhelmimg awareness of standing at a new beginning from which entirely new horizons of God's saving activity have become visible: the kingdom of God is here.'[57] Yet, as we know, that step proved to be one which only a small proportion of the people of Israel felt able to accept and it fell to the Gentiles to carry their vast insights forward. In the centuries which followed, however, the unified vision of the Old Testament which permeated also the New Testament and took personal form in Jesus Christ, began to fall apart and, as we shall seek to show, that process has continued to the point at which current interpretations of the New Testament, of Christ and of the world have become so limited, fragmented and diverse that there is little in the way of consensus on which we can rely in carrying the story forward. Before, therefore, we can seek to show something of the context within which Jesus came to be understood by his followers and the New Testament writers, we need to make some comments bearing on current interpretations of their testimonies.

---

[57] *Old Testament Theology*   vol II   p 328

CHAPTER THREE

JEWISH AND GREEK UNDERSTANDINGS OF GOD AND THE WORLD

Whereas we today tend to picture creation as an act of will by God involving a process which in some mysterious way takes place across the great gap between him and the world and gives it virtual autonomy, both the Jews and Greeks of the time of Jesus, as well as the early Christians, saw the world as a dynamic process which was in some sense bedded in and sustained by, the divine as a feature of his life: and the mutual indwelling of the New Testament implied just that.

What is more, whereas for us that act of creation is seen as essentially an act of will somehow producing a largely mechanical world governed by inflexible laws and chance, for earlier thinkers it was seen as essentially an act of thought. God created by his Word. This change is well illustrated by Lynn White Jr. who notes that during the first Christian millenium, in both East and West, God at the moment of creation is represented in passive majesty, actualising the cosmos by pure power of thought, Platonically. Then shortly after the year 1000, a Gospel book was produced at Winchester which made a great innovation: inspired by Wisdom of Solomon 11:20, 'Thou hast ordered all things by measure and number and weight', the monastic illuminator showed the hand of God — now the master craftsman — holding scales, a carpenter's square, and a pair of compasses. This new representation spread and, probably under the influence of Proverbs 8:27 'When he established the heavens I was there, when he drew a circle on the face of the deep', the scales and square were eliminated leaving only the compasses — the normal medieval and renaissance symbol of the engineer — held in God's hand.[1]

That the Jewish view of God as creator and sustainer of the universe did not markedly conflict with Greek ideas is widely recognised but it seems that many Christian scholars have seriously underestimated the accessibility — the closeness — of the divine in Jewish thinking of the time of Christ. It has been a common view among Christian scholars that in the period after the return from Babylon, in Judaism generally and in Rabbinic Judaism in particular, God became very remote. He is supposed no longer to have been spoken of familiarly, but only by circumlocutions; and angels were necessary as intermediaries. Yet, it is claimed, Judaism possessed no means of access to their remote God save obedience to the Torah, and this was manifestly

---

[1] Cultural Climates and Technological Advance in the Middle Ages *Viator* vol 2 (1971) pp 171-201 esp. p 189, quoted by Heiko Oberman *The Dawn of the Reformation* (1986) p 180

insufficient and inadequate. This situation led on the one hand to a religion of anxiety and on the other to smug self-reliance.[2] In two important works, *Paul and Palestinian Judaism* (1977) and *Jesus and Judaism* (1985) E P Sanders refutes this view strongly and quotes weighty support for his refusal to equate the transcendence of God with his remoteness. He suggests that the standard theological terms, transcendence and immanence, lead to misunderstanding and are not appropriate. In particular, they do not respond to the question of God's accessibility.[3] He asserts that the Rabbis viewed God as accessible and that this has now been shown with great clarity and thoroughness by numerous scholars. He refers particularly to George Foot Moore's major work on Judaism written over 50 years ago.

It is worth quoting some of Moore's statements. 'We have seen that the idea of God was eminently personal. He was supramundane but not extramundane; exalted but not remote. He was the sole ruler of the world he had created, and he ordered all things in it in accordance with his character, in which justice and mercy were complementary, not conflicting, attributes. His will for men was righteousness and goodness; and that they might know what he required, he had defined his will in two-fold law. His far-reaching and all-embracing plan had for its end the universality of the true religion in an age of universal uprightness, peace, and prosperity — the goal towards which all history tended — "the reign of God".' And Moore summarises this chapter on the idea of God by saying: '... The exaltation of God was not his exile. He who dwells in the high and holy place, dwells no less with him that is of a contrite and humble spirit. His almighty power and his humility go together; he is lofty enough to think nothing beneath him, great enough to count nothing too small to be his concern. The conclusive proof of this is the whole character of Jewish piety in those centuries, and the intimacy of the religious relation which is expressed by the thought of God as Father.'[4] The background for Jesus' peculiarly intimate term for God, 'Abba', stands out clearly from these passages — an intimacy that was to be lost in much Western theology, as will emerge in due course, together with its momentous consequences.

One major feature of these understandings of the Jews, as we have seen, was the belief that God had chosen Israel to be his people because, on one understanding, Israel was receptive to him. He had covenanted that he would look after them and lead them into his life if they in righteousness were faithful to him. There was, however, no sense that God would cancel the covenant if man failed to offer obedience. Despite widespread claims

---

[2] E P Sanders *Paul and Palestinian Judaism* (1977) p 212

[3] *op cit* pp 215

[4] *Judaism* vol 1 pp 423 & 442

to this effect among Christian scholars, Sanders says that there is no hint of such a view in the whole of Tannaitic literature. An individual might withdraw from the covenant by disobedience but this in no way implied cancellation on God's side.[5] The covenant was in this sense unconditional, though it clearly implied the obligation to obey.[6]

What is more, in allowing man to return within the covenant, God was seen as unfailingly merciful. Though, as Sanders says, the Rabbis never said that God was merciful in such a way as to remove the necessity of obeying him, they did think that God was merciful toward those who basically intended to obey, even though their performance might have been a long way from perfect.[7] For those who had transgressed, there was a means of atonement for every transgression, an atonement that restored the right relationship with God. As for the obligations that this imposed on people, these were not regarded as onerous but as a blessing, to be fulfilled with joy, as being accompanied with strength and peace, and as being a sign of God's mercy. It is important to recall, therefore, that as we have seen, the Rabbis did not have any doctrine of original sin or of the essential sinfulness of each man in the sense prevalent in Christian teaching.[8] Yet righteousness, Moore says, in the conception of it which Judaism got from the Scriptures, had no suggestion of moral perfection. What distinguished the righteous man who had fallen into sin was his repentance — 'a remedy which God, in knowledge of man's frailty and foresight of his sin, mercifully created before the world. ... God was too good, too reasonable, to demand a perfection of which he had created man incapable.'[9]

The Greeks also had a strong sense of the presence of the divine. The Greek language and Greek ideas had spread widely throughout the Eastern Mediterranean by the time of Jesus. A major contributing factor had been the conquests by Alexander some three centuries earlier. The Jews outside Palestine, the Diaspora, had been deeply influenced. The Septuagint, the Greek translation of the Old Testament, was widely used by them and this in itself was an instrument of change.

What, then, were the general characteristics of Jewish and Greek thought and the contributions that they made to Christian understanding and in particular to the conceptual framework within which experiences of Christ came to be interpreted by the early Christians?   As von Rad says:

---

[5] E P Sanders *Paul & Palestinian Judaism*   p 95

[6] *op cit*   p 97

[7] *op cit*   p 125

[8] *op cit*   p 114

[9] *Judaism*   vol 1 (1927) pp 494-5

'Certainly Israel was aware of the laws of nature; ... but the laws were seen only as the relative principles of a world embraced and held, at times disturbed, but always and unceasingly controlled by God. It was this divine control, for weal or woe, that Israel found beauty in its most exalted degree.'[10]

For the Greeks, however, whereas the ordinary world was seen as mutable, its divine origin was seen as immutable. That origin was seen as basically intellectual so it was reason that ordered the world; and reason was understood to strive inexorably towards the greatest possible unity of understanding. (e g Phaedrus 249b) There was, therefore, more emphasis on the unchanging natural laws in which the Divine could be discerned and less room for the personal initiatives to which the ordering of events responded which the Jews attributed to Yahweh.

In the later Platonism of the Christian era, the making and direction of the world by the Divine source or, more usually, by a second divine intelligence, was emphasised, as was the understanding that the Platonic Ideas or Forms that moulded the world existed in the mind of God. These Forms or Ideas were seen as the objects of true knowledge and the standards by which judgements of value were made. The objects of the sense world derived such reality and value as they had from in some way participating in them. They were the really real. Thus Plato pictures human life as a pilgrimage from appearance towards that reality. This process, which took place through the dawning insights of *gnosis* changed people's lives and led them towards goodness. For Plato, the best, though not the only method to achieve this change, was 'dialectic', that is philosophy regarded as a spiritual discipline — described in The Sophist (230c) as a purgation of the soul by scrutiny, argument, refutation and cross-questioning: a process which prepared the mind for *gnosis* leading the mind to greater integration and wholeness.

Some Greek thinking used Jewish ideas to lead towards *gnosis*, but *gnosis* itself was in no way solely a Greek phenomenon for we have seen the same emphasis on achieving 'openness' to insights and inspiration in the Wisdom literature of Israel. Louis Bouyer notes that Jewish *gnosis* is a product *sui generis* of Judaism, and he adds that it is the indubitable heir both of the great prophetic tradition of the eighth to seventh centuries and of Israelite Wisdom.[11] It was also, as we shall see, a fundamental feature of the early Christian Church.

This contrast between rational knowledge and the 'illumination' or 'insights' associated with *gnosis* is so important that it is worth quoting

---

[10] *The Problem of the Hexateuch and other Essays*   (1966)   p 152

[11] *A History of Christian Spirituality*   vol 1   (1968)   p 16

what Philip Sherrard says about it: 'The whole Christian Way, like that of any other genuine religious tradition, is intimately linked with the acquisition of knowledge, with a *gnosis*, and this is in accordance with Christ's own words, "know the Truth and the Truth will make you free". But the knowledge here indicated is not a rational, or philosophical, knowledge, and its acquisition is not a matter of abstract or theoretical speculation. Gnostic realisation, or illumination, which is at the same time one with the end of the Way, is dependent on following the Way. It cannot be acquired, as rational or philosophical knowledge may be, through mere learning and study, but only by means of an initiation through which the aspirant is prepared, and put in a position, to receive, stage by stage, and according to his or her capacity, spiritual understanding. It is, in short, another and higher order than the knowledge accessible to the human intelligence or reason alone, and may even be said to "confound" the latter altogether.'[12] Several points need to be made on this, though they will have to be developed later.

Because, in the Jewish, Greek and early Christian traditions alike, the whole of reality was seen as permeated and structured by the Divine, no sharp line is to be drawn between religious illumination and what we today would regard as more secular fields of inspiration as in, for instance, science and the arts. Iris Murdoch notes how Plato speaks more than once of the artist's inspiration as a kind of divine or holy madness from which we may receive great blessings and without which there is no good poetry.[13] It follows, therefore, that, as we have already said, though we would not normally regard as instances of such 'initiation', the formal instruction and learning in the sciences and arts that precede and have to allow for the leaps of insight that are essential to the process, this is what they are. What is more, in gaining such insights, and in so rendering more meaningful our understanding of the world and our place in it, we are developing our own minds towards wholeness and maturity. As we shall see, this process applies to such learning at all levels and at all stages of life, though insights at rudimentary levels and in highly specialised fields of learning may have only very limited relevance to this end, especially if any wider context for such learning is lacking.

Dodd's conclusion about the interaction and convergence of Jewish and Greek thinking provides the relevant context for the development of early Christianity: 'It was into a religious world in which this kind of cross-fertilization of thought was going on that Christianity came. It started from the Jewish side, accepting the authority of the Jewish Scriptures as a

---

[12] P Sherrard *The Greek East and The Latin West*   (1959)   p 28

[13] *The Fire and the Sun*   (1977) p 2 referring to Phaedrus 224-5

divine revelation, and yet, by virtue of the original religious impulse from which it began, free to criticize, reinterpret and enlarge its Jewish heritage. Its creative theologians, Paul, the author of Hebrews and the author of the Fourth Gospel, betray acquaintance with the generally diffused popular philosophy, partly Platonic, partly Stoic, whether this acquaintance was due to direct study of Hellenistic thought or to its infiltration into their own Hellenistic Judaism. ... Within the New Testament, however, such influences are always secondary. The regulative motive is that supplied by the originating impulse of Christianity itself.'[14]

The Gospels were written in Greek and it is in this context that we have to understand St John when, in the Prologue to his Gospel, he calls Christ the Word, Logos. He is there saying that Christ is that ordering and reasoning principle or aspect of God through whom the Father created the world as a whole and which has now taken specific form in Jesus. In Christian thinking, it was, of course, the Son, the Word of God, who was seen as Creator and not the transcendent Father, as is stressed in the Prologue to St John's Gospel where John says that the Word was with God at the beginning: through him all things came to be, and no single thing was created without him. According to Numenius, the second century philosopher, when in the Timaeus Plato speaks of the maker and Father of the universe, the Father is the supreme God who stands in some kind of paternal relationship to the second God who was, therefore, the maker of the universe. The closeness of the parallel is obvious.

It does not conflict with this, however, to note that, though the New Testament was written in Greek and, certainly within a few years of the death of Jesus, as the Gospel began to be taken outside Palestine to the Gentiles, Greek influences appear, there is none the less a question about how far Greek influences prevailed in the immediate environment in which Jesus grew up. Geza Vermes dissents strongly from a statement by Martin Hengel that, from the middle of the third century B C, all Judaism must really be designated 'Hellenistic Judaism' and quotes Fergus Millar as emphasising the uniqueness of the phenomenon of an original and varied non-Greek literary activity developing in a small area only a few miles from the Mediterranean coast. Vermes goes so far as to claim that the uprooting of Christianity following the death of Christ from a Jewish to a Gentile environment was so thorough that 'as a source for the historical understanding of Jesus of Nazareth, the reliability of the Gentile church, together with all the literature composed especially for it, can be ruled out.'[15] As has been noted, however, Paul, while completely rejecting the Greek

---

[14] *The Bible and the Greeks* (1935) pp 247-8

[15] G Vermes *Jesus and the World of Judaism* (1983) p 26

religions and disavowing use of their philosophy, shows at least a general acquaintance with them, as do the writers of St John's Gospel and of Hebrews. The rejection of pagan polytheism and idolatory was to remain constant among the Fathers of the Church but, as we shall see, the Pauline attitude towards the use of philosophy changed and by the end of the second century Greek philosophical thinking had penetrated deeply into Christianity as a vehicle for the faith.[16]

It is in the context of these understandings that we need to consider claims about Jesus.

---

[16] see e g H A Wolfson *The Philosophy of the Church Fathers,* Part 1, 3rd edn (1970) especially ch 1

CHAPTER FOUR

CHRIST IN HIS CONTEMPORARY SETTING

It would seem natural at this point to embark on a full discussion of Jesus Christ for the long conceptual odyssey with which we shall be concerned in the next few chapters, starts with the followers of Jesus and their understandings of his life and teaching, of his resurrection and post-resurrection appearances, and with the sense of his continuing presence. They are recorded for us in the New Testament; but even at that early stage, they had to be interpreted in the light of concepts available to his followers.

Not surprisingly, therefore, despite the views of many Churchmen that the only approach to Christianity is through Jesus, any such understanding depends crucially on the framework of thought we bring to it. In no way is that of twentieth century man similar to that of Jesus and his contemporaries. For reasons that will become clearer, therefore, we shall limit our comments on Jesus at this stage to certain very basic factors and defer further consideration until the last chapter of this book. We need to recognise from the outset, however, that to understand anything of Jesus Christ, we need to look wider than his teachings. Clearly it was not only what he said but what they thought he *was* that convinced the early Christians. Yet, as E P Sanders notes, '...Most studies of Jesus focus on Jesus as a teacher or preacher — at any rate primarily a messenger — and thus move immediately to try to establish the centre of his message.'[1]

Sanders criticises this position first because 'scholars have not and, in my judgement, will not agree on the authenticity of the sayings material, either in whole or in part'; but also and more basically because, 'when the study of Jesus is equated with the study of his sayings, there is an unspoken assumption that what he really was, was a teacher. He is then either a clear, straightforward teacher whose parables make his message about God and the kingdom plain, or, as in some recent studies, a difficult, riddling teacher, whose meaning is not and was not altogether clear, or even one who intended to be ambiguous. Whatever sort of teacher he is held to have been, it is difficult to move from "Jesus the teacher" to "Jesus, a Jew who was crucified, who was the leader of a group which survived his death, which in turn was persecuted, and which formed a messianic sect which was finally successful." It is difficult to make his teaching offensive enough to lead to execution or sectarian enough to lead to the formation of a group which eventually separated from the main body of Judaism.'[2] This view is

---

[1] *Jesus and Judaism* (1985) p 4

[2] *op cit* p 4

reinforced by Sanders' further comment that those who presumably know most about Judaism, and about the law in particular — Jewish scholars — do not find any substantial points of disagreement between Jesus and his contemporaries, and certainly not any which would lead to his death.[3] To the extent that attention is concentrated on Jesus as a teacher, however, there is, not surprisingly, a temptation to concentrate on the perceived ethical implications of his teachings and to allow other problems, including those of the relationship of his humanity to his divinity and the conceptual gap it seeks to fill, to become peripheral.

The problems arising from the conceptual gap between his humanity and divinity have, however, been avoided or minimised in other ways. Sanders shows how earlier generations of scholars sometimes made Jesus so unique (and Judaism so inferior) that the reader is now forced to wonder how it could be that Jesus grew up in such an environment. Thus Sanders points to W Bousset, for example, who while conceding some formal similarities between Jesus and his contemporaries (e g the use of parables), denied any similarities in all essentials.[4] And Sanders speaks of the tradition established by F Weber and followed by Bousset and others that 'Judaism was the antithesis of Christianity. Judaism was a legalistic religion in which God was remote and inaccessible. Christianity is based on faith rather than works and believes in an accessible God.'[5] The conflict between this view and that of Judaism presented earlier is stark and, indeed, the Christian claim to belief in an accessible God has for many people today a rather hollow ring. Having given such illustrations, Sanders adds that it is clear simply from the tone of these passages that Bousset's contrast is dictated primarily by theology and has little to do with historical description — a comment which Sanders supplements in a footnote where he says that this view of Judaism cannot be simply regarded as a period piece and passed over for two reasons: '(1) the use of a denigrating view of Judaism to set off Christianity as superior, which is so clear in Bousset, has continued; (2) his depiction of Palestinian Judaism is still cited as authoritative and "standard"'[6] As we have seen, Sanders, both in this book and in his *Paul and Palestinian Judaism*, has sought to redress the misunderstandings of Judaism that have become so prevalent and to set Jesus firmly in his historical setting. In so doing, he has sought to establish a clear link

---

[3] *op cit*   p 55

[4] *op cit*   p 18

[5] *Paul and Palestinian Judaism*   p 33

[6] *Jesus and Judaism*   (1985) p 360

between the life and intentions of Jeus and, following his death, the response of his followers in establishing the Church.

Accordingly, on the basis of strictly historical considerations, Sanders presents, with strong supporting evidence, a picture of Jesus which places him within the contemporary movement of Jewish restoration eschatology — hope for the restoration of Israel — and shows him as believing that the end was at hand, that God was about to establish his kingdom, that those who responded to Jesus would be included, and (at least by implication) that he would reign: and Sanders sees in the response of his disciples after the death and resurrection, their continued expectation of the restoration of Israel, of the inauguration of the new age, and their continued belief that Jesus would occupy first place in the kingdom. 'They continued to look for an otherworldly kingdom which would be established by an eschatological miracle, though its locale may have shifted from this world to the heavenly one. The person of Jesus was also progressively interpreted: he was no longer seen just as "Messiah" or "Viceroy", but as Lord. Some who were attracted to the movement began to win Gentiles to it. The work of the early apostles, which is so well reflected in Paul's letters, fits entirely into known expectations about the restoration of Israel.'[7] We shall have to discuss the basis for and implications of these beliefs in a much later chapter.

One feature that is quite clear, however, both from the sayings of Jesus and from the events associated with him, is his great sense of the intimacy of his relationship with the Father. If, however, as is normally understood by the Western Churches today, one sees this intimacy against a picture of a relatively remote God who has sent his only Son into the world in a special act of supreme grace to carry out a unique mission of saving the world, then that intimacy will tend to be seen as special to Jesus not only in degree but in kind, and the remoteness seen in the Jewish idea of God appears to fall into place by contrast. But if, as seems clear, the entire Jewish environment in which Jesus grew up had a great sense of the intimacy of the Father with every man who tried to maintain a right relationship with him, then the difference between Jesus and other Jews becomes, at any rate in his earlier years, one of degree. What is more, if we allow for God's love to be dynamic and creative and if we give due weight, not just to the humanity of Jesus which he shared with other men, but also to his special openness and intimacy with and obedience to the creative will of the Father, then a process of growth and development in Jesus becomes not only natural but inevitable and this, as will emerge in due course, can allow for his attaining that uniqueness on which so many Christians rest

---

[7] *op cit*   p 334

their faith. As has already been suggested, therefore, and as will emerge more fully later, on these divergent understandings of the closeness or distance of the relationship of God to the world and of the way in which the uniqueness of Jesus is to be understood, there rest profoundly different world views.

Given the intimacy of God prevailing in Judaism, and that the early followers of Jesus had been profoundly impressed by his personality, his powers, his resurrection and by a strong sense of his risen presence, the sense of God in the form of Wisdom being present in him becomes intelligible: and indeed, as J D G Dunn says: 'In the early stages of this development at any rate it would be inaccurate to say that Christ was understood as a pre-existent being become incarnate, or that Christ himself was thought to have been present and active in creation ... With Matthew there seems to have been no thought of pre-existence involved and in the Pauline letters and probably the introduction to Hebrews also, the thought is primarily of Christ as the eschatological embodiment of the wisdom of God, as the one through whom the creator God in all his fulness had revealed himself most clearly and definitively for man's salvation and creation's renewal.'[8]

Dunn reiterates this important finding thus: 'He who espouses a Wisdom Christology does not assert that Christ was a pre-existent being, but neither does he assert that Christ was simply a man used by God, even in a climactic way. He asserts rather that Christ fully embodies the creative and saving activity of God, that God in all his fulness was in him, that he represents and manifests all that God is in his outreach to men. We can express this as the divinity or even the deity of Christ, so long as we understand what this means: the deity is the Wisdom of God, for the Wisdom of God is reaching out and active in his world. So the deity of Christ is the deity of Wisdom incarnate ... While we can say that divine Wisdom became incarnate in Christ, that does not mean that Wisdom was a divine being, or that Christ himself was pre-existent with God, but simply that Christ was (and is) the embodiment of divine Wisdom, that is, the climactic and definitive embodiment of God's own creative power and saving concern.'[9] With the Fourth Gospel, however, Dunn suggests that we can speak of a full-blown conception of Christ's personal pre-existence and a clear doctrine of incarnation.[10]

However this may be, and there will be more to say on these issues later, Dunn goes on to show that there is a considerable overlap between the

---

[8] *Christology in the Making* (1980) p 211

[9] *op cit* p 258

[10] *op cit* p 258

earliest Wisdom Christology of Paul and the subsequent Son Christology of the classic creeds, and that the Logos Christology provided a bridge between them. In the pre-Nicene period in the East the concept of the Logos was the main vehicle for developing Christology but from Nicea onwards, the Son becomes the standard formulation of Christian faith in the East as well as the West. Throughout this early period, however, the intimacy seen between Wisdom and creation in the New Testament carried forward and so did the intimacy of Wisdom with the Father carry forward in the intimacy of the Risen Christ, the Son, with the Father.

C H Dodd illustrates that intimacy by showing the intentional parallelism in St John's Gospel between expressions used in regard to the mutual indwelling and the mutual knowledge of the Father, of Christ and of man.[11] He tabulates such expressions and these can be set out (in somewhat different form) thus:

The Father knows the Son (x 15)	The Son knows the Father (x 15)
The Son knows men (x 14)	Men know the Son (x 14)
Men know (see) Father and Son (xiv 7-8)	
The Son is in the Father (xiv 10-11,20, xvii 21)	The Father is in the Son (xiv 10-11, xvii 21,23)
Men are in the Son (xiv 20; xvii 21)	The Son is in men (xiv 20, xv11 23,26)
Men are in Father and Son (xvii 21)	

Dodd comments that 'It challenges the mind to discover a doctrine of the personality, which will make conceivable this combination of the universal and the particular in a single person. A naive anthropomorphism regarding God, makes nonsense of Johannine Christology.'[12]

It must suffice at this point to make two observations on this: first, it is hard to conceive of a greater intimacy than is implied in this tabular statement; and secondly, the challenge referred to by Dodd is largely met if we think of the physical world as a process within the mind of God, evolving to participate more fully in his life, and of men's minds as rooted back into the mind of God — perhaps with the picture of a developing whirlpool in a (boundless) lake as a very limited analogy. This way of thinking of God and the world conflicts with Western ways of thinking of them — ways which we shall have to consider presently in more detail — but, as we have noted, the New Testament has many examples of phrases implying such intimacy, or the need for it, and, in particular, incorporation

[11] C H Dodd   *The Interpretation of the Fourth Gospel*   (1953)   p 187

[12] *op cit*   p 249

in God; and these are in keeping with the intimacy of God as seen in Judaism.

Though Western theologians have read into the teaching of Jesus and Paul that the prime concern of both was with morality and repentance, these, though seen as pleasing to God, carry no obvious implication of any structural change in man's relationship to God. As we shall find later, therefore, and as Sanders shows, there are strong grounds for suggesting that these were the prime concerns of neither Jesus nor Paul. Jesus appears to have substituted for the Jewish concern with repentance, acceptance of him[13] — an acceptance that, as we shall see, opened the way to greater wholeness and salvation which itself entailed greater participation in the life of God. Similarly, Paul's prime concern was with the participation of the faithful in Christ or the Spirit — a participation which likewise entailed a real change in personality which in turn implied greater participation in and manifestation of the life of God.

This emphasis on and concern with the growth and development of the personality to participate in Christ and so in God, and the intimacy that this implied, carried forward into the early Church but before long, it appears to have been lost in some groups, though it remained of central concern in orthodox teaching. Tensions emerged rapidly and were prominent in the heresies which plagued the early centuries of the church. Thus by about the year 300, Arius and his followers sought to bridge the gap that they saw between God and the world by seeing Christ as basically a creature but a creature through whom God created all other things. The Arians therefore saw a sharp distinction not only between Christ and creation but between Christ and the Father: in so far they detracted both from the humanity and the divinity of Christ. On the other hand, Apollonarius, in denying a human soul to Christ, denied his human rational and volitional characteristics and so detracted from his human nature. The Church met these and other deviations by insisting at the Council of Chalcedon in 451 that Christ was both fully God and fully man. But though in thus balancing the two aspects, the Church adopted a position that it has since officially maintained, it has not suceeded in reconciling the tensions that arose in interpreting it. It set the parameters within which a solution might be found without establishing a durable framework of thought in which it could be understood. Indeed, we shall find grounds for suggesting that within the framework of understanding that the Western Church came to hold, a fully coherent solution was impossible. Not surprisingly, therefore, in recent years, traditional claims of the Churches about Jesus Christ have increasingly been questioned, explicitly or implicitly.

---

[13] see *Jesus and Judaism*   (1985)   p 210

In considering ways in which the divine and human in Jesus Christ have been thought of it is worth noting the comment of James Barr: that it is to be suspected that, within the Gospels themselves, incarnation is a secondary concept rather than a first-line one. The first-line question about Jesus is whether he is the Messiah expected in Israel.[14] As we shall see, it was changes in the wider understanding of the relation of the divine to the human that led the later Church to develop doctrines associated with the Incarnation which would have seemed strange to early Christians. In particular, it was Augustine, through whom Western understandings of Christian doctrine were largely channelled, who saw Creator and creation as quite different orders of being for which any mutual participation was impossible, so offering a context in which the uniqueness of Jesus stood out.

We shall need to discuss in later chapters the difference between these Patristic and Western views for our understanding of Christ, but the main point at issue was prominent in Anglican theology in the earlier years of this century. It was well crystallised in the contrasting thought of Charles Gore and Hastings Rashdall. Indeed, this issue provides a major theme in Michael Ramsey's *From Gore to Temple* — an account of the development of Anglican theology between *Lux Mundi* and the Second World War. Thus according to Ramsey, Gore in his view of the two natures of Christ '.. insisted that the essence of the doctrine was that the one Christ was both human and divine; and was not the one because he was the other, for deity and humanity are not identical but distinct, as creator and creature must needs be distinct. That was for Gore the supreme issue. The difference between incarnation and immanentism was absolute. Though God is significantly manifested in the created world, though there is the affinity between God and man implied in the creation of man in the divine image, none the less the most saintly men are not in virtue of their saintliness divine and the creature is not the creator. It is this which has been for Anglican divinity the supreme significance of the doctrine of the two natures.'[15]

The contrasting view is well brought out in a passage which Ramsey quotes from Rashdall's *Philosophy and Religion*[16]: 'We cannot say intelligibly that God dwells in Christ, unless we have already recognised that in a sense God dwells in and reveals himself in humanity at large, and in each particular human soul. But I fully recognise that, if that is all that is meant by the expression "divinity of Christ", that doctrine would be evacuated of nearly all that makes it precious to the hearts of Christian

---

[14] J Barr Some Thoughts on Narrative, Myth and Incarnation in *God Incarnate* ed A E Harvey (1981) p 22

[15] M Ramsey *F rom Gore to Temple* (1960) pp 22-3

[16] (1909) pp 180-1

people. And, therefore, it is all-important that we should go on to insist that men do not reveal God equally.'[17] In the same passage Rashdall speaks of Christ as 'the one in whom the ideal relation of man to God is most completely realised.' Also, speaking of the views of C E Raven, Ramsey says: 'In the emerging universe God discloses himself everywhere and always, but in varying degrees of significance. In this process of the growing divine self-disclosure and the growing unity of God and man, Jesus has a unique place, for which the Nicene definition of his person is the due expression. But it is a process in which creation and redemption are one and the same thing, and the distinction of nature and supernature has no validity.'[18] F W Dillistone notes the theological isolation felt by Raven in his later years,[19] and, not surprisingly, therefore, Ramsey, speaking of the Report of the Archbishops' Commission on Doctrine in the Church of England which was published in 1937, says, with obvious approval: '... there is within this comprehensive speculum of contemporary Anglican teaching no place whatever for that view of deity and manhood which in the hands of Rashdall and Bethune-Baker had loomed so large in the Modernism of two decades earlier. ... It was no longer in view. That is the supremely important fact.'[20]

It is worth noting a passage quoted by Rashdall in his *The Idea of the Atonement in Christian Theology*[21] and taken from Origen's *Contra Celsum*, that puts that Modernism into a longer perspective: 'We say that the Logos was united and made one with the soul of Jesus in a far higher degree than any other soul, seeing that he alone was able completely to receive the highest participation in the true Word and the true Wisdom and the true Righteousness.'[22] Speaking about theology today (i e 1960), however, Ramsey adds euphemistically that 'With less concern about the biographical aspect of the Gospels and less willingness to give their minds to questions about the consciousness of Christ, theologians have been the more willing to rest in the affirmation of his deity and humanity, and to leave mystery at the core of the Gospel.'[23]

We cannot here seek to pursue the obscurities into which the idea of two quite separate natures leads and to which the last references point. Suffice

---

[17] *op cit*   p 69

[18] *op cit*   p 26

[19] F W Dillistone *Charles Raven* (1975) e g p 398

[20] M Ramsey *op cit*   p 90

[21] (1920) p 257

[22] *Contra Celsum*   v 39

[23] M Ramsey *op cit*   p 42

to say here that for Gore, as for many other Western theologians, 'The Incarnation was inherently miraculous, and the miracles accompanying it stood attested by good historical evidence, unless blind prejudice against the miraculous gave bias to an historian's mind. Miracle was to him the vindication of the living God intervening to restore a created world wrecked and disordered by sin.'[24]

This question of interventions by God in the world has, however, long been the subject of protest by some theologians. Maurice Wiles notes the much quoted saying of Aubrey Moore that 'a theory of occasional intervention implies as its correlative a theory of ordinary absence.'[25] What is more, in the light of present day preconceptions, the idea of miracles seen as special initiatives of God, presents very serious problems. Not surprisingly, therefore, some theologians appear to have concluded that traditional Christology must be misconceived. Thus Maurice Wiles entitled a much discussed essay 'Does Christology rest on a Mistake?' and in guarded terms concluded that it did;[26] and John Knox has said, 'We can have the humanity without the pre-existence and we can have the pre-existence without the humanity. There is absolutely no way of having both.'[27]. It tends also to follow that the other extraordinary events associated with the life and death of Jesus, and which form such an integral feature of the New Testament records, have also to be discounted or explained away, often as in some sense 'myths'.

We shall find strong grounds for dissenting from such conclusions as these but before then, a long journey lies ahead: a journey which must build on the Old Testament understandings which we have already illustrated and which are far removed from many prevalent today. These understandings provided the framework of thought in terms of which the life and death of Jesus, his resurrection and post resurrection appearances and those subsequent experiences of the early Christians which they attributed to the Divine Christ, must have made coherent and compelling sense: for it was on this basis that they came to be recorded in the New Testament and developed in the early Church. Notwithstanding, therefore, the views of many Churchmen, as we have noted, that Jesus Christ provides the obvious and even the only approach to Christianity, we shall find that that approach is not obvious, if only because, as we have seen, any interpretation of Jesus Christ raises fundamental and divisive issues stemming from the very

---

[24] M Ramsey *op cit* p 21

[25] M F Wiles *Working Papers in Doctrine* (1976) p 124

[26] M F Wiles in *Christ Faith & History* eds. S W Sykes & J P Clayton (1972) p 3

[27] J Knox *The Humanity and Divinity of Christ* (1967) p 106

preconceptions of our current thought. For these reasons, therefore, it has seemed best to move straight to the understandings of the early Church about Jesus Christ and the relationship of God to the world and then to pursue their later development and implications, only at the end of this book bringing to bear our findings on to his life, death, resurrection and ascension.

CHAPTER FIVE

GOD & THE WORLD: THE EARLY CHURCH FATHERS

The Pre-Augustinian Understanding of God in Relation to the World

It would be beyond the scope of this study to attempt to show in any detail how the concept of God and the understanding of his relationship to the world developed during the early years of the Church. We have already seen how, at the time of Jesus, Judaism, notwithstanding its strong sense of the transcendence of God, had also a strong sense of his accessibility and intimacy, in particular in the form of various personified aspects of God himself, such as the divine Wisdom, God's 'glory' or 'presence' (Shekinah), his Word and his Spirit. The Greeks, too, had a strong sense of the presence of the divine in the world, in particular in the form of the Logos and the divine love — as both *eros* and *agape*. Such concepts are referred to in the New Testament and are applied to Jesus so that there are present in the New Testament, as well as in the Old Testament, the concepts that gradually took shape in the understanding of God as Trinity.

The form that this understanding took can be illustrated by reference to the work of Irenaeus who was born only about one hundred years after the crucifixion and who dominated Christian orthodoxy before Origen. Irenaeus' understanding of God and his relationship to the world, like that of the other early Fathers, is summed up in the formula 'enclosing, not enclosed', which enshrined both the transcendence and the immanence of God.

Kelly, describing the theology of Irenaeus, notes that he approached God both as he exists in his intrinsic being, and also as he manifests himself in the 'economy', i e the ordered process of his self-disclosure in the world. From the former point of view God is the Father of all things, ineffably one, and yet containing in himself from all eternity his Word and his Wisdom. In making himself known, however, in exerting himself, for creation and redemption, God manifests these: as the Son, his Word, the principle of reason and order, and his Spirit, his energy and love, they are his 'hands', the forms of his self-revelation. Thus, as Kelly says, Irenaeus could claim that 'by the very essence and nature of his being there is but one God', while at the same time 'according to the economy of our redemption there are both Father and Son' — and, Kelly notes, he might easily have added, Spirit.[1]

Having remarked on the emphasis which Irenaeus placed on the uniqueness and transcendence of the Father who is also the author of

---

[1] J N D Kelly *Early Christian Doctrines* rev edn (1977) pp 104-5

whatever exists, Kelly quotes Irenaeus: "'Being altogether mind and altogether Word, God utters what he thinks and thinks what he utters. His thinking is his Word, and his Word is his intelligence, and the Father is that intelligence comprising all things." More briefly, "since God is rational, he created whatever was made by his Word."'[2]

Kelly goes on to note that Irenaeus closely associated the Spirit with the Son. The Father reveals himself only by the Son in creation but it is only through the Spirit, whose work is sanctification, that knowledge of the Son can be obtained, for the Spirit purifies man and raises him to the life of God. Thus if we think of the Word as the ordering principle of the world and so of our minds, and of the Spirit as the divine energy or love which energises and guides the world and our minds towards fuller participation in the life of God, it may be seen how the Spirit energises those leaps of insight which offer progressively deeper participation in the life of God, and at the same time make the mind more whole and so more aware of, and rationally responsive to, the work of God in creation.

As we shall see throughout this book, therefore, there is entailed in the thought of Irenaeus and the other early Fathers an understanding in which every positive attribute of creation at every level — its form and energy, its life, consciousness, understanding, love and holiness — has its source as an attribute of God in which creation, as it has evolved and continues to evolve, progressively participates, in however limited and distorted a form. It is, however, only man who is in the image of God, because whereas the rest of creation has not attained the level of participation in the Logos, the order and reason of the life of God, that allows all these attributes to be manifested, man has the potential to develop to manifest them all, though in finite measure.

We have, therefore, in the thought of Irenaeus, the benevolence of the Father who, as the source, creates the world within his life in order that it may participate in it; the Word through whom this is carried out, and who progressively reveals himself through the deepening participation of the world in his order and reason, and who, in so far, reveals the life and work of the Father who in himself remains invisible; and the Spirit who, though also present in an energising, vivifying and sanctifying role throughout creation, has the special task of seeking lovingly to guide the process of developing — or evolving — participation towards completion.

Several points deserve comment about this understanding which, broadly, was shared by the other Church Fathers before Augustine. First, as has been noted and as will emerge more fully presently, Irenaeus and the other early Church Fathers have a very different understanding of the Trinity and of its

---

[2] *op cit*   p 105   quoting   Haer. 2 28 & Dem. 5

relationship to the world from that of Augustine and the subsequent Western Churches, including those of the present day. The Augustinian and so the Western understanding of the Trinity sees all three persons as 'internal' to and as constituting God's transcendent life and sees the world as 'outside' his full life — though Augustine continued to see the world as immersed in and penetrated by God's infinity as a sponge soaked in an immense sea.[3]

Whereas, therefore, in the West all three persons are equal manifestations of one underlying divine essence and constitute the internal life of God, the Trinity of the early Church Fathers, including Irenaeus, is of the Father as the divine source and as himself the essence; and the other two persons are seen as those aspects of the Father that act as his instruments in creation within his life. For the early Fathers, therefore, it is the Father who transcends the world, and though the other two persons share in his transcendent life, they are those aspects of the divine that are immanent in the world, structuring and energising it as a process within the divine life. In contrast, in the West, all three persons are transcendent and the persons carry out the work of creation simply by an overflow of the divine benevolence which takes the form of the divine missions outside his life. When, therefore, the early Church Fathers speak of God, or more specifically of God transcendent, they are speaking primarily of the Father, whereas in Western theology, to speak in this way of God is to speak of all three persons and their single underlying essence. Naturally, therefore, for the early Fathers, creation is an integral feature of the totally free life of God whereas, as we shall see, in the context of the Western picture, God's freedom came in due course to be seen in terms of freedom of choice whether and in what form to create, so that his creation of the world became, in effect, an optional extra.

The early Patristic context can be viewed also from a somewhat different angle. As Sherrard notes, a distinction which was crystallised by St Gregory of Palamas in the fourteenth century but was explicit already in the Patristic tradition, was drawn between God's ultimate nature or Essence and his uncreated powers and energies by which he created the world and which are present in all he creates — a distinction to which we have already pointed in the case of Irenaeus. It is the Essence that is totally transcendent, simple and unknowable whereas God's energies take the multiplicity of forms of the created world.[4] We shall have later to consider how there can be this distinction within God. In contrast, however, in the West, in the Augustinian and, to a greater degree, in Scholastic thought, emphasis was placed on the idea of the absolute simplicity of the Divine Essence

---

[3] *Conf*   7 5

[4] *The Greek East and the Latin West*   (1959)   pp 38ff

considered more or less exclusively as pure Being.[5] This precluded the earlier understanding of the Trinity and of creation within the life of God which was replaced by the idea of creation *ad extra*. The distinction is summed up by Sherrard thus: 'One might say that while for the Greeks there is one God because there is one Father, for the Latins there is one God because there is one Essence, one divine and entirely simple being'[6] — a being who had the Trinity within his life and the world outside it.

One other implication of this fundamental difference is worth noting here. Whereas for the early Church, creation, and in fuller measure man, participated in the Divine life, for Augustine, God and the world were utterly different. As a result, as Sherrard says, by a limitation of their thought to what amounted to a dualist conception of, on the one hand, God considered exclusively as Creator and, on the other hand, creation itself, the West eliminated all notion of an intermediary intellectual world, or world of Ideas, acting as a link, or bridge, between the two.[7] Although the conception of an infinite distance separating Creator and creation was to emerge only in the Middle Ages with Albert Magnus, the potential for this gulf was inherent in the change of understanding of the Trinity. Later we shall meet some implications of this change which are very important for understanding current thought, one particular implication being the normal present day understanding of minds as isolated from each other, save for the senses, in contrast with the idea of minds rooted back into the mind of God and so into what amounts to a form of collective unconscious.

The contrasting implications of the earlier understandings and those of the West can be further illustrated by reference to the Incarnation. For the earlier Fathers, God was present throughout creation which was being given form by the Divine Son, the Word of God, the Logos. The Son was, therefore, 'incarnate' throughout creation, creating and seeking to redeem it. Jesus was not special in *this* respect but, as we shall see, in his responsiveness and obedience to the creative powers of the Father and in the vast implications that flowed from this. In contrast, since for the West, creation lay outside the full life of God and normal man had no share in his divinity, and since Creator and created were utterly different, not only was there the virtually insoluble problem of the relationship of the human and divine natures in Christ, but it was natural for Jesus to be thought of as bearer of the divine nature being sent into the world from the outside in a special miracle to save it. In Western theology, therefore, the Incarnation is primarily the Incarnation in the world of God (as distinct from the divine

---

[5] *op cit*   p 68

[6] *op cit*   p 70

[7] *op cit*   p 122

Son) in whom, in principle, the roles of the three persons are seen as interchangeable; but for the earlier Fathers, the Incarnation is specifically the role of the Son, the Word, the Logos or the Divine Christ, though he is, of course, inspired by the Spirit and both are aspects of the Father who is present in them.

It will be apparent, therefore, that in this earlier understanding of the Trinity, through the Son and Spirit, God the Father is here and now in creation in the most intimate way possible: though invisible, through his Son and Spirit, he is structuring and energising the world and seeking to redeem it by making its order, through participation in his order, more complete and perfect. Man 'passes through all things' with safety only by union with — by participation in — Christ, who, with the Spirit, at each successive stage in the development of the individual and in each successive age of the world, offers him that knowledge and help that he needs at that time. The Gospel thus is no new thing, but the completion and fulfillment of a long chain of revelations of the Saviour; the last and best stage in the education of the world.[8]

The Idea of Developing Participation in the Life of God

We, as parts of his creation, are, therefore, within the creative life of God and in that sense embraced, structured and energised by the Trinity, though partially shut out by finitude and by sin — which we shall see more fully later is to be understood within this picture, not just in terms of moral failure but in the more basic and all-embracing sense of deviation from and foreclosing against the creative order and reason of God, the divine Christ, and so from and against the Father and his life and love, the Spirit. As we shall also see, therefore, the claims often made that the admission of the world 'within' the life of God entails admitting sin into the life of God miss the mark for this entire understanding of creation is in terms of greater or lesser participation in the life of God and sin entails the reduction of existing — or the frustration of greater — participation of creation in his life. This understanding is confirmed by the vigorous protests levelled by Irenaeus and others against the Gnostic views on the ground that they do admit imperfection into the being of God. Clearly, therefore, the process of overcoming sin and disorder and allowing us to approach oneness with the Father in Christ has to be thought of, not just as entailing moral purification but as increasingly sharing in his creative order and reason and depth through *gnosis:* for, as we shall see, the Divine process is basically one of the evolution of the order of the world and in particular our personalities to

---

[8] C Bigg *The Origins of Christianity* (1909) p 218

higher and higher levels of order and so to fuller participation in the Divine
Christ, thereby allowing him to work in and through the world and, more
specifically, in and through us and to manifest the attributes of God more
fully. In so far, we ourselves become more rational and whole and healthy
and so more transparent also to the creative love of God, the Spirit.

The idea of participation in the divine life through *gnosis,* leading to
'deification', which is a feature of the thought of virtually all the early
Church Fathers, has been the subject of profound misunderstandings in the
West, in large measure because some Western commentators have sought to
understand it within the Western picture of creation 'outside' the life of God
with God and man as utterly different: a picture which suggests that if man
were to be deified and entered the life of God, he would necessarily lose his
creaturely status and cease to be man, while God would cease to be God —
for God and creation are seen as exclusive categories. Within the earlier
picture of creation within the life of God, however, the whole of creation
necessarily participates in the life of God though in different degrees, and
develops by overcoming the disorder of sin to grow and develop in the life
of God more fully, while the transcendent life of God is itself unaltered.
The attainment by man of deification is, therefore, to become God, not by
ceasing to be man, but, by developing to share fully in the unchanging life
of God, to become fully man. But, as we shall see more fully later,
although man thereby shares more fully in the life of God, in no way does
he 'become' God in the sense of totally identifying with God, for God is
always the infinite, transcendent source, the Creator, whereas man is always
finite, sustained by and utterly dependent on, God.

This idea of developing participation in the life of God had strong roots
also in Greek thinking. Plato sees human life as a pilgrimage from
appearance to reality and, as Iris Murdoch remarks, his work is 'largely
connected with ways to salvation.'[9] As she says: 'The defeat of illusion
requires moral effort. The instructed and morally purified mind sees reality
clearly and indeed (in an important sense) provides us with the concept.'[10]
For Plato that reality was not, of course, this world of the senses but of the
Forms which lay in the mind of God. It is on this basis that Plato saw God
as the great educator. It was basically growth of insights and understanding
that morally purified the mind. This idea extended to Greek culture as a
whole and was taken over by Christianity in which the Divine Christ, the
ordering principle and reason of God who is active in us and in the world
and who, in conjunction with the Holy Spirit, inspires leaps of insight,
gnosis, to even deeper levels of order, came to be seen as the great Educator

---

[9] *The Fire and the Sun*   (1977)   p 32

[10] *op cit*   p 47

of the early Church. This was an important feature of, for instance, the work of Clement of Alexandria. Werner Jaeger comments that when Christ is visualised as 'the educator of mankind', he is contrasted with the Greek idea of culture as a whole, for that is the exact meaning that the word *paideia* had developed in the course of its history. He notes that Plato in the Laws had defined God's relation to the whole world by saying that 'God is the Pedagogue of the whole world' and he adds that it is this Platonic theological dignity that made it possible for Clement to introduce Christ as the Paedogogus of all men.[11]

Similarly, Jaeger notes that philosophy was for Origen both Logos and Bios [way of life] as it was for all ancient philosophers, and he adds that he suspects that the failure of modern interpreters to recognise the religious capacity of philosophy, in the broad sense in which it was interpreted by Origen, as by Plotinus and Porphyry, is partly due to the fact that for those thinkers, philosophy did not have the same meaning as our modern word but denoted a religion of the spirit. 'The modern psychology of religion seems to have difficulty in understanding this variety of religious mind, because under the influence of a Protestant concept of faith it has narrowed the field of religious experience and excluded the mind as mere intellect. But such an *a priori* concept of what "true religion" is would make late ancient religion in its higher forms quite ununderstandable to us and would limit religion to the irrational.'[12]

Charles Bigg speaks of the theology of Origen thus: 'Origen regards the world as existing in God as its cause, in such a way that the cause, being vastly superior to its effect, spreads out into inconceiveable heights and depths beyond the world. Thus God is partly and in a way comprehensible; partly incomprehensible, yet again in such a way that by moral and spiritual assimilation, we may draw ever nearer and nearer to him until at last we become able to behold him as he is. It is the teaching of St Paul. Here we know but in part; we see as in a glass darkly; but there will come a time when we know even as we are known ... God is pure Spirit, eternal, immutable, immaterial. The laws of time and space do not apply to him and no language which, however remotely, involves ideas of time and space can be used of him with truth. Thus it is only by a metaphor that we can speak of him as in heaven. Heaven is, on the contrary, in God, and is not a place, but a spiritual condition. Again, to say that God is immanent in the world is sheer Pantheism, unless the expression is most carefully guarded. The right manner of statement is that the world is in God; it is in God, Plotinus says, "as a net is in the sea," contained but not containing, pervaded by an

---

[11] *Early Christianity and Greek Paideia* (1961/9) p 133

[12] *op cit* p 130-131

element which it in no way restrains or bounds; and this is the meaning of
Origen also ... In other words, our own natural knowledge of God is true
as far as it goes. There are depths which we cannot as yet fathom, not
because they are unreasonable, but because as yet they lie beyond our
experience. Nothing is "against nature", nor can be so. But there are things
which are "above nature", which are in our present condition
uncomprehended.'[13]

And Henry Chadwick says that throughout his writings, Origen's theology
presupposes that 'providence' is another way of speaking about divine
immanence within the power and beauty of the cosmos which is not
indifferent to value. He notes that not everything that happens is the direct
will of God. '"Some things occur by his will, others are by his good
pleasure but other things by his permission." (Frg. in Luc. 57, p 261 Rauer).
But all is ultimately absorbed within the grand design.'[14]

We approach these understandings from another angle in the works of
Gregory of Nyssa who died about 395. Jaeger comments that in spite of
God's transcendence, there is a long way of gradual approach to him. This
is the path of knowledge. In this process, knowledge and virtue are
inseparable. Without knowledge it is impossible to discern the goal of the
'philosophic life'. In this sense religion is *gnosis* of the divine good or 'will
of God' towards which man's will must be directed. But, as we have seen,
'knowledge' in this sense is not just factual or abstract knowledge but
'insights' or 'understanding' or 'wisdom' which increase only with the
growth of man's entire nature and with his spiritual coming of age.
Gregory, Jaeger continues, visualises this process as a sequence of steps or
stages marking the advance towards the goal of perfection. This process of
salvation is the mystery of the new religion. It is interpreted as the gradual
purification of the soul from the stain of the material world and its final
liberation from the servitude of the passions. The goal of this lifelong
struggle is the freedom of man from the tyranny of evil.[15]

Later Jaeger notes that all Gregory's characteristic terms depict the ascent
of the soul to God by way of assimilation to him: and having commented
on the influence on Gregory of his brother Basil, he notes the the supreme
goal of human appetition according to Basil is 'to become God'.[16] This
understanding of the Cappadocian Fathers is thus basically in accord with
that of the other early Church Fathers, including Irenaeus, who, as Gustaf

---

[13] C Bigg *The Origins of Christianity* (1909) pp 430-1

[14] Freedom and Necessity in Early Christian Thought about God in *Cosmology and Theology* Concilium 166 (1983) p 12

[15] W Jaeger *Two Rediscovered works of Ancient Christian Literature* (1954) pp 78-9

[16] *op cit* p 102-3

Wingren notes, claims that God is one but man becomes, and for him there are many stages of development[17] — a view of man's development that has been, (and, as we shall see, should be) represented as an instance of virtually the modern theory of evolution.

The Pre-Augustinian Idea of the Incarnation

Basically the same kind of understanding of the relationship of God to the world is to be found in the work of Athanasius who died in 373. A few quotations from *De Incarnatione* show this and at the same time make clear the place of the Incarnation of Jesus within it. Speaking of the Divine Christ or Word who sustained the whole of creation while being specifically incarnate in Jesus, he says: 'He was not enclosed in the body, nor was he in the body but nowhere else. Nor did he move the latter while the universe was deprived of his action and providence. But what is most wonderful is that, being the Word, he was not contained by anyone, but rather himself contained everything. And as he is in all creation, he is in essence outside the universe but in everything by his power, ordering everything and extending his providence over everything. And giving life to all, separately and together, he contains the universe and is not contained, but in his Father only is he complete in everything. So also being in a human body and giving it life himself, he accordingly gives life to everything, and was both in all and outside all. And although he was known by his body through his works, yet he was not invisible by his action on the universe.' And speaking of the Incarnation he adds, 'For he was not bound to the body but rather he controlled it, so he was in it and in everything, and outside creation and only at rest in the Father.'[18] And later Athanasius says: 'The philosophers of the Greeks say that the world is a great body; and rightly they say so, for we perceive it and its parts affecting our senses. If then the Word of God is in the world, which is a body, and he has passed into it all and every part of it, what is wonderful or what is unfitting in our saying that he came in a man? If it is completely unfitting that he should be in a body, it would be unfitting that he should come into the whole and illuminate and move the universe by his providence, for the universe also is a body. But if it is suitable for him to come into the cosmos and be known in it all, it would also be suitable that he should appear in a human body, and that it should be illuminated and moved by him. For the human race is part of the whole; and if the part is not suitable to be his instrument wherewith to make known his divinity, it would be most unfitting that he should be known

---

[17] *Man and Incarnation* (1959) p 8

[18] *De Incarnatione* 17

through the whole universe.'[19] Thus life in the Father, in the world and in Jesus were brought together in the one conception.

By becoming incarnate in Jesus, Pelikan says, 'the Logos had enabled human beings to transcend themselves and, in the pregnant phrase of the New Testament, "to become partakers in the divine nature" (2 Pet:1 4). "The Logos of God has become human", one Greek Father after another would say, "so that you might learn from a human being how a human being may become divine."[20] The original creation in the image of God, in which all true human greatness consisted,[21] had been brought about through the Logos; that creation would now achieve not only restoration but consummation and perfection through the same Logos: his incarnation would achieve our deification. And the whole cosmos would have its proper share in that consummation; for "the establishment of the church is a re-creation of the world," in which "the Logos has created a multitude of stars", a new heaven and a new earth.'[22] The understanding of the Father primarily as God transcendent, of the divine Son (and Spirit) primarily as God immanent, and of the Incarnation as the supreme specific instance of the general activity of the divine Son in creating, ordering and sustaining the universe as a whole, should be plain from these quotations. So should the idea of Jesus Christ as God and man. Though the precise way in which his attributes should be allocated between his divinity and his humanity might be the subject of prolonged and subtle debate, the essential point is that the divinity and humanity of Christ are not seen in this account as inherently exclusive but his humanity is seen as developing within his divine life to bring the process to full participation in the life of God: a process of which Jesus Christ is the first fruits, the forerunner.

In other words, in the understanding of the early Church Fathers, Christ became man so that in incarnate form he might show us how we might participate in his divinity. This flowed from the creative nature of God and entailed the 'recapitulation', the showing of the way to the restoration and perfection of creation, carried through by God in Jesus as the supreme instance of the work in the world of the Divine Son and Holy Spirit. However, in the understanding of Anselm who died in 1109 and who is seen as the theologian who first crystallised the main Western view of the atonement, the sacrifice of Jesus as a man on the cross had to be made on

---

[19] *De Incarnatione*   41   (trans R W Thomson) (1971)

[20]   e g   Clement of Alexandria *Exhortation to the Greeks*   1 8 4 ;   Athanasius *De Incarnatione* 54 3

[21]   Gregory of Nyssa *On the Making of Man*   *16 2*

[22]   J Pelikan *Jesus through the Centuries* (1985)   p 68 quoting Gregory of Nyssa *Sermons on the Song of Songs*   13

behalf of all morally sinful and guilty men to God; and a worthy sacrifice could be made only by a man who was himself free from moral sin and guilt. In the earlier understanding, the atonement was made by God through a man who was sinless in the sense of whole and so transparent to the creative powers of God and who was therefore able to use the creative powers of God to grow so as to complete that journey of assimilation into the order and life of God on which the whole of creation is labouring. In the later understanding, because creation as a whole and man in particular are seen as having some autonomy, the atonement is achieved, not by growing and developing into the life of God by use of the creative powers of God, but by the conscious personal sacrifice of Jesus, albeit that this was made in accordance with the plan of God. Death in this view is important in itself as the price that has to be paid as the satisfaction demanded by God's justice. It is not primarily the path entailing the overcoming of the disorder of death in the resurrection, so showing men the way to victory over the forces of sin and evil: it is instead an offering of vicarious suffering which admits a 'non-personal' transference of Christ's merit to men but does not in itself make men more whole.

It is this change of meaning that leads to the devotion to the passion and the desire for identification with the sufferings of Jesus which became such a strong mark of religious life in the later Middle Ages and subsequently. The early Fathers understood sin as deviation from the creative will and order of God and as something organic detracting from the state of the whole of creation; sin had, as one of its implications, the breakdown of order in death, and salvation entailed the restoration or development of the order of the divine Christ and so the bestowal of the life of the Holy Spirit. In contrast, the understanding of Anselm and the main Latin tradition allowed for the remission of punishment: but did not lead thereby to the overcoming of sin itself. Not surprisingly, therefore, in the earlier tradition, Christ is seen as overcoming sin and death in a series of sequential steps which lead through his life on earth, his death and resurrection to his ascension. His death is one crucial step in this process but it is not all-important. The emphasis lies on the obedience of Jesus to the creative will of God which, as we shall see more fully later, at each stage opens him further to the creative powers of God and leads ultimately to the overcoming of the bounds of finitude and to his full identification with the Divine Christ.

The Augustinian Understanding of God in Relation to the World

We do not need to dwell here on the devotion of Augustine to Jesus as the perfect man and the fact that he saw Jesus, and, 'out of honour to the Lord', the Virgin Mary, as alone morally sinless. Suffice to say that, not surprisingly, in view of the sharp distinction drawn by Augustine between God and creation, this distinction was drawn in his Christology. Eugène Portalié quotes Harnack: 'According to the Bishop of Hippo, the inhabitation of the divinity in Jesus Christ can be conceived on the analogy of its presence in the just man as in a temple, even though he firmly maintained that the Word was made flesh.'[23] Portalié speaks of the evident falsity of any other explanation.[24] The distinction between the just man and the temple, between the humanity and the divinity, is clear.

As for the Trinity, in illustrating how it came to be understood by the early Church Fathers, it has already been necessary to contrast it with the understanding of Augustine and of the subsequent Western Church. Much of what needs to be said about the Augustinian Trinity for present purposes has, therefore, already been presented. Kelly comments that the Greek Fathers treated it as axiomatic that the Father alone was the source or fountain-head of Deity, and that both the Son and the Spirit derived, in the only legitimate sense of the word, from him, the one by generation, the other by procession.[25] On the other hand, Augustine's Trinitarianism did not start with the Father as the source of the other two persons who carried out his work in the world, but with the idea of the one simple Godhead to whose life all three persons were internal and in which whatever could be predicated of one of the persons could be predicated of the others. God thus came to be seen as complete in himself in the fellowship of the Trinity and creation came to be seen as being undertaken 'outside' the full life of God, though sustained by his 'missions', as a result of the overflowing bounty of his goodness. As Kelly says, this Augustinian understanding of the Trinity came to be universally accepted in the West in the fifth and sixth centuries; and he adds that there could be no more illuminating instance of the hold the great African had on Latin Christianity.[26]

As Bernard Piault says: 'Theologians say that creation is a procession *ad extra* or outside God because it does not affect the divine life.'[27]   Karl Rahner notes the resulting isolation that has developed between the doctrine of the Trinity and the doctrine of creation. 'Unlike the great theology of the past, as we find it in Bonaventure, today's theology hardly ever sees any connection between the Trinity and the doctrine of creation. This isolation is considered legitimate, since the "outward" divine operations are

---

[23] *History of Dogma* (1894-99) vol iv   p 183

[24] *A Guide to the Thought of St Augustine* (1960)   pp 153-4

[25] J N D Kelly *The Early Christian Creeds*   (1950)   pp 359-360

[26] *op cit*   p 359

[27] B Piault *What is the Trinity?*   (1959) p 120

"common" to the three divine persons, so that the world as creation cannot tell us anything about the inner life of the Trinity.' And he adds 'In the final analysis, all these statements say explicitly in cold print that we ourselves have nothing to do with the mystery of the Holy Trinity except to know something "about it" through revelation.'[28] Rahner, like Piault, is, of course, concerned here with the understanding of the Trinity as it has developed in the West: but that understanding is fundamentally that of Augustine. Rahner insists that this understanding of 'the isolation of the Trinity has to be wrong. There must be a connection between the Trinity and man.'[29] And he notes that 'The Greeks thought quite naturally that the Trinity was connected with salvation history. They felt, and rightly so, that their whole theology was a doctrine of the Trinity. ... Should we not say, then, that the West has taken over from the Greeks the formal part of the theology of the Trinity as if it were the (whole of) theology of the Trinity ..?'[30]

Sherrard comments that what came to occupy a central and overriding position in Latin theology was the idea of the eminent and absolute simplicity of the divine nature. But, he says, if the Divinity is considered to be absolutely determined in this way, then not only will the idea of a distinction of Persons in the Trinity be reduced in significance, but also, as a consequence, the sense of each sacramental centre [local church] participating through the ever-present and all-pervasive energies of the Spirit in the life of the Logos, the Principle of Unity, will be correspondingly weakened. Essence, he claims, implies entire simplicity, indivisibility, non-manifestation, absolute transcendence of all relationship and all created beings. Hence, if the Divinity is envisaged mainly from this point of view, it becomes difficult to understand how at the same time it can be fully present in, and invisibly sustaining, the multiplicity of created beings; it becomes difficult to understand how at the same time it can be fully present and indivisibly divided, in the sacramental life of the many local churches.[31] And Sherrard notes later that for the Latins, who tended to regard all distinction and multiplicity in God as irreconcilable with their conception of his entirely simple, undifferentiated nature, it became difficult to understand the full reality of that idea of participation on which the Greeks insisted.[32]

---

[28] K Rahner *The Trinity*   (1970)   pp 13-14

[29] K Rahner   *op cit*   p 21

[30] K Rahner   *op cit*   p 18

[31] P Sherrard   *The Greek East and The Latin West*   (1959)   pp 83-4

[32] *op cit*   p 85

The implications of this change initiated by Augustine proved, therefore, to be extremely far-reaching. We need not here pursue in detail the theological implications of the change, many of which will emerge later. It will be clear, however, that this separation of the life of God from that of the world meant not only reliance on revelation, as distinct from reason based in the knowledge of the world, for any understanding of the life of God, but also the abandonment of the Patristic view that the revelation of the divine nature 'has to be inferred from God's works, and apprehended by the exercise of the rational faculties' — by *gnosis*.[33] God's rational ordering work thus ceased to be the unique function of the Logos, the Word or divine Son; there was little scope for the doctrine of the Logos incarnate in all creation and, as we shall see, created beings came to be seen as having been created and being sustained to exist in their own right in a sense quite different from and apart from the divine. Not surprisingly, therefore, the Incarnation, instead of being seen as the culminating, perfect and in that sense unique instance of the continuing work of this rational principle which was leading to the evolutionary development of the entire created order within the life of God to participate in it, became in due course, a special and miraculous intervention into the created and sustained but largely self-subsisting order of the world on the part of God whose life lay outside it.

The Pre-Augustinian Understanding of Sin

This change found its counterpart in a change in the understanding of man's fallen nature and of sin. We indicated earlier that Judaism of the time of Jesus had no doctrine of original sin though the weakness and fallibility of man was fully recognised. Similarly, in general tenor, the early Church Fathers before Augustine, particularly in the east, were relatively optimistic about man's plight, though they were much preoccupied with the need for moral purity of man. Thus Irenaeus saw man as created perfect but weak. Daniélou says about his theology that on the one hand there is perfection of a certain kind in the beginning, the perfection involved in the fact that God gave his spirit to the first man. Any progress there may be, therefore, is not a movement from natural to supernatural Man. On the other hand, the first human being is but a child of a Man, still at a very elementary stage. Consequently only as much of the Spirit is given to him as he can bear, and what he does receive he can very easily lose. 'The plan of God is therefore a single whole. Neither the Spirit nor the Word (which are the hands of God) ever ceases to be present to Man, but Man can only receive them by

---

[33] G L Prestige *God in Patristic Thought* (1952) p 56

progressive stages. On this view, sin introduces a disturbing element into the story, but it does not change its essential outline.'[34] Indeed, Charles Bigg can say: 'The Fall did not strike Irenaeus as an unmixed calamity. Man created immature can attain to perfection only by completing his experience and "passing through all things". (Against Heresies iii 20 2)'[35] Because for Irenaeus there is in created things order that is the work of the Son and is nourished by the Spirit, in no way can man be cut off from God for the Son and Spirit are within him, giving him being and fashioning and developing him in so far as man can resist temptation and the wiles of Satan. The presence of all three persons was thus a *sine qua non* of man's existence and that of the world. On this basis, as Wingren says, Irenaeus saw the Church, not as a group but as a manifestation of Christ's progressive dominion,[36] and his dominion as embracing the whole of humanity and, indeed, the whole of creation.[37] It is in this sense that the Church was seen as the Body of Christ in which he lives and which lives in him.[38] In the words of St Anthony the Great, it is the house of 'truth': a word which has lost its implication of being well founded and trustworthy and has now the more abstract sense of 'knowledge' — an implication still reflected in current English language as when we speak of twelve good men and true.

Somewhat similarly, Athanasius saw man called into being by the Word in which he participated. This communion with the Word bestowed divine knowledge upon man, made him rational and whole, and had given him incorruption and immortality. Adam and Eve had allowed themselves to be distracted by the material world so they lapsed into ignorance and idolatory but the disintegration was not total for if man lost the immortality of the body, he retained that of the soul and his will remained free to throw off the entanglements of sensuality and recover his vision of the Word. Man shared in the consequences of this débâcle but not in Adam's guilt.[39]

For the early Fathers generally, therefore, there was a strong central concern with, as it were, 'structural' development of the personality through *gnosis* leading to fuller and fuller participation in the life of God, and morality found its place as a precondition and consequence of it. Thus for Irenaeus sin is to be seen in terms of the corruption of man by Satan who destroys man's 'growth': 'the child' ceases to progress towards his destiny

---

[34] J Danielou *Gospel Message and Hellenistic Culture* (1973) p 402

[35] C Bigg *The Origins of Christianity* (1909) p 217

[36] G Wingren *Man and Incarnation* (1959) p 141

[37] *op cit* p 142

[38] *op cit* p 160

[39] c f J N D Kelly *Early Christian Doctrines* (1977) pp 346-348

appointed by God which is to grow in conformity with God to his likeness.[40] Similarly for Origen man is put on earth to educate him to return to his maker and sin frustrates this. God takes care not only of the universe as a whole but of every rational being, and even if some parts, by sin, become very bad, God purifies it and, after a time, brings the whole world to himself.[41]

The Augustinian Understanding of Sin and of the Nature of the Church

As we have noted, for Augustine, any participation of creation in the Creator was impossible: they were quite different orders of being. Therefore, the idea of structural growth by *gnosis* to participate more fully in the life of God and of sin as the frustration of that structural growth was lost with Augustine and was replaced by a more psychocentric, directly moral concern. Because for Augustine, the world was as God ordered it and there was no room for chance, Augustine located the source of evil in man's rational will which was free to choose between good and evil.[42] It therefore applied only to men and angels, for the beasts could behave only in accordance with their God-given natures. If man were what he ought to be, there would be no need for change in him: it was a property of the good to be static. Evil was associated with change for the worse and it was the role of grace to seek to restore man to his original state of goodness. G R Evans notes that in *On the Christian Life*, Augustine emphasises that there are many qualities a good man must possess to be perfect before man and God: 'He must be just, pure, devoted, spotless, simple, gentle, dignified, prudent, devout, irreproachable, undefiled. He must avoid evil-doers and keep the commandments. In all these things he is perfect before men. He must fix his mind upon divine and heavenly subjects. Then he will be perfect before God.'[43] The difference between fixing one's mind on the divine and coming to participate in it will be obvious.

Augustine paints a glowing picture of the original gifts of Adam; but Adam, entirely by his own fault, fell. Yet, despite the hideousness of man's sin, Augustine does not see this as marring the perfection of the work of God, for man's failure, which is seen to be primarily sexual, is always offset by appropriately dreadful punishment. Such was the gravity of this fall that it resulted in the ruin of the entire race, which became a *massa damnata*,

---

[40] G Wingren *Man and Incarnation*   (1959)   p 51

[41] Origen *Contra Celsum*   trans H Chadwick   (1980)   IV 99

[42] G R Evans *Augustine on Evil*   (1982)   p 95

[43] *op cit*   p 159

sinful itself and propagating sinners. Westermann's comment about the way in which the Church isolated the first three chapters of Genesis, thus deeply misunderstanding the Biblical accounts of creation, will be recalled. On this Augustinian basis, therefore, henceforth, man is seen as unable to avoid sin without God's grace, and without an even more special grace he cannot accomplish the good. His choice remaining free, he, spontaneously, as a matter of psychological fact, opts for perverse courses.[44] Naturally, given Augustine's understanding of creation *ad extra*, that grace came from outside and had normally to be channelled through the Church. The Church was the realm, the body, of Christ and there was no salvation apart from it, though God was free to confer grace outside the Church in appropriate circumstances. These special circumstances aside, therefore, Augustine saw the Church as the necessary channel for grace. But the 'church' as so understood was no longer the entire world in so far as it participated in the order of the Divine Christ, for, as Kelly says, 'It goes without saying that Augustine identifies the Church with the universal Catholic Church of his day, with its hierarchy and sacraments, and with its centre at Rome.'[45] The radical implications of that change need no stressing.

It is not essential for the purpose of this sketch to show how Augustine developed and refined these understandings. Just as he saw the Trinity as internal to the life of God and the world as lying outside it, so he saw man, as a result of sin, inherently outside the mystical body of Christ which he saw as present in the Church centered in Rome, into which man had to be drawn by grace mediated by the sacraments. Naturally, therefore, though Augustine recognised the goodness of nature, he saw it 'as but solaces of man's miseries in no way pertinent to his glories.'[46] Galloway, in commenting on this passage says that even the goodness of this world has no significance whatever when we speak in terms of the benefits bestowed in Christ. The hope we have in Christ bears no relation to this world whatever. And Galloway sees Augustine, more than any other, as the founder of what he claims as this covert dualism of the Middle Ages.[47] Conceptually, therefore, the world and God were substantially separated by Augustine and the role of the Divine Christ in the world was in practice reduced and narrowed to a role manifested in the Church. The earlier view of sin had been in terms of disorder and decay and foreclosing on the creativity of God and in this process, not only humanity but the cosmos as

---

[44] J N D Kelly *op cit* pp 362-4

[45] *op cit* pp 412-3

[46] *De Civitate Dei* 23

[47] A D Galloway *The Cosmic Christ* (1951) p 127

a whole had lost its hold on the creativity of the Divine which sought to promote the growth of creation to participate more fully in the life of God. The later Western view of sin, however, became one of moral turpitude and guilt and so as affecting man rather than creation as a whole. Correspondingly, the role of Christ in showing the way in which the fracture caused by deviation from being could be repaired by building wholeness and order, tended to be replaced, as we have seen, by his role seen mainly in terms of expiation of man's guilt before God: an expiation which, as we have noted, left the cause of the guilt itself unhealed.[48]

Similarly, the role of the Church changed. It had been basically a fellowship of truth and love in which the growth and development of each person into the order of the Divine Christ and so into the life of God took place through openness to progressively deeper insights, guided by their ministers. These insights led to the progressive development and ordering of the personality by participation in the Son and Spirit which were potentially inherent within the community as a whole and each person in it. The Church instead now came to be identified with the Church of Rome which came to be seen as the mediator between a God whose life was inherently self-sufficient and external to the world and man who, without grace conferred on him through the Church, was hopelessly immoral and destined to eternal damnation. Naturally, implicit in this new understanding of the Church, was a different and profoundly enhanced — indeed a supernatural — role for the clergy and for the sacraments which were seen as the point where grace penetrated nature from the outside. Faced with the Donatist controversy, it was Augustine who developed the idea that the authority of the clergy depended not on their qualities of wholeness and maturity but, irrespective of their personal qualities, on an infusion of grace at ordination, channelled through the church hierarchy. As Eugène Portalié says, in the Augustinian theory of the priesthood, it is Jesus Christ himself who has instituted an order of clerics essentially distinct from the people, the laity. 'The hierarchical powers are not conferred by the will of the multitude but by ordination, which consecrates the minister and separates him from the laity forever.'[49]

It is largely on this understanding that the claims for the unique authority of the Roman Catholic Church rest and which maintains the gulf between that Church and other churches and between the clergy and laity. The implications of all this were thus to carry through into every aspect of Western mediaeval life including politics; and they were eventually to play an essential part in forming our present Western framework of thought with

---

[48] see e g J Pelikan *Jesus through the Centuries*   (1985)   pp 67-8

[49] E Portalié SJ *A Guide to the Thought of St Augustine*   (1960)   p 236

its profound separation of spiritual and temporal in which the spiritual, when recognised at all, is seen largely in terms of the struggle to overcome immorality, and of individual salvation. As we shall see, these and other changes wrought by Augustine were to be developed and extended in the Western Mediaeval Church and were in due course to provide a kind of lens through which the Protestant Reformers were to look back and seek to understand the early Church Fathers and the Bible.

CHAPTER SIX

CHANGES IN THE MEDIAEVAL CONCEPTION OF GOD

The Augustinian Separation of God and the World

As we have seen, despite many indications to the contrary in the Old Testament, Israel came to think in terms of God's reliability and constancy. This emphasis, which was balanced by emphasis on his mystery and plenitude from which sprang all things new, entered, and provided an important theme in, Christian thinking. For the Greeks, too, the divine rule over cosmic and human affairs was perfect and rational so that every act of divine rule over the universe was but a detail of a comprehensive and perfectly rational programme by which was caused the order, beauty and usefulness of the cosmos.[1] For the early Church, therefore, God, though living and dynamic, could not change the direction of his act for such a change could lead only to something worse; though this did not, of course in any way preclude deviation from his will on the part of creation within his life. Furthermore, there was no separate divine will to interfere with the process. God's will was simply a reflection of his unchanging nature and his nature included the order and reason that took form, albeit imperfectly, in the world. As E P Meijering notes of Athanasius, his major problem was how the eternal and unchangeable God could act here in time without changing his nature: something we consider later.[2]

The idea that the existence of the Supreme Creator was to be discerned from the rational structure of the universe was given great weight, yet since there was nothing other than God, the divine will was seen to be subject to no external limitations and was thus totally free; nor was there anything to divide or fragment the divine nature, which was thus seen as simple. Accordingly, Irenaeus saw God as almighty, omniscient, and not subject to affections that could impair his entirely spiritual activity. God thus enjoyed boundless freedom and sovereignty, and his will was, at one and the same time, cognition and action.[3] For Irenaeus, as for Clement, Origen or Justin, because man had been made in the likeness of his Creator, his freedom, too, was to be found in the gift of reason.[4] Similarly, Gregory of Nyssa stressed the rational aspect of God's freely made plans and arrangements for leading

---

[1] A Dihle *The Theory of the Will in Classical Antiquity* (1982) p 2

[2] *Orthodoxy and Platonism in Athanasius* (1968/74) p 194

[3] A Dihle *op cit* p 112

[4] *op cit* p 112

mankind through history to salvation. And the rationality of the will of God reflected, of course, his rational nature.

As we have seen, with St Augustine, there was a fundamental shift from the understandings of the early Church and this shift was in due course to reveal its major implications for the understanding of the freedom of God in relation to creation. Whereas the earlier understandings had been of creation within the life of God, with the divine Christ, the very order of God, structuring the world and with the Spirit energising it, for Augustine, creation was outside the life of God — creation *ad extra*. All things were made through the Word of God, the Son, who perfectly manifested the Father, but whereas in the earlier understanding, man's creation in the image of God implied *participation in his life*, it now came to mean a *participation in his likeness*, and the lower orders of creation which were further removed from God simply manifested his 'vestiges'.[5] Therefore, though for Augustine the life of God and the life of man were to be seen as directly related, they, and *a fortiori* the rest of creation, were not integrated into one order of being, for he considered that any direct participation of the created in the uncreated was impossible.[6]

This was a change of the greatest significance and one which was to have very large consequences. Sherrard comments that all that is possible, from the Augustinian point of view, is for the intellectual soul to be illuminated, so to speak, from above, and in this light, which remains separate from it, and outside it, and in no way becomes its own nature, to perceive the rightness and wrongness of its own rational conclusions.[7] Accordingly, in the creative overflow of the divine love that embraced the whole of creation, 'truth is not born in us or with us, although it precedes our birth and has attended us from birth; nor does it come from within, although it is there that we find it and through there that it must pass. Truth comes from God and since it is truer to say that we are in God than that God is in us, the Augustinian soul passes through itself, so to speak, on its way to meet the divine master and thus passes through itself only to go beyond.'[8] In other words, for Augustine, the divine did not dwell naturally in the mind of man, it reached down to it, and man, with the help of grace, could reach up to it. Whereas for the earlier Fathers, God was to be discerned in the world around and so spoke directly through creation, therefore, for Augustine the action of the divine ideas on the mind was seen as intuitive.

---

[5] c f J E Sullivan *The Image of God* (1963) p 19

[6] c f P Sherrard *Greek East and Latin West* p 144

[7] P Sherrard *op cit* p 144

[8] E Gilson *The Christian Philosophy of St Augustine* (1960) p 76

Accordingly, for Augustine, although, given the grace of understanding, man could find evidence of God in the world around him, it was only by a process of introspection that the clearest insight into the life of God could be found: and for this to happen, illumination of the mind was dependent on moral purification of the heart and this, for Augustine, depended on the will. There was no question, therefore, as with the Greek approach, of participation in and assimilation to God by developing insights, by *gnosis*. The Greek, Socratic, understanding that no one, knowing the full implications of his action, does wrong, was thus superseded. Augustine assigned this role to the will which thus was separated from both potential and achieved cognition and became prior to and largely independent of it. And, because of the Fall, in the absence of grace bestowed by God, man was seen in practice, always and inevitably, to exercise his freedom perversely. Not surprisingly, therefore, because of the separation that he saw between the life of God and the world, and the need that thus arose to understand the love that God bestowed on the world as an overflow of the utterly self-sufficient divine life, Augustine became the initiator of a new, comprehensive, understanding of grace.

Whereas for the earlier Greek Fathers, grace had been seen in terms of God's 'kindliness' and 'favour' which provided intellectual and moral illumination which extended throughout the created realm, for Augustine there was a much stronger sense of grace as a 'power' whose influence over men, if God so willed, would be 'irresistible', so leading to Augustine's belief in predestination. Grace was seen as normally transmitted to man, initially through baptism, by the appropriate officers of the Church, and the individual who had received this grace, by becoming part of the Church, thereby entered a new life. The realm and action of grace was thus separated from the realm of nature and the creative and sustaining powers of God were separated from his redemptive powers. The aim of all this lay, not in this world but the next. It was thus only by the sacraments administered by those who had been ordained, that salvation could be attained.

Although, therefore, in Augustine's thought the life of God and his creative activity in the world had been conceptually separated, and so, in their different ways, had redeemed man, unredeemed man and the rest of creation, God remained close to creation. In some sense he continued to structure and sustain the world *ad extra*. The idea of 'created grace' as some kind of intermediary between man and a distant God still lay in the future so that, in his grace, God was seen as present. If, with the help of the sacraments, therefore, one penetrated to the depths of the mind, one found God. As Steven Ozment says: 'According to Augustine, to have true knowledge, one must not concentrate on the sensory world outside oneself, but retreat into the eternal world within oneself, through which one can rise above oneself to truth. "Do not go abroad. Return within yourself. In the inward man dwells truth." ... "Concerning universals of which we can have knowledge, we do not listen to anyone speaking and making sounds outside ourselves. We rather listen to truth which presides over our minds within us. ... Our real teacher is he who is listened to and is said to dwell in the inner man, namely Christ, the unchangeable power and eternal wisdom of God."[9] We might perhaps say, therefore, that whereas in the earlier tradition, man looked outward to discern God, though his gaze was illuminated from within, for Augustine, that gaze turned inward and, with the help of the sacraments, could open man direct to God. None the less, for Augustine, the mind was seen as a potentially open-ended channel leading through its depths to God, whereas, as we shall see, in later Western theological thought the mind was to become a cul-de-sac: a difference which, we may add, was to reappear between Jung and Freud.

Though, therefore, Augustine based so much on man being made in the image of God and so related to God, he emphasised the fundamental difference between man and God and between man's will and God's will. Whereas man's will was deeply perverted, Augustine continued to see God's will as unchanging and unchangeable and identical with his substance. But this emphasis on the will of God led to it, rather than the reason of God, the Divine Christ, being seen as the structuring and preserving power of the universe and this in turn led to the gradual emergence of a very different understanding of the freedom of God in relation to creation: a difference between, on the one hand, freedom to do whatever flowed from the goodness and rationality of his own nature in which his reason and love, the Divine Christ and Holy Spirit, participated, and, on the other, freedom to choose to do virtually anything whatever.

Mediaeval Developments of Augustinianism

In the centuries following Augustine, theology developed slowly in the West and though, as we have noted, the conceptual separation of God and the world implicit in his thought carried profound implications for the understanding of the freedom of God in relation to creation, a long time was to elapse before the issue became one of great significance. Oakley points to the occasion, probably in the year 1067, when Peter Damiani embarked on a discussion of the implications of a passage in a letter of Jerome, written some 650 years earlier, in which, in stressing the grandeur of virginity, Jerome had commented that not even God could raise up a virgin after she had fallen. Jerome's had been a moral concern for the greatness of the loss

---

[9] S Ozment *The Age of Reform* (1980) pp 46-7 quoting *The Teacher* ch 11/38

of virginity but that of Damiani was about the limitation on the powers of God implied in Jerome's statement: a limitation which he sought to deny.[10]

Dilemmas concerning the freedom and omnipotence of God were to come to a head some seventy years later than Damiani's disputation, with the condemnation of Abelard at the Council of Sens in 1140; but the issues had already been considered by Anselm who died in 1109. In his works we find a searching consideration of the ideas of necessity and freedom in the conception of God. Whereas for theologians of the next century, God was to be seen as having the ability, though not the desire, to will many things different from and even contrary to what he had in fact willed and would uphold, for Anselm, God did not have the ability to will what he did not will or what was contrary to his nature. As W J Courtenay says: 'For Anselm only one way was ever really correct or possible, for God's will has to express God's nature, and God's nature, in turn, can never have been subject to multiple possibilities, since in such a case God's nature would have no consistent meaning. Anselm's entire theological method depends on the fact that there is one best way of doing things — the way God did them, consistent with his nature and wisdom — therefore, one should be able to establish that the way God did act was the only valid way, otherwise God would not have done it that way.' And Courtenay notes Anselm's refusal to differentiate the divine nature from the divine will or the possibilities open to God before he acted from what he actually did, notwithstanding passages in the Old Testament — as well as in some Islamic thinking that was available to him — that could be read as pointing to a God whose actions could not be understood or questioned and which might be regarded as the result of arbitrary or even chance decisions.[11]

In Anselm's understanding, therefore, God's will was eternal and unchanging: the human soul was separate from but was in the image of the Trinitarian life of God and in so far could be directly related to it. The gap implicit in the thought of Augustine between supernatural and natural, theology and science, faith and reason, had not yet opened up. Already, however, the change in the understanding of the relationship of God to the world was leading to a change in the understanding of the role of Christ and so of the atonement. As we have already seen, it was Anselm who crystallised the Western view that only Jesus was worthy to atone for man's sin and guilt as a sacrifice to the justice of God who stood conceptually apart. Already, the earlier unified understanding that it was God in all men

[10] F Oakley *Omnipotence Covenant and Order*   (1984)   pp 41-4

[11] W J Courtenay   Necessity and Freedom in Anselm's conception of God   *Analecta Anselmiana*   iv/2   (1975)   pp 39-65

who fought against sin and who in Jesus victoriously overcame it, had thus been superseded.

The conceptual separation of God and the world which was taking place and which was, at least in part, the result of a desire to exalt God and separate him from this sinful world, was, conceptually a shift of the world to place it alongside though below God. The world was no longer seen as embraced within the life of a God who was himself free from any external constraint whatever, and instead, the freedom of God came to be seen as freedom in relation to a world which lay outside his life. Thus as regards this separation, Moeller and Philips note that Abelard had a tendency to reduce the indwelling of the Spirit in man to the *gifts* of the Spirit.[12] Not surprisingly, therefore, it was not long before God's freedom came to be seen as a freedom in relation to the world, and so to choose, and this became the subject of controversy which led to decisions being taken by the Church in a sense contrary to Anselm's thinking.

This, happened, as we have noted, in 1140, only some thirty years after the death of Anselm. The theologian who provoked these decisions, taken at the Council of Sens, was that controversial figure, Abelard. Various of his ideas were condemned there but the one that concerns us here was his claim that choice does not arise for God and hence that this is the best of all possible worlds. Abelard appears not to have distinguished the world as it is from the world as willed by God in the form it might have had but for sin, for sin was by now being seen in terms of a rejection of the grace of God whose effects hardly extended beyond the will of man. The idea of the whole of creation having been warped and corrupted by sin had therefore faded. Not surprisingly, however, Abelard's claim led to his being charged by Bernard of Clairvaux with teaching that 'God ought not to prevent evils, since by his beneficence everything that happens does so in the best possible manner.'[13] The details of the controversy need not concern us but the outcome of the Council of Sens was that the proposition that God can act and refrain from acting only in the manner and at the time he actually does act and refrain from acting, and in no other way, was condemned.

Most theologians since then have accepted that God does not just act totally freely in accordance with his own nature — to use a colloquial phrase, that he does not just do his own thing — but that he has choices in relation to the world. We shall have to consider this issue in greater depth later but suffice to say here that, as has been pointed out by the distinguished Benedictine theologian, Dom Illtyd Trethowan, the idea of God's choosing has some odd and disturbing implications: after all, choice

---

[12] *The Theology of Grace* (1961) p 14
[13] Quoted by A O Lovejoy *The Great Chain of Being* (1936/78) p 73

implies limitation — either/or — yet there is nothing other than God to require him to choose; unless, indeed, the world is thought to have some form of recalcitrant autonomy around which God has to negotiate: a view which implies an ultimate dualism and dethrones God. In any event, even if God is thought voluntarily to choose, this suggests that, in so far, he must channel and so restrict or withold his creative love, thus introducing a negative element into his wholly beneficient nature. Indeed, over 500 years ago, a major Renaissance figure, Gemistos Plethon, shrewdly pointed to the introduction of the idea of the arbitrariness of divine action, in the sense that God was 'free' to 'change his mind' not only in conformity to his unpredictable wishes, but also in response to prayers and supplications of the Church, or even individuals, as completely undermining all possibility of a divine science, and as one major factor leading to a failure of Christian society.[14]

However this may be, and we shall consider these questions further, Oakley notes that Albert Magnus, writing just over a century later than the Council of Sens, distinguished God's 'absolute' powers from his 'ordained' powers and implied that this usage had by then become customary. Aquinas, a pupil of Albert, explained in the *Summa Theologica* the position thus: 'What is attributed to [his] power considered in itself, God is said to be able to do by his absolute power. ... As for what is attributed to his power as carrying out the command of his just will, he is said to be able to do by his ordained power. ... Accordingly, it should be said that by his absolute power God can do things other than those he foresaw that he would do and preordained so to do. Nevertheless, nothing can come to be that he has not foreseen and pre-ordained, for his doing falls under his foreknowing and pre-ordaining, not the power of his doing, for that is his nature, not his choice.'[15]

Oakley points to reasons for the careful path that Aquinas was treading here and the distinction he was making and he quotes Courtenay: 'The absolute power refers to God's ability to do many things that he does not choose to do. It refers, that is "to the total possibilities *initially* open to God, some of which were realized by creating the established order; the unrealized possibilities are now only hypothetically possible. Viewed another way, the *potentia absoluta* is God's power considered absolutely, ... without taking into account the order established by God. *Potentia ordinata*, on the other hand, is the total ordained will of God, the complete plan of God for his creation." The stress, therefore, lies on the realm of the ordained power, which evokes the stable, concrete arrangements that the good God, who

[14] P Sherrard *op cit*   p 122

[15] S T Ia qu 25 art 5 as translated in Oakley *op cit*   p 49

never acts in a disorderly or arbitrary fashion, ... has actually chosen to effect. ... At the same time, the absolute power remains, as it were, on dialectical standby, a matter of abstract possibility periodically evoked to underline the contingency of creation, the world's dependence, that is, on the untrammeled decision of the divine will, the fact that it does not have either to be what it is or even to be at all.'[16]

The difficulties to which this distinction between the absolute and ordained powers of God give rise will be obvious. Both the quotation from Aquinas where he speaks of 'the power of God considered in itself' and Oakley's phrase 'the untrammeled will', imply an understanding, however theoretical, that the power and will of God can in some way either operate independently of his other attributes or mould them: that he is able to create by his power which is 'untrammeled' by reason and love. Even in the Augustinian understanding of the Trinity — in which the roles of the divine persons are in principle interchangeable — the reason and love of God are the attributes of the divine Christ and Holy Spirit who necessarily work in totally unified harmony with the Father. The idea that his will can operate 'untrammelled' by them cannot therefore be correct. What is more, the idea of such choices arising 'before' God, who is eternal, ordained this world, also raises serious problems.

However, notwithstanding the care with which Aquinas drew these subtle and highly theoretical, distinctions, they were soon to become blurred so that Pierre D'Ailly, writing towards the end of the fourteenth century illustrates the operation of God's absolute power by invoking the analogy of the king's absolute power; and he speaks of God as acting 'naturally' when he acts in accordance with his ordained power, and as acting 'supernaturally and miraculously' when he acts by his absolute power, breaching thereby 'the common law' or 'common course of nature'.[17]

The gradual change in the understanding of the relationship of God to the world was not, however, just a change from seeing the freedom of God — with the world as an integral feature of his life — as a freedom from limitation or interference by anything outside God — to seeing that freedom as a freedom of choice in relation to a world which itself lay outside his life. This change was also from seeing God as creative in his nature and as creating by the irresistible and eternal bounty of his goodness to seeing God as self-sufficient, complete in the internal fellowship of the Trinity, with the world as in some sense an optional extra, chosen by him to be the object of

---

[16] F Oakley *op cit* pp 50-1 quoting W J Courtenay Nominalism and Late Mediaeval Religion p 39 in C Trinkaus & H A Oberman (eds) *The Pursuit of Holiness in Late Mediaeval & Renaissance Religion* (1972)

[17] F Oakley *op cit* p 56

his creativity and goodness. In other words, the role of his creative love and understanding as eternal and intrinsic to his nature was displaced by an emphasis on his freedom seen as not just freedom from any external limitation and so as freedom to do whatever his nature demanded but as freedom to alter the incidence of his inherent attributes and their relationships, and even to withold them. In particular, the creativity of God, instead of being an intrinsic feature of the nature of God, became an optional feature of his will.

The changing understanding of the relationship of God to the world at this time is emphasised by the emergence of the idea of 'created grace' in the thirteenth century. Initially, this was thought of in terms of a disposition of man towards a present God but, when combined with the idea of an infinite distance between God and the world, it soon came to be seen as a kind of intermediary between God and men. C Moeller, who was later to become Sub-Secretary of the Sacred Congregation of the Doctrine of the Faith in Rome, and G Philips, both Professors of the University of Louvain, in an important report (from which we have already quoted) on an interdenominational conference in 1953, attribute this development to Albert Magnus. They speak of the idea of the infinite distance of God as introducing an extremely dangerous dualism, in which it is possible to recognise the source of an idea far too widespread during the period of the decadence of Scholasticism: that between God who gives himself, and man who is transformed, there is an infinite distance; there must, therefore, be an intermediary, and that is created grace.[18] Such ideas, however, which were already being incubated before Albert Magnus, have, as we shall see, endured to structure much Western theological thought, notwithstanding that Moeller and Philips claim that the 'indwelling' of God (uncreated grace) remained and remains an essential aspect of Christian doctrine.[19]

Aristotelianism

To this changing understanding of the relationship of God to the world there was added at this time one further outstandingly important influence. This flowed from the rediscovery of works of Aristotle mainly during the twelfth century. These works reached the West, mostly from Arabic and Jewish sources, and were accompanied by commentaries and other works by Arabic and Jewish writers and by a considerable flow of Neoplatonic material. All this led to great intellectual ferment and to fundamental reappraisals of traditional understandings of Christian doctrine. It would be far beyond the

---

[18] *The Theology of Grace*   (1961) p 18
[19] *op cit*   p 35

scope of this book to offer any appraisal of this material and its influence but one facet needs to be picked out for special comment.

Hitherto, the influence of Plato on Christian doctrine had been of the greatest importance. He was predominantly a philosopher for whom this sensory world in which we live lacked the ultimate significance of the unseen and eternal world of the divine, though the link between them was extremely close. Aristotle, however, was predominantly a philosopher of this sensory world. For him, nothing reached the mind save through the senses. The divine was seemingly for him relatively far less important. He understood God to be the summit of the scale of being, the unmoved mover of all things, but essentially self-contained, without care for creation which none the less aspired to him. Christian theologians could not accept his influence unchanged but his influence is undoubted.

The contrast between Aristotelian anthropology and what is normally regarded as the 'Platonist' anthropology of the early Church Fathers, (but which, as we have seen, has much closer links with the Old Testament than is generally recognised) is summed up by Moeller and Philips thus: 'An Aristotelian anthropology sees man as a self-sufficient unity enclosed within himself, his highest functions or actions never surpassing the limits of "nature". His elevation to a supernatural state would therefore appear as an elevation to an action or a mode of action, which he cannot attain in his natural state. .. On the other hand, Platonist anthropology, even as corrected by the Greek Fathers, in order to deal with the dynamic aspect of Christianity, sees in man a being capable from the very beginning of reaching the highest degree of spiritual life, union with God, although unable to reach it by his own efforts. What in the Aristotelian formulation is 'nature', always appears as a deficiency to the Platonist, but this means that there is no barrier between man and the supernatural; one might say that he has the potentiality to 'move' towards his goal; his essence is to ascend towards the highest end. He is essentially free to do this, and fails or succeeds according to his own decision.' And they add that according to the Aristotelian idea, freedom is *an extra faculty* given to man.[20]

Whereas the Augustinian tradition was carried by St Bonaventure, the new Aristotelian influence took definitive form in the works of his contemporary, St Thomas Aquinas. For Bonaventure, though the Divine was separate from the natural world, the depths of the mind were open to God and man's understanding had always to be illuminated by God. The separation did not, therefore, imply autonomy for the natural world. For Aquinas, however, the natural world was essentially self-sufficient: revelation was separated from reason just as theology was separated from

---

[20] *op cit*   p 39

philosophy. Natural knowledge came entirely from the senses and, as we noted earlier, mind was seen as a kind of cul-de-sac. Thus in the thought of these two profoundly important theologians, Bonaventure and Aquinas, who became Doctors of Theology on the same day in Paris in 1257 — the one, though seeing Creator and created as separate, nonetheless seeing the divine directly illuminating the world and all experience, the other seeing natural and supernatural as only causally related — there were thus divergences which were to prove of lasting significance.

Gilson contrasts Bonaventure and Aquinas thus: 'In conformity with the ruling idea of his master Albertus Magnus, St Thomas co-ordinates philosophy and theology, subordinating philosophy but in such a way that it would appear to be sufficient to itself within its own sphere. For him while it would be difficult to know all the truths of philosophy without the aid of faith, it would not be theoretically impossible, and it is the proper function of the philosopher to regard things otherwise than as a theologian. ... From this conception of philosophy immense things were to be born: for the first time in the modern world it restored the idea of a discipline of the mind dependent only upon itself and competent by its own method to explore the field assigned to it. For St Bonaventure, on the other hand, reason is only competent in its own field if it keeps its gaze fixed upon truths beyond its competence. As this works out in practice, there is no field that belongs to reason alone: and with that St Bonaventure turns his back upon the modern separation of philosophy from revelation.'[21]

Aquinas thus saw theology as dealing with revelation which came to man by divine grace whereas philosophy dealt with natural experience. The senses were for Aquinas the source of all human knowledge. Faith and reason were largely separate realms. As Ozment comments: 'Whereas for Augustine, the discarnate Christ mediated all true knowledge, for Aquinas, man's natural powers of sensation and reason sufficed. For Augustine, to speak of reason was to speak of the mind of man illumined by the mind of God. For Aquinas, to speak of reason was to speak of the mind of man naturally exercising its own innate talents.'[22] Instead of starting with God and attempting to explain the world as a direct manifestation of him, Aquinas started with the world which he saw as God's work and as providing man's surest evidence of God. As Leff says: 'The whole of Thomist thinking is governed by the primacy of being, and this, for St Thomas, meant sensible reality. This was the starting point in all

---

[21] E Gilson *The Philosophy of St Bonaventure* (1965) p 103

[22] S Ozment *op cit*   p 51

knowledge.'[23] As Aquinas himself says: 'nothing exists in the intellect unless first in the senses.'

For Aquinas, therefore, God did not see things in themselves, for they lay outside him and he was related to them only causally: he saw only their resemblance which was contained eternally in his being. Also, because the knowledge possessed by the human soul came from the senses and because it was devoid of innate ideas, it was dependent on the body. Whereas the Augustinian tradition had seen the soul as a spiritual being and the Forms, the Divine Ideas, as giving form to all reality, the Thomist approach was to make the soul the form of the body and so of individual man and to make matter, not form, the individuating factor. God was in everything but as its cause. Though, because of this relationship between God and creation, people could, by analogy, know and speak of God, this severed the soul's direct link with the Divine and made spiritual knowledge dependent on abstraction from sensible objects.

This assimilation of Aristotelianism to Christian thinking amounted, therefore, to another fundamental shift in outlook for, as we have seen, earlier thinking had found reality in the stability of the divine Ideas as against the flux of the sensible world. As for the nature of the intellect, Sherrard notes that 'in effect, the intellect, as visualised by Aquinas, is no more than a kind of extension of the discursive reason. ... The type of knowledge which Aquinas regards as the highest accessible to man is of quite a different order from that of the *gnosis* of the Christian Fathers. ... Aquinas regards the direct intuition of divine essences as beyond man's reach: the human intellect as it works in this earthly life can know only by turning to the material and sensible.'[24] For Aquinas, therefore, reality lay in being — the two different states of being, namely potency which was an unrealized state of being and act which was being as actualized: and it was form that gave things being. God himself was the fully actualised: he was pure act, the first act which causally moved all other things from potentiality to actuality.

It will be apparent, therefore, that whereas for Bonaventure, though the soul and God were separate, God was directly present to it, for Aquinas, not only was the conceptual separation between man and God emphasised, but the entire approach turned over from starting with God and seeing the world as an imperfect reflection of him, to starting with this world and building up to an imperfect intimation of God. To build up towards God, man needed to be infused with grace which came from God, which could overcome original sin which was seen as privation.

---

[23] G A Leff *Mediaeval Thought* (1958) pp 215-6

[24] P Sherrard *op cit* pp 149-50

Grace, therefore, sought to perfect nature by realising being. When, therefore, the Thomist conceptual distancing of God from the world by seeing the relationship between them as causal and as conferring a relatively independent status on the world, is seen as a development from the Augustinian separation of Creator and creation while allowing the divine to be so close to the depths of the mind of man as to illuminate his understanding; and when both Thomist and Augustinian understandings are seen in contrast to the understandings of the earlier Church Fathers of the *participation* of creation in God, the significance of these changes in bringing about the progressive evacuation of God from the world becomes clear: and one fundamental feature of this process was the Augustinian change in the understanding of the Trinity which became internal to the life of God while the world came to be seen as outside the divine life. When that conceptual distancing is then related also to the development of the idea that God 'chooses' whether and in what form to create, so that the nature of the world reveals God's choice rather than his nature, it will be clear that the conceptual separation of God from the world was by this time well under way. In particular, as Plethon appreciated, the very idea of God's 'choosing' itself placed a serious barrier to any attempt to understand God from coming better to understand the world or to any attempt better to understand the world from coming to know more of God: for it was henceforward natural to assume that, if it was simply the product of God's 'untrammeled' choice, howsoever man came to see the world, that must be the way God had chosen to make it. In effect, therefore, whereas, in the understanding of the early Fathers, as we shall see in later chapters, the scientific investigation of the order of the world would have been an attempt to investigate the order and reason of God, the Divine Christ, who was revealed, however incompletely and imperfectly, in it, henceforward, the investigation of the natural world could reveal only what God had chosen: and, we may add, given all the suffering and evil in the world, that in itself gave little knowledge of the 'chooser' and only very ambivalent support to the Christian understanding of the God of love.

The Trend Continues: the Reaction against Aristotelianism

Of course, the new understandings did not prevail without opposition and it was only later that Thomism became the standard by which orthodoxy tended to be measured in the Roman Catholic Church. A large number of Aristotelian propositions were condemned by the Church authorities in Paris 1270 and 1277 but this did not halt a growing trend. In particular, they condemned the Aristotelian idea that God cannot immediately and freely produce a plurality of effects. Gilson makes clear the importance of this when he says that this 28th condemned proposition is to be carefully noted, for it is of capital importance for the understanding of the subsequent history of mediaeval philosophy and theology: he claims that to maintain this principle was radically to deny the liberty and omnipotence of the Christian God. In Gilson's view, the Jewish and Christian God was not only able to create at a single stroke the world, with the multiplicity of beings it holds; he still could intervene in it freely at any instant, either directly to create in it human souls or to act miraculously and without the intervention of secondary causes. Not surprisingly, therefore, for Gilson, between what he understood as Yahweh and what he saw as the Greco-Arabian god from whom effects proceed one by one and according to a necessary order, no conciliation was possible.[25] Such assertions of Gilson, as will already be appreciated, are not those of the early Church as we have outlined them above; they can be read as a manifesto for later Western theology and we shall find that they need to be qualified at almost every point. But that is not to deny the importance of the Paris condemnations: as Oakley says: *'The condemnations marked the formal beginning of a theological reaction that was to vindicate the freedom and omnipotence of God at the expense of the ultimate intelligibility of the world.'* (my italics)[26] We are still living with the implications of that change.

What is more, as Ozment says of these condemnations: 'The church did not challenge bad logic with good logic or meet bad reasoning with sound; it simply pronounced *anathema sit.* Theological speculation, and with it the mediaeval church itself, henceforth increasingly confined itself to the untestable sphere of revelation and faith.' And he notes that Gilson believed that in subsequent centuries rational demonstration and argument in theology became progressively unimportant to religious people while faith and revelation held increasingly little insight into reality for secular people. 'In the Gilsonian vision, reason and revelation, nature and grace, philosophy and theology, secular man and religious man, the state and the church — all progressively lost their common ground and went their separate ways after 1277.'[27]

Indeed, the progressive changes in the understanding of the relationship of God to the world were reflected in changes in the understanding of the nature of the Church itself. The early Church had been understood in terms of the Body of Christ, *Corpus Christi,* who was himself seen as the order and reason which structured the life of God and, in so far as they came to participate in the life of God, structured the world and the mind of man. The Church was, therefore, an organisation devoted to helping men and

---

[25] E Gilson *History of Christian Philosophy in the Middle Ages* (1980 edn) p 407

[26] *The Crucial Centuries* 2nd edn (1979) pp 164-5

[27] S Ozment *T he Age of Reform 1250-1550* (1980) pp 14-5

women to develop insights into and so participation in the life of Christ and in so far, the Church was that progressive fellowship in Christ. But as the role of Christ as the Logos, the Word of God in the world and of man's participation in Christ, faded, so did this conception of the Church. It was seemingly in Carolingian times that the eucharist came to be known as the mystical body, *corpus mysticum*, as distinct from the 'proper and true body' of Jesus.

Gradually, however, a change took place, particularly around the middle of the twelfth century. *Corpus Christi*, which had originally designated the Christian Church and its participation in the order and reason of the Divine Christ, came to be applied to the eucharistic host and *corpus mysticum* which had been applied to the host, came to be applied to the Church. As Ernst Kantorowicz says, 'It was finally in that relatively new sociological sense that Boniface VIII defined the Church as "one *mystical* body, the head of which is Christ."'[28] This was is 1302. Meanwhile a new emphasis had been laid on the real presence of Christ in the eucharist — the doctrine of transubstantiation — and it became the real body — *corpus verum*. Around the middle of the twelfth century, therefore, the distinction began to be drawn between the 'Lord's Two Bodies': the individual *corpus verum* on the altar, and the collective *corpus mysticum,* the Church: a distinction which was, of course, quite different also from that of the two natures of Christ, human and divine. Aquinas, therefore, in speaking of the mystical body of the Church, is showing that the Church was becoming a mystical body in its own right. This, in turn, led to the Church itself becoming thought of as a mystical 'person' with strong legal and juristic overtones and this led to the idea of the Pope as the head of the mystical body of the Church. Finally, with William of Ockham, the Church as the mystical body of Christ came even to be referred to as the mystical body of God, and, as Kantorowicz says, *The Corpus Mysticum* 'came to be less and less mystical as time passed on, and came to mean simply the Church as a body politic, or, by transference, any body politic of the secular world.'[29]

Of course, other factors played a role in this separation of divine and human and were very diverse. Tendencies towards secularisation of society can be traced quite early. As Walter Ullmann noted: 'To a large extent historiography in the earlier Middle Ages down to the twelfth century was an extended biblical exegesis, the core of which was that everything happened "by the determinate counsel and foreknowledge of God." (Acts 2 23) and that events took place which demonstrated God's plan... Christ was seen as the centre of things and therefore as the saviour in the literal

---

[28] *The King's Two Bodies* (1957) p 196

[29] *op cit* p 206: pp 194-206 summarise succinctly details of this change

meaning of the term.'[30] Changes within and from that position mostly came gradually and almost imperceptibly and many factors which arose from these changes contributed to further changes. Thus Ullmann puts weight on the impact of the Investiture Contest, the famous dispute over the claim of the Emperor to invest an abbot or bishop-elect with the ring or staff and to receive homage before consecration. This dispute which took place over the later years of the eleventh and the early part of the twelfth centuries, had the particular effect of widening the intellectual horizons of observers from the rather rigid framework of biblical exegesis and fixed divine design to mundane causes and effects observable by man with his own natural gifts.

Later Mediaeval Developments

Though many and complex forces were thus at work, some working for continuity and some for more radical change, the general trend towards the separation of the divine and the natural and the distancing of God was gathering pace throughout the later Middle Ages. Only fifty years after the death of Aquinas, another key figure in this process of change, William of Ockham, was being summoned by the Pope to the papal court at Avignon to defend errors in his philosophy and theology. How far William of Ockham had moved from the Thomist understanding of the absolute and divine powers of God has been a matter of dispute amongst scholars but he made other changes of no less significance. For him, the universal Forms had no independent existence outside the mind of man: they arose from the mind's abstraction of common features of many individual objects of experience. These Forms were thus no longer seen as rooted back into the mind of God as part of God's nature for he saw such forms as dissolving the unity of the Christian God into a heathen multiplicity, as well as implying an unacceptable qualification of God's omnipotence and freedom. There was no hierarchically ordered world of 'real' relationships between God, man and the world. The Divine ideas no longer interlocked the nature of God and creation. The world was contingent, not necessary. As H A Oberman comments, by ensuring that the established reality of God's ordained powers is never divorced from the possibilities of his absolute powers, 'we are reminded that this, our world, is contingent, not an ontologically necessary outflow or reflection of eternal structures of being, but the result of a decree, a contract, a *pactum Dei.*'[31] Individual things were there simply because God willed them.

---

[30] W Ullmann *Mediaeval Foundations of Renaissance Humanism* (1977) p 61

[31] *The Dawn of the Reformation* (1986) p 27

Oakley comments that Ockham's world, accordingly, is not so much a "living" organism possessed of its own inherent intelligibility and order as an inanimate machine operating in accordance with the norms of behaviour imposed upon it by its maker. And he comments that there are simply no necessary relations or connections between distinct things in nature, not even between cause and effect.[32] As Ozment says, if one cannot believe that the particular things of the world are essentially connected with their ultimate cause, then it becomes difficult to argue confidently from finite effects to the existence of God. And he emphasises that for Ockham, there was no more rational basis for belief in God's existence than there was for the existence of intelligible species and common natures. All such things became genuine matters of faith.[33] Similarly Oberman says that in this emphasis on covenanted and not necessary relationships between God and his world, as well as between God and his Church, man is no longer primarily a second cause moved by the prime mover and first cause. And of an important development of this understanding, he says that in the nominalist view man has become the appointed representative and partner of God responsible for his own life, society and world, on the basis and within the limits of the treaty or *pactum* stipulated by God.[34] Clearly, in man's efforts to understand the world, such a *pactum* added little and it was not a large conceptual step for the world to be seen as completely autonomous.

More immediately, it followed that it was not possible to deduce the order of the world by any form of *a priori* reasoning, for being completely dependent on the choice by God, it corresponded to no necessity and could be discovered only by empirical investigation. Oberman comments that in Nominalist thought we encounter the sternest opposition to the claims of intellect and reason when not verified by the tests of experience. On this basis, nominalism provided the setting for modern science, replacing the authority-based deductive method with the empirical method.[35] Ockham's rejection of necessary conditions in nature and of final causes, and his concentration on efficient causality also eliminated the possibility of any organic view of nature which had prevailed hitherto: something which, as we shall note, science has in recent years been rediscovering. As Oakley shows, the idea of the laws of nature as imposed by God was common coinage in the sixteenth and seventeenth centuries, even before Descartes,

---

[32] *The Crucial Centuries*   (1979)   pp 165-6

[33] S Ozment   *op cit*   p 61

[34] *op cit*   p 29

[35] *op cit*   p 28

Boyle and Newton made it a commonplace of scientific thinking.[36] Oakley claims that it became so widespread precisely because it was the expression of a tradition in natural theology which started back well beyond the late thirteenth century. In the thought of Ockham, all this applied to ethics, too, where reason was seen to have little basic role and where the main issues turned on arguments about the commands and prohibitions of God. Even in theology itself, the dogmas of revealed religion could be known only under the supposition of faith.

On such presuppositions, Christ's life, death and resurrection found their significance simply in God's decision to value them so highly. And, as for the effect on the Church, with its claims to its exclusive and necessary mediatorial role between supernatural and natural, and with its sacraments and revelation seen as indispensable to this process, it had long ceased to be seen as the Way, the educational source that helped man to grow towards wholeness and maturity, towards participation in God, through *gnosis;* it had now ceased to be regarded as an essential link in the metaphysical chain of being; and its role came to be seen simply as the result of a special covenant with him that God happened to have willed.

Recent scholars have tended to put greater emphasis than did their predecessors on the continuities between earlier and later mediaeval thought.[37] Wherever the balance may come to lie in this much disputed field of scholarship, however, the general trends seem clear. There was increasing emphasis in the fourteenth century on the total freedom and sovereignty of God and it was even thought that to see God as first cause itself implied limitation of his actions. It was thought that God should have such perfect freedom as to defy explanation and analysis. In line with this, the distinction between reason and faith tended to make each increasingly self-contained so that natural and supernatural were regarded not just as at different levels but as having no meeting point. A hostility came to be seen between reason and faith so that reason was regarded as undermining faith which became increasingly independent of rational support, leading to scepticism about rational knowledge and increasing weight being put on men's reading of the scriptures. Indeed, the late mediaeval mystical movement, *Devotio Moderna,* believed that all the efforts made by men to commend themselves to God were simply reflections of a sinful vanity and that the aim of the faithful soul must be to remain passive in its acceptance of God's grace: a belief that became fundamental to the understanding of

---

[36] Christian Theology and Natural Science   in *Creation: the Impact of an Idea* ed D O'Connor and F Oakley (1969) p 75

[37] W J Courtenay Nominalism and Late Mediaeval Religion in C Trinkaus & H A Oberman *op cit* pp 26-59

Luther. The range of issues seen to be of direct relevance to theologians thus contracted. There was growing emphasis on God's distance and otherness; and God's will, not intellect, became the central theological category. What God and man did was more basic than what they were in themselves. The primary object of faith ceased to be God as he revealed himself in the world and became God as he revealed himself to man in Scripture. And the latter, particularly the Old Testament which came into increasing prominence, was seen as requiring trusting acceptance from man, not rational understanding. Popular piety thus placed increasing emphasis on devotion, directed particularly to the host in the mass, to the crucified Saviour and to the Virgin Mary; and as Ozment says, monastic traditions drew freely on themes from Dionysian mysticism, which placed God so far beyond the reach of mysticism that "ignorance" was said to be the surest route to him.[38]

A variety of movements thus developed, some looking back to important figures in the past of the Church, some looking forward in the light of new trends of thought, and some heretical. The separation of reason from faith placed more weight upon authority. As early as the latter part of the eleventh century the Inquisition as an instrument of coercive judicial authority had emerged, pointing to the contrast between the earlier freedom that was necessary for *gnosis* and these later requirements of conformity; yet, as we shall see, there was great uncertainty as to what these requirements were and who was to enforce them. And, as if to emphasise the growing distance between God and the world, mystical writings became the most universal literature of the Middle Ages.[39] At the same time, however, the elevation of theology into the realms of faith and so of tradition allowed room for a strong interest in humanism based particularly on classical learning to develop. The ground was being prepared both for the exuberant creativity of the Renaissance and for the anxious devotion of the Reformation.

---

[38] S Ozment *op cit* p 89
[39] S Ozment *op cit*   p 115

CHAPTER SEVEN

RENAISSANCE AND REFORMATION

As the Middle Ages wore on there emerged the new ethos which characterised the Renaissance. The Renaissance has been variously described and defined in the course of intense scholarly debate which it would be inappropriate to attempt even to summarise here.[1]

The Renaissance was the outcome of wide-ranging and far-reaching changes — cultural, social, political and, as we have seen, theological. Religious and secular life were separating. Laymen were wresting political control from the clergy. The economies of those areas most affected by the Renaissance were becoming increasingly dependent on commerce rather than agriculture. The boundaries of the known world were fast receding and man was increasingly becoming a little freer from those natural changes into which agriculture was inexorably tied. For many people, religion had become oppressive of the spirit of man and secularisation was accompanied by a sense of liberation and exuberance which is most clearly seen in the art of the period but which penetrated all other aspects of life. Yet all this had also another, darker side, for, in separating man from the regulated, organised structure of the world, it left him in a world of more unpredictable and often hostile forces and, because the Church was losing its omnipresent grip, it left him personally responsible for his own destiny.

The early Church had for many people been liberating and creative, but this sense had long since faded. Thus whereas in earlier Christian thinking, revelation and reason had been integrated and, later, at least coordinated, Renaissance thought tended sharply to distinguish ultimate truths altogether inaccessible to the reason of man from that practical knowledge and reason that man needed to get along in the world. On this basis, philosophy could no longer contribute to theology. What is more, a hierarchical conception of the Church and of society which was rooted back into the very order of creation lost favour and a conception of a broad equality of men, including clergy, emerged, where differentiation was by individual effort and achievement. In the process, worldliness and fallibility in the Church came to be judged by worldly standards. Thus the Church found itself straddling two worlds that conceptually were moving apart. The best ordering of life became that which worked best in practice. Man came to be seen as a complex unity in which the will, responsive to the passions, was central. Human happiness and virtue came to be defined in relation to other men and the community rather than God. The life of action rather than contemplation

---

[1] see W K Ferguson *The Renaissance in Historical Thought* (1948) conveniently reviewed by J H Hexter *On Historians* (1979) pp 45-59

became the ideal. All this, of course, placed great strains on traditional Catholicism for it was felt that in ultimate terms neither the mediation of the Church nor of reason could be counted on; man was left dependent on grace in an immediate and personal relationship with an essentially free, mysterious and inscrutable God who, though active in the world, was mainly known through Scripture.

This sense of the limitations of human understanding and its associated separation of philosophy from religious belief was to find its counterpart in the Reformation claims that Scripture alone could communicate what was needed for salvation; that sin penetrated all aspects of the personality; and that what was needed for salvation was thus neither intellectual gifts nor theological expertise but an act of faith, an act in which the layman was at no disadvantage in comparison with the clergy. Life in relation to God came to be seen in terms of conflict and change. God ceased to be revealed through the order of the universe and came to be seen as the God of history. But, whereas the Renaissance attitude was in many ways optimistic and idealistic, there was, as we shall note, in Reformation thought, and notably that of Luther, a sense of the utter sinfulness of man, of judgement and of the need for reconciliation that gave a dimension to the Reformation uncharacteristic of the Renaissance.

This difference carried through into later thought. In the following centuries the spirit of the Renaissance survived in the humanism of the sixteenth and seventeenth centuries, in the new philosophy of the seventeenth century and then in the Enlightenment, whereas the Reformation had its continuation, at least in spirit, in the evangelical churches, in the seventeenth century school theology and in Pietism. It will be clear, therefore, that though many of the same underlying historical factors came to form them, and there were many basic ideas common to both Renaissance and Reformation thinkers, particularly their common view that God was distant and mysterious and known not by reason but primarily through the Scriptures, none the less, the ethos developed and promoted by Luther was vastly different from that characteristic of Renaissance thinkers.

As with the Renaissance, the Reformation was the outcome of extremely complex forces and it would be beyond the scope of this work to attempt a balanced sketch of them. As we have seen, the roots of that momentous change, too, lay back in the Middle Ages. By the late Middle Ages there had arisen a number of schools of theology each with differing interpretations of major theological doctrines and there was neither clear authoritative teaching nor was there authority able or willing to enforce it.

Walter Ullmann sought to show, perhaps at the expense of some over-simplification, how two opposed concepts of government and law had struggled against each other in the Middle Ages. On the one hand, there was the idea of power 'ascending' from the people to the sovereign — a view which found support in the works of Aristotle and in Germanic laws and customs. On the other hand, there was the theocratic idea, referred to earlier, of power 'descending' from God through the Pope and clergy to the laity. The picture was more complex than this might suggest, however, for even within the Church there were supporters of the 'ascending' view who sought to promote the powers of the Church Councils in limiting the powers of the Popes. The position was greatly complicated also by the concerns of the papacy as a territorial state and by the struggles for dominance between the papacy and the secular rulers who sought to limit the Church to sacramental functions and to make it an agent of the state. Within the Church, great confusion was caused also by schism. When the Council of Constance met in 1414, there were no less than three duly elected Popes — one in Rome, another in Avignon, and a third in Pisa — each with a supporting college of cardinals and political allies and each claiming to be the true Peter. It took months of argument and confusion, before the council could pass legislation declaring itself the supreme authority within the church.[2]

By 1460 the conciliar idea was fading but the consequences in undermining belief in 'the divine authority of a thousand years' were far-reaching. Dissenting forces within the Church were becoming increasingly significant and the burning at the stake of Huss did not quell them. The successful papal monarchies of Gregory IX (1227-41) and Innocent IV (1243-51) left behind an example of Peter's pre-eminence which their successors 'could neither forget nor repeat'. By seeing God in the Church rather than in the natural order of the world, faith was placed in an institution which, though it claimed to partake of the Divine, gave every sign of human fallibility. By the later Middle Ages, the idea of unity and harmony throughout Christendom was fading; the secular and natural worlds had achieved substantial autonomy; and the spiritual was being forced back into the realm of faith; indeed, by the sixteenth century, religion was itself proving to be a key factor in the promotion of political division and of social change.

The forces that converged to bring about these changes that were in train in the later Middle Ages were diverse. The growth of nation-states was crucially assisted by the spread of lay education. This contributed to the displacement of ecclesiasical administrators whose allegiance had been to the Church, and their replacement by lay administrators whose allegiance lay to the monarchs and their states. At the same time, clerical power was being checked in many other ways. By 1500 the population of Western Europe

---

[2] S Ozment *The Age of Reform 1250-1550* (1980) pp 155-6

as a whole was growing fast and though it was still predominantly rural, towns were rapidly developing, though most were very small. Within them, however, were the merchants, bankers, skilled craftsmen and scholars. Such men played a major role in the Reformation, so much so that the Protestant Reformation, especially in its Zwinglian and Calvinist forms, has been termed an 'urban theology'. Increasingly, a money economy was developing and with it, so were both inflation and taxation which gave rise to many problems, not least the often oppressive exploitation of the new opportunities for taxation by the Church which intensified resentment against it.

The development of printing had enormous influence. It has been estimated that more books were printed in the 40 years between 1460 and 1500 than had been produced throughout the entire Middle Ages, and a growing literate public awaited them. The mediaeval Church had forbidden the circulation of vernacular Bibles amongst the laity but with the development of printing such a ban became impracticable. The ability of laymen and scholars to obtain access to books broke the monopoly of the Church in such matters and raised both their self-esteem and their critical abilities. Divisive theological issues could be defined and disseminated widely. There was a persistent Protestant ideal of everyone being able to read the Bible which, with pamphlets and sermons, was not only read but read to the people. A deep thirst for such understanding combined with a deep dissatisfaction with what the Church had to offer. But despite such dissatisfaction with the Church, there was a strong interest in things spiritual and this showed itself both in anxiety and in idealism and piety. As Ozment comments, 'The road to the Reformation was paved both by unprecedented abuse and long-unsatisfied popular religious yearning.'[3]

That the factors leading to the Reformation and the forms it took were complex is, therefore, obvious. But two influences on the form of Reformation thought appear to be especially noteworthy in the context of this book: the influences of Augustine and of the nominalism of Ockham. In rejecting many aspects of Scholasticism, the Reformers turned back to Augustine. It was especially through his eyes that they read the early Fathers and the Bible, though how far he had moved from them will already be apparent. Moeller and Philips express this when they speak of St Augustine as at once genius and yet incomplete, whose influence is always of very mixed value. And they add that the misfortune, the tragedy, was that the Reformers, instead of being faced with a theology in the authentic tradition, which united St Augustine and the Greek Fathers, found

---

[3] S Ozment *op cit*   p 221

themselves up against a scholasticism in decay, and St Augustine's thought seemed much more biblical and Christian.[4]

Moeller and Philips point also, however, to another factor which was of no less significance — what they term 'the unconscious nominalism' of the Reformers. 'The idea of extrinsic salvation which in spite of everything that has been said, is present in Reformed theology, comes from the way this system sees God — he is too inaccessible, and unable to have any real dealings with man, except by lowering himself and becoming "something created"'. And they quote Louis Bouyer as saying that the essential characteristic of Ockham's thought, and so of nominalism in general, is a radical empiricism, reducing all being to what is perceived, which empties out with the idea of substance, all possibility of real relations between beings, 'and ends by denying all intelligibility to the real, conceiving God himself only as a protean figure impossible to apprehend.'[5]

The third factor to which Moeller and Philips point is a basic difference in Christology. Whereas the earlier understanding was of deification through participation in Christ as the very order and reason of the world and of the minds of men, the West emphasised more the inspiration of the Spirit; and Moeller and Philips suggest that this leads to the risk of losing sight of the cosmic aspect of redemption, as well as its relation to the community, and so to the Spirit being thought of as 'a kind of mysterious and inestimable force exerted by God alone.'[6] This picture finds support in the conclusions of Oakley about the way in which natural law came to be seen as imposed, as it were from without. He notes that Luther was well acquainted with the works of d'Ailly and Biel and through him the theory of imposed natural law seems to have made its way into Protestant thought.[7]

Oberman comments that in claiming that nominalism was the cradle of Luther's theology, Roman Catholic scholars have sought to explain his 'defection' in terms of the un- or anti-catholic nature of nominalism, and Oberman has himself sought to counter this by showing that on certain issues Luther had discarded nominalism at an early stage. It does appear, however, that, at least in terms of his overall framework of understanding,

---

[4] *The Theology of Grace*   p 43

[5] *op cit*   pp 43-4   quoting L Bouyer *The Spirit and Forms of Protestantism*   (1956) p 153

[6] *op cit*   p 48

[7] Christian Theology and Natural Science   in *Creation*   D O'Connor and F Oakley eds (1969)   p 65

Luther did have much in common with the nominalists and owed much to them.[8]

It is clear, then, that Protestantism shied away from any idea of divine laws as immanent in the world, and indeed of the world as having such immanent laws; it shied away, too, from any idea of man's sharing in the Divine nature, of deification, and it emphasised the distance of God, notwithstanding the power of his influence imposed from without. But, among many other factors which played a role in forming Protestantism, not least was the personality of Luther.

The factors that moulded the personal development of Luther have been much discussed and so in particular have the weights to be put on personal, parental, social and religious forces. In whatever ways these contributed to his development, it seems clear that he had a strong sense of his own unworthiness, of tension between the divine mercy and the divine wrath, and of personal responsibility with the aid of grace, to solicit the former and to placate the latter. But his conversion experience was more than a breakthrough of personal conflicts. Ozment notes that we are so accustomed to think of the young Luther as a melancholy monk preoccupied with his own salvation that we sometimes lose sight of the fact that he was the age's most brilliant theologian. Luther's breakthrough was a breakthrough in his theological understanding for, Ozment claims, at the base of all the religious changes brought about by the Reformation lay the new theology of justification by faith.[9]

It had been the traditional teaching of the mediaeval Church, including of Aquinas, that a man who freely did good works in a state of grace cooperated in his attainment of salvation. An infusion of grace preceded every meritorious act and if a man did his best with that he would be rewarded with eternal life. The Ockhamists, however, preoccupied as they were with the freedom alike of God and man, modified this understanding, for if man was moved to love God by an infusion of grace, there arose the question whether man was really loving God freely. They felt that God's gifts of natural reason and conscience had survived the Fall and they were impressed by passages in the Bible implying that man had the ability and duty to turn to God and, if he did so, that he would be rewarded by God. (e g Zechariah 1 3 and Luke 11 9) They therefore came to see the initiative as lying with man to make moral effort which was rewarded by God with an infusion of grace with whose aid man had then to do his best. His reward would then be eternal life, though it was not man's efforts that

---

[8] H A Oberman *The Dawn of the Reformation* (1986) pp 97 et seq, and especially p 102, n 104

[9] S Ozment *op cit* p 231

determined his salvation but God's willingness to value these efforts so highly.

This understanding was attacked by Luther who on this lined up with Augustine. For both, man by nature lacked the freedom of will to do good. Luther condemned Aristotle's *Ethics* for defining moral virtue as acquired by effort and he equated scholastic theology with Pelagianism for in both the traditional mediaeval and Ockhamist views, whether before or after grace, man had to make an effort to do good. Similarly, he rejected the earlier Scholastic desire for a rational theology modelled on Aristotelian philosophy and sought to exclude the competence of reason from matters of faith. The truths of Christian faith were not to be treated as objects of intellectual curiosity without reference to the Cross and the benefits that flowed from Christ.

Similarly, despite the influence of mysticism on his thinking, Luther rejected not just the idea of participation in the life of God but the idea even of a divine spark in the depths of the soul and showed no interest in man's union with God as 'deification'. More specifically, despite the separation of natural and supernatural, it had been an axiom of mediaeval understanding that likeness to God was necessary both for saving knowledge of and a saving relationship with him. In that mediaeval picture, God had become man so that man could become like God. This likeness had to be achieved by grace infused by the sacraments. The central mediaeval concept was, therefore, that grace in the form of love formed faith; faith alone was simply assent to the data of revelation which had not yet done their transforming work and which left man still distant from God: it was love, the work of the Holy Spirit, that provided the internal dynamics of the Trinity and bound man to God and man to man.

Luther rejected all this. Man had no such claim on things divine. The attainment of these was entirely contingent on the promises of God and on man's faith in Christ. Luther denied that man could be like God: the basis of salvation lay in man's recognising his vileness and yet trusting and believing that, through the sacrifice of Jesus on the cross, God would save him. Man's union with God both presupposed and confirmed the greatest possible dissimilarity between man and God: not likeness but unlikeness to God. Only total humility and faith could prevent the justice and so the wrath of God. This Divine justice created horrible torments of the heart and fury of conscience. Man had no resources for the establishment of a saving relationship with God. This depended on Christ coming to men where they were in response to faith in him. It was in and through faith in Christ that men found his presence in righteousness, peace, mercy and salvation — in grace. There was no natural covenant between God and man but a historical covenant which was dependent on man's recognition of his total discongruity with God. God's response depended not on man's good works and merits but his awareness of his sinful works and unrighteousness. Humility was the receptacle of grace. Only as men sank in humility could they rise in power. Man found no grounds for hope in himself or in the world but only in Christ: such righteousness as was 'imputed' to the believer from Christ was thus 'alien righteousness'. The essential link lay in man's recognition of his unlikeness to God and his unworthiness and of God's trustworthiness in fulfilling his promises to man. The Church was no longer essential; reason was no longer essential; even love was not essential; the idea of faith as entailing the growth and development of the personality in the order of the Divine Christ so as to participate more fully in the Divine life had long since been lost; it was faith thought of in terms of subjective belief in God's words spoken though the Bible that mattered. In the thought of Luther the separation of God and the world had progressed so far that only such total trust and faith on the part of man and freely given grace by God could bridge it.

The immutable, eternal, infallible will of this hidden God was omnipotent, ordaining everything that happened in the world, yet was incapable of being comprehended by man except in so far as God had chosen to reveal himself in his Word. God's commands had to be obeyed, not because they seemed just or relevant to the ordinary welfare of man but because they were God's commands. For Luther, God had strictly forbidden speculative investigation of his divinity which would remain hidden except in the Christ crucified, the Word of God: nor could we know anything of Christ had it not been revealed by the Holy Spirit in the word of the Gospel supported by the Law, both of which were to be found in the Bible. What was more, because the omnipotence of this God was such that he must have had complete foreknowledge of all future as well as all past events, men must all have been already predestined to be either saved or damned. Man was totally helpless; only totally passive faith in the righteousness of God could save him. It was God's righteousness, available through Christ — an 'alien righteousness' — that alone could save him. It was this clear distinction between the total unworthiness of man and the saving righteousness of God through Christ that for Luther marked the distinction between the Old and New Testaments. The contrast with the pictures of the Old and New Testaments presented earlier in this book could hardly be starker. For Luther, it was Christ's sacrifice on the cross that provided the key to salvation, releasing the faithful from the demands of the law by his redeeming merit and love.

On this basis, therefore, there was no place for the Church as an authority mediating between God and the individual believer and the idea of a separate and sacramental priesthood was replaced by the idea of the 'priesthood of all believers'.

It will be apparent from all this, however, that by now, though the primitive apostolic church was regarded as the essence of perfection,[10] the relationship between God and the world envisaged by the early Church Fathers had been utterly transformed, narrowed and distanced. The role of the Divine Christ in the world was not denied. Calvin formulated it thus: 'For although the boundless essence of the Word was united with human nature into one person, we have no idea of any enclosing. The Son of God descended miraculously from heaven, yet without abandoning heaven; was pleased to be conceived miraculously in the Virgin's womb, to live on earth, and hang upon the cross, and yet always filled the world from the beginning.'[11] Even Luther did not ignore the role of the Divine Christ in the world. But the emphasis was placed first on the conceptual gap between God and the world; secondly on the Son of God descending miraculuously from heaven, the emphasis having moved from the role of the Divine Son as the order and reason of the world to the self-sacrifice of Jesus; thirdly on the scriptures as the supreme or even sole revelation of the Word of God; and fourthly, in the case of Luther, on an elevation of the humanity of Jesus which took specific form in his belief in the *communicatio idiomatum*; the special mark of Lutheran Christology, by which the properties of Christ's divine nature, among them ubiquity, were attributed also to his human nature. Hence, whenever Christ was spiritually present, he could also be thought of as corporeally present so that the partaker of the Eucharist received the one, whole, crucified and risen Christ.[12] The blurring of the lines between the humanity and the divinity of Christ was thus well under way. Luther's position was thus in line with his criticism of scholastic theologians that they were 'theologians of Christ's glory' rather than of his cross, and that they were so enamoured of the Christ who reigned in eternity that they neglected his incarnation and crucifixion.[13]

We are not here concerned with the political forces that lined up for and against Luther when he was condemned by the Church and in 1521 refused to recant, or with the complex factors that led to his survival and the success of the movement that he initiated. Suffice to say that, though Luther, like Zwingli and Calvin, drew a clear line between religious and secular powers and responsibilities, Luther saw the Devil as seeking to extend his authority over both areas and therefore expected Christians to support law and order and justice as divinely sanctioned goals.[14] Not surprisingly, therefore, he

---

[10] J Pelikan *op cit* p 118

[11] *Inst* II 13. 4

[12] c f S Ozment *op cit* p 336

[13] S Ozment *op cit* p 337

[14] S Ozment *op cit* pp 260-272

sided with authority in the repression of popular uprisings in 1525 in which it is estimated that between 70,000 and 100,000 people were killed.

As for Calvin, he arrived in Geneva just after the city had accepted the Reformation and quickly put forward a thorough-going plan to ensure that the inhabitants lived according to his view of the Gospel and the Word of God. Following opposition, he left the city. When he was invited back, some three years later, he was more careful to distinguish religious and secular issues. Ozment notes that his thoroughness for moral discipline was not matched by severity of punishment, save in a few cases of doctrinal heresy.[15] And Ozment adds that all Protestant theologians shared the common problem of giving good works a constructive role within the believer's life without at the same time succumbing to a Pelagian covenant theology of the Middle Ages, in opposition to which Protestant theology had been born.[16] Whereas for Luther, however, justification was by faith alone regardless of works, for Calvin, though works did not help salvation, they were evidence of it and so of man's eternal destiny. This had been predestined and, therefore, though one's own place might be uncertain, the ultimate course of history and success of God's cause was certain. The Fall loomed large in Calvin's teaching, but Christ's redemption of mankind and at least gradual and partial recovery by the true Christian was thus a possibility.

The sixteenth century reform of the Catholic Church in the Counter Reformation has increasingly been seen by scholars less as a reaction to Protestantism than as a response to the breach that opened in the fourteenth century between lay piety and official church religion. In a sense, reform was made more difficult by the Reformation for any criticism of the Church and its abuses led to suspicion of Lutherism, and the vested interests of the Papacy and hierarchy thwarted reform for a long time. The Council of Trent convened in 1545 and had three sessions over a period of almost twenty years. All the important Reformation doctrines were rejected. The Council reaffirmed, against justification by faith, the traditional view that faith formed by works of love saved people, salvation coming to man on the basis of an acquired, inherent righteousness, not an imputed, alien righteousness. Against Protestant belief in the sole authority of the Bible, Trent upheld two sources of church authority: Scripture and tradition, the rulings of the Popes and councils. The Council reaffirmed the seven sacraments against the Protestant reduction to two. It reiterated the traditional belief that the Mass repeated Christ's sacrifice and that the consecrated bread and wine of the Eucharist became the very substance of Christ's body and blood. Trent

---

strictly forbade clerical marriage and took harsh measures to end the surrogate status of clerical concubinage. Purgatory, indulgences, the worship of saints and the veneration of relics and sacred images were given a new endorsement. Efforts to supplant the traditonal scholastic education of priests with humanist studies were rejected.[17] The Council's special agent in promoting these claims became the newly formed Society of Jesus.

Despite the efforts of the Roman Catholic Church to reform itself and reassert its values, however, the Reformation endured and it clearly hastened the conceptual separation of God and the world and of religion from secular culture. Secular concerns were developing and drawing the constructive creative energies of men and women in ever new directions. Though religion remained a major force in the lives of individuals and society, its need to accomodate itself to being one element in an increasingly secularised culture was already becoming evident. How far the sustained secular creativity which has been exhibited in the West since that time and which appears to have been concentrated particularly in those countries where secularisation proceeded fastest, was due to the Reformation ethos and how far to the escape from it which secularisation provided, we need not seek to determine. What is clear is that henceforward interest and attention were concentrated on the world itself and organised religion became increasingly peripheral and disoriented. It is this process that we must glance at in the next chapter.

---

[17] S. Ozment *op cit* p 407

CHAPTER EIGHT

LATER DEVELOPMENTS IN UNDERSTANDING GOD AND THE WORLD

The Heirs of the Reformation

For the heirs of the Reformation, the conceptual separation of faith and reason and of theology and science were increasingly taken for granted and it was the changes in the understanding of the world itself that emerged into prominence. For much of the Middle Ages, explanations had been sought in terms of the true form or intelligible essence of objects and of the purpose they fulfilled. Objects had been seen to change to attain an end state — a stone fell to find itself a natural resting place; an acorn grew in order to become an oak. The actual processes attracted less attention. The aim was to understand the rightful purpose of each thing within the cosmic hierarchy created by a purposeful God. Within this hierarchy everything had its place according to God's plan and in it man was unique and central — in importance as well as in location — within the Ptolemaic universe. Natural Law was the form taken in the world by the divine reason in which all things participated and which was therefore immanent in the world which was thought of as a product of craftsmanship and by analogy with an organism.

Within this picture nature was seen as essentially static and, though attitudes to nature varied, its being seen at times as a seat of evil forces and at other times, as amongst the Franciscans, as a sacrament of the divine, the general understanding was matter of fact. Yet though God was seen as Creator and sustainer of all things, they had, as we have seen, a certain autonomy, though in exercising it, his concurrence was needed. As for the natural world, it was seen as subordinate to man and as there largely to serve men's interests: it thus provided the stage on which the cosmic drama of man's creation, fall and redemption was taking place. Man was therefore quite unlike other creatures.

By the seventeenth century, following the Reformation, this understanding had changed radically. Interest was shifting to the world in itself. Both mathematical reasoning and experimental observation were coming into prominence in the form of theories to discern the underlying mathematical harmonies and of experiments and of observations to test them. Whereas the Greek and later view of the world was as an organism, the paradigm was changing from the organic to the mechanical. The emphasis was thus moving from the purpose of events to the processes involved.

Whereas such concepts as mass, time and space had been relatively unimportant in mediaeval thought for they were seen as accidental to the essential character of objects, as change ceased to be seen as change from potentiality to actuality and came to be seen in terms of rearrangement of particles, these concepts assumed a central importance. What is more, because the world came increasingly to be thought of in terms of a machine, instead of being capable of ordering its own movements according to its immanent laws, the world came to be thought of as devoid of intelligence and life and, as we have seen, as operating according to laws which were not intrinsic to it but were imposed from without. This shift in turn contributed to the radical dualism of matter and mind that was crystallised by Descartes and which was to become of central significance in the succeeding centuries.

For Descartes, the entire world other than mind thus came to be seen in terms of self-sufficient matter extended in space. All animals and even the bodies of men were seen as machines or automata. The mind, an unextended thinking substance, was seen as having all the qualities with which the new science could not cope and it was so different from matter that interaction was difficult to envisage: hence the conceptual chasm that has troubled almost all subsequent philosophy. What is more, the consciousness envisaged by Descartes was a solitary one — the consciousness of a philosopher meditating alone in his room. But, as William Barrett notes, having extracted the mind from its world, Descartes was hard put to get it back into the world: he had to rely on a good God who would not have created our minds in such a form that they were deceived about the world around them. But that mind was only the abstract *ego cogitans* — the thinking mind, not the concrete self: and feelings and emotions came to be seen as objects to be noted, rather than lived and suffered. What is more, the body as Descartes conceived it, was not such as could be penetrated by the soul: the body was a piece of matter, the concern of physics, and the soul was in only external contact with it[1]

Even in the time of Descartes, such dualistic ideas had wider implications. Thus they were seen as challenging the Bible which had increasingly come to be viewed by many people as not just the witness to the redemptive acts of Christ but as a source of information, including scientific information, dictated by God. Against this view, Galileo, a contemporary of Descartes, saw nature as the sole source of scientific knowledge which, with Scripture as the main source of theological knowledge, together provided knowledge of God. It was not to be long before this natural basis of religion was largely to displace the Biblical understanding of creation. As this emphasis

---

[1] William Barrett *Death of the Soul* (1986) pp 18-20

developed, though God continued to be seen as the originator and therefore the first cause of interacting atoms and so of the causal processes of the universe, these came to be seen as largely autonomous. The idea of God sustaining the whole and all the processes within it, from being a presupposition, increasingly dropped from sight. As for the central role of man, with the invention of the telescope, his displacement from the centre of the universe became inevitable.

In Britain, the alliance of mathematics and experimentation came to fruition with Newton. For him, the task of the scientist was descriptive, and scientific concepts were understood to be literal representations of the world. A single system of forces and masses was replacing the mediaeval hierarchical system of purposes. Man was becoming a largely irrelevant spectator of a silent, dead and colourless world of forces and particles and the sensuous world of experience was retreating inside the head. A method was becoming a metaphysic.

For many people, however, the evidence of design was so strong that God was still seen as the great designer. That design was, however, thought up by God and was seen as in a sense external to the system itself. The purposes lay in God and not immanent in the events themselves. In this way of thinking, the world was seen as having been created in its present form at one moment, and suffering and evil were seen simply as anomalies or as part of the design of God hidden from men's understanding. Religion was understood as having to be based on reason and as depending primarily on the existence of a supreme being, on the immortality of the soul and on the obligation towards moral conduct. Religion became more a matter of intellectual demonstration than living experience. God was thought of as the divine architect and creator rather than the redeemer and a Christ-centered Christianity ceased for the time being to be fashionable. The idea of divine immanence also passed out of sight. But though the idea of God was so reduced, man retained his dignity because of his powers of reason. The inherent link of mind with the mind of God was, however, dropped and the picture of mind imprisoned in the brain and in only indirect contact with the world came into prominence.

As we have seen, the steady development of empirical knowledge and understanding of the world was accompanied by and was, perhaps, in large part a consequence of, the increasing sense of distance, of the otherness and transcendence of God. This in itself pointed towards the de-sacralization, the disenchantment, the objectivization of the world which removed from it any idea that in itself it was expressive of the divine. This emphasis had been greatly accentuated by the weight given by the Reformers and notably by Calvin, to the sinfulness and depravity of natural man and to the omnipotence of God. As Charles Taylor says: 'For the majority of non-philosophical men, the sense of being defined in relation to a larger order is carried by their religious consciousness, and most powerfully for most men in most ages by their sense of the sacred, by which is meant here the heightened sense of the divine in certain privileged places, times and actions. Catholic Christianity retained the sacred in this sense, both in its own sacraments and in certain pagan festivals suitably "baptised". But Protestantism and particularly Calvinism classed it with idolatory and waged unconditional war on it. It is probable that the unremitting struggle to desacralize the world in the name of an undivided devotion to God waged by Calvin and his followers helped to destroy the sense that creation was a locus of meanings by which man had to define himself.'[2] Not surprisingly, the very different emphases on the evil of the world and the sinfulness of man as seen by the heirs of the Reformation and those supporting the essentially optimistic views of the emerging Enlightenment tended also to widen the already marked divergences in Christian belief.

The Age of Reason and the Heirs of Kant

The eighteenth century saw itself as the 'Age of Reason' — as a time when enlightenment and rationality were within the grasp of men, though there were, of course, differences in the manifestations of this ethos in the different countries affected by it. It was particularly during this period that the very existence of God came seriously into question; when nature came to be seen as a deterministic system of natural forces and man appeared to be perfectible. Thus Laplace saw the world not just as deterministic: he saw it also as impersonal, self-sufficient and in terms that were essentially reductionist. Associated with the view of God as a questionable hypothesis, there was, as we have seen, a strong tendency to minimise the existence of evil. The idea of the great chain of being in which every possible creature was created still had a powerful influence on men's minds and offered some explanation of why some creatures might be less than perfect. But the basic understanding was full of optimism about the future of man and society and this was associated with a sense of liberation and a concern for toleration. But, of course, such an approach could not and did not endure. The very remoteness and impersonality of the Deist's God limited his appeal to the intellect and meant that if that was all there was to God, his existence was indeed an unnecessary hypothesis.

Particularly influential for subsequent ways of viewing the world was Hume. Edward Craig has argued in an important study that hitherto the conception of man as in the image of God underlay both scientific and philosophic thought. Hume, however, 'aimed at no less than the destruction

---

[2] C Taylor *Hegel* (1975) p 9

of the doctrine of the image of God, and substituted for it an anthropology which looked not to the divine but to the natural world for its comparisons, and to the sciences for its methods'.[3] Man was a natural object and in seeking to weaken or demolish grounds for finding an analogy between the mind of man and the cause or causes of order in the universe, he was wanting to establish a science of the mind on the Newtonian model — 'an associative mechanism in accordance with his quasi-Newtonian theory of the workings of the mind, often given the general title of "the imagination"'.[4] What is more, in common with Locke and in contrast with Kant, it was an essentially passive, responsive, view of mind.

Not surprisingly, before the end of the century there followed the Romantic reaction, with its emphasis on man's emotional and imaginative powers and with its idealisation of freedom and personal fulfillment. Equally, there was a revival of concern for the immanence of God especially in nature and in beauty. Earlier, reaction had already taken the form of strong revivals of religion, first among the Pietists in Germany and later in the British Methodist movement; and by the time of the great religious revivals in the United States in the early nineteenth century, Deism was dead. The scepticism of Hume had contributed to its demise as well as proving of more lasting significance.

A new approach to the relationship of religion and science was, however, to be offered by Kant. For him, as for Hume, all knowledge started from sense experience, but he believed that it was mind that organised these experiences within a framework of space and time. As we could never know 'things in themselves' other than through our mental processes, Kant considered that we could not prove or disprove God's existence on any such basis. As Basil Mitchell notes, 'So far as religion is concerned, his policy was "to deny knowledge to make room for faith."'[5] Instead Kant saw the need to postulate God in the quite different field of moral obligation — in the field of values. He saw as 'categorical imperatives' such formulations of the moral law as the need always to treat persons as ends and never means, and to act only in ways one would agree to being adopted universally by other people. Such moral laws required a lawgiver and guarantor who could only be God. But though such moral experience provided the justification for regarding God as real, it did not in itself offer the basis for religious knowledge. Our certainties about God had to come, not from theoretical, metaphysical, reasoning, but from practical experience. In this way Kant emphasised from quite a different angle, the separate

---

[3] E Craig *The Mind of God and the Works of Man*   (1987)   p 70

[4] *op cit*   pp 74 & 87

[5] *Morality, Religious and Secular* (1980)   p 27

realms and functions of religion and science. Whereas for ancient thinkers there was no severance of the rational and the moral, morality being, for instance, in Aristotle's ethics, the fulfilment of human nature, in the new picture, the natural world was seen as a vast impersonal machine, indifferent to human purposes, whereas morality had to find its roots elsewhere. To this Kant's answer is divided: on the one hand duty — the call of conscience — is the voice of God within us; but on the other hand, he seeks a logical or formal explanation in the rationality of our nature — responses reflecting piety rather than any deep passion for the presence of God.

None the less, these ideas took root and their rationalist elements proved highly influential both in the development of philosophical idealism, whose most distinguished proponent was Hegel and in some strands of Protestantism where Kant's moral interpretation of religion reinforced their understanding of Biblical ethics. In a very different way, Kant's rejection of metaphysics and his emphasis on the role of God in practical life, came to have a strong influence on Kierkegaard and the existentialists, though they rejected his rationalism. What is more, the rejection of the constraints of any comprehensive metaphysics and the conception of God as the author of the moral life allowed for the emergence of the idea of God as 'a person'.

Two nineteenth century developments had particularly far-reaching implications for the understanding of the relationship of God to the world. The first of these was the idea of evolution. This appeared to strike at the roots of any idea of the world created by God according to some preconceived plan and it has taken a long time for it to be at all widely appreciated that though it killed the static conception of God as like a watchmaker and the world as like a watch, it left room for a much more adequate and subtle conception of directivity in life and the gradual realisation of God's purposes in the world — a theme to which we shall have return later. But, of course, the idea of evolution did more than that to damage received ideas. Man had already ceased to be seen as the centre of the universe: his dignity was further shattered by the idea that he was simply the product of a natural evolutionary process and that he had evolved from the apes. Even his moral sense appeared to be the product of evolutionary processes and the idea that competition promoted progress in some measure sanctified the individualistic ideas of the period.

Meanwhile, however, the growth of scientific and particularly geological knowledge, which came together with the evidence of evolution, was badly shaking those who insisted on reading the Bible literally. The responses were diverse and there is no need to outline them here. Linking with this was the strong growth of Biblical scholarship which undermined more and more of the preconceived ideas in terms of which the Bible had been read and substituted others which were often equally inappropriate and misleading. Again, reactions were various but one noteworthy and influential response was that of Schliermacher who saw the basis of religion not primarily in revelation through the Bible nor the Church nor through the application of reason in natural theology nor even in ethics as seen by Kant, but in religious experience. Yet all the approaches discounted by Schliermacher found their supporters amongst his contemporaries and successors.

Some Features of the Current Scene

To try to summarise the many different forms taken by Christian thinking during the present century would be too large an undertaking to be fruitful for the purposes of this book. Twentieth century Protestantism has been deeply influenced by Karl Barth who saw God as 'wholly other' — as the transcendent Lord who is known only when he chooses to reveal himself. Barth saw God as a person wholly distinct from the world, separated from sinful man by a chasm which only God could cross in response to man's obedience which alone could overcome sin. The basic revelation of God was seen in Christ but God was seen as revealing himself also as judge and redeemer, especially in the preaching of the Word. There was thus no bridge between theology and science yet there was no conflict provided natural theology was seen as an aberration. Other leading theologians, notably Bultmann, developed forms of Christian existentialism. For Bultmann, though the Bible spoke of God in terms of time and space, any such ways of speaking had to be read as revealing of eternal truths. They were therefore to be seen as 'mythical' statements bearing on the central theme of understanding ourselves in relation to God. Modern philosophers who have been influenced in various ways by language analysis, have also joined the fray, sometimes with destructive intent and, as we shall see later, have sought either to sustain or undermine modern understandings of God which the New Testament writers and the early Church Fathers would have regarded as simplistic parodies of their beliefs.

At another extreme, however, Process Theology, under the influence of the mathematician and philosopher, Alfred North Whitehead, has sought to bring theology and science together in ways which allow full weight to the immanence of God in relation to the evolving universe while seeking to maintain his transcendence. This theology has sought to reemphasise the idea of creation 'within' the life of God which, as we have seen, was the understanding of the early Church. There are many parallels to the thinking of the Process Theologians as well as original insights in the ideas of Teilhard de Chardin. But, of course, differing widely from all of these have been the more traditional approaches. Thus various forms of Thomism are alive and well within the Roman Catholic Church and influence some

Anglican thinkers. There has also been some development of interest in the teachings and forms of the Eastern Orthodox Churches which were little affected by St Augustine and which were for a long time shielded from the radical developments and the destructive fragmentation of the beliefs of the Western Churches. But, of course, many, particularly young people, have turned outside the Christian faith to seek fulfilment, notably in the religions of the East and in a vast range of cults. Yet, however important all these movements have been, the prevailing ethos has been predominantly of life enclosed within this material world and as ultimately purposeless.

Thus Edward Craig, in his *The Mind of God and the Works of Man*, has noted how in the nineteenth century, the view of man as a spectator of events in the natural world gradually gave place to a more active conception which placed man within the world and saw his salvation in his power to change it. 'It was also a period in which the purely contemplative values, the idea of the intrinsic desirability of knowledge, found it more and more difficult to make their way unaided by at least the arguable prospect of some beneficial connection with practice.'[6] It is not surprising, therefore, that the idea of man as the shaper of his own world, with its associated ideas, became increasingly influential; that what we ought to believe ceased to be independent of what we wanted and truth became less an end in itself and more an instrument for the attainment of other ends. Yet as Craig shows in later chapters of his book, there has been no joy, only discomfort, in the thought that there might be a final goal of history:[7] and he quotes some leading churchmen of today for whom religion seems to have come to be valued mainly for sincere and committed participation in the activity of religion. Noting that whereas the symbol of faith was formerly a rock and had now for some commentators become a sea, he relates this to a quotation from William James: 'Humanism is willing to let finite experience be self-supporting. Somewhere being must immediately breast non-entity. Why may not the advancing front of experience, carrying its immanent satisfactions and dissatisfactions, cut against the black inane as the luminous orb of the moon cuts the caerulean abyss?'[8] As Craig comments, many will find the vivid imagery of William James, which was presumably intended to show the brighter face of human autonomy, 'as terrifying a feeling of the

---

[6] *op cit* p 227

[7] *op cit* p 254

[8] *op cit* p 27 quoting 'Humanism and Truth' in *Pragmatism and The Meaning of Truth*

trackless void surrounding human life as anything ever produced by any purveyor of existentialist *angst.*[9]

It is not, therefore, surprising that, embedded in such an understanding of the world, the Churches have in recent years suffered a serious loss of theological nerve. This has manifested itself in a shrinking from traditional tenets of belief; a retreat into relativism; a seeking refuge in anodyne religious formulae which have been voided of clear content; and a rush to substitute as central to the Churches' role, an often undiscriminating and largely secular concern with the social welfare of minorities which, though fully justifiable in itself, has left both those minorities and the remainder of the population almost totally ignorant of, and largely indifferent to, the entire spiritual content of this life. Yet, as we shall see, this scene of fitful and fragmented activity in a tundra of spiritual decay and triviality is also a scene of hope, for it offers an unprecedented opportunity to rebuild the Christian faith in the light of our vastly increased knowledge of the natural world and of the worlds of the Old and New Testaments and the early Church.

The Conflicting Pressures for Fragmentation and Unity

The main purpose of these cursory and necessarily inadequate historical chapters has, therefore, been to illustrate how the understanding of God and of his relationship to the world has changed over the almost 2000 years since the birth of Christ and how we have reached our present state. We have seen that, though the language of theology has had great continuity, and adherence to the Gospel message has been continuously proclaimed, the form and content of the ideas lying behind and enshrined in this language have continuously altered, and have gradually lost coherence and fragmented. All this suggests that the problems facing Western theological thinking, and, indeed, Western thinking as a whole, must be very deep-rooted. It may not be surprising, therefore, if we now turn back to the insights of the early Church and seek to demonstrate the broad coherence of its understanding of God and the world; to expose some of the fundamental incoherences into which its Western heirs have been led; and then to show how it offers a coherent context for the emerging framework of modern scientific understanding and for much other modern thought and experience. In so turning back, therefore, we return to a world of which God is seen not only as creator, sustainer and redeemer, but in which he is to be found, if we know where and what to look for: a world which God seeks to guide into his life as it unfolds, though always respecting its freedom to damage

---

[9] *op cit*   p 271

and destroy itself. But since the very idea of God and of his relationship to the world has been so debased, we need next to sketch the framework of that earlier understanding of God and his relationship to the world on which we can build in later chapters.

PART II

GOD AND THE WORLD

SOME IMPLICATIONS OF THE CHANGES BETWEEN BIBLICAL
AND EARLY CHURCH IDEAS AND THOSE OF THE WEST

CHAPTER NINE

THE CONCEPT OF GOD & HIS RELATIONSHIP TO THE WORLD

Though Israel appears to have reckoned for a long time, not only with the existence of other Gods, but also with the idea that other nations belonged to these other Gods and not to Yahweh, for Judaism the universality and uniqueness of Yahweh's deity came to be taken for granted and is assumed by early Christianity; the Father of Jesus Christ is seen as the only true God (John 17 3) and he is the God not only of the Jews but of the Gentiles. (Romans 3 29)

But if only because Christianity at a very early stage ceased to be a Jewish religion and moved out among the Gentiles, Christian beliefs had to take account of the strong Greek cultural influences which prevailed around the Mediterranean. This translation of Jewish thought into Greek philosophical terms was aided by strong tendencies in Greek thought towards 'philosophical monotheism' and, as we have seen, by a certain degree of correspondence between the Platonic ideas of God and the ideas of Judaism. But this translation and assimilation was by no means simple for Greek religious ideas took many different forms, only some of which were relevant and many of which had to be modified. James Barr warns against over-simplified contrasting of Hebrew and Greek thought. Far from being a dilution or corruption of the Christian message in order to make it palatable to the Gentiles, it is arguable that Greek ideas were selectively appropriated and changed to allow ideas inherent in the Christian message to be developed and articulated more clearly. Thus as Barr says: 'The role of Greek ideas may have lain not in communication to the outside, but in appropriation for the needs of concept formation.'[1]

Though the contributions of Jewish and Greek thought to the formation of Christian doctrine had, therefore, much in common, they were also in many ways different and both were important. Pannenberg remarks that the philosophical idea of God (including even the Platonic) was shaped differently from the Biblical idea because of its origin in Olympian religion, with the specifically immanental character of its deities. The guiding idea of the Greek concept of God was, he says, that of the origin of everything presently in existence. Accordingly, philosophy could construct its concept of God by inference back from the world. This corresponded to the peculiar character of the ancient Greek understanding of God, but not to the Biblical

---

[1] J Barr *Old and New in Interpretation*   2nd edn   (1982)   p 61

God's essential freedom in relation to the world. And Pannenberg quotes Jeremiah 32 27; 'Behold, I am the Lord, the God of all flesh; is anything too hard for me?' and comments that such freedom on the part of God for ever new, as yet unheard of works in his world was beyond the scope of Greek philosophy.[2]

In contrast, although the Biblical God was thus the unitary origin of present reality, and came to be seen as consistent, rational and just, he was also seen as the unitary, free, creative source of the ever new and unforeseen. He was free because there was nothing other than God to limit him in any way, and he was able to bring about the new and unforeseen because of the very plenitude and so the mystery of his life. He was the God 'who gives life to the dead and calls into existence all things that are not.' (Rom 4 17) It was because of his plenitude that his freedom to bring about the new and unforeseen could be be reconciled with his utter reliability. And since the Biblical God could not be known by ordinary discursive reason from the world, he could be known only by the creative insights — *gnosis* — which were seen as coming by special gifts of God: gifts which themselves presupposed a fellowship between God and men — an idea equally foreign to philosophy.[3]

Linked with this idea of the divine as the source or origin of the world was the idea of its being essentially intellectual. By about 450 B C Diogenes of Apollonia had taken the step of seeing in the purposeful order of the world an argument for its being the product of a thinking, planning mind and thus the idea of the origin of the world as intellectual — as a divine mind — became an essential feature of Platonic and also Stoic thinking; even Aristotle attributed to the divine some of the features of personality. But this was not inconsistent with Jewish ideas of a God of whom his Word and Wisdom were aspects.

Associated with these ideas was that of the unity of the divine. In particular, God was seen in the early Christian understanding as the unitary source of order and meaning in the world and as that unity from which, in some sense, all the multiplicity of the world derived. Indeed, most of the characteristics attributed to God can be seen as implications of that unitary status. The idea of the unity of God has itself several facets, although such distinctions may not have been clearly recognised by the ancient writers who helped to formulate the concept. Thus G C Stead, in his discussion of early thought about the divine unity, notes the distinctions between the oneness of God in the sense that there is no other God; the oneness of God in the sense that he is simple and undivided; and the oneness of God in the sense that he

---

[2] W Pannenberg *Basic Questions in Theology vol 2 (1972)* pp 137-8

[3] W Pannenberg *op cit* p 138

is unchanging: all three of which play a very important role in Christian doctrine.[4]

The idea of the divine as the unique source and origin of the world and as essentially intellectual found support in an idea that was prevalent throughout the whole development of philosophical theology — the idea that reason strives towards the greatest possible unity of understanding. Thus Plato thought of the Forms or Ideas as arranged in a hierarchy and as being crowned by the most universal Form of all, the Form of the Good, which he eventually identified with the One. This idea of the unity of the divine was carried forward by Aristotle and the Stoics and, of course, found its counterpart also in the strict monotheism of the Jews. Associated with this idea of the divine as the ultimate and unified source of the cosmos was an appreciation that it must be quite unlike this world and inaccessible to human conceptualisation. The appreciation of its incomprehensibility and otherness was, therefore, implicit not only in the Jewish but also in the Greek conception of the divine; though various claims have been made that this Greek understanding was itself influenced by Oriental mystery religions, by Gnosticism or Judaism. This sense of the unity and otherness of the divine was in turn linked with the idea of the simplicity of God, partly because everything composite was seen as mutable and partly because everything composite was seen as having a ground outside itself so that it could not be ultimate — which again pointed to God's singularity and unity.

Because his creation could not detract from the uniqueness and freedom of God, for, as we shall see later, this would be self-contradictory, the freedom of God needed to be distinguished from the freedom of what he created. God was unique and free in that he was not constrained by anything self-subsisting — anything which was independent of him in the sense that if *per impossible* God ceased to exist, it could remain in existence. God's freedom was therefore unconditional. What he created was created and continuously sustained by him and where he was, he was in his full plenitude, though his creation could not, of course, share fully in or fully manifest it. In so far as it was able to share in his life, however, as we shall find later, creation had also to share in his freedom. And because at all normal evolutionary levels it had not developed so as to share fully in his life and so in his attributes, that freedom lacked, wholly or in part, his guiding reason and his love and so was forever deviating from so much of his life as it had attained. What is more, that freedom of creation was not unconditional for it was totally dependent on God and any deviation from his creative and sustaining will and act was a deviation from his order and was therefore self-diminishing and ultimately self-destructive. It followed

---

[4] G C Stead *Divine Substance*   (1977) p 181

also, because creation was totally dependent on God for its very existence and other attributes, it did not constrain the freedom and sovereignty of God: nor, as we have seen, did anything else. Deviation on the part of creation from the will and act of God, though self-diminishing, could not, therefore, diminish or detract from the sovereignty of God, notwithstanding that it lay within his life.

God did not, however, having created the world, seek just to maintain it in a static relationship. God was seen as essentially creative and the creativity of God demanded also an openness and responsiveness on the part of creation, if it was to develop to participate more fully in his creative life. This need for openness to new insights — to *gnosis* — and so to the development, the education, of man — *paideia* — is, as we shall see, fundamental to the entire evolutionary process at all levels. Therefore, 'foreclosure' to God's creativity on the part of creation was as much a departure from the will of God and so a mark of 'sin' as other forms of deviation from his order. Yet that sense of the need for openness to the creativity and self-disclosure of God was largely lost by the Western Churches and replaced by closed systems of belief. Whereas purification of the mind was for the early Church basically an intellectual ordering of the mind through participation in Christ, the Logos, the reason and order of God, this understanding was replaced in the West by an emphasis on purification of the mind by moral cleansing to allow entry of a distant God whose creative work was often thought of as complete and who now had the rather different task of redeeming man who had fallen from a prior perfect state.

The unity, simplicity and freedom of God as the source of creation themselves precluded there having been uncreated matter out of which God might have fashioned the world, and though there seems to have been some uncertainty on this issue amongst the earliest Church Fathers, the idea of creation *ex nihilo* quickly came to be assumed. What precisely was understood by this doctrine is a question to which we shall have to return, for the answer is not as simple as is assumed by many modern commentators influenced by Western understandings. None the less, the rejection of any idea of matter eternally co-existing with God did mark a decisive step in establishing the essential freedom of God. Irenaeus, writing before 200 A D, was thus able to attribute the substance of created things to the will and power of God.[5] Similarly, the spirituality of God was contrasted with man's matter-bound spirit and because God was the Creator of matter and of the spirits bound to it, he was seen as himself immaterial. The spirituality and simplicity of God in turn pointed to his

---

[5] *Against Heresies*   2 10 4

incomprehensibility and ineffability for he could not be fully comprehended by any concept or category though by deepening insights that came to him, man could move towards that aim. As Pannenberg says: 'Patristic theology for the most part maintained that man cannot know God by his own efforts but only by means of divine illumination.'[6]

That God's uniqueness and so his freedom and sovereignty, were linked with his otherness and spirituality was part of Israel's faith. A variety of texts speak to this, including Isa 45 15, Isa 40 28 and Deut 4 12ff. Holiness was the Old Testament name for God's otherness. These ideas found a parallel in Middle Platonism where it was generally accepted that God was ineffable and could not be caught by any name. As Armstrong notes, the idea that God is wholly other, different from and better than everything that we are or can know, is at least hinted at in Plato and begins to appear in the later Platonic philosophy of the first centuries A D.[7]

The uniqueness, freedom, mystery and depth of God, ranging from the closest possible intimacy to the remoteness of his supreme majesty, was linked with his simplicity. There is, as we have noted, a deep tendency in human beings, the theological roots of which we shall seek to identify later, to try to unify and simplify their understanding. This tendency, which motivates scientists to unify their understanding of the natural forces of the world, is accompanied by a deep-seated faith that there really is an underlying unity and simplicity in the order of the world of which we ourselves are parts. This unifying tendency can be seen also as an effort to penetrate through to what is ultimately durable in a world of change — durable in the sense of outside time, and so eternal and everlasting, and durable in the sense of unchanging, immutable. Thus in Greek philosophy, it was commonly held that composite things are liable to perish through loss of their distinctive structure, whereas the indivisible or simple was seen as indestructible, perfect and unoriginate. This idea of the unoriginateness of God in turn underpinned ideas of his eternity and immutability which themselves pointed to his impassibility as well as his constancy and faithfulness: yet this idea of the indestructibility and immutability of God had to be understood in terms of the creative plenitude and the dynamic character of the living God in a way which will become clearer later. These features of God linked with his omnipresence and so his providential guidance of the world in every detail, though it could also imply that all changes in man's situation in relation to salvation had to lie on man's side.

Quite apart from the emphasis in the Old Testament on the personality of God, the idea of God as the source itself led back to the idea of God as

---

[6] W Pannenberg *op cit* p 152

[7] A H Armstrong & R A Markus *Christian Faith and Greek Philosophy* (1960) pp 8-9

personal. This was because he was the source of all personality and so more perfect than the impersonal. What is more, because God was seen not only as personal but also as simple and as creator of everything that existed, he was seen as omniscient and omnipotent, though the context in which these have to be understood will have to be considered later. What is more, because there was nothing other than God and the world which he created *ex nihilo* within his life, this pointed not only to his uniqueness but his infinity; another term on which we shall have to comment later. But though there was this tendency to seek a simple source in terms of which the world could be understood, this still left room for differing views about the nature of that simplicity and how it related to the world. Stead, having referred to such ideas in Greek philosophy and their developments in the work of Philo and Eudorus, notes that finally the doctrine of the divine simplicity became conventionalised; and it was protected from attack by the elusive character of the word 'simple' which could mean either 'excluding all differentiation' or merely 'not composite', 'not constructed out of parts.'[8]

Underlying this discussion about the character of the divine simplicity was the question how, if God was simple and unchanging, he could be endowed with a variety of attributes and credited with a varying succession of actions and relationships for, as Stead notes, if the various powers are in any real sense possessed by the ultimate Godhead, they must give expression to various distinct purposes or activities, and he must be variously related to them. And he point to the difficulty of reconciling the exercise or employment of a number of powers with the requirement of absolute simplicity.[9]

We shall have to return to this theme later, but suffice at this point to say that in whatever way the divine simplicity is to be understood, it is in no way a simplicity of emptiness but needs to be thought of in terms of supreme richness or plenitude: an idea which was, of course, to be found also in Greek thinking. Furthermore, as we shall note presently, that simplicity needs to be thought of as in some way incorporating the order of the divine Christ and the creativity of the Holy Spirit.

If, then the world attains its being through participation, albeit a totally dependent participation, in the divine nature, we shall find that, as order builds up in the evolutionary process, including in the development of the mind of man, (or falls away), the attributes of God are in finite measure unveiled (or are veiled) in the specific cumulative order or sequence which we find in the evolutionary process, including in the development of man; a process which finds its culmination when the mind is fully ordered, and,

---

[8] G C Stead *Divine Substance* (1977) pp 93-4

[9] G C Stead *op cit* p 186

in the full mystical experience, we meet God face to face in all his plenitude.

How we can understand the divine simplicity so as to allow for differentiation arises also in attempts to reconcile the unity of God with his Trinitarian nature. That issue, too, will fall to be considered presently but the contribution of Leonard Hodgson to the doctrine of the Trinity is relevant also to the present question. Hodgson sought to present a view of the Trinity which went further along the road towards tritheism than the views of most theologians. He sought to justify this by contrasting the idea of mathematical unity with that of an 'internally constitutive unity' to which the atom and the self are more analogous than the unity of arithmetic.[10] He claimed that mathematical unity means the absence of multiplicity whereas in the internally constitutive sense, the degree of unity is measured by the intensity of the unifying power. He went on to note that the idea of organic unity is but one instance of the class of internally constitutive unities.[11] Much of the work of Teilhard de Chardin also has this idea of complexity in unity in the coming together of the multiplicity of creation in the unity of God. Thus speaking of the consummation of the world (what Paul calls the Pleroma)[12] he says 'What is the supreme and complex reality for which the divine operation moulds us? It is revealed to us by St Paul and St John. It is the qualitative repletion and the quantitative consumation of all things: it is the mysterious pleroma, in which the substantial one and the created many fuse without confusion in a whole which, without adding anything essential to God, will nevertheless be a sort of triumph and generalisation of being.'[13]

The relevance of Hodgson's example of the simplicity revealed in the operation of all living things finds strong confirmation, as we shall see, in the role of cybernetic forces and, indeed, of open systems as a whole throughout the natural world: a feature which is becoming central in modern scientific thought.[14] And Hodgson gives the particularly apt example, albeit imperfect, of some very mature, whole person who manages to bring together vitality, understanding, love and holiness in a kind of massive simplicity, so that in whatever circumstances we meet him, we meet essentially the same person.[15] We shall find that it is on the basis of such

---

[10] L Hodgson *The Doctrine of the Trinity* (1943) pp 105-7

[11] L Hodgson *op cit* p 108

[12] *Le Milieu Divin* (1969) p 28

[13] *op cit* p 111

[14] see e g Paul Davies *The Cosmic Blueprint* (1987)

[15] c f L Hodgson *op cit* p 91

ideas that we can best gain some idea of a perfect simplicity and unity of the life of God in which there is richness which is perfectly coordinated and integrated.

In the idea of the divine simplicity of the Christian God, there must, therefore, as we have seen, be the idea of order, *perfectly coordinated, coherent and self-integrating*, for the divine order and reason are the prerogative of the Son. It needs, therefore, to be specifically recognised that the order and reason of the Son not only take form in the world but are inherent in the simplicity of the Father. This is entailed in the coinherence of the persons of the Trinity and it was recognised specifically by the early Church Fathers. As Stead notes, 'Tertullian pictures God as a mind which contains within itself the Word as its "plan" or "thought", yet this latter is sufficiently distinct to be addressed as a "partner in dialogue".[16] At the moment of creation, however, this thought is uttered, and becomes *sermo*, the spoken word, in place of *ratio*, and now for the first time can be regarded as "Son" in the full sense.'[17] Later Stead draws attention to a passage in *De Synodis* 51 in which Athanasius clearly means that in some sense the reality of the Father, including his Wisdom and Word, is comparable to a single personality.[18] It is clear, therefore, that for the early Fathers, there was implicit in the divine simplicity not only plenitude but also reason and order: an idea on which we shall presently find grounds for putting considerable weight, particularly when developed to have regard to its creative and sustaining, self-regulative character. It is this reason and order which issue from the the Father as properties of the Son which structure and sustain creation within his life.

This at once poses the question of what causes the generation of the Son and so causes the divine simplicity to issue in the multiplicity of creation. In Western theology these tend to be quite different questions. The Trinity, like the divine plenitude, is a feature of the internal nature of God which we know about only by revelation and which is a fundamental aspect of the divine mystery for which no further reason can be sought. The question why God has created the world is, however, to be answered in terms of his *choosing* to do so as a feature of his divine beneficence. On the other hand, in the early Patristic understanding, it would be natural to say that creation takes place through the second and third persons of the Trinity as a feature of the eternal but totally free creative nature of God for whom choice does not arise. As we shall see, the question why God's nature takes this

---

[16] *Adv Prax*   5

[17] G C Stead   *op cit*   p 228

[18] G C Stead   *op cit*   p 265

threefold form and therefore why creation occurs, lends itself to explanation. This, however, suggests that on this basis creation should be eternal — which itself calls for further consideration. Clearly, therefore, there are very different implications of the early Christian and Western understandings of God and his relationship to the world and we need to explore some of these in some detail.

CHAPTER TEN

CREATION *EX NIHILO*

If creation lies within the life of God, how are we to understand creation *ex nihilo*? What is this 'nothing' within the life of God? In considering this question, we may turn first to some modern theological views: though these are often hard to ascertain precisely as most theologians appear to regard *ex nihilo* as self-explanatory. Eric Mascall, who, like most modern theologians, thinks in terms of creation *ad extra* and who accepts the Thomist position 'if it is interpreted in a broad sense', says that creation is, in the scholastic definition, 'the production of the whole substance of a thing in the previous absence both of itself and of any other subject.'[1] And he adds that it is literally *making out of nothing* where 'nothing' is not some kind of *ungrund* or formless prime matter co-eternal with God, as much Greek philosophy taught, but the entire non-existence of anything.[2] Mascall does not say how the 'entire non-existence of anything' is to be reconciled with the infinity of God. On the other hand, A D Sertillanges, in his *Foundations of Thomistic Philosophy* says that we must not start with nothing at all and say: (1) There is nothing; (2) God makes something. That, he claims, is the sort of explanation that does harm and holds us up to the derision of philosophers. Instead, he says, 'Starting with God, we argue like this: God is, and God is not alone. He has given a sort of extension of his being which we call the world.'[3] Here, too, the question arises as to the sense in which there can be an extension of an infinite God. Somewhat less explicitly, Gilson says: 'Without any preexisting matter God willed that things exist and they did exist; and this is precisely what we call creation *ex nihilo*.'[4] The implication of some form of materialisation in a void seems clear.

There is also relevant comment in the report *Man and Nature* by a group of Anglican theologians: 'The model of "making" is already used in the biblical narrative. ... Theologians have often maintained that the analogy finally breaks down because God makes creatures out of nothing, whereas all human making works with an already existing material. But the real problem about the adequacy of the model is different. It has often been claimed that something which is made is entirely external to the maker and the product of his will, and it has therefore been argued that the creation is entirely external to God. It was by a free and sovereign act of will that the

---

[1] cf *S T* 1 lxv 3c

[2] E L Mascall *He Who Is* (1943) pp 97-8

[3] A D Sertillanges *Foundations of Thomistic Philosophy* (n d) pp 98-9

[4] E Gilson *The Christian Philosophy of St Augustine* (1961) p 190

creation was brought into existence, and it is usually implied that God might equally well have refrained from creating. Indeed, herein lies the contingency of creation. This view received classic statement from Calvin and more recently in those writings of Barth and Brunner in which the difference and distance between Creator and creation are stressed to the limit. The most recent advocates of this view are the so-called "theologians of the secular", both Protestant and Catholic, such as F Gogarten, Harvey Cox and J Metz. They have been insistent in declaring that the world is quite external to God and is therefore stripped of any numinous quality and so available for exploitation.'[5]

We must leave aside for the moment the highly questionable suggestion in this passage that the contingency of creation lies on the side of God rather than in creation itself. But so far as creation *ex nihilo* is concerned, understandings of creation in or from some kind of void run first into criticisms that they are logically absurd on the ground that nothing can be made from nothing; but apart from this very general criticism, there is secondly the difficulty which we have already noted, of how there can be anything 'external' to God if God is infinite. Even granted that the term 'external' is metaphorical, it is far from clear how it can be given any 'cash value' so as to imply either extension or separateness from God. Thirdly, there is the major question how the will of God can be separated from his creative and sustaining act and so from God himself so as to be able to act outside himself, for God is one and simple — a question to which we must return. Later we shall also have to consider Anthony Kenny's claim that he knows of no successful treatment of the philosophical problems involved in conceiving a non-embodied mind active throughout the universe: and he adds that it is rare to find among theistic philosophers even an attempt to solve the problem.[6] But these issues aside, there remains the implication of this approach that if it is to achieve the desired aim of separating creation from God, in so far creation must seemingly limit God: for separation implies limit. Of course, as we have seen, the whole of creation is not-God in the sense that it lacks the full transcendence and plenitude of God but, as we shall see more fully later, this need not imply a total 'otherness' or separation of creation from God. It is difficult, therefore, to see how these attempts to regard creation as separate from God can be successful in their aim and it seems that in so far as they succeed, they must limit and diminish God.

Later, we shall find confirmation of the earlier view that creation needs to be understood not as a single act but as a process 'within' God's life that

---

[5] H Montefiore (ed) *Man and Nature* (1975) p 23

[6] A Kenny *The God of the Philosophers* (1979) p 127

allows creation freely to order itself using God's powers so as to lead to fuller participation in his life; yet that that freedom entailed in the process allows also for deviation and so for loss of order and, in so far, for a warping of that dynamic process and a loss of his powers. We shall find, therefore, that that warping needs to be understood, not in terms of the twisting of some kind of static entities materialised outside the life of God but in terms of dynamic forms which can increase or diminish their 'order' (in a sense of order which we shall have to discuss later), and so increase or diminish their participation in God's life and so in the life of the Divine Word, the Divine Christ, and Spirit in so far as they open themselves to the dynamics of his life or shut themselves off from it. And yet, as we shall see, they can never totally merge with it nor can they dissipate themselves so as to leave a void. A loss of order can thus be seen as a movement towards nothing, not as a void, but as the limit of disorder and non-participation in God's life — of chaos. But that chaos still lies within the life of God, emerging as a first step in the process of creation. In so far, creation participates in the life of God in differing degrees but, while diminishing and warping its own life, it neither warps nor diminishes its source in God. How God comes to take that first step in the process of creation by an act of abnegation, we shall see.

Some of these issues have been faced by Jurgen Moltmann in his book *God in Creation.* As he notes, 'ever since Augustine, Christian theology has called God's work of creation an act of God outwards. ... It distinguished this from an act of God inwards, which takes place in the divine relationships within the Trinity.' He notes that 'theologians have made this distinction between God's "inward" and his "outward" aspect so much a matter of course that no one has even asked the critical question: can an omnipotent God have an "outward" aspect at all? If we assume an *extra Deum,* does this not set God a limit?' Moltmann then goes on to assert that there is one possible way of conceiving an *extra Deum* without contradiction: namely by assuming a self-limitation by God himself, preceding creation, by which the omnipotent and omnipresent God withdraws his presence and restricts his power: and he adduces support from the Kabbalistic doctrine that develops the ancient Jewish doctrine of the Sheckinah, according to which an infinite God can so contract his presence that he dwells in the Temple. Moltmann sees the space so created as a 'God-forsaken' space, which is outside God but still remains in God. In this way Moltmann seeks to maintain the idea of creation *ad extra* and the seeming spatial distinction between God and creation that so many Western theologians consider vital.[7]

---

[7] *God in Creation* (1985) pp 86ff

Other theologians also have sought to maintain and develop these Western understandings, though sometimes this requires a balancing act more skilful than revealing. Thus in a review of Arthur Peacocke's *Theology for a Scientific Age* (1990), in *The Times Higher Educational Supplement* of 14 June, 1991, John Polkinghorne notes that Peacocke 'has until now seemed to characterise himself as a panentheist — that is, someone who believes that the world exists in God, though God exceeds the world. From an extended footnote we learn that what Peacocke actually means by panentheism is simply that he wishes to maintain a due balance between divine immanence and divine transcendence, an eminently sensible theological ambition. Panentheism has usually been understood as implying a more intimate relationship than that,' Polkinghorne goes on to note that Peacocke recoils from the idea of divine embodiment in the universe. And Polkinghorne claims elsewhere that 'Only by breaking the tie implicit in embodiment can God be let be to be God and his creation be let be to be itself. ... To the extent that they emesh God in the world, all pantheistic theories are going to threaten the mutually free relation of God and his creation.'[8] This claim we shall have cause to question. Peacocke himself denies that in his usage at least, the world is in some sense a *part* of God, that is, of the same kind of being as God. 'This would indeed deny the ultimate otherness of God from that which he has created and imply that the world is of the same stuff or "substance" as God himself.' Peacocke thus desires to affirm that 'God is causally independent of the world, that the world has a derivative existence, and is thereby dependent on God, *and* that God interacts continuously with the world.'[9]

Such claims thus raise issues about the nature of the relationship of God to the world and, in particular, the nature of the freedom of creation. They also entail questions about the relationship of spiritual to mental and physical; all of which are issues to be discussed presently. The Western concern to stress the separateness and difference of God and the world was not, however shared by the New Testament writers or the Fathers of the early Church, as their emphasis on *participation* in Christ and the ideal for man of 'deification' reveal. As Henry Chadwick notes, 'Underneath the cold language much of the detail of Origen's use of philosophy is in line with the programme laid down by Justin and developed by Clement. "Every wise man, to the extent that he is wise, participates in Christ who is wisdom."'[10] Such ideas have direct bearing on the context within which we need to understand creation *ex nihilo*.

---

[8] *Science and Providence*   (1989) p 22

[9] *Theology for a Scientific Age*   (1990)   pp 208-9

[10] *Early Christian Thought and the Classical Tradition*   (1966) p 103

Not all modern theologians, however, see the relationship of God and the world in typically Western terms. Thus J V Taylor says in a passage, each sentence of which is of direct relevance to the claims of this book: 'To envisage creation in terms of life-giving energy and inspiration is a far profounder insight than the earlier image of God the potter or builder who remains outside and essentially separate from his handiwork. The poets and mystics have always been aware that the whole earth is full of his glory. "We are all in him enclosed", said Julian of Norwich, "and he is enclosed in us". And the pagan Plotinus anticipated the same thought: "We must not think of ourselves as cut off from the source of life; rather we breathe and consist in it, for it does not give itself to us and then withdraw itself, but ever lifts and bears us." Creation, providence and redemption are aspects of one action.'[11]

Julian of Norwich is not alone amongst mystics in her insight. Many mystics, inspired by their experiences, have spoken clearly against a sharp conceptual gap between God and the world such as has arisen in Western theology and they have done so in a way which has direct bearing on the interpretation of creation *ex nihilo*. G G Scholem, in his book *Major Trends in Jewish Mysticism*, when writing about the Kabbalist tradition, bears this out. Having said he will not go into the difficulties with which orthodox theologians found themselves faced when they tried to preserve the full meaning of creation out of nothing, he notes that the mystics, too, speak of creation out of nothing: in fact it is one of their favourite formulas. But in their case, the orthodoxy of the term conceals a meaning which differs considerably from the original one. This nothing from which everything has sprung is by no means a mere negation: only to us does it present no attributes because it is beyond the reach of intellectual knowledge. 'In truth, however, this Nothing — to quote one of the Kabbalists — is infinitely more real than all other reality. Only when the soul has stripped itself of all limitation and, in mystical language, has descended into the depths of Nothing does it encounter the Divine. For this Nothing comprises a wealth of mystical reality although it cannot be defined. ... In a word, it signifies the Divine itself, in its most impenetrable guise. In fact, creation out of nothing means to many mystics just creation out of God.'[12]

The closeness and omnipresence of God is of course, a constant theme of many mystics. Julian of Norwich has already been quoted. God, says Meister Eckhart, 'is nearer to me than I am to myself; he is just as near to

---

[11] J V Taylor *The Go-Between God* (1972) pp 26-7

[12] G C Scholem *Major Trends in Jewish Mysticism* 3rd edn (1961) p 25

wood and stone, but they do not know it.'[13]   Bett, in his account of the
teaching of John Scotus Erigena says: 'God created all things out of
nothing, is a precisely equivalent statement to: God created all things out
of himself.'[14]

All this has been forcefully reiterated by P Sherrard who, having
discussed criticisms of Christianity made by Plethon, refers also to Scotus
Erigena and develops their claims thus: 'The creation *ex nihilo* does not
mean that God creates the world out of mere nothingness, for there can be
no privation of relationship before relation exists, nor negation of existence
before existence; on the contrary, what is signified by "nothing" in this
context is the negation of all habitude, existence, being, accident, of all that
can be said or thought; in other words, what is signified is the
pre-ontological nature of God which precedes all determination.'[15]   As
Scholem, speaking of the reports of mystics, says: 'Creation out of nothing
thus becomes the symbol of emanation, that is to say, of an idea which, in
the history of philosophy and theology, stands furthest removed from it.'[16]

We have already seen that ideas about the constant struggle between the
creative powers of God which seek to build order out of chaos and the
destructive tendencies to disorder were a feature of many primitive religions.
They were fundamental to the belief of Israel and underlay all parts of the
Old Testament.   Creation was, therefore, to be seen in terms of God's
ordering forces which had constantly to seek to overcome the forces of
disorder, of chaos.   God's creative forces therefore operated, not only to
originate the world, but to sustain it.   B W Anderson, in his book *Creation
versus Chaos* (1987 edn), has shown the pervasiveness of this theme in all
parts of the Old Testament, with chaos being often represented in terms of
the waters and oceans.   But it is always clear that that chaos did not exist
alongside God; it is the product of the act of creation.

A Ehrhardt discussed the Old Testament and Greek backgrounds to the
doctrine of creation *ex nihilo* and the New Testament understanding of it, in
an article in 1951.[17]   He sought to show that the claim that God created the
world out of nothing and the claims of Genesis 1 1 that in the beginning
God created heaven and earth are largely contradictory.   He argued that the
idea of nothingness, in so far as it has any meaning at all, demands that all
things, i e the universe, should be opposed to it and consequently limited,

---

[13] Meister Eckhart *Pred* lxix (quoted by E Underhill *Mysticism* (12 edn) (1930) p 101)

[14] H Bett *Johannes Scotus Erigena*   (1925) p 34

[15] P Sherrard *The Greek East and The Latin West*   (1959) pp 136-7

[16] G C Scholem *op cit*   p 25

[17] *Studia Theologica*   IV   pp 10ff

whereas the idea of 'universe' demands that it should embrace all things and so be without limit. He considered the relevant Biblical references. He notes 2 Macc 7 28ff where the Maccabean mother encourages her son to martyrdom and says: 'I beseech thee, my son, look upon heaven and earth and all that is therein, and consider that God made them of things that were not; and so was mankind made likewise; fear not the tormentor, but being worthy of thy brethren, take thy death.' This passage, which was the only Biblical passage which Origen could find to support creation *ex nihilo*, emphasises the lack of reality of the cosmos as an encouragment to martyrdom. In Acts 17 22-31, where the role of God as creator is also stressed, Paul says that in God we live and move and have our being for we are indeed his offspring, and goes on to point to the resurrection of Christ as according a new level of reality to the world. In all such passages, Ehrhardt claims, and even in the passage from Maccabees, there is always the divine reality behind the apparent world. He quotes a line from Porphyry's version of an Orphic poem: 'For all this is lying in the great body of Zeus' as representative of a trend in Greek philosophy and claims any amount of contemporary philosophical support for the Pauline formula in Romans 11 36, 'For of him and through him and in him are all things'; and for the similar comment of Paul in Acts 17 28 where, as noted, when addressing the Athenians, he quotes the words '"In him we live and move and have our being": as even some of your poets have said.' Ehrhardt refers also to 1 Cor 8 6; Col 1 16ff; Eph 4 5 and Heb 2 10 as relevant to this way of thinking.

Von Rad, in his discussion of the first verses of Genesis, having noted that the word *bara*, 'create', contains the idea both of complete effortlessness and *creatio ex nihilo*, since it is never connected with any statement of the material, says: 'Verse 2 teaches one to understand the marvel of creation, therefore, from the viewpoint of its negation; thus it speaks first of the formless and abysmal out of which God's will lifted creation and above which it holds it unceasingly. For the cosmos stands permanently in need of this supporting Creator's will. We see here that the theological thought of Ch 1 moves not so much between the poles of nothingness and creation as between the poles of chaos and cosmos. It would be false to say, however, that the idea of *creatio ex nihilo* was not present here at all (v 1 stands with good reason before v 2), *but the actual concern of this entire report of creation is to give prominence, form and order to the creation out of chaos.'* (my italics)[18]

---

[18] G von Rad *Genesis*   rev edn   (1972)   p 51

R M Grant treated the doctrine of creation *ex nihilo* more widely in his *Miracle and Natural Law in Graeco-Roman and Early Christian Thought.* He too noted that there is no statement in the New Testament that God made creation out of nothing and he quotes particularly 1 Cor 8 6 as suggesting that God is himself the 'matter' out of which the universe emanates: 'For there is one God the Father, from whom are all things ... and one Lord Jesus Christ through whom are all things.' He notes also Col 1 16 which in the RSV reads: 'He is the image of the invisible God, the first-born of all creation; for in him all things were created ... all things were created through him and for him. He is before all things and in him all things hold together.' Grant notes, referring to Cullmann, that this is the same teaching as in John 1 3 and Heb 1 2-5.[19] Grant claims, however, that such passages do not imply a philosophical analysis of causes but religious faith in God who is the cause of all, and that because in ordinary Greek language of the period 'out of' is used for both the origin and cause of events, 'therefore Paul's language in 1 Cor 8 6 cannot be pressed to prove his teaching of an emanation doctrine.' On the contrary, Grant claims, 'it looks forward to the eventual expression of the doctrine of creation "out of nothing"'[20] However, he does not offer any explanation of what creation *ex nihilo* would come to mean or means or where it differs from creation out of God.

How, then, did the Church Fathers themselves understand creation *ex nihilo*? First, we can turn again to Augustine. Having made clear that God created heaven and earth out of nothing, Augustine goes on to qualify 'nothing' to mean 'almost nothing'. 'It was not yet like the world which we now see and touch. It was invisible and without form. It was a great chasm, over which there was no light. ... But in those days the whole world was little more than nothing, because it was still entirely formless. Yet by now it was something to which form could be added. For you, O Lord, made the world from formless matter, which you created out of nothing. This matter was almost nothing, but from it you made all the mighty things which are so wonderful to us.'[21] And earlier he had said, 'Nor was it in the universe that you made the universe, because until the universe was made there was no place where it could be made. Nor did you have in your hand any matter from which you could make heaven and earth, for where could you have obtained matter which you had not yet created, in order to use it as material for making something else? Does anything exist by any other cause than that you exist? It must therefore be that you spoke and they were

---

[19] R M Grant *op cit* (1952) pp 138-9

[20] *op cit* p 139

[21] Augustine *Confessions* Trans R S Pine-Coffin (1961) xii 8

made. In your Word alone you created them.'[22] The Word of God, so
spoken of by Augustine, is, of course, the ordering principle of the world
and the Divine life, the Divine Christ. As we have seen, however, the
predominant and lastingly influential view of Augustine was that there could
be no participation of creation in God so, not surprisingly, Gilson notes the
ambiguities in Augustine's doctrine of creation. He comments that:
'Augustine undertook an undoubtedly impossible task, namely that of
explaining creation in terms of participation', something which, Gilson says
apologetically, would be incomprehensible in a Father of the Church as great
as Augustine were it not for the very impeccability of his theology: and he
adds that his theology of creation is as irreproachable as his theology of the
Trinity.[23] But Gilson spoke within the Western tradition as a convinced
Thomist.

Henry Chadwick describes the views of earlier Fathers on creation *ex
nihilo* thus: 'Three times Clement declares that the world is made "out of
nothing" but in each case the phrase he employs is *ek me ontos*, not *ex ouk
ontos;* that is to say, it is made not from that which is absolutely
non-existent, but from relative non-being or unformed matter, so shadowy
and vague that it cannot be said to have the status of "being" which is
imparted to it by the shaping hand of the Creator. Philo had used virtually
the same language. Justin is ambiguous but could be taken to suggest, like
Tatian, that the Logos first created needed matter as raw material and then
ordered it into cosmos. Athenagoras, on the other hand, makes no attempt
to interpret creation as anything other than the ordering of pre-existent
matter by the divine artist.'[24] Christopher Stead notes that for Athanasius,
God calls things into being out of not-being, 'but the latter is conceived, not
as sheer nothingness, but as a sort of limbo of unreal being.'[25] As for the
Cappadocian Fathers, I P Sheldon-Williams describes the views of Gregory
of Nyssa thus: 'It is not necessary to follow the scriptural order of events,
since the Creation was a single act of the Divine Will outside time. From
it sprang instantaneously the potentialities of all things, which being seminal
.., develop, without further divine intervention, successively into all the
phenomena which can and will constitute the world. Regarded as a single
seminal power these potentialities ... or "surges" ... or causes ... are the
Logos, whose unity is eternal and therefore is never wholly lost in the
multiplicity of creation but holds it together and is the means by which it
may in due course ... ascend from the less to the more perfect, from the

---

[22] *op cit* xi 5

[23] E Gilson *The Christian Philosophy of St Augustine* (1960) p 202-3

[24] H Chadwick *Early Christian Thought and the Classical Tradition* (1966) pp 46-7

[25] *Divine Substance* (1977) p 237

minimal being of purely potential matter to its information, vivication ...,
sensitivization, rationalization and deification.'[26] This is a view closely in
accord with that which we shall be presenting later.

One further implication of these claims which conflicts with the Western
understanding should also be pointed out. Even if one ignores the problem
of how to reconcile the idea of a void with the infinity of God, and assumes
that there can be some form of void whether within or outside God, if God
is simple, where the will of God is, there will have to be other attributes of
God and so God himself. Insofar the void will no longer be a void and we
come back to creation as an ordering process from that state of formless
disorder within the life of God which is furthest removed from his ordered
plenitude. How that disorder got there is separate question to which we
shall refer later.

From this survey it seems fair to conclude that at the very least there are
grave difficulties in interpretations of creation *ex nihilo* as being creation
from some form of void and that it is a view that gains any plausibility that
it may have from the idea of creation *ad extra* — for it has little plausibility
if seen in terms of creation within the life of God. We shall find even that
limited plausibility undermined as we proceed to consider the wide range of
related doctrines that cluster around this idea of creation *ad extra*. There
remains, however, the question whether we can find any reconciliation
between the views of 'nothing' as signifying some form of as yet formless
matter and 'nothing' as signifying the life of God itself. This is precisely
what we shall find for, as we have seen, the world cannot be a part of God
in the full sense implied by his transcendent immutability. Rather, we shall
find, the act of creation, instead of being understood in terms of some form
of materialisation, needs to be understood in terms of a dynamic ordering
process — in other words, in terms of the evolutionary process which can
be seen as entailing a progressive revelation of the attributes of God as order
develops from a state of formlessness, yet one which is constantly the
subject of warping and deviation to lower levels of order.

This emerging process involves, at the furthest remove from the full life
of God, his act alone, which, being unguided by his reason and his love,
deviates from his life and so passes out of existence randomly; then his act
vivified and in some measure guided by emerging cybernetic forces; then by
consciousness, then by various levels of understanding which become
progressively informed by love, leading to holiness and, in the culmination
of the process, when mind is fully integrated and stilled, to the full mystical
experience in which the mind comes face to face with, but is never totally
absorbed by God. These stages are, it will be appreciated, cumulative in

---

[26] *Camb. Hist. of Later Greek and Early Med. Phil.* Ed A H Armstrong (1970) pp 447-8

that life entails the act of God but not vice versa; consciousness entails life and act but not vice versa; understanding entails consciousness, love entails understanding and so on. The reasons for creation taking this cumulative form will become clear later but the crucial element in the answer, when widened to creation as a whole, again lies in the ideas of Gregory of Nyssa: 'Human nature as it is now, cannot be as God intended it in the beginning, and as it will surely be in the end ... How then did this new state arise ... The ultimate cause is man's freedom. For freedom is a divine quality, and God may not create man in his image without giving him free will.'[27]

As for the immutability of God, we shall suggest that this is a feature of his full dynamic life when his act is an aspect of, and so directed by, his full life including his understanding, love and holiness, all of which direct the Divine life so as to maintain it in the best and fullest conceiveable state. Thus, in proportion as these attributes are lacking or are subtracted in creation, his dynamic act becomes in its outcome undirected and so deeply mutable, and so tends, with less than full knowledge and love to guide it, to deviate from fuller participation in his life to lower levels of order with the consequent progressive loss of his attributes. Here, as we shall see, lies one essential form of sin, the other being when creation lacks the faith to open itself to the creativity of God and so to fuller participation in his life which has always to be understood in dynamic terms. The act of God when operating on its own without his other attributes, thus becomes, at the limit, what remains a manifestation of the life and being of God at the furthest possible remove from his immutable ordered plenitude, for there cannot be a void from which God is totally absent. Indeed, we shall go so far as to suggest that that ultimate state of disorder in which matter keeps coming into and promptly deviating out of existence may be identified with the vacuum field of quantum physics.

This, however, is to look ahead. At this point we need note only that even if, as is suggested by Gregory of Nyssa, God in the process of creating has in his nature to give freedom to creation to deviate from his will and, by implication, also from his act and life and love and understanding — issues that remain to be explored — such deviation by creation from the will of God has to be distinguished sharply from any idea of change in the will of God itself. As we have noted, God's will has traditionally been considered to be immutable, an attribute that is inherent in the early Patristic understanding of the concept of God. We need, therefore, as a next step to consider some of the implications of the idea of God's 'choosing' — a concept that seemingly must allow for change in the will of God.

---

[27] J Daniélou *From Glory to Glory* (1961) pp 11-12

CHAPTER ELEVEN

THE IDEA OF GOD'S CHOOSING

The Incoherence of the Idea of God's 'Choosing'

We have already seen how the idea of God's 'choosing' gradually emerged into prominence in the Middle Ages. That God is totally free in the sense that there is nothing whatsoever external to him or other than him which could limit him in any way — not even a void or any form of original matter — was clear to the early Church and has been steadfastly adhered to since. And for some centuries after, the picture of creation within the life of God — a picture that did not lend itself to the idea of God's choosing — had been superseded in the West, the immutability of the will of God appears to have been maintained without serious challenge.

The idea of God's choosing does, however, raise issues quite different from those raised by change within the life of God, for whereas *change* can occur within God in the course of implementing his unchanging will in the process of creation, and so without God in his essence changing, *choice* by him would imply a change in God 'as a whole' and so in the Son and the Spirit, his order and love, and so in their relationships to one another: relationships which, as we shall see, in the West constitute the very structure of the life of God. Thus the idea of God's choosing implies not only a change in the implementation of the will of God but in his will itself and so in his consciousness and act and understanding and, indeed, in the direction of his love. We need therefore to consider some of these implications.

That God is free in the sense of being totally unconstrained by anything other than God and so by anything which is self-subsisting, we have already stressed. God can, therefore, do whatever is in his nature to do without any such constraints whatsoever: that is not at issue in this discussion; and his nature includes, of course, his reason and understanding and his love. If we could imagine a time when God, before starting his creative activity, considered a range of possibilities and then decided entirely freely to choose one, we might think of his immutable act coming into play at that point. But for most theologians, God is eternal, outside time, for time is to be seen as associated with this changing world — a view which finds support in modern physics — and this changing world is itself the product of his creative act. If, therefore, God is outside time, there cannot have been a time before God's creativity commenced. Indeed, if time — and so some form of sequence — applied to God, this would seemingly imply some form of constraint on God which restrained him by requiring such a sequence. In any event, arguably, the very idea of sequence only makes sense if there is some independent observer or point of reference against which it can be measured; but that would seem to point directly towards dualism.

It might be felt, of course, that God might still need to choose between the creation of two incompatible goods, but this seems very questionable for God cannot create anything independent of himself for to do so would destroy his supremacy, and if all real goods flow from the simple plenitude of God, they cannot be ultimately incompatible: it is (necessarily) destructive deviations from his will that make them so. Also, the idea of God 'considering' before he acts, separates his thought from his act and so destroys his simplicity: indeed, the very idea of 'considering' alternatives may be seen as implying some form of discursive or at least divergent thoughts and this seems incompatible with his immutability, simplicity and eternity.

What is more, ideas of God doing only some of the things open to him seemingly introduce potential and witholding and so a negativity into the idea of God — though God is always considered to be wholly positive. If, however, we accept that in whatever way God acts, he acts eternally, outside time, having always 'foreseen' the implications of his acts; and that there could not have been a time when God considered what to do before starting, the problems of conceiving of God's choosing to implement these ideas as he 'goes along' are no less serious. First, in its very nature, choice implies limitation — either/or — and it is unclear why God should have to choose instead of doing everything his nature allows, given that there is nothing other than God which could restrict him. The alternative is that God should voluntarily withhold some of his goods, but this seems incompatible with his wholly beneficient goodness. But if, notwithstanding, God is still thought to choose, his choice would presumably have to be rational. Apart from the fact that he would presumably have to consider a range of possibilities that are not carried out, thus separating his thought from his act, God himself creates reason by the ordering of his act and he is not governed by it. Whatever he chose would, therefore, provide a different basis for reason: yet his choice would not itself be based on reason — which would seemingly make God transcend reason and so non-rational in his nature. Yet reason, which is the prerogative of the Divine Christ, the Word of God, the Son, is inherent in the life of God. God cannot choose different Sons. These incoherences and contradictions are not comprehensive and some may be surmountable, but at the very least they should not only make any idea of God's choosing highly questionable but also make clear the highly anthropomorphic character of the God so implied. What is more, we shall find good grounds for saying that such an idea is quite unnecessary.

Part of the difficulty here seems to be that we today, in line, as we have seen, with much modern philosophy, tend to identify the self with the will and the will is thought of in terms of the exercise of choice. Kenny notes that concepts of freedom can for philosophical purposes be divided into two main classes. 'Some analyses of freedom lay most emphasis on the notion

of choice or desire, others lay most emphasis on the notion of ability or
power. Some define freewill as the capacity to do what one wants, others
define it as the power of alternative action. On the one account, a person
does something freely if he does it *because he wants to*; on the other
account, he does something freely if he does it *though it is in his power not
to do it*.[1] If, however, we can do what we want to do — fulfil ourselves
in the way we wish — whether there are other options open to us becomes
irrelevant. As Iris Murdoch says: 'Freedom is not strictly the exercise of
the will, but rather the experience of accurate vision which, when this
becomes appropriate, occasions action. It is what lies behind and in between
actions and prompts them that is important, and it is this area which should
be purified. By the time the moment of choice has arrived the quality of
attention has probably determined the nature of the act.'[2]

Arguably, therefore, in the case of God who is under no external limits
and whose love and knowledge are perfect, what matters is that he can do
what he wills. Thus if nothing other than his own nature constrains him
from choosing alternatives or witholding his act so that he does not want to
exercise alternatives, which therefore do not arise, his freedom cannot be
constrained. But 'not choosing' can so easily seem to imply constraint, that
we may wish to say, with equal force, that God infallibly chooses what is
best, subject only to any limits of self-consistency or self-contradiction.
Indeed, what God infallibly chooses is the best for, since God is all-in-all
and since there is no reference point outside God by which any alternative
could be judged, in principle any alternative at this level, when considered
with all its implications, is literally inconceiveable. Whatever God chooses
is the best because there could be no other. But this is fully compatible with
God's creative act being always necessarily associated, at all levels save the
highest, where necessity and freedom coincide, with the freedom of what is
created by his act to deviate from his act in countless different ways, and so
towards self-diminution and conflict. This is an idea of God's relationship
to the world which can cause difficulties to those who think of God as in
some sense existing alongside the world and 'intervening' in it. But for a
God who is already in the world, creating, sustaining and seeking to redeem
it, in so far as it freely responds to him, no question of 'intervention' arises:
instead, God seeks continuously to develop, sustain and reconcile the world
to himself and so its parts to each other, so as to realise in the world the
harmony of the Divine life within which it develops.

That God was free to do whatever he willed was the position of the early
Church, though the ways of God were regarded as shrouded in mystery. But

---

[1] A Kenny *Freewill and Responsibility* (1978) p 25

[2] *The Sovereignty of the Good* (1970) p 67

the Platonic idea of the fecundity of the divine taking every possible form carried through into Christian doctrine. Thus Origen speaks of the good God and kindly Father of all creation, 'at once beneficent power and creative power, that is, the power that does good and creates and providentially sustains': and Origen adds: 'It is absurd and impious to suppose that these powers of God have been at any time in abeyance for a single moment. Indeed, it is unlawful even to entertain the least suspicion that these powers, through which chiefly we gain a worthy notion of God, should at any time have ceased from performing works worthy of themselves and have become inactive. For we can neither suppose that these powers which are in God, nay, which are God, could have been thwarted from without, nor, on the other hand, when nothing stood in their way, can we believe that they were reluctant to act and perform works worthy of themselves or that they feigned impotence. We can therefore imagine no moment whatever when that power was not engaged in well-doing.'[3]

The limit which Origen sees to the powers of God is not choice but stems from the fact that God cannot act in a way which is incompatible with his other attributes — for, as we have seen, Origen claimed that God could create only what he could comprehend and make subject to his providence, and the infinite was in its nature incomprehensible.[4] In other words, as we shall see further, order and reason which were understood in terms of the Divine Christ and so as inherent in the life of God, were necessary for comprehension and in that they were inherent in the life of God, God's powers were necessarily limited, not by anything other than God, but by that order and reason that lay within his very nature.[5] Apart from this, Origen saw God acting in accordance with the full beneficence of his own nature. Henry Chadwick sums up Origen's position by saying that if for Origen creation is not eternally necessary to the being of God, it is certainly an eternal consequence of his nature.[6]

As we have seen, however, the question whether God chooses came into prominence in the Middle Ages as the concepts of God and the world drifted apart, and it became enshrined in almost all subsequent Western theological thinking. It is therefore worth pointing to the problems seen in the idea of God's choosing by several modern theologians. Thus E Lampert claimed that the differentiation of freedom and necessity in God contradicts the absolute character of the divine life, for God 'who has in himself the power to create, cannot but be creator. God is love: he cannot either not love at

---

[3] *De Principiis* trans G W Butterworth (1971) I iv

[4] *op cit* II ix i

[5] c f C Bigg *The Christian Platonists of Alexandria* 2nd edn (1913) p 198

[6] H Chadwick *Early Christian Thought and the Classical Tradition* (1966) p 83

all, or love to a limited extent; on which account he might have abstained from creation partly or altogether. And in God love is just as "necessary" as his own being, in which love is inherent. The creation of the world is not a sort of supplementary "extra", a certain "plus" to God's own life. Nay, it enters the divine life with all the power of "necessity", which in God is wholly identical with freedom.'[7]

A much fuller discussion of the issues was undertaken by the highly respected Benedictine theologian, Dom Illtyd Trethowan, in his book *Absolute Value,* He notes first, by reference to A O Lovejoy's *The Great Chain of Being,* what Lovejoy says about the position of Aquinas on this issue: that on St Thomas's general principles we should expect him to say that nothing less than the sum of all genuine possibles could be the object of the divine will.[8] Aquinas is, however, under the necessity of affirming the freedom of the absolute will.[9] And so he adopts the solution that 'though the divine intellect conceives of an infinity of possible things, the divine will does not choose them all; and the existence of finite things is therefore contingent and the number of their kinds is arbitrary.'[10] How, Trethowan asks, could God leave a possible good unrealised? And he notes also that John Hick in *Evil and the God of Love* similarly draws on Lovejoy and repeats his argument with emphasis. The conclusion that Trethowan draws is clear: there are no possible worlds; there is simply the world.[11] He had noted earlier that E L Mascall in *Existence and Analogy*[12] had attempted to refute this by reference to Lampert's claim quoted above, on the ground that it cut away the contingency of the created world and led to an unbalanced immanence. Trethowan had discussed Mascall's criticisms in his earlier book *An Essay in Christian Philosophy*[13] and had concluded that for God to will both himself and the world did not mean that God was identical with the world and that Mascall still had to show that to say that God's knowledge of the world is included in his nature involves identifying the world and God.

Most of Trethowan's subsequent discussion in *Absolute Value* is devoted to clarifying his position in relation to the Church's condemnation of

[7] E Lampert *The Divine Realm* (1944) p 39

[8] I Trethowan *Absolute Value* (1970) p 110 (quoting Lovejoy *op cit* (1936/64) p 74 who quotes *SCG* 1 75, *SCG* 1 81 and *ST* 1 19 4)

[9] A O Lovejoy *op cit* p 74

[10] A O Lovejoy *op cit* p 75

[11] I Trethowan *op cit* p 117

[12] (1949) pp 130-1

[13] (1954) pp 96-100

Abelard, in relation to the Vatican Council's condemnation of Guenther for teaching the necessity of creation, and in relation to possible objections by Thomists. Trethowan first denies the 'necessity of creation' in the sense that creation contains within itself the reason for its own existence: for God is that reason. He notes a claim by Victor Cousin that without the act of creation, God would not be God because (as all agree), he is his act.[14] Trethowan denies that it follows that the term or outcome of that act in the sense of the created universe, adds anything to God. He notes that it is good Thomism not to allow that there are relations in God to creatures, but only in creatures to God. And he says that he can think of choosing only as a response in a state of affairs upon which the chooser is in a sense dependent. 'If God is described as choosing, this can mean for me only that he finds himself faced with "possibles" soliciting his will and therefore in a certain respect acting upon him and so making him dependent on them.'[15] The idea of God's choosing seems to introduce this lack of necessity into the creative act of God which is God himself; for, as Trethowan says, how can we avoid the conclusion that if God had chosen not to create, there would have been something 'unrealized' in him.[16] The act of God 'makes no difference' to God only in the sense that it is identical with his nature. God cannot have a better purpose for his creation than the communication of himself in knowledge and love to his creatures. And Trethowan sums up the discussion, which is a lot more detailed than indicated here, by suggesting that our ordinary notions of freedom and necessity coincide at infinity.[17] Trethowan's claims will receive amplification and support in later pages of this study.

It needs, in the light of this discussion, to be stressed that though the creative act of God, which is one aspect of his simple and totally free nature, carries with it freedom for what is created to deviate from his act, and so what is created is always contingent, it is quite a different step to introduce that contingency into the divine life itself, with the radical incoherence it implies, including in the relations of God's triune life. It was basically for this reason that we expressed reservations at an earlier point when, in the passage which we quoted from the report of a group of Anglican theologians, *Man and Nature*, they specifically ascribed the contingency of creation to God's ability to create or refrain from creating.

Trethowan's discussion of God's choosing had been introduced by reference to some perceptive words of C S Lewis in *The Problem of Pain*.

---

[14] *op cit* (1970) p 111

[15] I Trethowan *op cit* (1970) p 112

[16] I Trethowan *op cit* (1970) p 113

[17] *op cit* (1970) p 118

Lewis perceptively commented that with every advance in our thought, the unity of the creative act and the impossibility of tinkering with the creation as though this or that element could have been removed would become more apparent. He suggested that perhaps this is not the 'best of all possible' universes but the only possible one. Possible worlds can mean only 'worlds which God could have made but didn't.' The idea of that which God 'could have done' involves a too anthromorphic conception of God's freedom. Whatever human freedom means, he stresses, divine freedom cannot mean indeterminacy between alternatives and choice of one of them. And, he continues, 'Perfect goodness can never debate about the means most suited to achieve it. The freedom of God consists in the fact that no cause other than himself produces his acts and no external obstacle impedes them — that his own goodness is the root from which they all grow and his own omnipotence the air in which they may all flower.'[18]

The Implications of the Anthropic Cosmological Principle

These precient words of Lewis have found remarkable support in evidence which has in recent years been exciting interest amongst cosmologists and which has led to what is known as the Anthropic Cosmological Principle. Earlier assumptions that man occupied the central role in nature were largely overthrown by the Copernican principle that man did not occupy a privileged position in the universe. What is more, there seemed no compelling reason for assuming that there might not be many different possible forms of universe. The improbability of life evolving in this one was thus set in the context of this very wide range of possibilities and could thus be seen as accidental. It has now become clear that such views are open to serious question.

In 1974 Brandon Carter pointed out that 'our location in the Universe is necessarily privileged to the extent of being compatible with our existence as observers.'[19] Carter formulated two versions of the principle that are known as the Anthropic Cosmological Principle. There appear to have been widely differing interpretations of his ideas but the underlying point is clear. He was pointing to the correlation that exists between some very remarkable and unlikely pieces of evidence about the universe which all appear necessary for the emergence of intelligent observers. However, he appears to have started with the existence of intelligent observers and used this fact to highlight these remarkable features of the universe without which there

---

[18] C S Lewis *The Problem of Pain* (1940) p 23

[19] B Carter in *Confrontation of Cosmological Theories with Observation* ed M S Longair (1974) quoted by J D Barrow and F J Tipler *The Anthropic Cosmological Principle* (1986)

would have been no intelligent observers: he was not starting with these remarkable features and arguing from them to the likelihood or necessity of intelligent observers.[20]

These observed properties of the Universe, however improbable they may initially seem, can be understood in perspective only when we have noted that certain properties of the Universe are necessary prerequisites of the evolution and existence of any observers at all. Thus Barrow and Tipler point out that we are a carbon-based intelligent life form and that the environment necessary for the evolution of such life-forms is a Universe that is at least several billion years old and hence at least several billion light years across. They comment that the realization that the possibility of biological evolution is strongly dependent upon the global structure of the Universe is truly surprising and perhaps provokes us to consider that the existence of life may be no more, but no less, remarkable than the existence of the Universe itself.[21] Far from there being many possible universes compatible with the emergence of intelligent observers, therefore, they point out that that the implications of the Anthropic Cosmological Principle suggest that the number of possible universes must be very small; and that many cosmologists are coming to the view that logically there is only one possible universe which could have led to such observers.[22] In particular, the investigation of the relevant constraints has led to the identification of a number of unlikely coincidences between numbers of enormous magnitude that are, seemingly, completely independent, and which all appear to be essential to the existence of carbon-based observers in the universe. So numerous and unlikely did these coincidences seem that Carter proposed a stronger version of the Anthropic Principle than the Weak form of self-selection principle: that the Universe *must* be such as to admit the creation of observers at some stage.[23] That 'must' is open to different interpretations, but these arguments appear at least to suggest that, given certain universal constants, if God wanted a universe with intelligent observers in it, the constraints on the form which such a universe could take were so strict that there may have been only one possible broad form that it could take: that of our present universe. Clearly, however, as we shall see, this view that there is only one possible broad form of universe is not necessarily incompatible with countless more detailed variations.

---

[20] see e g M K Munitz *Cosmic Understanding* (1986) pp 254-5

[21] *op cit* p 4

[22] *op cit* p 20 and p 105

[23] *op cit* pp 5-6

Despite this trend of opinion amongst cosmologists, however, Barrow and
Tipler note that, in contrast to the cosmologists, a consensus exists amongst
biologists that the evolution of intelligent life on earth was not foreordained
and is so improbable that it is unlikely to occur elsewhere in our galaxy.[24]
Barrow and Tipler themselves assert that the emergence of *homo sapiens*
was not an inevitable outcome of any one of the primate species which
existed ten million years ago; that the modern view of nature stresses its
unfinished and changing character;[25] and that 'there is no generally
purposeful pattern in the collection of all lineages. Most lineages have died
out, a few have regressed in the sense of becoming less complex, while
some — including the branch of the evolutionary tree which has led to man
— have increased the complexity of their nervous systems dramatically.[26]
Barrow and Tipler thus claim that had the environmental pressures or the
sequence of mutations been slightly different at any point during this period,
the human species would never have arisen.[27] Accordingly, whereas many
cosmologists go so far as to think that only one form of universe was
possible, a form that could and did produce observers, biologists think of the
evolution of observers as so extremely improbable that it might never have
occurred. Thus the cosmologists and the biologists appear to be pointing in
opposite directions. Closer scrutiny of these positions appears, therefore, to
be desirable.

Barrow and Tipler show that the role of natural selection is by no means
so wide-ranging as is often thought and that the gross size and structure of
almost all natural objects are determined by certain fundamental features of
the natural world. They comment that there has grown up, even amongst
many educated persons, a view that everything in Nature, every fabrication
of its laws, is determined by the local environment in which it was nurtured
— that natural selection and the Darwinian revolution have advanced to the
boundaries of every scientific discipline. Yet, they say, in reality, this is far
from the truth. Twentieth century physics has discovered there exist
invariant properties of the natural world and its elementary components
which render inevitable the gross size and structure of virtually all its
composite objects. 'The size of bodies like stars and planets, and even
people, are neither random nor the result of any progressive selection
process, but simply manifestations of the different strengths of the various

---

[24] *op cit*   p 124
[25] *op cit*   p 30
[26] *op cit*   p 128-9
[27] *op cit*   p 135

forces of nature. They are examples of possible equilibrium states between competing forces of attraction and repulsion.'[28]

It appears, therefore, that in considering possible universes, we should distinguish, first, universes where the constants of nature might be different from those of this universe. There are grounds for questioning whether any such universe is possible and particularly whether any such universe could develop observers. This suggests, therefore, that probably only a universe with the same laws and constants as ours could develop at all. Our own universe, however, though it is seemingly quite closely determined by these laws and constants of nature, has, none the less, a significant area of uncertainty and contingency where the interplay of the various forces under the influence of natural selection can and does produce constant variations. It is within this framework that Barrow and Tipler follow the biologists in envisaging that the universe might have taken many different forms and that slight variations in environmental pressures or the sequence of mutations might have prevented the emergence of the human species.

Within this framework, Barrow and Tipler distinguish between determinate natural teleology where the outcome is quite closely determined, as in the development of an embryo into a baby, and indeterminate natural teleology where the outcome is not so determined — and they cite the development of *homo sapiens* as an example of this.[29] But given that our universe *is capable of* producing us as intelligent observers, it seems reasonable to assume that the pressures for development, when combined with the processes of natural selection, would have led to the emergence of some form of intelligent observers akin to, if not identical with, *homo sapiens*, given sufficient time: and indeed, it seems reasonable to assume that given all the wasteful and protracted processes entailed in natural selection, there may have been, historically, many such developments which were in fact frustrated. While, therefore, it is clear that the evolutionary process has been extremely protracted, hesitant and wasteful, there is a big step from claiming that changes in environmental pressures or in the sequence of mutations could have *hastened or delayed* the emergence of the human species (or a species with essentially similar intelligent characteristics), to claiming that had there been slight changes at any point, the human species *would never have arisen* and, by implication, that there is no such underlying teleology.

This point is of importance theologically for the idea that God, by virtue of the requirements of self-consistency, gives to his creation freedom to find its own way into his life, while recognising that any use of that freedom to

---

[28] *op cit*   p 289
[29] *op cit*   p 135

deviate from his will must be self-diminishing or self-destructive, implies that, despite constant deviation in the process of development into his life, given time, the outcome is (virtually) foreordained. Questions of probability are, therefore, built into the process. By implication, there was an infinitesimally small chance that, had there been virtually no deviations from the fully ordered development of the universe, the entire evolutionary process might have taken place in a very rapid succession of steps; there was a chance, probably also infinitesimally small, that had there been too many deviations thwarting development, given the time scales allowed, this world would become too hostile for life before intelligent observers emerged. The strongest probabilities, however, presumably lay somewhere between these two extremes. It is noteworthy that Barrow and Tipler ignore the evidence, on which we comment later, notably that marshalled by James Lovelock in his book *Gaia*, that cybernetic forces operate to maintain not only individual organisms and groups of organisms, but the environment of the earth as a whole in a state favourable to the development of life and man. What is more, the theological picture being sketched here itself *requires* an indeterminate evolutionary process but a (virtually) determinate outcome. By implication, therefore, assuming that the evolutionary process is incomplete, though further progress may well depend on psychological rather than biological developments, it seems that there is nothing here that rules out an underlying teleology. Barrow and Tipler themselves say about teleology: 'In general, ... teleology failed, and gave either incorrect predictions or untestable nonsense, when it was applied in the small, to the details of the evolutionary history of the single species, *homo sapiens*, or to the physical structure of living things, which is to say, when it degenerated into vitalism. ... When teleology was restricted to global arguments — its true domain, according to Kant and according to T H Huxley, ... its predictions have ... been by and large correct.'[30]

The Anthropic Cosmological Principle has, however, been widely assumed to show that the appearance of design and so of teleology in the universe derives from the fact that our own existence as observers imposes on the evidence a self-selection factor and that this explains its seeming design. However, if we start from the fact that observers exist in this evolutionary universe, it is hardly surprising that it has features, ordinary and extraordinary, which allowed for their emergence. But this offers no explanation of why the universe has taken a form that allows observers to emerge. What it does show is that the extraordinarily complex processes involved, with chance playing an eliminating role at countless stages, makes the emergence of observers, unless there is some strong teleological process

---

[30] *op cit* p 127

operating, virtually inconceiveable; and the extraordinarily tight constraints on any such emergence reinforce this view compellingly. What is more, the highly integrated character of the universe leaves virtually no room for intervention, either.

From all this it should be apparent, therefore, that the idea of God's 'choosing', not only fails to enhance his supremacy, and indeed jeopardises it in that it implies either a negativity, a witholding, and a lack of foresight on the part of God or something other than his own nature that requires him to choose; not only does it render the concept of God radically incoherent; but it rests very uneasily with the very remarkable scientific evidence for the tightly interlocked underlying structure of the world, which, we shall seek presently to show, flows from the requirements of self-consistency in the life of God. So important are these issues, however, that we need now to approach them from another angle: namely whether, if God's will directs itself in accordance with his other attributes, this introduces a necessity into God which prejudices his freedom; or whether, to preserve his freedom, we need to think of God's will as a separate faculty somehow free to direct those attributes while being unconstrained by them.

CHAPTER TWELVE

THE WILL OF GOD AND EMANATION

We need now to consider rather more closely whether the will of God in Christian theology needs to be thought of as able to operate in some measure independently of his nature, and in so far as free to change; whether, if it is to be regarded as an aspect of his nature, this is a restriction on the freedom of God's will and so of the freedom of God; and if it is not, whether or how, when applied to the process of creation by God, creation is to be distinguished from emanation and in particular from emanation as understood by Plotinus.

H A Wolfson claimed to identify three differences seen by the early Fathers between Neoplatonic emanation and their own belief in creation. These were (1) emanation is from God; creation is from nothing; (2) emanation is an eternal process; creation is an act in time; (3) emanation is by nature; creation is by will.[1] It seems, at first sight, therefore, that there must be two very different understandings of the relationship of God and the world entailed here; which is how they have been seen by most commentators. Yet if, as we have found, creation is to be thought of as a process within the entirely free life of God; if such creativity is to be regarded as an intrinsic feature of the eternal entirely free nature of God; if, as we shall see, time is a feature of creation that arose with it; and if his will also is to be regarded as one facet of the entirely free nature of God rather than as in some sense having a freedom separate from his nature, as we must now show, the sharp distinction seen by Wolfson will be greatly diminished.

In this chapter, therefore, we shall be primarily concerned to consider the will of God in relation to his nature, and we shall have to leave until later the question whether, if creation is a feature of the eternal nature of God, this does not imply that the world must itself be eternal. But, of course, we need to distinguish clearly the question whether there can be changes in the will of God itself from the question whether there can be deviations by creation from the will of God and so from his love and understanding and so from his act and being. Such deviations are the essential feature of sin.

We may start with Greek understandings of the will and note first that they had none. E R Dodds remarks that the intellectualist approach to the explanation of behaviour set a lasting stamp on the Greek mind: the so-called Socratic paradoxes that 'virtue is knowledge' and that 'no one does wrong on purpose' were formulations of a long-ingrained habit of thought.

---

[1] H A Wolfson The Identification of *ex nihilo* with Emanation in Gregory of Nyssa *Harvard Theol. Rev.* 63 (1970) pp 54-5

Such 'intellectualism' was 'merely the inevitable result of the absence of a concept of the will'. And he comments that 'to ask whether Homer's people are determinists or libertarians is a fantastic anachronism: the question has never occurred to them, and it would be very difficult to make them understand what it meant.'[2] Similarly, A Dihle says that whereas our term 'will' denotes only the resulting intention, leaving out any special reference to thought, instinct or emotion as possible sources of that intention, Greek is able to express intention only with one of its causes, but never in its own right.[3] And later he says that the twofold psychology that explains human behaviour on the basis of the interaction of rational and irrational forces and which has no room for the concept of the will prevails throughout the Greek tradition from the time of Homer onwards. But emotion and reason are always clearly distinguished and their mutual interaction carefully described when the motives of human action are being discussed, analyzed, or simply mentioned in Greek tragedy and comedy.[4]

An example may make this clearer. A child, having considered what he wants for a birthday present, decides he wants a transistor radio. This, we may assume, is the result of a rational and free appreciation of the alternatives. If pressed to feel free to choose something else, in the absence of some better option presenting itself, he will stick to his choice. Given that range of choice, if pressed to feel free to choose something else, he would rightly feel that any other choice would be worse and limit his freedom. Naturally, therefore, if left free to choose, he will always choose what seems best to him. If he did choose something that seemed to us less than the best, we should look for some other, probably irrational, motive; for example, envy of his sister. But even in that event, he would be choosing the best as he saw it even though he was not conscious of the envy that was motivating him. Given that he chooses the best as he sees it, and given an understanding of the rational and irrational factors guiding his actions, if we understand his intentions, we do not need to introduce a separate understanding of the will. As Dihle comments of Greek law, 'Emotion or passion provides the only psychological alternative to the knowledge of the objective with regard to the ensuing impulse towards action. Good and ill-will, though well-known in its various appearances such as envy or benevolence, did not become a factor separated from its origin in either intellect or emotion, as the legal and moral evaluation of human activities operated according to the criterion of intentionality.'[5]

---

[2] E R Dodds *The Greeks and the Irrational* (1951) pp 7, 17 & note 105 (p 26)

[3] A Dihle *The Theory of the Will in Classical Antiquity* (1982) p 24

[4] *op cit* p 27

[5] A Dihle op cit p 32

The Greek understanding appears to have been broadly shared by the early Church Fathers. As we have seen, for Origen the fact that there is a world was a direct consequence of the eternal creativity of the nature of God, though he clearly saw the world itself as contingent in the sense that it was of such a nature as to allow for the Fall. Indeed, he ascribes the diversity of rational beings to the fact that they declined from unity in different ways.[6] Dihle notes similarly that for Athanasius, God's substance is identical with his activity and his will. As he says: 'the will of God ... cannot be split up into single decisions. It is inseparably linked to or indeed identical with God's eternal and unchangeable substance.'[7]

We can view this from another angle by noting that for us, because of our finitude, our view of the world is always partial, and different views often offer different satisfactions so that we are constantly faced with choices. But God creates all things and sees all thing *sub specie aeternitatis*: no such need for choice therefore arises. In any event, we have seen the incoherence that such an idea leads to.

It seems clear, then, that any idea of a 'double contingency' entailing contingency within the full life of God would have been alien to the understanding of the early Fathers. But, as we have already seen, such an understanding, which is one implication of the idea of God's choosing, has become standard in the Western Churches. The earlier understanding was that God does whatever he freely wills; that he freely wills whatever is consistent with his nature, including his understanding and his love; and that since there is no alteration or succession in the nature of God, he is immutable, unchanging. There was, therefore, no contingency in the nature of God nor was there any external necessity, for God was seen to act entirely freely in accordance with his own unchanging nature. The resolution of the seeming conflict between the eternal and unchanging nature of God and the contingency and temporality of the world thus had to be sought, as we shall see, in the claim that whereas the Son is God, being an aspect or form taken by the Father as source, creation is derived from and is totally dependent on God: and that time took its beginning only with creation. God as eternal is, therefore, antecedent to the world, not chronologically but ontologically and logically: something which, as we shall note, makes sense if the world lies within the life of God but little sense if it lies outside and so alongside him.

That it was Augustine who introduced the will as a distinct factor in human personality appears to be widely agreed. He still held fast to the immutability of the will of God, albeit recognising that its operation was in

---

[6] *De Principiis* II 1 1

[7] A Dihle *op cit* p 227 n 84: the discussion on pp 116-7 and notes are relevant

many ways shrouded in mystery, but as regards man, according to Dihle, 'A distinct notion of the will was conceived by St Augustine ... in order to clarify which part of the human personality is concerned with freedom, sin, and divine grace, since it turned out to be difficult to describe these experiences of religious life in terms of intellect and sensuality.'[8] For Augustine, therefore, lust, pride and curiosity resulted, not from the immaturity of man, who had not yet grown sufficiently into the reason and love of God to respond to him unfalteringly and whose personality was thus distorted, but from the perverted will. This linked with the idea that though man had been created fully made and perfect, including perfectly rational, yet he had had chosen to disobey God. The direction of the will was thus thought of as dependent, not on a more or less adequate appreciation of, and participation in, reality as a manifestation of the divine, for God and the world were seen as separate substances, but on an awareness of, and desire for better or worse. This superseded the Socratic idea of nobody doing wrong on purpose. The response to God in faithfulness thus ceased to be a matter of growth through *gnosis* to participate freely in the plenitude of God, including his reason and his love, and became a moral decision of the will: and since the will had been perverted by the Fall, only humility could open the soul to the grace of God and allow it to respond as it should. Augustine's understanding of the will thus carried with it new understandings of the relationship of creation to God and in particular of freedom, grace and salvation — understandings that were to play a prominent role in subsequent Western theology.

It would be beyond the scope of this study to attempt to chart later changes in the understanding and role of the will: they are outlined briefly by Dihle on pp 194-5 of his valuable study. Suffice to say here that, as Dihle notes, though the Greeks never developed a distinct concept of the will, the relevant issues came to be handled in all European languages with the aid of such a concept. More specifically, we have already noted Pannenberg's statement that 'Christian theology set the freedom of God above his "nature" (in the constricted sense of the philosophical method of causal inference), and thus, at least in principle, subordinated metaphysics to redemptive history.' As Dihle says, however, the Greek approach to explaining human action and moral responsibility is apparently in agreement with some recent attempts to handle the problem philosophically, whereas various schools of modern psychology still seem to need the concept.[9] He draws attention in particular to G E M Anscombe's *Intention* (1963) and to Kenny's *Action, Emotion and Will* (1960) and quotes Kenny as speaking in

---

[8] A Dihle *op cit*   pp 194-5
[9] A Dihle *op cit*   p 68

his *Freewill and Responsibility* (1978)[10] of the triad intellect-emotion-will as separate abstractions from the 'observable entity' of an acting human being.[11] We have noted the role of the separated will in much modern philosophy — an issue discussed by Iris Murdoch in her valuable study *The Sovereignty of the Good*. As she says: 'Man is not a combination of an impersonal rational thinker and a personal will. He is a unified being who sees, and who desires in accordance with what he sees, and who has some slight control over the direction and focus of his vision.'[12]

If, then, man is to be seen as an, at any rate potentially, unified being; if, as Kenny says, intellect, emotion and will are abstractions from a human being acting in certain ways; and if the will in man need not, and ought not, to be thought of as independent of cognition, the case for regarding the will of God as independent of his other attributes — which produces the incoherence which we saw when considering the idea of God's exercising his will by 'choosing' — is diminished further.

There are, however, some specific facets of this issue which are worth commenting on and we may do so mainly by reference to the acute analysis by J M Rist of emanation and necessity in the case of the One of Plotinus: a case of particular illustrative value as emanation as conceived by Plotinus is constantly contrasted with with creation *ex nihilo* of the Christian God. Though we are not concerned with Rist's detailed analysis of the relevant passages in the works of Plotinus, we are with his main arguments and if, with Rist, we can conclude that 'Necessity is in fact the One's own will which by its very act is its own accomplishment' and 'Creation is as free, no more and no less, than the One itself',[13] then, any such criticism levelled at the concept of God as understood by the early Church Fathers should be largely met and any support for the Western understanding of God on such grounds will be corresponding diminished.

The Western viewpoint reveals itself clearly in a comment by Daniel O'Connor: 'God created all things not from any necessity of his nature, but freely ...'[14] In what adverse sense, we may ask, does God's nature impose necessity upon the freedom of God's will? There is similar comment by Mother Mary Clark about the freedom of the will in the understanding of Plotinus where she says: 'In this consideration of freedom, the reader is conscious of the intense intellectualism of the Plotinian system. The intellect is itself desire of the Good, of the One. This is the intellect in its

---

[10] pp 39 and 44

[11] A Dihle *op cit* p 196

[12] *The Sovereignty of the Good* (1970) p 40

[13] J M Rist *Plotinus* (1967) p 83

[14] *Creation: the Impact of an Idea* ed D O'Connor and F Oakley (1969) p 4

willing-phase. There is necessity here and spontaneity but, according to Plotinus, no coercion. The mind confronted with the truth would never be unwilling to adhere to it, according to Plotinus. The synthesis of the metaphysical and the moral viewpoints leaves no gap for the contingent factor of free will.'[15] As Rist, who quotes the passage, says: 'In what sense is there "no gap for the contingent factor of free will?" Is Plotinus then a determinist after all?'[16]

In an earlier work Rist had sought to show that for Plotinus the soul, which is impelled by desire (*eros*) in its ascent to the One, when it attains that state of union, insofar, shares in that giving-out of love which is still called *eros* but which at that point has more of the character of what Christians called *agape*, the dispassionate, caring love that gives being to the world.[17] It is this process of giving out of love, which is in its nature creative, that is our concern here.

Rist notes first that we must not separate the 'existence' of the One from its activity for the two are identical — as are God's being and act. Rist then quotes a well-known account by A H Armstrong of this 'activity' — the emanation process — an account that Rist describes as 'traditional'. Armstrong says first that the Nous — which broadly we may describe as the equivalent of the Logos[18] — proceeds from the One without in any way affecting its source. 'There is no activity on the part of the One, still less any willing or planning or choice (planning and choice are excluded by Plotinus even on a much lower level when he comes to consider the forming and ruling of the material universe by the Soul). There is simply a giving out which leaves the Source unchanged and undiminished. But though this giving-out is necessary, in the sense that it cannot be conceived as not happening or as happening otherwise, it is also entirely spontaneous: there is no room for any sort of binding or constraint, internal or external, in Plotinus' thought about the One.'[19]

Rist comments first that there can be no external constraint on the One: the question therefore turns on how 'no internal constraint' is to be understood. He quotes an earlier passage from Armstrong: 'The production of each earlier stage of being from the higher is not the result of any conscious act on the part of the latter, but is a necessary, unconscious reflex

---

[15] M T Clark *Augustine: Philosopher of Freedom* (1958) p 26

[16] J M Rist *Plotinus* (1967) p 130

[17] J M Rist *Eros and Psyche* (1964)

[18] see J M Rist *Plotinus* (1967) pp 84-5

[19] A H Armstrong *Plotinus, a Volume of Selections* (1953) p 33, quoted by J M Rist *op cit* p 67

of its primary activity of contemplation.'[20] The One is in some sense fully self-conscious yet the implication of 'necessary unconscious reflex of contemplation' seems to be that the One contemplates and that, as it were, an automatic by-product of this is the emanation of the Nous. This therefore raises the question whether the One is fully free in the sense of willing what it is, or whether in some sense it must be what it is — an unconscious source of emanation — because it could not be anything else.

Rist notes that 'We must recognise that no distinction of more than a purely abstract kind must be allowed to enter into the One. The act by which the One is what it is must be allowed to be identical and indistinguishable in fact from the act by which it does what it does.'[21] We can see why in the case of anything other than the One, its act is necessary because it is made that way because of something above it: but that does not apply in the case of the One. Armstrong reads Plotinus as pointing to 'the evolution from the One to the sense world as an evolution from potency to act, a passage to greater fulness and extent of being.' This leads Armstrong to speak of a 'serious inconsistency' in the thought of Plotinus.[22] But, as Rist points out, if the One or Good is what it is, emanation 'must' be a fact: and that 'must' is a logical 'must'. It is not an extrinsic necessity bringing pressure on the One but a deduction from the One's nature. The products of the One will not be a realisation of the One's own nature for when they are realized they are not-the-One: it is part of the nature of the One to produce these products and it is totally unaffected by it. The problem comes down to why the One is as it is. To say that the One acts 'according to its nature' has to be ruled out for the act is indistinguishable from and indeed is its nature. 'But if the One does not exist because of its own nature, it certainly does not exist by chance ... or by any kind of automatic action. .. Nor can it be said that it "happened to be". .. Nor, of course, can we say the One is free to choose between contraries. Such a description would clearly be detrimental to its unity...'[23] Rist then quotes Plotinus: 'It is therefore in a sense determined — determined, I mean, by its uniqueness and not in any sense of being under compulsion. ... It is what by a necessity prior to all necessities it must be.'[24] Plotinus then indicates that the One is what it wills to be but he qualifies this by saying that it

---

[20] A H Armstrong *The Architecture of the Intelligible Universe in the Philosophy of Plotinus* (1940) p 111

[21] *op cit*   pp 70-1

[22] A H Armstrong *The Architecture of the Intelligible Universe in the Philosophy of Plotinus* (1940) pp 62-3

[23] *op cit* (1967) p 77

[24] Enneads 6 8 9 10-17

flings out into existence what it wills while remaining greater than all willing. The One did not will itself to be such a thing of a kind which would conform to what was willed. The will and the accomplishment are one and without distinction: the One's will is its act and this, Rist suggests, is its true and unique kind of mastery of itself. The will is not, of course, a power of choice: it is the One's own accomplishment which is already all-embracing. He is his own cause: he is as he wills to be, not as he happened to be. The nature of the One is its will and is also its accomplishment. Emanation is thus necessary to the One because it so wills it. 'Necessary' is not to be contrasted with 'free' but with 'by chance'. Necessity is the One's will which by its very act is its own accomplishment. Creation is as free as the One itself and there is nothing that can constrain the One.[25]

If, then, Rist's analysis is accepted, its relevance to our understanding of the Christian God should be plain. If the internal necessity of his very nature by which the One gives rise to the world can be seen as itself freely willed by the One, then any criticism of an understanding of the Christian God as creating the world by the necessity of his very nature ought to be met by seeing it equally as creation by an entirely free act of his eternal will: any claim that it is essential to disengage God's will from his other attributes in order to preserve his freedom cannot in these circumstances be sustained. Trethowan's claim that necessity and freedom coincide at infinity is thus borne out. What is more, this is the understanding of the early Fathers. E P Meijering shows this in a full discussion of the issue as it appears in the works of Athanasius. He notes that Athanasius is the first Christian author of whom we have extensive speculations on God's will, and not only does Athanasius identify the will of God with his immutable being, but he holds that whilst the opposite of freewill is necessity, nature or essence transcends freewill.[26] *Pace* Gilson, the Christian God is a God whose very existence is to be a creator.

Of course, it will also be said that there must be a difference in the freedom of the wills of the One and the Christian God because, in contrast to the One, the Christian God is deeply personal or is 'a person'. Just how far the One of Plotinus is to be seen as personal we do not need to consider here for it is no part of our case here to try to equate the One with the Christian God: it suffices to show that if the One creates by free will, this must be no less true of the Christian God. Having said this, however, it is perhaps worth quoting Rist's comment that 'we may assume that there are in Plotinus' concept of the One a number of "personal" characteristics. In

---

[25] *op cit*   p 83

[26] *Orthodoxy and Platonism in Athanasius*   (1968/74) p 72

general, the One is viewed more in the personal light of a God of religion than as an Absolute of metaphysics.'[27] And on the other side, we need also to recall that, as Tillich claimed, the Christian God became 'a person' only in the nineteenth century; and if he is to be seen as, for example, immutable and eternal, and if the world is to be seen as being created within his life to share in it, some qualification of 'a person's' attributes when applied to God — not by diminution but enhancement — becomes essential, too. On this basis, distinctions, such as those drawn by Wolfson between emanation and creation and quoted at the beginning of this chapter, are further diminished.

Now this understanding of the will of God as a manifestation of his nature carries through into the understanding of the Trinity, for the will of God is common to all three persons and indeed, for some of the early Fathers, the Logos, the divine Christ, was understood as himself the will of the Father. We need now, therefore, to turn to consider some aspects of the Trinity as understood by the early Church Fathers and the Western Churches, and this will lead us to a crucial point in the argument of this book: a consideration of the implications of the limits of self-contradiction on the life of God and his work as creator.

---

[27] J M Rist *Human Value*   (1982) p 151

CHAPTER THIRTEEN

THE TRINITY AND THE LIMITS OF SELF-CONTRADICTION

The Early Patristic Trinity

We have seen how, from the New Testament and early Patristic understandings of God and creation, the Western tradition diverged and how, in keeping with this divergence, the meaning of creation *ex nihilo* changed, the idea of God's 'choosing' emerged, and the idea of the freedom of the will of God became conceptually separated from the understanding that God acts entirely freely but by his own nature. Central to this divergence of the Western from the earlier understanding was the change in the understanding of the Trinity effected by Augustine. We need, therefore, now to consider certain features of these two understandings of the Trinity and how it comes about that God should have this threefold nature.

As we have seen, the Christian doctrine of the Trinity is that God is one but also three. As the so-called Athanasian Creed says, we worship one God in Trinity and Trinity in unity. There is thus one God but three persons: the person of the Father who is unbegotten; the person of the Son who is begotten; and the person of the Holy Ghost or Spirit who proceeds from the Father and (or through) the Son. Yet these three persons are all one, co-eternal, uncreated and almighty. The word 'persons' is not, therefore, being used in a sense that would imply three centres of consciousness: which for Christian orthodoxy is the heresy of tritheism. In the early Church, the corresponding terms related to the outward appearances, 'persons' as seen and understood by others, as it were from the 'outside', and so able to be translated as 'presentations', 'aspects', or even 'modes'. In the doctrine of the Trinity we have, therefore, one God presenting himself eternally in three aspects, modes or forms.

It may help the reader again to suggest how this may be understood. If we are considering an eddy or whirlpool in a lake or stream, this can be considered from three aspects: the water itself; the form taken by the eddy or whirlpool; and the energy that stirs it up. It all involves the water and is in so far unitary, but in taking this specific form, it is triune. Of course, this analogy has severe limitations: in particular, in so far as the energy that stirs the water comes from an outside source such as the wind, the analogy fails, for the living God is, as we have seen, dynamic and creative in his nature.

Bearing this analogy in mind, however, the early Patristic picture of the Trinity as it emerged, could, therefore, be described in broad terms thus. The absolute, the source of all things, God transcendent, was the Father, and as the source of all personality, he was himself living and personal. The second person of the Trinity who in some way derived from, or was begotten by the Father, was the divine Son, the Logos, Word, the divine Christ. He was that aspect of the living and personal God which was his reason and so the order of God, and who gave form to and sustained the whole of creation. And the Holy Spirit was the divine energy or love which issued or proceeded from the Father through the Son and energised and inspired the forms taken by the Son in creation. Since the Son and Spirit were seen as derived from the Father, they were in that sense subordinate to the Father, but in that they were with the Father eternally and were, in effect, those aspects of the Father that related to the world, they were no less God than the Father. All three thus coinhered, all were equally divine and equally personal for all were aspects of one personal God.

Not only, therefore, were the Son and Spirit to be seen as divine in themselves and as expressions of the divine in the creation and sustaining of the world: they expressed the reason and order and energy and love of God in the world and so in man. And so men came to know of the Father through the reason and love of God in the world, and particularly in each other as the highest and fullest manifestation of God in the world, insofar as they came to participate in and manifest them truly. Christians, Athenagoras insisted, taught a God 'who is apprehended by the understanding only and the reason', who, 'as eternal mind, had the Reason within himself, being from eternity endowed with reason.'[1] Not only, however, was his reason within God: it was also within creation and in particular within man, in so far as man developed within the life of God. Hence the mutual indwelling and hence also the words of Prestige: 'The Fathers are emphatic that the revelation of the divine nature is not made directly to the mind of man, but is to be inferred from God's works, and apprehended thus by the exercise of the rational faculties.'[2]

On this point, it is worth stressing, in view of later developments, that for the early Fathers, although the human reason can be regarded as a copy or imitation of the divine Logos, its kinship was closer than such terms might imply: it was a specific instance of, a specific form taken by, the divine Logos. Thus Lilla claims that for Justin 'human reason is represented as a "seed", i e as a particle of the divine Logos, and in this sense, it also partakes of him ..., and is his imitation ...' Lilla refers to the Platonic teaching which regarded the human mind (nous) as a divine fragment;[3] he also speaks of Clement's understanding that reason is something divine in man.[4]

---

[1] Leg 10 1

[2] G L Prestige *God in Patristic Thought* (1936/52) p 56

[3] S R C Lilla *Clement of Alexandria* (1971) p 22

[4] *op cit* p 15

The idea of the Son as subordinate was largely met by the Cappadocian Fathers. That the Father is the source of the Son and Spirit remained a feature of understandings of the Trinity, but any subordination that that might imply came to be balanced by an emphasis on the coinherence of each of the persons. To use a term adopted by Prestige, there is in this picture one 'psychological centre' of God so there is a single consciousness and will.[5] There are, however, three objective presentations: the Father as source, the Son as the formative principle and the Holy Spirit as the energy or love which inspires the forms taken by the Son. As Prestige says: 'The whole unvaried common substance, being incomposite, is identical with the whole unvaried being of each person; there is no question of accidents attaching to it; the entire substance of the Son is the same as the entire substance of the Father; the individuality is only the manner in which the identical substance is objectively presented in each several person.'[6]

What has remained obscure so far is how it came about that the divine unity took Trinitarian form, and so gave rise to the multiplicity of the created world. It is this question that we need now to approach, notwithstanding that in so doing, we shall be venturing on to ground that, with the Western Trinity in mind, is normally regarded as part of the forever inscrutable mystery of God's life. The critical issue appears, therefore, to be to seek to identify and understand how it comes about that the very nature of God can itself so limit and form the creative activity of his life as to issue in this world while his essential self remains unchanged.

The Limits of Self-contradiction or Self-consistency in God

That there are limits on the life of God which derive from his nature is well recognised in Christian doctrine. The general understanding of these limits was stated in clear and forthright terms by O C Quick when he spoke of 'the ridiculous notion that "an omnipotent God" ought somehow to mean a God who is capable of being and doing any conceivable thing. No sane theology ever intended to affirm anything of the kind.'[7] What limits God is that he cannot do anything that is logically impossible or which would be inconsistent with his own nature — self-contradictory. It is, therefore, generally accepted by theologians that the limits of self-contradiction do not impair the perfection of God — his freedom, omnipotence, his omniscience, his simplicity and so on: nor do these limits detract from his transcendence. It is recognised that this means that God cannot create another God or

---

[5] G L Prestige *op cit*   p 284

[6] G L Prestige *op cit*   p 244

[7] O C Quick *Doctrines of the Creed*   (1938) p 61

jeopardise his own supremacy, do anything evil or make a circle square; but beyond this, the conclusion seems to be that of Quick: 'It is evident that with our imperfect knowledge we are unable to say, except within very narrow limits, what is and what is not intrinsically possible, and which of our highest hopes may turn out to involve self-contradiction.'[8]

Despite this agnosticism expressed by Quick, it is important to pursue this question of the limits of self-contradiction further for we have seen good grounds for saying that God does not limit himself voluntarily by *choosing* to limit or withold his act so as to create the finite forms of this world; and there is, of course, nothing other than God which could limit him in any way. If, however, in the nature of God, the very richness and perfection of his life were to require that his creativity could take only specific and limited forms, this might structure the Trinitarian dynamics of his life and the form which it takes in creation.

In approaching the question of the limits of self-contradiction, we need first to consider what is meant when we describe God as infinite. The significance of the infinite in theology has been the subject of much discussion. The primary implication of the infinity of God is that there is nothing independent of God in the sense of self-subsisting that could limit him in any way. Claims that God is infinite might need to be qualified, however, on quite other grounds. Thus Origen contended that God could not be infinite on the ground that 'if the divine power were infinite, of necessity it could not even understand itself, since the infinite is by its nature incomprehensible'.[9] Origen thus links with the need for self-consistency in God, the order and reason which is the role of the Word of God, the Son or Divine Christ, and which is therefore inherent in the life of God.

Origen argues, therefore, that notwithstanding the unquestioned uniqueness, supremacy and sovereignty of God, neither he nor creation can self-consistently be infinite.[10] As Charles Bigg points out, the God of Origen is no longer the unconditional: he is not absolute but perfect, and perfection is itself a condition. Thus he sees God as perfectly wise, perfectly just, perfectly mighty; but the perfection of these attributes has to have regard to the fact that they are limited by one another. Bigg develops Origen's conception thus: '... like the English Platonist Henry More, Origen finds the idea of God in that of perfect being. .... Hence all the so-called negative attributes sink at once into a secondary place. The more the reader reflects on this, the more important I feel persuaded he will see it to be. What an absurd yet mischievous word is "infinite", purely material in all its

---

[8] O C Quick *op cit* p 60

[9] *De Principiis* II ix 1

[10] *De Principiis* II ix 1

associations, and as unmeaning when applied to spirit as "colourless" or "imponderable" would be. Yet it is habitually used as if it were the highest term of reference. To a Platonist "infinite" means almost the same as "evil". Limitation is the essence of truth and beauty.'[11]

Notwithstanding what Bigg says, we shall continue to speak of God as infinite, but this will point only to the fact that God is supreme and that there is nothing that is not-God to limit him in any way. Infinity in this sense does not, however, preclude limits arising from the ordered richness and perfection of God's own dynamic attributes. This opens the way, therefore, for us to understand the world as the product of the inner dynamics of the life of God — dynamics that operate with the totally free consistency of the logic of his life; yet to see that logic as that of the living, conscious God of love.

It is difficult to see how anything which has order inherent in it can be without any limits what so ever, for anything totally without limits must, it seems, be totally formless, and this cannot be true of God in whom the Divine Christ inheres. An infinite God in that sense would be a God without the Divine Christ and, indeed, without reason or purpose, let alone beauty; and such a God could hardly be the creator of an ordered world. What is more, the inherent order in the life of God need not imply boundaries to God: the very order of the life of God may itself render his life self-contained in the sense that an Einsteinian universe, though finite, also is without boundaries.[12] But even if this is so, in which case the analogy of the life of God with the Einsteinian universe may be more than an analogy, it leaves unanswered the question how such order comes to be inherent in the utterly simple life of God for it presumably flows from the very dynamics of his life.

Now since God is simple in the sense that in his full life all his powers inhere together, it would seem, if we leave aside the effects of sin (in the sense of deviation from the order of God), that God's creative act must carry all his other attributes except insofar as these attributes limit each other. We have already suggested how the freedom which is an essential feature of the life of God allows his plenitude to separate out into his different attributes and into the many facets of creation, as a result of deviation from the order that is inherent in his life and which is the province of the Son. It would seem, therefore, such deviation aside, that all God's creative powers, including that order, must potentially inhere in an ordered way with each other in creation, and all must potentially be involved in his creativity. On this basis, therefore, we need to ask whether we can ascertain anything about

---

[11] C Bigg *The Christian Platonists of Alexandria* 2nd edn (1913) p 198

[12] see e g P W Davies *Space and Time in the Modern Universe* (1977) pp 151-2

the form or forms that God's creative act must take in the absence of
deviation, to meet the needs of self-consistency. The traditional answer,
framed in the light of the Western picture of God creating *ad extra*, is that
the potential number of such forms is infinite, depending entirely on the
choice of the divine will. But if creation is thought of as lying 'within' the
life of God and is, as it were, 'embedded' in it and is the product of his
reason, the Divine Christ, it would appear that this cannot be true. There
cannot be more than one Christ. Indeed, this understanding points directly
to one Christ — one world. We can approach this from another angle.

First, God cannot create anything independent of himself in the sense of
self-subsisting: for that would be self-contradictory in that it would limit
and so destroy God's supremacy: what God creates, therefore, must be
totally and continuously dependent on him so that if, *per impossible*, there
were no God, there would be nothing there. Secondly, we have found
strong arguments against the idea that God *chooses* whether and in what
form to create, for that, too, would be incoherent and self-contradictory: not
only as a result of his very nature must he choose the best but the best is
what he chooses. And since God is perfect as well as creative in his nature,
it would seem, as we have noted, that he cannot consistently withold his
powers, including his goodness, nor can he use his creativity just to increase
his powers — his love, reason, and so on — for that would imply a lack of
perfection and a potential in God, as well as change. In other words, if God
cannot create anything independent of himself in the sense of self-subsisting,
this suggests, as has been said, that anything he creates must be totally and
continuously dependent on him; if he cannot restrict himself voluntarily in
the sense of choosing, this suggests that what he creates must flow freely
from his nature; and if he cannot add to himself, this suggests that whatever
things he creates must be eternally within his life which therefore sets limits
to their life so that they cannot be infinite. And since anything that he
creates within his life will have to be as perfect as the limits of
self-contradiction allow, since they cannot equal God, they will have to be
— or seek to become — microcosms of God — a term used here in the
extended sense of a miniature representation of anything, for a term is
needed that suggests a dynamic, fully working, reproduction of God within
his life: a sense for which the customary word 'image' seems too static.

At this point we reach a crucial step in the explanation of why the world
has to take the finite, wasteful, painful evolutionary course that it is taking.
For these potential microcosms, if they are to attain that state of sharing
fully in the life of God, have to partake also in his freedom. God cannot,
consistently with the freedom that is inherent in his life, impose his will and
other creative attributes upon creation: one cannot force a person to
understand or love. For God to seek to do so would be inconsistent with the
nature not only of God but of the microcosm that he is seeking to create.

God can, therefore, only offer himself to creation to allow it freely to make use of his powers to grow within his life. In a sense, creation has to use his powers to create itself within his life. Yet the freedom of these microcosms, or potential microcosms, must be constrained, just as is the full life of God, by the limits of self-contradiction; and, in particular, since they are totally dependent on God, any exercise of that freedom in any way incompatible with the total supremacy of God, must be self-destructive.

It follows, therefore, that if creation is to partake of his attributes, it has to assimilate them into itself entirely freely, and in practice, this means step by step, using powers it has already assimilated, to open itself freely to each further influx of the divine energy and other attributes. And because of the very plenitude of God, the creative paths open to it are legion; each offering assimilation into different aspects of the divine plenitude. But these paths of progressive assimilation are by no means infinite in number for all must lead progressively into the life of God and, in practice, by far the largest number of possible paths deviate from the will of God and so detract destructively from the order and reason of both the organism itself and others around it. What is more, it is only as organisms develop freely, step by step, to higher and higher levels of order that they become responsive to the guiding forces of the Holy Spirit which take the form, not only of new insights and leaps to higher levels of order, but also of the cybernetic forces, including healing forces, which seek to maintain, restore and develop order and at higher levels, reveal themselves in reason, love and holiness.

In other words, every facet of creation stems from and manifests aspects of the plenitude of God and every facet of that plenitude has to be accepted unconditionally and unconstrainedly before it can become part of creation and subject to divine guidance: it cannot be thrust upon creation by God. This is equally true at levels where random mutations play their role and at higher levels where man has to open himself to receive the inspiration that deepens his understanding and his love. To take a simple example, if I want to obtain some understanding of Quantum Physics, it is no use my sitting back and waiting for God to teach me. I have to do my own study, assimilating the necessary material. But as I study that material, it has to take shape in my mind and I come to understand it only in so far as I allow the elements of learning to fall into place, to order themselves, or, in the terms being developed here, in so far as I allow God to order them through the power of the Holy Spirit. I cannot command this process — it happens to me: but I have to prepare the way; and in so far, I am developing not just my understanding of the world, but the very structure of my mind.

By so assimilating into my personality the forms of creation, however, not only am I ordering my understanding and bringing meaning to my experiences: I am finding meaning in them. The ordering process and the rendering meaningful of my experiences are inseparably linked. In current thought, man makes events meaningful — imposes meaning upon events that are inherently meaningless. The plenitude of God, however, has within it meaningfulness, as every mystic asserts. The meaning is objectively there and I find different facets and depths of it, in so far as I open myself to the order and reason and understanding of God which are part and parcel of his life. Man is not just a meaning-creating but a meaning-discovering being.

In the light of this discussion, we can then ask how far God is changed by the process of creation and how far he is unchanged. In Western understanding, God is self-sufficient and simple; his creativity is an optional extra to his life. The world lies outside his life, sustained by his missions. In broad terms, we might say that there is in this picture virtually no difference between God and the Godhead. If God as so envisaged is to be unaffected by creation and unchanging, creation has to be extraneous to God.

In the picture being presented here, however, the world is a process within the life of God. It is the Godhead that is unchanging: the still centre of the turning wheel: the creative source which is creative in its nature — giving out love and compassion but totally unaltered by what is given. This is the distinction between the essence and the energies of God; between the Godhead and the Mind of God; between God transcendent and God immanent. Necessarily, if a changing and evolving creation lies within the life and mind of God, in so far there must be change and evolution within God: but this creative process is the changing and evolving outcome of the unchanging giving out of the source, the Godhead, which is eternally seeking to share its life with its creation and is in so far unchanging, for creation adds nothing to God that is not already present in the Godhead. In this as in so many other respects, it is the attempt to apply the Western understanding to these eternal verities that produces so many incoherences and misconceptions.

More generally, we can say that the attributes of everything that God creates must be manifestations of, and flow from, his own attributes and so cannot conflict with his own attributes. On this basis everything created by God derives from him and is totally dependent on him. He can thus 'give' his love in the sense that his love itself, together with his other attributes, themselves constitute creation which is thus created and sustained by his love: but he cannot 'give' his love in any sense that implies divesting himself of it: he is his love. And the same applies to all his other attributes. In other words, this, too, suggests that whatever God creates must, in the absence of deviation from his life, potentially be 'microcosms' of God formed within his life. As we have said, these potential microcosms will not be infinite in their powers because of their total dependence on God; because he cannot self-consistently create anything equal to himself; and because their order will have to reproduce his order within his life. They will also have to share, at any rate potentially, in all his other attributes, including his life and love and understanding. Yet, as we have seen, that 'sharing' implies neither diminution of God for God 'gives' his creative love freely as a feature of his nature, nor does it imply 'dividing'; for in 'sharing' or 'giving', God gives himself and he is therefore present in creation for it is within his life.

This, however, suggests that the creative process should flow from God down through his creation: yet in practice, as we know, the process is of a slow evolution up into the life of God. But this poses the question, the answer to which has already been pointed to, why God created the world in this seemingly unhappy and indirect manner. Leon Askenazi, speaking of the Creator's ultimate intention, says that the Jewish tradition is that God wanted to create the soul, man as distinct from himself, and for man to be situated somewhere in existence, there had to be a world. The Jewish Kabbalistic teaching elaborates on this with an explanation which coheres with the logic of the life of God as it is emerging in these pages. Askenazi describes how the traditional interpretation of Jewish Kabbalism is that creation did not take place in six days but in a flash and the result of this creation was chaos. 'The Kabbala explains that in order to make a place for what was to be human consciousness, that is to say the place of man, it was necessary for God (and when I say God, this is not yet the manifested God of revelation, but the root of absolute being), to empty himself, in one point of his Being, and that a withdrawal of his divinity should take place. ... In fact, creation takes away from Nature the unveiled presence of God, for if the latter were manifested in its total intensity, the world of Nature would be reabsorbed in it and there world be no room for men. So there is a screen, a barrier between God, the Creator, and the world so that man could have his place in freedom.'[13]

In other words, because freedom is inherent in the sharing in the life of God, God could not force creation upon man or the world and subsequently confer freedom: creation had to be accepted freely and that required a sequential, step by step — a temporal — evolutionary process dependent on undetermined mutations and conceptual leaps. But that in turn implies that, by the very logic of his life, God must 'at one point' have stripped himself of every attribute short of creating a void, (for a void would limit him; would be inconsistent with his supremacy; and would lack the creativity essential if creation is to create itself by progressive participation in his powers within his life). Creation could, therefore, start only at the bottom. But at that lowest level of his eternal life where only his act remains and time began, because it lacks his understanding, love and holiness, it can no

---

[13] The Relationship between the Soul and Creation in *Science and Consciousness* ed. M Cazenave (1984) pp 282-4

longer direct its growth into his life, and so deviates randomly, falling back into his life, whilst the creativity of God constantly restores it. Gradually, however, order develops, the slowness of that development reflecting the plenitude of God and the richness of creation. So creation is able progressively and cumulatively to manifest the attributes of God: to his act, as order develops, his life is added, then consciousness, understanding, love, holiness and ultimately, when perfect order is attained, creation comes face to face with God in the full mystical experience. At that point, as we shall see, perfect freedom coincides with the absolute necessity of participating in the life of God, for to reject it would entail a rational creation irrationally and pointlessly being self-destructive: it would, in fact, be self-contradictory.

But, of course, as we look lower down the evolutionary scale, we find that the order attained does not allow the guiding love and understanding of God to be accepted or manifested by creation; hence, irrational, blind, deviation occurs, and so, at the lowest levels, the world takes the form of a virtually random process of coming into existence and deviating from it. It is this lack of full participation in the order of God, of Christ, that provides the screen, the barrier, which allows creation that freedom to grow freely into the life of God: but the price of this is more or less blind destructive deviation which is, as we shall see, the basis of sin. What is more, as we shall find, it is these deviations around the order that has been attained that constitute the physical world. We can see, therefore, from this sketch, something of how the utterly unconstrained logic of the creative plenitude of God issues in the creative plenitude and the destructive misery of this spatial and temporal world.

There is another implication that needs to be made more explicit here. It is difficult within this picture to envisage the role of God, who is creative in his nature, without creation: yet since God is eternal, that suggests that creation must be eternal, too. But that would make creation equal with God, at least in that respect, and the limits of self-contradiction forbid that in any respect whatever. As we shall see, the world does not exist in time: God created time with the world: the world is an opening up of the eternal life of God to allow for a sequential developmental process within it. However hard it may be to envisage this, there is, quite literally, no 'before' creation and, when the process is complete, there will be no 'after'. God remains, therefore, eternal yet the world within his life is temporal.

It may, then, be asked why all this matters. There lies deep within the make-up of most human beings a desire to order, explain and understand the world, themselves and their place within it; and for such people, unanswered questions are a challenge. It is here that we find the motivation of scientists. What is more, deep unanswered questions about the nature of reality and our place within it can give rise to a deep and disturbing unease, or even anxiety. Yet each answer that we find normally gives rise to yet further questions in a kind of infinite regress. Thus scientists have traced back the origins of the universe to some form of big-bang when not only the physical world but time and space began. But this does not stop questions arising in various sophisticated forms about what caused the big-bang. From another angle, as evolution has taken place and systems have grown in complexity, there have emerged life, consciousness, various levels of understanding and love, and, it seems, holiness and, with full integration, the mystical experience of coming face to face with God. Associated with this development of systems is the emergence of cybernetic forces which seek not only to maintain these systems but to lead to their further development and integration. Yet although scientists may in time be able to specify ever more precisely the defining characteristics of systems at each level which lead to the emergence of these attributes, there remains a question whether an explanation of the character of these attributes, as distinct from the conditions under which they arise, can fall within the realms of science, at any rate in its present form.

It is, of course, open to theologians and to those scientists who are religiously so inclined, to seek to explain all this in terms of the action of an all-powerful God who has *chosen* to create the world in this emerging form. This, however, adds little to our understanding for such an explanation can be offered for virtually any state of affairs what so ever; and we have seen the incoherences entailed in it. More specifically it leaves unanswered the question why an omnipotent God of love should have chosen to create the world in such a protracted and wasteful way with so much suffering and evil. Of course, not all scientists and others see the need to ask such questions, but even for those who do, there seems little prospect of an answer with the current frameworks of science and theology.

In this situation, the postulation of a God who creates the world within his life through the ordering and energising activities of his Word or Son and Holy Spirit offers a context in which the evidence of evolutionary science, including the attributes of emerging organisms and their origins in the big-bang, appear all to find, at any rate in principle, a unified explanation. In particular, given the dynamics, as well as the other attributes of the life of God, for whom choice does not arise, the form of this emerging world can be seen to flow from his creative nature. Even the protracted wastefulness and suffering that afflicts not only man but the entire natural world, appalling as it certainly is, finds at least an explanation. Not everyone will be convinced, at any rate on this side of the grave, that the price of such development is worth paying. That, however, is the world we find ourselves in, and whatever choices we may have, particularly if there is an after-life, these do not allow us to opt out. It can, therefore, reasonably be claimed that the postulation of a God in the form being

offered here, offers a unified and ultimate explanation of the world that is
at one and the same time, both scientific and theological.

The implications of this tentative account of the limits of self-consistency
deserve, of course, to be developed, but it will be apparent that it is a lot
more revealing than Quick's comments quoted earlier would suggest
possible. It offers a picture of creation evolving from and into the plenitude
of the life of God to allow the rational soul to develop into the image and
likeness of God. Yet it retains the absolute distinction between Creator and
created.

This point needs to be emphasised for the conceptual gap between God
and the world that has developed in Western theology will certainly lead
some of those brought up in the Western tradition to claim that this book is
'pantheistic' — a term of execration amongst many theologians. However,
as should be apparent from all that has been said and will be said here,
despite the fact that creation needs to be thought of as 'within' the life of
God, if the distinction between Creator and created were not absolute, God
in creating the world would destroy his own supremacy and that would be
self-contradictory: creation is always totally dependent on God: but in no
way does this prevent God being personally directly present in the world, in
atoms as well as persons, though in varying degrees, and veiled from us.

Paradoxically, much Western theology, in seeking to emphasise the
transcendence of God, has moved a long way towards conferring autonomy
upon the world, and, in so far, it has moved a long way towards dethroning
God by allowing the world autonomy to exist alongside him: a process
which materialism and atheism merely take further. The only way in which
the utter transcendence of God can be maintained is by recognising that it
requires also his immanence. Transcendence is not to be contrasted with
immanence but includes it. What is more, though creation derives all its
positive attributes from God, because the distinction between the
transcendence of God and creation is absolute, this leaves ample room for
creation to develop in its multifarious forms, each reflecting different facets
of the plenitude of God and manifesting the enormous number of ways in
which it can fall short of that plenitude. It therefore leaves ample room for
each creature to approach God from its own individual roots while never
losing its identity by absorption into God: something forbidden by the limits
of self-contradiction.

If, then, it is the limits of self-contradiction that channel the development
of these potential microcosms, it must be these limits that allow also the Son
and Spirit to proceed, to issue from or be begotten by the Father. On this
basis, the Son and Holy Spirit are the specific and eternal forms taken by the
creative dynamic interactions of his attributes within the life of God: the
Father as the source begets the order and reason of the Son yet the Son is
of one substance with the Father and the Spirit proceeds from the Father.

Yet all three are one infinite God who creates the finite and temporal world within his life: a world which is not only finite but utterly dependent on all three Persons. The Son thus forms and structures these potential microcosms in a way which, subject to deviations from the order of God, should allow them to manifest in finite form the attributes of God: and, in particular, the order and reason of God, the Divine Christ, his Son.

This, of course, implies a view of the Son that is far removed from the views of theologians like Hodgson who, as we shall note, seek to endow the Divine Son with some sort of personality of his own apart from that of the Father; but that moves towards not one God but tritheism. It implies also a view that is far removed from the Western tradition that has sought to maintain a deep conceptual gap between God and his creation. But, as we have seen, the basis of both these Western understandings is highly questionable and, as has been stressed, their abandonment does nothing to confuse the absolute distinction between God and the world, Creator and created, or to deviate from the Christian faith towards pantheism: unless, of course, pantheism is defined in terms of any understanding which, while keeping that absolute distinction, removes that conceptual gap.

As for the creative energy and love which is the Holy Spirit and which energises the entire life of God and so guides and inspires the forms taken by the Son, since it issues from the Father, we can say that it 'proceeds' from the Father and in that it manifests itself in creation, it does so through the Son. However, on this view, the Spirit does not also 'proceed' from the Son as in the Western Trinity. Clearly, however, since the Son and Spirit are both the products of the internal dynamics of the eternal life of the Father and are of one substance with him, all three must operate in creation inseparably and all three are aspects of the one living God and all of them are living. What is more, since on this view, the unity of God is more strongly stressed than in some understandings of the Trinity, and since it is, it seems, in the nature of God freely to create microcosms of himself to share in his life — microcosms which, in the case of man, despite the warpings of sin, are 'persons', it follows that God, as the macrocosm and as the ultimate source of all personality, must himself in some relevant sense be 'a person'. But this has to be understood in an even more qualified sense than in the Western Trinity, given the view that creation lies 'within' the life of God; whereas on the Western view it lies in some sense alongside or below him.

If 'pictures' are as influential in our thinking as we have suggested, it is worth while trying to form some 'picture' of these different understandings of the Trinity, however inadequate they may be. It seems that the early Church Fathers thought in terms of a hierarchy or pyramid, with the Father at the top extending his reach down to and including creation at or near the base: but at some way down, his work of creating and sustaining creation was taken over by his 'hands', the Son and Spirit. The Cappadocian picture was rather different in that the subordination of the Son and Spirit seems to have been largely eliminated. We have already offered the picture of a vast pool of water with a whirlpool within it as some form of relevant analogy. Better is the picture of the child in the mother's womb: the mother being the source of all life, the form of the child being the work of the Son and its energy and life being the work of the Spirit; a picture that also does something to symbolise the feminine which encloses its offspring and which has been unduly overshadowed by the Western emphasis on the maleness of God with the separation of progenitor and offspring that this analogy implies. In contrast, in the Augustinian picture, we return again to some form of hierarchy but instead of the Father being at the top, all three members of the Trinity are there complete in their own life but creating and sustaining a deeply alienated and separated world by a kind of 'overflow'. This is a picture in which, while man is in the image of God, albeit deeply marred, the lower the level of creation, the more it is seen as removed from God and as manifesting only his 'vestiges': an understanding which may well have contributed to the devaluing of the natural world and encouraged its exploitation and abuse, the costs of which we are only now becoming aware and which, in theological terms, can be seen as the wrath of God.

CHAPTER FOURTEEN

THE AUGUSTINIAN-WESTERN TRINITY

From various angles we have found the early Christian understanding of the Trinity taking an integral and natural place within the picture that is emerging in this study. Since, however, it is very different from that which has been prevalent in the West since the time of Augustine, this Augustinian understanding needs to be explored further. Whereas the Greek Fathers had seen the Father alone as the source or fountain-head of deity, from which both Son and Spirit, who did his work in the world, derived, Augustine's understanding of the Trinity started with the idea of one simple Godhead to whose life all three persons were internal, so that whatever was predicated of one person could be predicated of either of the other two. And because the primary role of all three persons was seen to lie in their mutual relations within the Godhead, creation was seen as a kind of optional extra undertaken by his 'missions' out of the overflowing bounty of God outside his life.

As regards these internal relations of the members of the Trinity, Augustine saw these as constituting the very life of God. The persons actually became those relationships. As Bernard Piault says: 'God is eternally Father because his Son is eternal.' The Father thus is the relationship of Fatherhood. 'God the Son is the relationship of Sonship. God the Holy Spirit is the relation of "Love-between-Father-and-Son". There is, then, "relationship" in God, but in it each of the divine persons can be discerned. It follows that since relationship in God is God, and since there are three related Persons in God, Father, Son and Holy Spirit, then each of them (though related to each of the others) is God too.'[1] Jaroslav Pelikan, quoting a work by Noesgen, confirms this understanding. Speaking of Augustine's reasons for arguing for the procession of the Holy Spirit from the Son as well as the Father, he says that those reasons are to be found in the very structure of Augustinian Trinitarianism, for 'since according to Augustine the three persons to whose common essence it also belongs to be a "person", are distinguished from one another solely through the functions that pertain to each in relation to the other two, the "procession from the Father and the Son" is regarded by him as the specific property of the Holy Spirit within the immanent essence of God.'[2]

This idea of 'relations' came to Augustine from Aristotle. For Aristotle, 'relation' was one of the ten 'categories' — terms which may be predicated of a subject. Of these ten, one, 'substance', was different from the others in that it could be predicated of the others but the others could not be

---

predicated of it; and another, 'relation', was different from the others in that it implied not only subject but also object. Of Augustine's use of 'relation', Mascall, who strongly supports the Western understanding, says: 'Now Augustine's stroke of genius was to locate the three persons in the category of relation, while at the same time raising them from the level of accidents to the level of substance: he thus introduced the notion of person as subsistent relation or, as Fr Jean Galot has preferred to say in his brilliant use of it in the realm of Christology, relational being.'[3] In other words, for Augustine, the persons are relations not of separate entities but of or within one entity, God.

The problem to which this gives rise, however, is that though the Father is thought of as giving of himself, the Son, instead of being thought of as one of the modes or forms through which the Father gives himself, becomes thought of as responding as though he was a separate person in the sense of having a separate personal existence: and the Spirit is then thought of as that mutual internal relationship of the other two persons who were themselves defined in terms of their mutual relationship. Of course, the Son and Spirit are personal as the Father is personal, for they are forms in which the Father reveals himself. But that does not give them a personal status sufficiently separate to respond any more than the fact that my words are the personal form of my self-expression, allows them to respond to me. As Karl Rahner says: 'The Logos is not the one who utters, but the one who is uttered. There is properly no *mutual* love between Father and Son, for this would presuppose two acts. ... There is only one real consciousness in God, which is shared by the Father, Son and Spirit, by each in his own proper way.'[4]

Not surprisingly, therefore, given these difficulties of understanding the persons as 'relations' — and in the case of the Holy Spirit, relations of relations — in any relevant sense of the term 'persons', the mystery of the Trinity and its basis in revelation have been greatly stressed. As Piault says: 'Theologians would never have been able or have dared to penetrate so far into the mystery of God, would not have dreamed even of lifting their eyes to the eternal processions of the Son and Holy Spirit, if Scripture had not led them to do so.' Piault hastens to add, however, 'Not that Scripture has anything at all to say about the eternal processions....'[5] He goes on to explain how this understanding of the Trinity can be read into the Scriptures. Obviously, however, it was not found there ready-made, so that even if support can be claimed from the Scriptures for such a view — and this is

---

[3] E Mascall *The Triune God* (1986) p 12

[4] K Rahner *The Trinity* (1970) pp 106-7

[5] B Piault *op cit* pp 131-2

at least questionable — the initial justification must be found elsewhere. In practice, that justification lay, not in the Scriptures but in the personal authority of Augustine and the institutional authority of the Church.

Much of the plausibility of this understanding of the Trinity stems from the idea of the internal fellowship of the persons. Thus Hodgson describes as the main thesis of his lectures on the Doctrine of the Trinity 'that the act of faith required for the acceptance of the Doctrine of the Trinity is faith that the Divine unity is a dynamic unity actively unifying in the one divine life the lives of the three divine persons.' (The plural 'lives' is to be noted.)[6] He thus distinguishes from mathematical unity, the idea of an organic unity of basically separate entities and, referring to C C J Webb's *God and Personality* (1918), he claims that we cannot think of any life as truly personal unless it is a life of intercourse between persons. He then notes that if we are to think of God as unipersonal, we must think of him as related to some object of his personal attention: and he suggests that for this reason the idea of creation as the eternal object of God's personal love and care has always been congenial to unitarian theology. He does not note here that creation has been regarded as an object of such supreme love by God that he gave his only begotten Son (John 3 16) and that this is the basis of the Christian understanding of the Incarnation. Instead he continues: 'But the doctrine of creation, in orthodox Christianity, asserts that the created universe is not necessary to the being of God. It is entirely dependent on God for its being, but God has no need of it in order to be entirely himself in all the full richness of his Godhead. The doctrine of the Trinity implies that in the eternal being of God, quite apart from creation, there exist all the elements necessary for a fully divine life. ... Taken together, the doctrines of the Trinity and of creation expressly forbid us to assert that this whole vast universe, let alone this world and the life of man upon it, are the centre of interest in the life of God.'[7] As we have already noted, Gilson puts the issue more succinctly: 'It is quite true that a Creator is an eminently Christian God, but a God whose very essence is to be a creator is not a Christian God at all.'[8]

We have seen the powerful objections raised by Trethowan to the idea that the creativity of God is some form of optional extra for God and that it is thus separable from his nature. Of course, God does not need creation in the sense of filling any lack in him, for it is wholly dependent on him: but the realisation of his creativity is a basic feature of his totally free nature. What is more, as Trethowan has said, the contingency of creation

---

[6] L Hodgson *The Doctrine of the Trinity* (1943) p 95

[7] L Hodgson *op cit* p 190

[8] E Gilson *God and Philosophy* (1941) p 88

on which Western theology has put so much stress, cannot lie in the act and so in the nature of God but must lie in the term or outcome of his act and so in creation itself. As we have seen, however, and shall see further, this contingency comes about because God, in his very nature, in giving being, gives of himself and so has to give freedom to creation to deviate from that being. The contingency of creation lies not in God but in the outcome of his act in creation because that act necessarily carries freedom to deviate from it.

Karl Rahner stresses the tendency in the Western view towards tritheism in his valuable study *The Trinity*. As he says: 'There can be no doubt about it: speaking of three persons in God entails *almost inevitably* the danger ... of believing that there exist in God three distinct consciousnesses, spiritual vitalities, centers of activity, and so on.'(my italics)[9] And later he comments that 'when nowadays we hear of "three persons", we connect, *almost necessarily*, with this expression the idea of three centers of consciousness and activity, which leads to a heretical misunderstanding of the dogma.' (my italics)[10] Rather, as he says, there are not three spiritual centers of activity, three subjectivities and liberties — not only because in God there is only one essence, hence one self-presence, but also because there is only one self-utterance of the Father, the Logos. And we have already quoted Rahner as saying: 'The Logos is not the one who utters, but the one who is uttered. And there is properly no mutual love between Father and Son, for this would presuppose two acts. ... There is only one real consciousness in God, which is shared by Father, Son and Spirit, by each in his own proper way.'[11] But on this basis, much that makes the Western understanding of the Trinity plausible has to be discarded.

The objections to this understanding of the Trinity extend much further, however. We noted earlier the essential irrelevance of this understanding of the Trinity to the remainder of Christian doctrine. As Rahner says: 'It is as though this mystery has been revealed for its own sake, and that even after it has been made known to us, it remains, *as a reality*, locked up within itself. We make statements about it, but as a reality it has nothing to do with us at all.'[12] But, as Rahner goes on to stress: 'The isolation of the Trinity *has* to be wrong. There *must* be a connection between the Trinity and man. The Trinity is a mystery of salvation, otherwise it would

---

[9] *op cit* (1970) p 43

[10] *op cit*   pp 56-7:

[11] *op cit*   pp 106-7

[12] *op cit*   p 14

never have been revealed.'[13] And he therefore asserts time and again that the economic Trinity is the immanent Trinity and the immanent Trinity is the economic Trinity.[14] In other words, the Trinity that is inherent in the life of God *is* the Trinity that structures and energises the world.

Rahner develops this assertion by stressing an idea familiar in this book, that God's self-communication is truly a *self*-communication. 'He does not merely indirectly give his creature some share of himself *by* creating and giving us created and finite realities through his omnipotent *efficient* causality. In a *quasi*-formal causality he really and in the strictest sense of the word bestows *himself*.'[15] Earlier he had said that 'in the Christian's act of faith, as *salutory* faith, and in the Christian's life the Trinity is present and has to be present. ... The true and authentic concept of grace interprets grace (hence also salvation history) as a self-communication of God (not primarily as "created grace") in Christ and in his Spirit. Grace should not be reduced to a "relation" (a purely mental relation at that) of the one God to the elected creature, nor to a relation which is merely "appropriated" to the other divine persons. In the recipient himself grace is not some created sanctifying "quality" produced in a merely causal way by the one God.'[16] As Rahner says about the Divine Christ: 'The Word is, by definition, immanent in the divinity and active in the world, and as such the Father's revelation. A revelation of the Father without the Logos and his incarnation would be like speaking without words.'[17] And similarly he stresses that 'through what we call "Holy Spirit", God (hence the Father) really communicates himself as love and forgiveness.'[18]

What Rahner is stressing here is therefore the intimate and direct presence of all three persons in the world, notwithstanding that the Father reveals himself only through the Son and Spirit. But it follows that if, as he stresses, the immanent Trinity is the economic Trinity, then since the immanent Trinity is inherent in the life of God, so must be God's creative activity in the world. We are driven back, therefore, towards the understanding of the Greek Fathers. The contrast between that understanding and that of the West is summed up by Rahner, in a passage we have quoted already: 'The West has taken over from the Greeks the formal part of the theology of the Trinity as if it were the (whole of)

---

[13] *op cit* p 21

[14] e g *op cit* p 22

[15] *op cit* p 36

[16] *op cit* pp 22-3

[17] *op cit* p 29

[18] *op cit* p 67

theology of the Trinity, whereas its own doctrine of salvation has kept only the dogmatically indispensable minimum of theology of the Trinity.'[19]

To put the issue another way, the role of the transcendent Father in the earlier understanding of the Trinity was in some respects taken over, in the Augustinian Trinity, by the entire triune life of God. As the Son and Spirit came to be seen as primarily occupied in the internal life of the Trinity, creation, which had, of course, lain outside the full transcendence of the Father — though embraced by the Son and Spirit, and so within the life of God — now came to be seen as 'outside' not just the transcendence of the Father but outside the life of the Trinity and so outside God. What is more, although the Western Trinitarian God is not seen as static in that his internal life is dynamic though essentially self-contained, because there is no necessary link between this internal dynamism and the optional external overflow of the divine creativity, so far as the world is concerned, that internal dynamism is seen inherently as virtually static and as only optionally active.

The fundamental irrelevance of the Western Trinity to the rest of Western doctrine; the need to deny that the persons within the Godhead are separate centres of consciousness and can have subject-object relationships with each other within the life of God; the difficulty in understanding relations (and relations of relations) as persons in any relevant sense; the need to emphasise that in his relations with the world God is not just causally present in the world but is really present in all three modes or manners of the Trinity; and the need to deny any contingency in the act and so the life of God as distinct from its outcome; together with the criticisms of the idea of an 'overflow' of the creative divine activity as though there were a boundary to it — all these drive a coach and horses through not only the Western understanding of the Trinity itself, but also through a number of Western doctrines which have taken shape in line with it. We have already looked at several of these and have found radical weaknesses in them; and when these are taken in conjunction with the problems of the Western understanding of the Trinity, the edifice as a whole in the form it has taken in the West, must become highly questionable. We need now, however, to press these questions still further by drawing out yet more implications of the differences between the early Patristic and Western understandings of the relationship of God to the world by considering some facets of the different logical or conceptual relations implied in each and their implications for certain other basic Christian doctrines.

---

[19] *op cit* p 18

CHAPTER FIFTEEN

SOME CONTRASTS IN IMPLICATIONS OF THE EARLY PATRISTIC AND WESTERN PICTURES

We need now to explore some of the important differences in the conceptual implications of the early Patristic and Western ways of viewing the world and its relationship to God.

Some Implications of the Dominant Western Picture

Whatever its detailed complexities, the broad conceptual status or logic of the early Patristic picture of the relationship of God and the world is fairly straightforward. The evidence for God lies all around us in varying degrees in tables and chairs, in flowers and animals and human beings: and God manifests himself more fully in the Scriptures, in religious experiences, in special acts of grace such as healing, and above all in the Incarnation. In the Western picture, however, the evidence for God tends to be seen in special interventions. This is well illustrated in a widely discussed parable originated by John Wisdom.[1]

In this parable, friends who view a deserted garden cannot agree whether it is still being tended by a gardener whom they have failed to observe at work. They seek to resolve the question by reference to such order as still remains in the garden. More specifically, they are looking for evidence of someone who, by cultivating it, is intervening in the natural growth of the garden; and they do not agree whether there has been such intervention. They are thus looking for departures from the natural growth and exuberance of nature which, it seems, for them, itself needs no explanation. The theological parallel is thus seen in concern with divine interventions in the natural world. The natural growth is seemingly assumed to require no God to explain it. Whereas in the Patristic picture as it is being developed here, the question of the gardener would be secondary and at a different conceptual level from whether we can see God both in wild and cultivated gardens, in the Western picture the wild garden is seen as self-explanatory. God is seen as somehow existing alongside the world, and while it is acknowledged that he creates and sustains the world, since this is *ad extra*, this somehow gets lost so that we are led to enquire whether and how he 'intervenes' in the garden.

Such 'interventions' can, however, enter theological thinking in much more subtle form. This can be illustrated by a few examples from

---

[1] Gods *Proc. Arist. Soc.* (1944)

Christology where the relationship of the divine and human natures of Christ poses this problem particularly acutely.   Thus J A T Robinson noted this specifically when he said at the start of his essay 'Need Jesus have been Perfect?': 'The doctrine of the two natures has been one classic way of saying how Jesus Christ could be both a self-expression of God and at the same time a completely normal human being — in the words of the Chalcedonian definition, "of one substance with the Father" and "of one substance with us".   It is a way that today is subject to formidable objections.   Not only does it use categories that almost inevitably suggest that the human centre of consciousness in Christ was replaced or displaced by the divine, but it gives the impression to a modern man that Jesus was a hybrid.'[2]   He went on to say that no such isolating effect was intended. He added, however, that the incarnation was part of a continuous drama in which the two worlds of the natural and supernatural constantly *interpenetrated*. And in the next essay in the same volume, the writer can even say: 'Thus contemporary theology is faced with an apparently new dilemma; can it say precisely at what point the divine "entered" the human?'[3]

Of course, as we have seen, such views have deep roots in Western doctrine. Rahner, himself, notwithstanding his criticisms of the Augustinian Trinity and his stress that the immanent Trinity is the economic Trinity, can still say that 'The mystery of Jesus consists in the fact that he truly stands on both sides of the boundary separating God from creatures.'[4] And Francis Ferrier, in a careful exposition of the Incarnation from the Roman Catholic point of view, can say about the union of natures: 'The union is thus hypostatic or personal for the Person of the Word is the point of contact uniting the divine and human natures in a unity of being which is beyond any union known to man by experience.'[5]   And from a very different approach, Swinburne can speak of one particular event which God might be expected to bring about, a particular intervention of himself into the world which he made, an incarnation.[6]

In the wider Western picture, the relationship between God and the world can lead to great complications. It is worth illustrating this by reference to two relatively simple examples, chosen more or less at random. In an article on 'Evil and Omnipotence', J L Mackie claimed that theism could be refuted

---

[2] J A T Robinson 'Need Jesus have been Perfect? in *Christ, Faith and History* eds. S W Sykes and J P Clayton (1972) p 39

[3] S W Sykes 'The Theology of the Humanity of Christ' *op cit* p 59

[4] K Rahner and H Vorgrimler *Concise Theological Dictionary* (1965) p 240

[5] F Ferrier What is the Incarnation? (1962) p 92

[6] R Swinburne *The Existence of God* (1979) p 239

on grounds of inconsistency because the theist was committed to three assertions: (1) God is omnipotent; (2) God is wholly good; (3) evil exists. Given that someone eliminates evil so far as lies within his power if he is good and there are no limits on the power of someone who is omnipotent, these statements cannot be true together. We do not need to pursue the implications of this argument in the context of the Western theistic picture. It is discussed by Basil Mitchell in the Introduction to his book in which the article is reprinted.[7] One leg of Mackie's claim is discussed also by Plantinga in his article 'The Free-Will Defence' which is also reprinted in that volume.[8] Suffice to say here that the great complexities into which Mackie's claim is seen to lead turn primarily on ignoring the limits of self-contradiction as applied to God and on the view that God has a very wide choice of interventions in the world. This understanding is directly related to seeing God as in some sense a person and to the conceptual uncoupling of God and the world which we have noted and which seemingly allows each very wide room for manoeuvre in relation to the other.

It is worth referring here to a variant of the contradiction seen by Mackie. The instance is sometimes quoted of the man who claimed that when he visited a certain congested city 'on God's work', he always found a parking place waiting for his car. He attributed this to his faith and God's caring response to it. Such claims have been dismissed derisively even by devout churchmen on the ground that God would not get involved in such trivialities. Such dismissal of the claim implies, however, not only that God is able to intervene but has some system of priorities. But if these priorities do not include the trivial, neither do they include many personal tragedies nor do they include the prevention of the wider horrors that constantly afflict this world, sometimes on a gigantic scale. And it requires mental agility approaching 'double-think' to accept that a God who could stop such horrors but does not do so, is a God of love.

Such objections, however, no longer apply if, as is entailed in the picture being developed here, the dynamic plenitude of God is such that he is always present in creation, sustaining it and always seeking to redeem and guide it further into his life wherever and whenever it opens itself more fully to him. On this basis, normal life, with both its trivialities and extremes of good and evil, marks the continuously varying point of balance between the limits of where creation opens itself to the creative love and reason of God that seek constantly to sustain, redeem and guide it further into his life, and where, beyond these limits, creation shuts itself off and deviates blindly and often wickedly from his love and reason. On this basis also, we need to

---

[7] B Mitchell *The Philosophy of Religion* (1971) pp 3-4 and pp 92-104

[8] A Plantinga The Free-Will Defence *op cit* pp 105-120

recognise that creation is an almost infinitely complex system, interlocked one part with another at many levels; and that the scope for God's sustaining and guiding powers to prevail must depend not only on the openness of individuals but also on the openness and so on the responsiveness to the guiding powers of the Holy Spirit of the continuously varying situations in which they find themselves. In contrast, the Western view allows little room for such subtleties.

It is, perhaps, worth pausing here briefly to develop the idea, just stated, that the world manifests the line that marks the evolving but continuously varying balance between the creative love and reason of God and the deviations (or sin) of creation. This is necessarily so, for as we shall see, the creativity of God, which is inherent in creation as a whole and in all elements of it, seeks constantly to manifest itself in the world and succeeds in doing so in the growth and development of creation and its multifarious elements to the extent that their structure and other attributes allow. The more the limits of self-contradiction yield as a result of creation progressively and freely assimilating into itself the attributes of God, the more the plenitude and harmony of the divine life are able to manifest themselves. But the greater the self-destructive deviations from God's will, the more the scope of the creativity of God and his other attributes are curtailed and the greater are the destructive waste, suffering and evil that flow from the deviations from his creativity. We shall see something of how these ideas manifest themselves in the evolutionary process in the third part of this book.

Meanwhile, it is worth considering a second example of the complexities to which the Western understanding leads. This example is an argument by Kretzmann quoted by Kenny:[9] (1) A perfect being is not subject to change; (2) A perfect being knows everything; (3) A being that knows everything knows what time it is; (4) A being that always knows what time it is is subject to change; (5) A perfect being is therefore subject to change; (6) A perfect being is therefore not a perfect being; (7) Ergo there is no perfect being.

Within the early Patristic picture, this argument fails to bite for it is seemingly of a God who is unchanging in the sense of static, whereas the understanding which we have been presenting is of a God who is dynamic and creative — who is, in other words, living — but unchanging in the sense of constant, faithful. Change can and does occur within the life of God and so within the life of a perfect being who is omniscient, for change can occur within the life of God without God himself changing. Indeed, it is meaningless to talk of change except in relation to something else and the

---

[9] A Kenny *The God of the Philosophers* (1974) p 40

very supremacy, the transcendence, of God precludes there being anything else. But that does not preclude changes within the life of God and of these changes he is necessarily aware. The idea of change within something that is itself unchanging is not, of course, unusual when applied to any dynamic system. A jet of water may be (relatively) unchanging while the drops of water change continuously. But in any event, all these changes within the life of God are given form, we have suggested, by the operation of the limits of self-contradiction or self-consistency which themselves allow for freedom and so for deviations from the life of God. In this picture, therefore, God is seen as eternal, outside time, while time and change, of which he is, of course, aware, occur within his life.

An answer to Kretzmann's argument is not available within the Western picture, at any rate as interpreted by Kretzmann and Kenny himself: and we do not need to comment on the complexities to which it leads. Suffice to say that after some eight pages of discussion which draws on the work of other philosophers, Kenny concludes that a believer in divine omnipotence must give up belief in divine immutability.

Even if, however, God is still thought of as a person who can intervene in the world, there still remain deep obscurities about how this is to be conceived. On this Kenny has some important things to say at the end of his book. At that point, he has, he believes, established that there is no such being as the God of traditional (Western) natural theology and that the concept of God propounded by Scholastic theologians and rationalist philosophers is incoherent.[10] Given the sort of God on which he bases his work of demolition, I see no reason to question his conclusion.

Kenny goes on to note that he has not considered arguments for the existence of God, but that none of the arguments appear to him to be sound. He then raises the question whether such a divine being is conceivable. He asks, in particular, whether it is possible to conceive of a being which has no body but whose sphere of operations is the whole universe, as the minds which we know are embodied minds. He notes that for Aquinas immateriality entailed knowledge, and having remarked that most contemporary philosophers find immateriality a much more problematic concept and find it hard to conceive an immaterial knower, he asks if a disembodied mind is possible. The work of a disembodied mind is analogous, he says, to the traditional notion of the natural Word of God which was the world itself, considered as God's creation and as an expression of God's intelligence in the way that a work of art is the expression of an artist's skill. Most artists, however, work with their hands:

---

[10] *op cit*   p 121

but if the world is an artefact of God's mind, then nothing comes between his mind and his work.

Kenny goes on to say that we could think of the artistic work being created by telekinesis but even there, the agent has a body in a particular place. But, he says, 'in the case of a non-embodied agent whose sphere of immaterial operations is the entire universe, there seems no parallel Archimedean point from which the concept of agency can get a purchase.'[11] And he adds that he knows of no successful treatment of the philosophical problems involved in conceiving of a non-embodied mind active throughout the universe: indeed, it is rare, he says, to find among theistic philosophers even an attempt to solve the problem.

The need that Kenny sees to find an Archimedean point makes clear why there are these difficulties. He, like most contemporary philosophers of religion, has the Western picture in his mind — a picture of God seemingly in some way conceptually localised yet immaterial, creating the world outside himself, like someone effecting telekinetic changes at a distance. And this is also made clear when, in a brief earlier discussion, he notes that the world is not to be thought of as the expression of God's mind in the way that words and actions are the expression of our thoughts: 'To think that way would be to make the world God's body, which traditional theology would have regarded as objectionably pantheistic.'[12] Obviously, he is thinking at this point of traditional Western theology and presumably has particularly in mind a picture of God 'in' the world in a way in which our minds are in these days thought of as 'in' our bodies. But the Patristic picture was not pantheistic for it was of God 'enclosing, not enclosed': of God within creation but creation within the life of God which utterly transcends it. What is more, the problem of finding an Archimedean point from which the agency can get a purchase does not arise within the Patristic picture, for the world lies within God's life and is the direct product of his act.

Kenny goes on to say that the idea of the world as God's body has found an echo in recent philosophy, for Arthur Danto, in an influential article, has introduced the notion of a 'basic action'[13] A basic action is an action which one does not by doing anything else. I wind up my watch by moving my finger and thumb but I do not do anything else in order to move my finger and thumb. Danto suggests that a body can be defined as the locus of one's basic actions.   If God can act in the world directly, and without

---

[11] A Kenny *op cit*   (1979) p 126

[12] A Kenny *op cit*   p 126

[13] A Danto   'Basic Actions'   reprinted in *The Philosophy of Action* ed A R White (1968) pp 43 ff

intermediary, as traditionally he has been held to, then on Danto's definition, Kenny suggests, the world would be God's body. This is part of what the Patristic picture suggests, notwithstanding that, as Kenny says, most traditional (Western) theologians would have rejected such an idea with horror. Yet even the most influential of Western theologians, Aquinas, had not totally shed earlier ways of looking at the world for he himself says: 'The whole human soul is in the whole body, and again, in every part, as God is in regard to the whole world'[14]

The idea of the world as God's body is not one that I much like for we tend today to think of the human personality as in some way contained in, or as a by-product of, the body: and any such idea applied to God is far removed from the idea of God enclosing, not enclosed, being advocated here. Objections made to the idea of the world as God's body are, however, often made on wider grounds.

One such objection is that it seemingly requires that the world should be co-eternal with God. As we have already seen, however, that is forbidden by the limits of self-contradiction: the world has to be finite in all respects and so cannot be co-eternal with God.

A second objection is that such an idea entails that the world limits the freedom of God. In one sense this is, of course, true, for sin and evil constantly frustrate the will of God: but that is implicit in the freedom given by the will of God and applies also to the Western picture. It seems, however, that this Western picture also assumes that the world has in some sense an additional autonomy from God: a scope for activity that is neither fully in accordance with his will nor actively frustrates it. In the picture being presented here, however, this does not apply. The world lies within the life of God and is constantly dependent on him. The only freedom that the world has is to grow in accordance with his will and other attributes to share more fully in his life, or to deviate self-destructively from it. It is the very plenitude of God that allows the multiplicity of paths that are in accordance with his will and lead into his life and give this world its richness: an understanding that is not incompatible with there being only one 'right' path for any given person at any given juncture in his life — 'right' being not so much morally right as in accordance with the will of God and so leading to fuller participation in his life.

A third objection is that if the world is God's body, this introduces sin and evil into God. As we have seen, however, the entire picture being developed here is of the world developing within the life of God, despite constant deviations. Such deviations in no way change or detract from the will or act or other attributes of God though they limit their application in

---

[14] *S T* 1 93 3

the world. This said, however, we need to recognise that the world is
developing into the life of God at many levels and is to be thought of in
dynamic terms. Although sin entails deviation from the sustaining will of
God and so is self-destructive, it is sustained by other levels of being that
are in themselves good. This makes evil parasitic on the good and gives it
a power and perversity that it would otherwise be lacking.

Other Western Insights

Whether or not the world is thought of as God's body, the idea of his
presence in the world is not alien to all Western theology; nor is the related
idea that the opening up of creation and ourselves allows a present God to
reveal himself more fully. Despite the generally unfriendly structure of
Western theology to the older understandings, the important role of insights
more characteristic of that older tradition is recognised by some modern
theologians, though they are often seen as restricted to a 'religious' context.
Peter Baelz notes that: A man's coming to belief 'is like coming to
recognise the presence of something that has been present all the time but
to the existence of which one has been blind. ... It embraces and illuminates
all other experiences. The religious "object", correspondingly, is seen as the
ground of all other "objects". It is "the transcendent in the midst"'[15] And
Mascall, having claimed that for Aquinas, arguments for the existence of
God are exercises in syllogistic deduction, draws attention to another school
of thought, of which, in spite of their differences on points of detail, Dr A
M Farrer, Dom Mark Pontifex and Dom Illtyd Trethowan are representative.
According to their view, the function of the arguments is to direct the
attention of the mind to certain features of finite beings which can easily be
overlooked and from which the existence of God can be seen without
discursive process. 'There is no question of asserting that, in this
movement, we have a direct and immediate apprehension of God: direct, if
you like, but not immediate, for it is mediated by and in our apprehension
of finite beings. ... It is not denied that in making this approach there is a
great deal to be done in the way of argument and discussion; but it would
be held that the purpose of this argument and discussion is not to win assent
to a logical demonstration, but to put the hearer in the frame of mind in
which he will be able to apprehend finite beings as they really are, to get
behind both the superficial level of sensible phenomena and also beyond
even the particular individual existence of the finite beings themselves, to
the creator upon whose incessant activity their very existence depends.'[16]

---

[15] P Baelz *Christian Theology and Metaphysics* (1968) p 109

[16] E L Mascall *Words and Images* (1957) pp 84-5

The idea of the opening up of creation to reveal greater depths of significance is not however, always thought of solely as a religious phenomenon. The significance of the mind being open to such insights is stressed by J V Taylor: 'True attention is an involuntary self-surrender to the object of attention. The child who is absorbed is utterly relaxed. The adult mind, also, must be unstriving, receptive, expectant, before there can be any creative insight. Again and again, this is the state of mind in which new truth dawns. We do not work it out or think it out; rather we have the sense of waiting for the disclosure of something that is already there.'[17]

Anthony Storr, in his book on Jung, makes a similar point when he notes that for Jung, the supreme value, the goal towards which the individual's psychological development tends, is that of integration or 'wholeness'. The person who has achieved this goal possesses, in Jung's words, 'an attitude that is beyond the reach of emotional entanglements and violent shocks — a consciousness detached from the world.' In Jung's view, and here Storr says he thinks that Kleinians like Elliott Jaques would agree with him, such an attitude, achieved only in the second half of life, is a preparation for death. A certain degree of detachment from the world is, of course, valuable when one is preparing to leave it for ever: and this, Storr notes, has been amply recognised by both Christianity and Buddhism. And he records that Jung, and later analysts studying the mid-life crisis, have concluded that this preoccupation with death begins early, and that it a natural part of the individual's psychological development. 'The conscious attitude which accompanies the achievement of this new integration is essentially one of acceptance; more especially, of ceasing to do violence to one's own nature by repressing any side of it, or by overdeveloping any particular aspect.'

Storr illustrates these points by reference to a letter from one of Jung's patients which Jung quotes in his commentary on *The Secret of the Golden Flower*.

"'Out of evil, much good has come to me. By keeping quiet, repressing nothing, remaining attentive, and by accepting reality — taking things as they are, and not as I wanted them to be — by doing all this, unusual knowledge has come to me, and unusual powers as well, such as I could never have imagined before. I always thought that when we accepted things they overpowered us in some way or other. This turns out not to be true at all, and it is only by accepting them that one can assume an attitude towards them. So now I intend to play the game of life, being receptive to whatever comes to me, good and bad, sun and shadow for ever alternating, and, in this way, also accepting my own nature with its positive and negative sides.

---

[17] J V Taylor *The Go-between God* (1972) p 18

Thus everything becomes more alive to me. What a fool I was! How
I tried to force everything to go according to the way I thought it
ought to!'"

And Storr notes that Jung calls such an attitude 'religious', although the
person who achieves it may not subscribe to any recognized creeds. 'By
sacrificing the ego's mundane goals, and accepting what comes, the
individual is acknowledging dependence on something beyond the ego,
which lives in and through him.'[18]

Similarly, Iris Murdoch comments of the artist that he must surrender his
personal will to the rhythm of divine thought, as in the oriental doctrine of
the Tao;[19] and she notes that in the mythology of the Timaeus, only
passionate selfless unenvious mind can understand the world since
passionate, selfless, unenvious mind made it.[20]

The link of these insights with morality becomes clear when Iris Murdoch
notes that 'it remains Plato's (surely correct) view that the bad (or mediocre)
man is in a state of illusion, of which egoism is the most general name,
though particular cases would, of course, suggest more detailed descriptions.
Obsession, prejudice, envy, anxiety, ignorance, greed, neurosis and so on
veil reality. The defeat of illusion requires moral effort. The instructed and
morally purified mind sees reality clearly and indeed (in an important sense)
provides us with the concept.'[21] The sharp contrast in Western thought
between God and the world not only has dulled our sensibilities and often
prevented our recognising signs of God's presence in the world, but has
made us normally unaware of the richness of experience waiting to reveal
itself if we can but open ourselves to it.

Comments by Sir Peter Medawar give emphasis to this view. Having
criticised the idea of scientific thought as inductive and having
acknowledged his debt to Sir Karl Popper, Medawar says that science is not
logically propelled forward. Scientific reasoning is to be seen as an
exploratory dialogue that can always be resolved into two voices and two
episodes of thought, imaginative and critical, which alternate and interact.
'In the imaginative episode we form an opinion, take a view, make an
informed guess, which might explain the phenomena under investigation.
The generative act is the formation of an hypothesis.' And he quotes Pierce
as saying that we must entertain some hypothesis or else forgo all further
knowledge, for hypothetical reasoning is the only kind of argument which
starts a new idea. The process by which we come to formulate an

---

[18] A Storr   *Jung*   (1973) pp 87-8

[19] *The Fire and the Sun*   (1978) p 58

[20] *op cit* p 59

[21] *op cit*   (1978) pp 46-7

hypothesis, Medawar emphasises, is not logical but non-logical, i e outside logic. But once we have formed an opinion we can expose it to criticism, usually by experimentation; 'this episode lies within and makes use of logic, for it is an empirical testing of the logical consequences of our beliefs.'[22]

Scientists, and all other creative persons, are dependent on such insights 'coming to' them. As Einstein, having spoken of the search for those highly universal laws from which a picture of the world can be obtained, says: 'There is no logical path leading to these laws. They can be reached only by intuition, based on something like intellectual love (einfühlung) of the objects of experience.'[23] Indeed, Einstein regarded the search for these laws as the supreme task of the physicist.

This understanding relates directly to that of Gregory of Nyssa which is described by Werner Jaeger thus [Greek terms omitted]: 'In spite of God's transcendence, there is a long way of gradual approach to him. This is the path of knowledge [in the sense of "insight"]. In the treatise [De Instituto Christiano] as well as in the Vita Moysis and the In Psalmos Gregory depicts it as a toilsome ascent and a ceaseless struggle which we must carry on in the sweat of our brow. In this process knowledge and virtue are inseparable. Without knowledge it is impossible to discern the goal of the "philosophic life". This is why Gregory calls the life of the perfect Christian the true askesis. In this sense religion is gnosis of the divine good or "will of God" towards which man's will must be directed. But knowledge increases only with the growth of man's entire nature and with his spiritual coming of age. Gregory visualises this process as a sequence of steps or stages marking the advance towards the goal of perfection. This process of salvation is the mystery of the new religion. It is interpreted as the gradual purification of the soul from the stain of the material world and its final liberation from the servitude of the passions. The goal of this lifelong struggle is the freedom of man from the tyranny of evil.'[24]

Yet though Gregory emphasises the struggle entailed in this pilgrimage, man cannot command the outcome for it is basically a struggle to prepare the mind, to open it, in the absolute confidence that God is there, helping and awaiting entry.

As we have seen, however, with Augustine this profound influence almost ceased to have a role in religion in the West. Louis Bouyer says that whatever may be the importance of the elements that Augustine took from the Greek Fathers in order to plant them in the Latin world, his idea of

---

[22] P B Medawar *Induction and Intuition in Scientific Thought* (1969) p 46

[23] Quoted by K Popper *The Logic of Scientific Discovery* (1959) p 32

[24] W Jaeger *Two Rediscovered Works of Ancient Christian Literature: Gregory of Nyssa and Macarius* (1954) pp 78-9

wisdom brings out the fact that he did not transmit one of the most basic, the most traditional structures of Greek spirituality, *gnosis*. 'Augustinian wisdom, in spite of certain affinities, is something other than the *gnosis* of the Greek Fathers. It is distinguished particularly by its psychological, reflexive orientation: it is not the mystery of God in Christ that it has directly in view, but the mystery of ourselves, which God, which Christ, aid us to unravel. An element ... of anthromorphism and, if we dare formulate it, of psychocentrism has been introduced.' And Bouyer suggests that its emergence traces out the main line of the progressive alienation of the Latin West from the ancient Eastern tradition.

Bouyer goes on to note that the interiorisation of all Christianity is the first consequence of this change. But, as he says, when man, in his experience of God, comes to fix his attention primarily on his own experience, it is forseeable that, sooner or later, his experience alone will be enough to captivate him, whatever the object may be. And he comments that neither Protestantism nor the idealistic religious philosophies would have been conceiveable in a world in which the influence of St Augustine had not been practically predominant.

Bouyer then draws attention to another strand in this loss of the ancient tradition. He points out that the ancient type of asceticism, doubtless precisely because it was the work of minds radically objective in their orientation, is strikingly positive in its motivations: the question is that of freeing oneself completely from what is not God for God. However, 'with the young Chrysostom, still more with Jerome, we have seen an asceticism introduced that tended to justify itself by a disgust of the world, of the body and, what is even more serious, of woman seen simply as the intermediary by which the religious man finds himself wholly absorbed in the body and, as it were, nailed to the world.'[25]

Earlier, in carefully chosen words, Bouyer had noted that for Augustine, the vision of God was accessible only in the world to come when man will finally be freed from the weight of the flesh of sin. For him, contemplation is never given to us except in a way which cannot be grasped and that impels us, by its very instability, to struggle: and he speaks of the 'combat' associated with progress which is an incitement never to halt or take rest before entrance into eternal blessedness. He notes that throughout his career Augustine went from a mysticism 'more speculative than experimental, even though experience certainly had its part in it, to what Fr Cayré has happily called a mystical moralism' — a term which he explains as a development of charity in which an asceticism increasingly dominated by the pastoral care for the salvation of his brethren, inseparable in the Church from his own

---

[25] L Bouyer *A History of Christian Spirituality* vol 1 (1968) pp 493-4

salvation, remains none the less, for Augustine, moved by the mystical aspiration.'[26] The inheritance of Augustine that remains with us, has, however, further implications.

---

[26] *op cit* p 492

CHAPTER SIXTEEN

REDEMPTION, *PAIDEIA* AND THE CHURCH

The change from the understandings of the early Church Fathers to those of the Western Church, had other implications which were to have lasting significance and we need now to consider several of these.

Redemption and Paideia

Whereas in the West, redemption came to be thought of in almost entirely moral terms, as we have seen, the earlier understanding, though it had strong moral implications, both as a precondition and consequence of redemption, saw redemption as a wider aim of achieving fuller participation in the life of God. The early Church was relatively optimistic about man's ability to overcome sin and, amongst the Greek Fathers, there is little flavour of his sharing the guilt of Adam. For the Greek Fathers, as Kelly comments, their starting point was not that of Augustine for it was 'marked out by the ideas of participation in the divine nature, rebirth through the power of the Spirit, adoption as sons, new creation through Christ — all leading to the concept of "deification."' And Kelly quotes Cyril of Alexandria: 'We are made partakers of the divine nature and are said to be sons of God, nay we are actually called divine, not only because we are exalted by grace to supernatural glory, but also because we have God dwelling in us.'[1]

Essentially, therefore, if men were to be assimilated into the order and reason of the Divine Christ and the love of the Holy Spirit, they were seen as having to grow and develop in that order and reason which is objectively present in the world as well as in our experiences: they had in the widest sense to be *educated* into the Divine life by growing participation in it and gaining insight into it. Christians therefore saw Christ, the Word of God, as the Divine Educator, the Illuminator. In this understanding there was the belief that to achieve moral and spiritual maturity, wholeness and integrity, men had to grow and develop; that that development was a development of the person as a whole; and that there was in this process a profoundly important intellectual element involving far more than learning facts or reasoning: it involved a growth and development of insights and of wisdom that had to come *to* the person, and that led to a growth in ability to understand and love. It was in this sense that Jesus said in John 8 31-2: if you continue in my word, then you are my disciples and you shall know the truth and the truth shall make you free.

---

[1] J N D Kelly *Early Christian Doctrines* 5th edn (1977) p 352 quoting In Ioh 1 9

The implications of this understanding are so central to this study that it will be valuable to develop them by reference to the work of a modern philosopher, Iris Murdoch, for these ideas are far removed from much current thought: not only does the West tend to think of redemption almost entirely in moral terms but morality has come to be seen as accessible to all by an act of will in a value-neutral world.

We have already quoted some of the observations of Iris Murdoch and, in particular, we have noted the attention that she draws to the emphasis given in much current philosophy to the overtly choosing will which is seen as isolated from belief, reason and feeling, yet is also seen as the centre of the self. She notes that in this understanding, 'will does not bear upon reason, so the "inner life" is not to be thought of as a moral sphere. Reason deals in neutral descriptions and aims at being the frequently mentioned ideal observer. Value terminology is the prerogative of the will; but since will is pure choice, pure movement, and is not thought or vision, will really requires only action words such as "good" or "right"'.[2] And she points out that this is what may be called a democratic view, in that it suggests that morality is not an esoteric achievement but a natural function of any normal man.[3] In Basil Mitchell's words, 'the world is value-neutral. There is no mystery in it, and agreement about it can be reached in principle by any who are willing to attend to the facts.'[4]

This modern understanding, Iris Murdoch finds 'alien and implausible' and she finds empirical, philosophical and moral objections to it. What she regards as chiefly blocking our view of the world as it is is the 'fat, relentless ego' with its need for consolatory fantasies. We need some technique to purify our selfish wills, and allow us to see the world clearly and so to act well and thus necessarily, realistically.[5]

We can see the problem that she is posing if we ask how a person can become someone who understands and cares. Most people today would probably accept that this is something to which we should all aspire. But clearly, despite the view that morality is at every man's behest, we cannot command that state of mind. We have to grow and develop so that we become the sort of person who responds in that way spontaneously. As Iris Murdoch says, moral change and moral achievement are slow; we are not free in the sense of being able suddenly to alter ourselves since we cannot suddenly alter what we see and ergo what we desire and are compelled by.[6]

---

[2] *The Sovereignty of the Good*   (1977) p 8

[3] *op cit*   p 9

[4] B. Mitchell *Morality; Religious and Secular*   (1980) p 65

[5] *op cit*   pp 52-54

[6] *op cit*   p 39

If, she continues, we consider what the work of attention is like, how continuously it goes on, and how imperceptibly it builds up structures of value around about us, we shall not be surprised that at crucial moments of choice most of the business of choosing is already over.[7] True vision, she claims, occasions right conduct.[8] As she says, freedom is not strictly exercise of the will but rather the experience of accurate vision which, when this becomes appropriate, occasions action.[9] 'In a way, explicit choice seems now less important: less decisive (since much of the "decision" lies elsewhere) and less obviously something to be "cultivated". If I attend properly I will have no choice and this is the ultimate condition to be aimed at.' This, she says, is in a way the reverse of Hampshire's picture, where our efforts are supposed to be directed to increasing our freedom by conceptualising as many different possibilities of action as possible. Having as many goods as possible in the shop. 'The ideal situation, on the contrary, is rather to be represented as a kind of "necessity". This is something of which the saints speak and which any artist will readily understand. The idea of a patient, loving regard, directed upon a person, a thing, a situation, presents the will not as unimpeded movement but as something very much more like "obedience".'[10] We respond to 'the only rational thing to do in the circumstances'. It is precisely in this sense that we should understand obedience to the will of God.

Implicit in all this is the idea — the idea that motivates the creative scientist — that underlying the kaleidoscopically fragmented and warped multiplicity of the world there is order and that not only is that order ultimately a unity, but there are strong cybernetic forces that are seeking to extend that order. What is more that unity in some sense finds its counterpart in the ordering and, in the ideal, in the unification of the mind and so its intellectual and moral purification; and this itself has strong moral implications. On this basis, morality is not just at the behest of the will, nor is it at the behest equally of everyman: it is the outcome of a long pilgrimage of growth and development of insights and understanding which not only guides and strengthens the will, but in a sense largely supersedes the need for it.

It is on this basis that we can understand the Good as the centre towards which understanding and love naturally move.[11] The good man, Iris Murdoch notes, is humble, for humility involves a selfless respect for reality

---

[7] *op cit*   p 37

[8] *op cit*   p 66

[9] *op cit*   p 67

[10] *op cit*   pp 39-40

[11] *op cit*   p 102

and is one of the most difficult and central of all virtues.[12] Humility, she says, is a rare virtue and an unfashionable one and one which is often hard to discern. 'Only rarely does one meet somebody in whom it positively shines, in whom one apprehends with amazement the absence of the anxious avaricious tentacles of the self.'[13] Humility is, of course, linked with detachment. She thus sees 'the unsentimental, detached, unselfish, objective attention' characterising the great artist, as 'a kind of intellectual ability to perceive what is true, which is automatically at the same time a suppression of the self.'[14] Indeed, she regards appreciation of beauty as a completely adequate entry into (and not just analogy of) the good life.[15] The parallels between this and the views of Israel's sages will be obvious.

The views of Plotinus are relevant to this discussion. As Rist comments in an important article,[16] Plotinus is not particularly concerned to tell us directly what we ought to do, still less what it means to use the word 'ought'. 'For Plotinus, as for Plato, Aristotle and the Stoics, the good life is the life of virtue and virtue is a state of the soul.'[17] Plotinus comments that without virtue, God is just a name and those who use it without virtue are misguided if not hypocritical. Plotinus distinguishes the so-called civic virtues from those associated with the purification of the soul and sees purification as a progressive process of freeing the soul and enabling it to engage in its natural and proper activity.[18] Thus for Plotinus free action, natural action, rational action and good action ultimately coincide, so that when the soul is free, the need of a sense of moral obligation is superseded: for the virtuous soul, the sense of obligation disappears and it does what is good naturally. What it ought to do is simply what, in any given situation, it is rational to do. The fully rational judgement of what is expedient leads to a discovery and realisation of the good and this leads also to a state of happiness. But it follows also that growth and development have to be undertaken by each person for himself, however much he may be encouraged and assisted: it can be neither dispensed or imposed: each person has to face reality for himself: no one and no organisation, (including no Church) can do it for him.

---

[12] *op cit* p 95

[13] *op cit* p 103

[14] *op cit* p 66

[15] *op cit* p 65

[16] J M Rist Plotinus and Moral Obligation   XI *Platonism and its Christian Heritage* (1985)

[17] *op cit* p 218

[18] *op cit* p 219

It follows, therefore, that the priority is to attain the state of virtue from which rational and therefore good actions follow rather than to seek to obey externally fixed moral rules. But, of course, such rules are in practice necessary as everyone has to develop towards a state of virtue and most people are at best semi-free. We might view the matter from another angle by noting that to act rationally is not just to respond to every passing situation. To understand implies an understanding in some depth: it is thus a matter of degree — of depth of penetration — embracing deeper and deeper levels of wisdom and aspiring towards a vision *sub specie aeteritatis*. And such a vision in depth implies a corresponding development of, and so purification of, the personality.

As we shall see later, there are strong arguments for suggesting that Jesus, too, was not concerned primarily with teaching morality but with getting people to grow and develop towards that state of personal development in which they follow the moral rules of their society but feel free to apply and adapt them as the situation demands: they grow in rationality, 'in Christ'; and, as will be recalled, that in turn implied faith that God will organise events to meet them. 'Blest are the pure in heart for they shall see God' (Matt 5 8) is thus not to be understood just as morally pure but as 'whole'. 'A good man produces good from a store of good within himself' (Matt 12 35). It implies a faith and humility and a freeing of the self from worldly attachments. 'If a man will let himself be lost for my sake, he will find his true self' (Matt 16 25).

All this gives meaning to the idea of purification of the mind which we need to understand, not so much in moral terms, as in terms of clarifying and rendering more meaningful and objective our vision: though the attainment of this leads to largely spontaneous moral behaviour. In this process, obviously, we learn from other men and women from whom we imbibe our culture with its truths and its distortions. It was the early Christian claim to provide that Logos and *bios* (way of life) through the Church, the Scriptures and most of all through Christ. This was thus a process of gaining insights from the Holy Spirit, through the Divine Christ, about the implications of the Incarnation of the Divine Christ for men's lives, so that they could themselves grow and develop in the order and reason of the Divine Christ. It was precisely in this sense that we must understand their conception of Christianity as *paideia*, the education of man.

What is more, if, as we have seen, true morality is inseparably linked with utter realism which itself requires development to achieve, on the one hand humility and detachment, and on the other caring concern, then it is not surprising that, when we do see the world unclouded by personal prejudices or fantasies, the right response in those circumstances is also profoundly clarified. As Iris Murdoch says, the right course may appear so obvious as hardly to leave choice.

Such understandings were not those of Augustine, however. For him the emphasis on the Incarnation as a guide towards that state and so towards fuller participation in Christ, in God, was replaced by emphasis on the crucifixion. What is more, for Augustine, there was a move away from *apatheia* — the calming of all disordering tendencies allowing for charity to take over — and instead, to an emphasis on the trials and moral decisions to be faced by men on the way towards rest in God *after* this life.[19]

This was revealingly reflected in changes in the understanding of the spiritual life. Andrew Louth notes that during the Middle Ages there develops the idea that the mystical organ of the soul is not intellectual at all but affective. It is in virtue of the *principalis affectio*, which is the *apex mentis*, the summit of the mind, that the soul has contact with the divine. 'In the context of such a tradition, the teaching of Denys's *Mystical Theology* takes on a different light: the insistence that the intellect must be transcended is interpreted as a rejection of the intellect in favour of the will or feeling.'[20] And Louth finds support from both Vladimir Lossky and Mme Lot-Borodine in the contrast which he sees between the spirituality of Eastern and Western Christianity. 'It is a contrast between a passionate, tortured devotion to the sufferings of our Lord's sacred humanity in the West and a more austere, serene devotion to the royal Victor in the Byzantine East. ... The Byzantine (and Russian) East continues the tradition of the Fathers; but in the West the Church began to depart from this tradition with Augustine, and with him Mme Lot-Borodine finds the beginnings of a new tradition guided by poignant personal experience.'[21]

There arose as a result of this change two dangers, to both of which Iris Murdoch points. As she says, the idea of suffering confuses the mind and in certain contexts (the context of "sincere self-examination", for instance) can masquerade as purification;[22] and: 'It is in the capacity to love, that is to *see*, that the liberation of the soul from fantasy consists. The freedom which is a proper human goal is the freedom from fantasy, that is the realism of compassion. What I have called fantasy, the proliferation of blinding self-centered aims and images, is itself a powerful system of energy, and most of what is often called "will" or "willing" belongs to this system.'[23] And she had noted earlier that the great artist sees his objects (and this is true whether they are sad, absurd, repulsive or even evil) in a

---

[19] see e g G B Ladner *The Idea of Reform* (1959) p 160-1

[20] *The Origins of the Christian Mystical Tradition* (1981) p 183

[21] *op cit* pp 187-8

[22] *op cit* p 68

[23] *op cit* pp 66-67

light of justice and mercy. The direction of attention is, contrary to nature, outward, away from the self which reduces all to a false unity, towards the great surprising variety of the world, and the ability so to direct attention is love.[24]   Indeed, we can go so far as to say that, whether or not it is recognised as such, no one who fails to see and so respond to the divine which lies behind and within the twistings of human and even animal nature, can himself stand right with God.

If this is so, it becomes clear that reliance on our own wills which are dependent on our limited and short-range vision, to lead us into accordance with the will of God is misconceived: it points to a narrowly focussed, single-minded, imposed vision. In contrast, just as the will of God reveals and is revealed by the action and response of his entire nature, so we can know his will and find strength to follow it only by coming to participate fully in his reason and his love — in the Son and Spirit — in the actual affairs of everyday life. Such responsive participation is, of course, in line with the approach of the Wisdom writers; and it is noted by Iris Murdoch who, as we have seen, comments that the ideal situation is rather to be represented as a kind of 'necessity'. We have already quoted her as saying that this is something of which the saints speak and which any artist will readily understand. The idea of a patient, loving regard, directed upon a person, a thing, a situation, presents the will not as unimpeded movement but as something very much more like "obedience".[25] And Aquinas makes virtually the same point when he notes that it is impossible for any man either to will or do anything except to aim at what he sees as good; so that the perfect union of the created good with the uncreated good (and the perfect vision that accompanies this) renders him unable to sin.[26]

The Role of the Church

For Augustine, of course, such insights and guidance as come to men depended on grace bestowed *ad extra* without which they could not accomplish the good; and this was seen by him as 'an internal and secret power, wonderful and ineffable' by which God worked in the hearts of men.[27] For him, however, such grace could normally be attained only within the Body of Christ, his Bride, the Church, for the Holy Spirit was bestowed only in the Church. Exceptionally, God gave grace direct, but only on condition that the recipient did not attempt to by-pass the visible means of

---

[24] *op cit*   p 66

[25] *The Sovereignty of the Good*   (1970) pp 39-40

[26] *Summa Theologica*   I 62 9   pt 1   8

[27] *De Grat et pecc orig* 1 25

grace, the Church. And, of course, as we have seen, Augustine identified the Church with the Catholic Church with its centre at Rome.[28] As so understood, the Church included all who believed in Christ in the past and would do so in the future; what is more, it was a 'mixed community' comprising bad men as well as good. But the two groups within the Church would be separated at the final consummation when only those who constituted the 'congregation and society of saints' would attain salvation to which they had been predestined. And, of course, most of those without the Church were in any event damned.

It follows, then, as we saw earlier, that Augustine in effect separated God's creative and sustaining powers from his redemptive powers; he restricted the incidence of the redemptive powers; and, though they did their work internally and secretly, he saw them as normally channelled through the Church hierarchy and the sacraments. Christ for him had a triple mode of existence: as eternal Word, as God-man or Mediator, and as head of the Church, though he saw the whole as a single spiritual entity or person.[29] The Church was, therefore, one of these modes of Christ's existence. Redemption was no longer seen as one aspect of God's creative and sustaining powers working throughout creation. Rather, it was seen as 'channelled down' through the Church which was his instrument for redemption, so reaching ordinary men and women *ad extra*. And in a yet further narrowing of God's link with the world, the Pope himself came in due course to be seen as the specific point of normal access, and so as the Vicar of Christ, acting vicariously for him.

As for the Protestant Churches, in subsequently separating themselves, they did not discard Augustinian and post-Augustinian preconceptions and notably his subjectivism. But they added facets of their own. In particular, in Protestant orthodoxy, scripture was taken to be the central criterion for faith and the central source for doctrine, for the canon was seen as inspired by God. As James Barr has said, however, in so doing, the Church — and especially the Protestant branch of it — was actually taking its stand, to a considerable extent, outside the Bible rather than within it. 'Completed scripture was something that was not there until a long time after the central events, after the time — if we may so call it — of Biblical revelation was past: for the New Testament, one or two generations, perhaps more, and for the Old Testament, or almost all of it, some centuries.' Yet as Barr says, Protestantism continued to revere the *persons* of the Bible — Moses, Isaiah, Jesus, St Paul — and to see them in their own times and situation as far as limitations of historical perspective could permit, and to consider their

---

[28] J N D Kelly *Early Christian Doctrines* 5th edn (1977) p 413

[29] J N D Kelly *op cit* p 413

attitudes and actions as authoritative.[30] These men of the Bible were not, however, themselves controlled by a fixed, delimited and complete written scripture as Protestant believers were expected to be, for within the Bible itself, religion was not a scriptural religion in the sense that it later, and especially after the Reformation, became normal to suppose. Rather scripture derived from faith and only much later did faith derive from scripture. What is more, though by the time of Jesus, Judaism did have its collection of holy books — roughly what we know as the Old Testament — and Jesus regarded them as having continuing and inviolable authority, he did not hesitate to differ from them. And, of course, as we have seen in the case of the Western Trinity, the use made of the scriptures by the Churches has been highly selective, and the basis of selection has not itself derived directly from scripture.[31] What was totally lost was the sense that God spoke to man through creation itself and that this required of man a long pilgrimage of growth towards openness and an objective response to it.

Despite the incoherences and implausibilities built into Western Christian doctrine, however, some of which we have considered, the very separation of the main tenets of doctrine from the understanding of the natural world gave it some invulnerability to direct empirical falsification. This invulnerability did not apply to the older tradition which embraced the natural world, including the psychological and spiritual nature of man. But as we have seen, this tradition had lost its hold long before it could be systematically critically examined. It is, therefore, to the question whether, and if so how far, that tradition is confirmed or falsified by the empirical evidence of the natural world now available to us in science that we must now turn. But in so doing, we need to explore some implications of the Fall whose mark lies not just in the moral life but in all aspects of reality.

---

[30] J Barr *Holy Scripture* (1983) pp 3-4

[31] see J Barr *op cit* for a valuable discussion of such use of the scriptures

PART III

GOD AND THE WORLD

CONFIRMATION OF BIBLICAL AND EARLY CHURCH IDEAS IN MODERN
SCIENCE AND THEIR RELEVANCE TO SURVIVAL OF DEATH AND
JESUS CHRIST

CHAPTER SEVENTEEN

THE NATURE AND IMPLICATIONS OF THE FALL

So far we have seen something of how the understandings of God and of his relationship to the world have changed over the last two thousand years. But the framework of thought that has been emerging in this study is incomplete and lacks any adequate account of the actual world that lies around us: for whatever sort of world God has sought to make cannot be directly related to the world we know without showing further the way in which it is marred by sin and its consequences in suffering and evil.

The Nature and Scope of Sin

We have seen that laws of God are often thought of as mainly concerned with morality, and sin is often regarded as a moral failure in man to obey these laws. By implication, therefore, sin does not apply to other factors which lead to man's suffering and misery or to other parts of creation where, it seems, impersonal chance plays a major role around the impersonal laws and constants of nature. We need, therefore, to consider further the nature and scope of sin, including how the impersonal insensitivity and seemingly merciless indifference of the lower reaches of the world in which man is embedded can be reconciled with a personal and caring God.

Any view of sin which need have no direct moral connotation and which applies to the whole of creation at every level, may to some people be surprising. Yet both were features of Israel's view of sin. As G F Moore shows, 'It is a consequence of the fundamentally religious (i e non-moral) idea of sin that to constitute a sin it is not necessary that a man should know the rule of the law nor be aware that he is infringing it, still less that the intention to do an unlawful act should be present. Protestants in particular are so habituated to associate the word sin exclusively with the so-called moral law, and to regard knowledge and intention as of the essence of sin, that it requires some effort to put themselves at the point of view of the Old Testament, consistently maintained by Judaism, of which none of these things is true.'[1]

Not only was sin not in itself seen primarily as a moral failing, but it affected the whole of creation. Speaking of the Fall, Claus Westermann comments that 'When the serpent shares in the punishment, then this is an indication that man and the rest of Creation are drawn into a common

---

[1] *Judaism* vol 1 (1927) p 463

relationship which is seen in the "groaning of all creation"[2] In other words, 'sin' involves deviation from the creative order and will of God at all levels of creation.

Linked with these understandings of sin was the further understanding that, as we have seen, God is present in creation in the most intimate possible way, and not only guides the man who is righteous and so open to him, but so orders events as they unfold that they come to meet him: indeed, it is God himself who comes to meet the righteous man in these events: an idea which is not only totally alien to our present mechanistic understanding of the world, but to theological understandings of the Western Churches. Even its pale replacement by ideas of God's 'interventions' in the world are by now sufficiently alien to be widely discounted. Thus whereas the providence of God is freely related by theologians to the order of the world which they see him as having initially established, any thought that that order changes constantly in response to the righteousness or unrighteousness of men would be regarded by them and others as totally incompatible with our scientific knowledge: so any such need for men to stand right with the will of God in the ordinary affairs of life, not just in a moral but a fully personal sense, hardly arises.

Yet, as we shall see, there is no conflict with scientific evidence in such a view, for there are built into the unfolding sequence of events, large areas, both in the natural world and in the lives of men, where events are not closely causally determined and where there is ample scope for variations to occur without any conflict with the laws and constants of nature. This freedom and openness to change which God gives along with his other attributes, allows also for deviations from his will at all levels of creation; and such deviations, which occur as a result of the blindness of all lower levels of creation, bring waste, destructiveness and suffering. What is more, because there are deep creative and integrative forces operating more or less blindly throughout creation, and these integrative forces organise themselves to take advantage of, and as far as possible, compensate for the warpings that occur in the system, this of itself restricts the openness to reordering and creative change in the system as a whole and in each part of it, so that any reorganisation in accordance with the will of God will often necessarily be fiercely resisted. Inherently, however, action in accordance with the will of God should be able to operate creatively and in harmony with all levels and all parts of the system; and this is what is looked forward to with the coming of God's kingdom.

An example may serve to clarify these issues which operate at all levels of creation. If one thinks of the current drought areas of parts of Africa, it

---

[2] *Creation* (1974) p 99

is only too sadly clear that neither plants nor animals nor human beings are able adequately to respond the the challenge offered by the blind changes that are occurring in the weather and, perhaps, the climate. Wars, insensitive farming practices, misuse of water resources, population too high for these and other available resources, and national boundaries are amongst the factors which point to the desperate, and possibly insurmountable, problems that these areas face, and to the rigidities that appear to preclude any rational solution. Sin, therefore, in this profound, amoral sense, is deeply rooted in the system as a whole and in all parts of it, so that its current state is always the outcome of the struggle between these warping forces of sin and the creative and sustaining forces of God, albeit at many levels operating blindly.

In this context, therefore, we can understand how for the Israelites, sin was a violation of the revealed will of God and though the will of God was crystallised in the Law, it was embodied in the order of creation: such violations, embedded in the world of which man is part, alienated the world and so man from participation in the creative life of God. It therefore invoked his wrath and entailed penalties which revealed themselves in the disasters and misfortunes of everyday life. Some of these man brought upon himself, as well as on the rest of creation, particularly if sin was persisted in. All this carried also the recognition that the activity of God escapes all calculation, for between the putting into practice of man's best plans and that which actually took place, there always lay a great unknown.[3] Hence the need was not only for man to obey the laws of God but to keep himself open so that he could respond to the constant creative initiatives of God.

It follows, therefore, that there were for the Israelites two aspects of sin, though each entailed the other: the transgression of the order laid down by God, primarily in the Law, but also throughout creation as a whole and so in the ordering of everyday events; but secondly and perhaps even more heinously, the shutting of oneself off from God and his creative guidance, at lower levels of creation, by the blindness inherent in its limited level of development, and in man, primarily by undue self-confidence and by self-glorification which imply lack of faith: for as von Rad notes, 'self-glorification cannot be combined with trust in Yahweh.'[4] Yet given a system that was open to God's creative powers, these powers could so order or reorder events as to overcome or circumvent these blockages. Von Rad sums up the aim of the Israelite sages by noting that a wise and understanding mind, a 'listening' mind, was the content of Solomon's royal request (I Kings 3 9). 'What he, the paradigm of the wise man, wished for

---

[3] G von Rad *Wisdom in Israel* (1972) p 101

[4] *op cit* p 102

himself was not the authoritative reason which reigns supreme over dead natural matter, the reason of modern consciousness, but an "understanding" reason, a feeling for the truth which emanates from the world and addresses man.' The sage was totally receptive to that truth, but this was not passivity; it was an intense activity, the object of which was response, prudent articulation. The way in which a sage arrived at his knowledge remained in obscurity, but was none the less full of promise. The sage ran no risk if he trusted it in advance.[5] The voice which spoke in these terms was the voice of the world-order itself which called man to itself and offered him every imaginable fulfillment. In fact, the concern here was with the redemption of man, and had all the signs of a doctrine of salvation. If a man was not constantly listening to the order established by God, then he was lost.[6]

There were, therefore, incremental and decremental processes operating here: the more fully a man responded to the will of God, the more he grew and developed; and the more he grew and developed the more responsive could he be to grow and develop further. Later we shall see the relevance of this for understanding Jesus. Contrariwise, the more man deviated from the will of God, the less responsive he became and the more destructive was his life likely to be, both of himself and others. But, of course, an implication of this is that, notwithstanding the survival of creation in its countless forms, each manifesting different facets of the plenitude of God, and each warped at many levels, in the longer run, as the outcome of the ultimately destructive character of deviation, the creative will of God alone endures and so necessarily prevails. We have here, therefore, a version of the survival of the fittest seen in terms of the need for everything that exists and survives to be sustained by the creative will and other attributes of God despite constant deviations; and an explanation, also, of that gradual speeding up of evolution that has taken place over the ages.

We shall also see later how these same understandings reveal themselves in the Gospels and indeed in the rest of the New Testament. Suffice to refer to Matthew 6 25-34 where Jesus, having pointed to the beauty of the lilies of the field, continues: 'But if God so clothes the grass of the field, which today is alive and tomorrow is thrown into the oven, will he not much more clothe you, O men of little faith? Therefore do not be anxious, saying "What shall we eat?" or "What shall we drink?" or "What shall we wear?" For the Gentiles seek all these things; and your heavenly Father knows that you need them all. *But seek first his kingdom and his righteousness, and all*

---

[5] *op cit*   pp 296-7

[6] *op cit*   p 314

these things shall be yours as well' — the echo of what God said to Solomon in his dream is clear.

As we have seen, the understandings of the early Church were in line with this. The Fall was seen as applying to, and God was seen as exercising his providence over, all facets of creation.[7] Instead of the doctrine that man was created finitely perfect and then wilfully and incomprehensibly destroyed his own perfection and plunged into sin and misery, Irenaeus suggests that man was created as an imperfect, immature creature who was to undergo moral development and growth and finally be brought to the perfection intended for him by his Maker. Accordingly, there is a strong emphasis in the works of Irenaeus on man's need for growth. Wingren points to the importance of this theme for Irenaeus and the way in which it links with terms which, for an interpretation of men, are central to the New Testament.[8]

When, therefore, the idea of development towards perfection entailed in this understanding is seen as itself entailing the overcoming of deviation from the creative will of God; and this is seen as expressed, not just in moral terms, but the very structuring of creation, such overcoming can be seen also as part of the far longer evolutionary process: a process by which the creative, sustaining and redeeming powers of God lead towards the overcoming of disorder and foreclosure and so to further development of order, which itself opens creation to fuller and fuller participation in the order of the Divine Christ and so in the life of God. And the fuller is that participation of creation in the order of the Divine Christ, the more God's attributes of life, consciousness, understanding, love and holiness are able progressively and cumulatively to manifest themselves in creation and, in particular, in man. The strong historical arguments for detaching from the idea of sin as deviation from the order and will of God, its normal limitation to man and its strong moralistic flavours thus come together with wider implications. This opens the way to an explanation of the blind, insensate, utterly impersonal lower levels of the world where chance, operating around the order of God, is king: and the gradual emergence of understanding and love which increasingly allow man to guide himself and creation into the ways of God, but also give him powers to pervert them. More importantly, whereas if man seeks to operate on his own, he is, sooner or later, inevitably lost, it also opens the way for God to respond to the righteous man, which also carries implications for an understanding of the power — and limitations — of prayer. These themes are so important that we need to develop them further.

---

[7] c f Irenaeus *Against Heresies* 3 25 1

[8] *Man and Incarnation* (1959) p 26 ff and note 81

Few people today would support Augustine's view that creation as a whole is perfect, and that God's retribution balances out departures from his will. But it does seem to be widely assumed that the world apart from man is broadly as God created it: that 'every prospect pleases and only man is vile.' As Chadwick notes, Augustine himself did not think chance or randomness played a part in the amazing order and design of the world. Augustine saw 'chance' as a term used when we do not happen to know the cause, for nothing occurs without a cause of some sort. 'Augustine was confident of the rationality of the universe; only the quirks of free choices introduced apparent irrationalities.'[9]   A thousand years later Julian of Norwich was to comment that 'Indeed nothing happens by luck or by chance, but all is through the foresight and wisdom of God. If it seems luck or chance to us it is because we are blind and shortsighted.'[10] And some six hundred years later still, Einstein was to comment that God did not play dice with his universe.

By implication, for those who have held this view, man desperately needs to sort himself out and become morally good, both in his own interests and to satisfy the moral laws of God: though the relationship of man's interests to these laws, at any rate in this world, is not obviously close. But such a view does not entail the need for any reordering of creation as a whole or, seemingly, given a change of will, even, in other respects, of man himself. In any event, moral deviation from the will of God is seen as quite different from chance deviations from the structure of reality, and creation including man himself, is to be seen (other than morally), more or less, as God intended it.

This concentration on the ill-effects of immorality and either the ignoring of the ill-effects of impersonal, blind chance or the assumption that they are all parts of God's deep-laid plans for the best, seem untenably implausible. Morality requires freewill: but hereditary and environmental factors combine to provide a context within which freewill operates. What is more, that context does not provide, as it were, a neutral space that is similar for everyone: rather, such space as it provides has many constrictions and biases within it, as the very idea of wishful thinking implies: and there seems little reason to doubt that some people have stronger, more resilient, personalities than others. These are all matters to which genetic factors, with their strong element of chance, contribute. Many other hereditary defects and limitations appear also to depend to a large extent on chance; and similarly, chance seemingly plays a major part in bringing about situations, good and bad, which may play a crucial role in our development.

---

[9] H Chadwick *Augustine* (1986) p 89

[10] *Revelations of the Divine Love*

A mere glance at a list of factors such as earthquakes, storms, droughts, floods, diseases, harmful mutations, accidents and so on which can blight or destroy men's lives — and exceptionally enhance them — should make it abundantly clear, not only that the boundaries of free will vary from person to person, but that their overlap with other chance factors is ill defined, so that man's moral defects are only one element contributing to his suffering and misery. It therefore seems totally arbitrary to recognise and give full weight to the ill-effects of man's immorality yet to regard the ill-effects of chance as unimportant or as in accordance with the benign will of God.

Increasingly, also, people are becoming more sensitive to the enormous suffering of animals. John MacQuarrie notes the vast amount of animal suffering, to say nothing of all the waste and frustration that seems to have gone into the evolution of the world;[11] and he remarks on the tragic element in the creative process in which man, as creature, shares. He comments that, in so far, there is truth in the view of Origen and others who have thought of creation as a kind of Fall.[12] Whether we describe such suffering as resulting from deviations from the will of God or from sin or natural evil is not, perhaps, of great importance; the essential point is that deviation from the will of God is entailed at all levels of creation and it is thus rooted in the very character of the world we live in.

It follows, therefore, that chance deviations and the underlying directive, integrating, ordering processes which observe the laws and constants of nature, both play a fundamental role in constituting the world as we know it; for without freedom allowing for such deviations there could be no freedom for development to higher levels of order; and without the underlying order, there could be neither preservation of that order nor a base for development to higher levels of order. Such deviations must not, however, be thought of as if they entailed some kind of mechanical breakdown. Even when they occur, there is always present the redeeming aspect of the creative activity of God, which itself implies a self-healing, restorative process, so that the outcome is normally of both forces and may be more or less protracted. But, of course, for these integrative forces to operate, they have to be assimilated into the dynamic processes that constitute creation, and in so far, they can operate blindly and destructively. As we shall see more fully later, this points to the world as more akin to a cybernetically controlled organism rather than a mechanism. But, according to the sages, even this is not an adequate understanding, for cybernetic forces are normally seen as impersonal in that they respond to the needs of the system as a whole rather than the units within it: whereas the sages

---

[11] *The Principles of Christian Theology* rev edn (1977) p 254

[12] *op cit* p 264

stress that that response is personal to each individual human being *in so far as he is open to it.* On the other hand, any such view of cybernetic forces is itself inadequate for it is these forces which organise an organism as a whole to restore injury or disease in any part of it. Obviously, however, the fact that there is freedom for deviation does not of itself require that such deviation should take place: such deviations occur only because creation, even at the level of man, is fully open neither to the reason nor the love of God and so is wholly or partially blind. Death itself is such a sudden loss of order and the importance placed in the New Testament on the need to overcome death, to which the resurrection of Christ bears witness, needs no stressing.

CHAPTER EIGHTEEN

THE NATURE AND DEVELOPMENT OF ORDER

At this point, we need to make clearer what is meant by 'order' in this context. This is a far from simple matter. We need to distinguish, for instance, the near-perfect order of a crystal from the ordered complexity that lies at many levels in living organisms. But order is reflected also in the cosmological laws of physics governing, for instance, electro-magnetism and gravity: we have already pointed to the far-reaching implications of the order entailed in these laws and in the constants of nature. Terms such as order, information, fitness, complexity, integrality and organisation amongst others feature in discussions of the subject. Developing studies of the role of cybernetic forces and of systems arising from dissipative processes are proving of the greatest significance in deepening our understanding of the world. Thus the newly developed studies, which go by the rather misleading title of 'chaos', have shown how, from states of disorder, vastly complex, highly ordered systems, often of fantastic beauty and richness, can develop spontaneously by a creativity embedded in the very nature of reality. Such emerging patterns, which are found throughout the natural world, and are exemplified in the myriad forms of snowflakes and leaves, exhibit a common form yet are individually unique. Within the current materialist paradigm, these processes have to be seen as mysteriously generating order and information from chaos; but within the picture being developed here, that state of chaos from which the forms emerge can be seen as a state of extremely sensitive openness which allows the order inherent in the plenitude of God to reveal itself. The importance of such openness at the level of man in allowing the emergence of order and so of participation in the Divine Christ, has already been stressed and will be developed further.

Some of the relevant features of 'order' or 'complexity' were identified by K G Denbigh in a valuable discussion of the subject.[1] He there distinguished degrees of 'orderliness' as manifested, for instance, in a crystal, from degrees of 'organisation' as manifested, for instance, in a cell: and he pointed out that we do not yet have a satisfactory measure of 'organisation'. He proposed what he called a measure of 'integrality'. Arthur Peacocke, who discusses these issues in his book *Creation and the World of Science*[2] and in more detail in his article 'Thermodynamics and Life',[3] notes specifically that in the various analyses of the nature of

---

[1] *An Inventive Universe* (1975) pp 89ff

[2] (1979) Lecture IV

[3] *Zygon* vol 19 no 4 Dec 1984

biological evolution which he discusses 'it is no longer simply the continuous tendency towards increased fitness that impels the development in evolution to more and more complex living systems, but, rather, the nature of the process itself is such that both increase in complexity and, concomitantly though not identically, increase in organisation, are inherent features of the process itself.'[4] How this process operates in practice, offering, in particular, increased freedom, can best be illustrated later at the level of the extended social order, by reference to the ideas of F A Hayek., though it applies at other levels also.

That there is a strong connection between 'complexity' and consciousness was claimed by Teilhard de Chardin: a claim summarised by B Towers as: (1) Throughout time there has been a tendency in evolution for matter to become increasingly complex in its organisation; and (2) with increase in material complexity there is a corresponding rise in consciousness of matter (or the organism it eventually becomes).[5] A comment of Peacocke is thus relevant here: 'mental activity and functions have been shown to be best regarded as emergent, and non-reducible, only with respect to a certain level of complexity in the organisation and pattern of the physio-chemical units.'[6]

There is one further aspect of these ordering tendencies which needs special comment. As we shall see, following the work of Piaget, human beings, as one fundamental aspect of their development from infancy, have the very remarkable ability to discriminate the underlying order in their constantly varying experiences, classify it and conceptualise it so as to develop highly complex conceptual models at many levels. These models not only allow us to find meaning to our experiences but they structure the personality and because they derive their order from the order of the world around them, they can thus be viewed as potential microcosms of the order and reason of God and so as participating more and more fully in that order and reason as they develop towards maturity and wholeness. This structuring process not only structures our personalities but actually enables us to see the order of the world of which we are part and to find in it its meaning. It is thus on the basis of these conceptual models that human beings interpret and find meaning in each new experience. In so far, not only are they enabled to see the order and reason of God in the world: as microcosms of that order, they participate in it.

Such models, however, which, as we have seen, form the very basis of the organisation of the human personality, do not, in practice, reflect entirely accurately the order of the world; and they may be more or less well

---

[4] *Zygon op cit* p 416

[5] B Towers *Teilhard de Chardin* (1966) p 32

[6] A R Peacocke *Creation and the World of Science* (1979) p 127

developed and more or less well integrated. Given the complexity of human beings and their environments, therefore, it is hardly surprising if, within such models, various sub-systems develop and, when these are imperfect and not adequately integrated, there arises mental conflict. This conflict can, therefore, be seen, not only as a division of the personality but as reflecting also a measure of alienation from the order of God and so, in the wider sense discussed earlier, of sin. Gradually, however, if the personality is open to deeper and deeper insights into the order of the world — the process of *gnosis* — these discordant sub-systems can be coordinated, reordered and brought into a deeper harmony: the process of integration, of making more whole, of maturing. That there is a link here between sin as so understood and moral failure will be obvious yet it will also be obvious that they cannot be identified, in particular in any allocation of guilt or blame.

It follows, therefore, that we need to think in terms of the evolutionary process as flowing from the logic of the life of God; as covering both physical processes and the development of the mind of man; and despite deviations and warpings at all levels, as leading to the development of more complex systems incorporating higher and higher levels of order. What is more, we can think of these increasing levels of order in terms of increasing participation in the order and reason of the Divine Christ and so as carrying with it, as man approaches wholeness and maturity, fuller and fuller manifestations of the attributes of God — attributes of life, consciousness, reason and understanding, love and holiness, culminating in the full mystical experience.

The Need for Openness to Development of Order

Within this emerging order, two specific features need in this context to be stressed. First and foremost, at every level of this transitory world, the systems are dynamic, involving changing standing patterns in an energy flux. And secondly, there are built into the developing process, complex 'areas' of 'freedom' or 'openness' where, even in the life of man, chance can play a crucial role in allowing higher levels of order to emerge. It would seem, therefore, that that 'freedom' which is inherent in the creative will of God, is a *sine qua non* of growth and development to higher levels of order and so into the life of God, in accordance with his will. At levels below the level of man, however, as we have seen, that freedom allows also for blind or largely blind deviations from the will of God and so to loss of order; and even at the level of man, his ability to respond to the reason and love of God is limited. The resulting blind or half-blind deviations are the most obvious forms of 'sin' and their self-destructiveness is a mark of the 'wrath' of God, of which the Jews and early Church were well aware, but which has in recent years tended to fade into oblivion.

At each higher level of order, there emerge also dynamic ordering forces of a cybernetic character which seek to stabilise and maintain it. As we have already noted, these cybernetic, ordering forces, in so far as they too lack reason and love, are themselves largely blind, and, as we have seen, tend in an important sense to operate blindly and so prematurely in that, in seeking to maintain the order so far established, they tend to prevent that openness that allows for the development of higher levels of order. The systems formed by such foreclosure have then to be broken up to allow for further development: so the very creativity of God as it operates in this corrupt world entails a measure of destructiveness.

All this finds confirmation in scientific ideas about the development of open systems. Both too great disorder in near-chaotic situations and too great order, as is found, for instance, in a crystal, preclude further development to higher levels of order, on the one side because there is insufficient stability to allow the cumulative process of development to take place; on the other because there is such a high degree of stability as almost to preclude mutations. Thus Denbigh notes that chance effects are essential to the life processes. They maintain the potential variability of the species, and also, when they occur in the environment of any individual organism, they provide it with *a set of possible futures*. This, Denbigh says, is especially important in the case of those organisms that are conscious. On the other hand, if an organism were subjected to chance disturbances (whether internally or externally generated) much too frequently, that organism might become unviable due to the overwhelming of its regulative system. Thus from these two opposing considerations it follows that living creatures require the occurrence of a certain state of balance in which there is neither too much freedom nor too little. And Denbigh sums up this discussion by saying that the most favourable conditions for the life processes are those which provide an optimum point of balance between order and disorder, between necessity and chance.[7]

Several points of importance follow from this account. Every step, whether large or small, towards full participation in the life of God has to be free in the sense of undetermined by forces which are external to the potential organism. But this does not, of course, preclude responsiveness to those emerging forces, particularly cybernetic forces, which are inherent in the growth which has already been freely attained. Nonetheless, such forces do not wholly preclude deviation and since every step before full participation is achieved is wholly or partially blind to its implications, deviations are seemingly so likely to occur that the only way to ensure that full microcosmic status is attained is for there to be vast over-production of

---

[7] *An Inventive Universe*   (1975) pp 161-2

potential microcosms and/or for there to be a vast time available: and in practice, the fecundity of God and the richness of his life with so many steps involved, seemingly requires both approaches.

Though on this basis God pre-ordains the ultimate form of a potential microcosm when it attains that full status, he does not pre-ordain which potential microcosms will attain it nor does he pre-ordain which warpings in their order will occur. He therefore does not pre-ordain the forms of all the countless manifestations of his life in the world which are the outcome of the interplay of his creative forces and the largely blind deviations from them. Nor does he pre-ordain how long the process will take, for it is sin, in the sense both of deviation from the order of his life and so from his will, and also premature foreclosure, that protract it. The process is channelled to its ultimate destination partly by the self-destructiveness of sin. The process is, however, more positive than this might imply for, as we have seen, at each higher level of order, stronger, cybernetic, guiding forces emerge and the higher the level of order that is attained, the more the potential microcosm is able to open itself to the grace of God that is always seeking entry and always seeking to guide it through reason and love, from whatever state it is then in, towards its ultimate fulfillment.

We must not, however, think of this developmental process as if it were the scaling of the rigid form of a mountain peak. As we have seen, the process is far more dynamic and flexible than this. Arthur Peacocke notes that some biologists have objected to any metaphor of unfolding on this ground. He draws attention to work by Richard Lewontin who stresses that organisms are consequences of themselves — that is of their state at any given moment, with all its dependence on historical accidents — as well as of their genotype and environment. He suggests, therefore, that the analogy is not that of climbing a peak with a fixed summit but rather impacting a trampoline that changes with the impact.[8] As we have noted, the same point is made another way by Manfred Eigen and Ruthild Winkler when they say: 'Everything that happens in our world resembles a vast game in which nothing is determined in advance but the rules, and only the rules are open to objective understanding. The game itself is not identical with either its rules or with the sequence of chance happenings that determine the course of play. It is neither the one nor the other because it is both at once.'[9]

None the less, as Peacocke himself says, 'As one goes up the scale of biological evolution the open-ended character, unpredictability, and creativity of the process becomes more and more focussed in the activity of the biological individual. For in the biological sequence, the increase of

---

[8] *God and the New Biology* (1986) p 47
[9] *The Laws of the Game* (1983) p xi

complexity becomes increasingly accompanied by an increase in consciousness culminating in human self-consciousness, the power of language and rationality. This aspect of the process reaches its apogee in man's creativity and his sense of freedom in taking responsibility for his decisions.'[10]

But clearly, such development in man is incomplete: none of us attains that full potential for rationality and love that is inherent in us. Nonetheless, as we have seen, the more clear-sighted and caring we become, the more there is a kind of necessity in our responses and initiatives.

One further implication of this account needs, however, to be made explicit. This is that any entity at any given level of order is not independent: it is part of larger microcosmic units and so of the total fabric of creation. The freedom of a unit such as a cell is therefore constrained, not only by its internal dynamics but by its place and role in the organism; the freedom of the organism is constrained by its place and role in the environmental systems of which it is part, and the different factors in each environmental system are similarly constrained both by the nature of its constituents and by the nature of the wider systems of which it is part. This applies no less at human level. But to regard these constraints just as constraints is inadequate for the interactions of organisms with their environment and of environmental systems with each other are also the source of order which, particularly at higher levels, is essential to their development and so to the realisation of the potential of creation as a whole. We must not think, therefore, of these interactions in static terms: rather, as we shall see, we need to think of these interactions taking place within a dynamic energy flow in which standing patterns are continuously forming and dissolving and so within a process whose evolutionary development can be seen in terms of a gradual unfolding of the plenitude of God in a vast hierarchy of systems, each within others and the whole within the life of God leading ultimately to its salvation.

Recent work by Prigogine and Eigen and their collaborators has shown how the subtle interplay of forces can be both indeterminate as regards precise courses of development yet determinate in its outcome: which is precisely the picture which, from a theological point of view, is emerging in this study.[11] Man alone has attained that level of order which gives him potential flexibility and freedom to respond to the creative will of God so as to develop the order of his own personality and voluntarily to bring himself more fully into the likeness of God. As Stead says: 'God can only

---

[10] *God and the New Biology* (1986) p 54

[11] See e g A R Peacocke *Creation and the World of Science* (1979) Lecture III for a discussion of this evidence

look down; but he looks down with creative love and authority, seeing in men both the reality of what they are and the possibility of what they may become: his life-conferring generosity restrained only by his care to preserve in each of his creatures their own authentic self-determination.'[12]

Never the less, this does not complete even the basic lineaments of the picture of the world in God, for not only has the Plenum, the life and mind of God, an inherent depth of order and meaning which is plumbed only in the full mystical experience and which far transcends our everyday experiences, but it must in some way contain within its timelessness, events embracing past and future as well as present. What is more, as we shall see, such patterns and events in the Plenum are not passive. The Plenum is living and is the source of life. Any organisation or reorganisation that takes place in the plenum may be manifested in and may influence the form of events as they emerge in the explicate order. Despite the claims of relativity, there are good grounds for believing that the unpredictability of the future leaves ample scope for this, whether in natural or personal affairs. This suggests, therefore, that there may be whole areas of life occurring in the implicate order, the Mind of God, which are related to, but largely independent of, the physical world of which we are parts. But this remains to be explored in a later chapter.

The Nature of the Creative Process

Science is still at an early stage in the understanding of these higher level systems. The understanding of their nature and importance has, however, been radically transformed in the last few years. Increasingly, it is being appreciated that predictable systems like the rotation of the planets which have dominated scientific thinking since the time of Newton, are, in the natural world, exceptional and that most systems are characterised by complexity and openness. Such dynamic systems are typically in a dynamic far-from-equilibrium state which they maintain by drawing energy from their environments. Such systems often appear rapidly rather than evolving slowly; they often have large numbers of components and many degrees of freedom; and they are typically non-linear and, within limits, unpredictable. They tend to operate as wholes and totally lose their character when taken to pieces. They are often hierarchically ordered and 'self-organising': and because of their interaction with their environments, they often form open systems within larger open systems and, indeed, often have within them

---

[12] G C Stead The Concept of Mind and the Concept of God in the Christian Fathers in *The Philosophical Frontiers of Christian Thelogy* eds B Hebblethwaite and S Sutherland (1982) p 53

open sub-systems. Because of their extreme sensitivity to external and internal forces, they have scope for developing to higher levels of order or for decay to lower levels of order, as well as interacting with higher and lower hierarchical levels.

Some of these systems are so sensitive as to be affected by chance events at quantum level but at higher levels, also, such systems are intrinsically unpredictable in their behaviour. Yet though so extremely sensitive and unpredictable, the behaviour of many of these systems is in fact causally determined. In particular, their behaviour depends critically on initial or 'boundary' conditions. These boundary conditions are typically set by the higher level systems of which they form parts.

This so-called top-down causation is not sequential but rather sets constraints within which the lower level systems operate. It is important to realise, however, that a 'top' system is not necessarily a system separate from those below but is the total system up to that level. This can allow great flexibility of response within such systems. Thus cybernetic forces within a living organism not only seek to maintain its state: they coordinate the parts of the organism: they can organise the organism as a whole to restore injury or disease affecting any part within it; and particularly where the system has the necessary flexibility and potential, they can operate creatively to increase the order of the system — as in the case of learning. There is, therefore, typically, constant interplay between the higher and lower levels of such systems. There are grounds for suggesting that such cybernetic forces operate, not only in living organisms and in some lower level systems, but in wider social and environmental systems also.

Thus although many scientists are resistant to, or are at least cautious about, accepting the evidence offered by James Lovelock for the cybernetic character of the earth's environment as a whole, this evidence needs to be seen within a context in which self-organising and self-maintaining processes have been found in every branch of science.[13] What is more, it seems extremely difficult to understand in any other terms how the different parameters of the environment of the earth as a whole have been maintained in a potentially unstable state over so many millions of years and in a form hospitable to life. That state has not been completely constant but has itself changed in response to the development of life within it. In other words, life as it has evolved has itself formed part of the system which has adapted accordingly.

Lovelock's claims do, however, meet also the objection that they cannot be true as the world lacks a nervous system which could effect such overall self-regulating functions. This, however, appears to be only one instance of

---

[13] see e g Paul Davies *The Cosmic Blueprint* (1987) p 1 & pp 131-2

the challenge that is increasingly facing scientists of demonstrating how localised interactions can exercise global control over a wide range of processes and systems.[14] It needs also to be pointed out that many low-level organisms lack a nervous system and if the earth is to be thought of as an organism, it is clearly a very low level organism, despite its size — indeed such a low level as to make the very word 'organism' questionable. Higher grade organisms maintain themselves at far higher levels of order. Typically, they have to grow and develop and respond to very varied, rapidly changing and often hostile environments and it is in response that they have developed specialised organs and the necessary coordinating systems. In contrast, changes in the earth's external environment are mostly very slow and not highly differentiated: and the internal changes to which the earth's system responds are mostly of a global character. Arguably, therefore, the earth has not needed to develop anything comparable to a nervous system. This suggests, in other words, that we need to see the development of specialised organs and nervous systems as specialised forms taken by more fundamental attributes inherent even in lower level entities of which the earth is one. We shall see how this idea finds a wider context later.

Faced with the evidence of the need for, and for the operation of, such dynamic cybernetic forces at a wide range of levels, it seems, therefore, extremely improbable that the evolutionary process can be explained entirely in terms of random mutations and natural selection, fundamental as these are. Rather, it seems that we must recognise the dynamic, integrating, forces which energise the process. What is more, those ordering forces seemingly operate over systems as a whole and are therefore in some sense non-local. But, of course, for such forces to operate, the systems have to have a considerable measure of freedom and that freedom allows for decay as well as for the creation of order.

When we seek to find how this understanding of the natural world finds a place within the theological picture being developed here, it is at once apparent that such open systems offer much more scope for God to 'intervene' than was seemingly available when science offered only deterministic systems. The idea of God 'intervening' in such open systems, however, assumes that the systems have some natural mode of operation without God. This is essentially the Western picture. In the picture being developed here, however, we cannot think of God 'intervening', as it were from the margins. Rather, God is in the system as a whole, sustaining it and seeking to restore and develop it. The system has evolved around the will and act of God: the will of God is in a sense central to such systems which

---

[14] see e g Paul Davies *op cit* p 104ff

use their freedom freely to explore within his plenitude. We may, however, think of the system deviating destructively when for some reason it closes itself off from the dynamic energies of God and we may think of God manifesting himself more fully as it uses his creative powers to develop its order; and at higher levels, God manifests himself in understanding, love and healing, in beauty and even in miracles, when the system for some reason opens itself more fully to him.

Whereas pictures of God 'intervening' in a largely autonomous world emphasise his living will at the expense of his sovereignty, but raise unanswerable questions about his priorities, a picture of God as unchangingly seeking entry to creation can easily see him as impersonal: as like a head of water behind a dam that flows wherever openings offer. This picture, too, fails, however, in that it gives insufficient weight to the almost infinite variety of personal responses that need to flow from the plenitude of God: responses that have to take account of the state of development of human beings and other systems. Thus at a physical level, the forces of God that can be accepted by a system are purely physical: they are the sustaining, creative and healing forces that we have termed 'cybernetic'. But equally, to meet the psychological and spiritual needs of human beings, there flow from the plenitude of God, understanding, intelligent, loving and guiding forces which manifest themselves in living creatures: in fact, in their full form, they *are* the Holy Spirit and so God.

It is important to realise, however, that God has always to respect the freedom of creation. He cannot force upon it more than it can accept freely. Thus prayer is not necessarily associated with humility and openness and however strong and piteous the prayer, God cannot force entry. God cannot, therefore, self-consistently change the orbit of the planets or even heal a person who, often far below the level of consciousness, at a purely physical level, is, perhaps instinctively, clinging to life and so is closed to him. We are not in full control even of our own minds and bodies, however much we may desperately want to be, though it is possible for us to influence them. What is more, God must be able to see the future for if he could not, he could respond to the situation of his creatures only as seen at that moment. But, as we often find in retrospect, that would be a recipe for disaster. That response by God to such openness has, therefore, in some way to include the future: something a little less mysterious when we realise that God is outside time and, indeed, in creating the world minute by minute, he is creating time with it.

This kind of understanding takes us a little way forward in understanding why God may be seen sometimes to act in trivial events yet to ignore great disasters. God does not, however, distinguish between important and trivial when creation opens itself to him: his plenitude embraces and surpasses both. And although the argument can be advanced only with many reservations and with great sensitivity, it is clear that the growth and development of the personality in Christ can in some circumstances be advanced by suffering: something that we shall have to face when we consider the implications of the crucifixion.

This then leads us to consider the form of God's relation to the world and in particular its relation to his will. It is easy to think of the will of God as some distant, unbending pathway. God, however, is the living God, dynamically seeking to create, sustain and heal. In other words, the analogy of God acting and behaving in the world cybernetically may be more than analogy. We have to use such knowledge of the world as we try to extend our understanding up to God. It is, therefore, tempting to think of God, not just as a person but as in some sense a vast living organism embracing the world: a view emphasised if we recall that God, though infinite in the sense of being unlimited by anything other than God, has as aspects of his plenitude, within his life, both the order and reason of the Divine Christ and the healing, sustaining, guiding and creating roles of the Holy Spirit. But God is not so much like a living organism as living organisms are in limited ways like him: and man has the fullest potential to be in his image and likeness. As Israel knew, God is actively present in the world, in its normal as well as in its exceptional phases, and the world is in God. To think of God as the all-embracing plenitude within whom the world finds its existence — sustaining, healing, guiding and creating it — thus becomes intelligible.

The Call of Love

As for the place of love within this picture, the dynamic forces of creation take this form only at the higher evolutionary levels, as an underlying creative force that can easily be blinded or distorted. In its full form, it is revealed in this world only in those men and women who have attained a large measure of maturity and wholeness. In its full form it is not, therefore, an attribute of everyman, and given the current ethos of experimental psychology and philosophy, it is not surprising that love proves to be an emotion that finds little place within such studies, at any rate in Britain. Iris Murdoch notes that contemporary philosophers frequently connect consciousness with virtue, and although they constantly talk of freedom, they rarely talk of love.[15] Yet love is a concept that is basic to Christian understanding. It can be described as a tendency towards ultimate union or unity: typically, therefore, it seeks fulfillment in union with another person of the opposite sex.

---

[15] I Murdoch *The Sovereignty of the Good* (1970) p 2

In practice, however, in the very nature of the evolving and developmental character of life, even the most fulfilling human relationship is temporary and incomplete. What is more, in any relationship where love is incomplete and takes the form of need or desire, it can impair growth, either if it is directly destructive of the integrity of one or both partners in a relationship or it becomes an end in itself, so foreclosing on further growth. Thus there are deep instinctive forces that lead to the sexual manifestations of love; and emotional insecurity and immaturity lead to a need to seek security by possessiveness towards whatever objects are felt to enhance it, even when such possession cannot rationally achieve this and may limit and even destroy its object and so be self-defeating. All such manifestations of love need, however, to be understood as limited and warped manifestations of God and, more specifically, of the Holy Spirit: indeed, all other emotions can be regarded as manifestations, in limited or warped form, of frustration of, or seeking for, union or unity. Love, including such limited and warped forms, can thus be recognised in the process of enhancement of order leading, in principle, to fuller participation in the life of God. In this sense, it is the activity of the Holy Spirit and the motivating force of creativity.

As for the form of love by man for God, it is at least questionable whether we should see its highest forms in rigorous, devout, intensely focussed dedication to God or Christ, expressing itself mainly in personal and corporate devotion: it is questionable, therefore, whether it offers any encouragment to potential 'athletes of God'. Rather, the highest form of the love of God is to be seen in an attitude that is relaxed though disciplined; open to the world including animals and even plants; an understanding, outward-looking, caring attitude that expresses confidence, joy, wonder and, when circumstances allow, playfulness; an attitude that sees the world as a revelation of an ever-present joyous God, even when his manifestations are so obscured and perverted as to evoke deep sadness and sorrow.

We can, on this basis, understand why the mature, rational person has little need to possess and control for his own immediate satisfaction, for he has considerable tolerance of uncertainty. In theological terms, he feels secure in the love of God and has little fear of being separated from him. He can thus open himself so as to respond to a much wider range of life-enhancing, creative, ordering and often unexpected experiences.

All such views need, however, to be qualified, for they may suggest a greater flexibility of response than is to be found in living creatures. It is, therfore, important equally to stress the many factors which can obscure and deflect any such response and the constraints to which organisms are subject. Though we might expect the intelligence and constancy of God to reveal themselves in the response of living creatures, God is himself subject to the all-important constraint that he cannot impose his will, even in the interests of the creature: the purposes of God must always be accepted freely. In practice, therefore, since all creatures lack freedom adequately to respond, the outcome will fall far short of the purposes of God. Given the extremely complex structure of say a living embryo, the parameters of growth deriving from that structure and the environment are very restrictive: but there is some flexibility and that may in some circumstances allow a damaged embryo to attain the same broad end as the undamaged embryo. Similarly, different organisms that have very different genetic endowments may tend to develop broadly to the same kind of structure. Perhaps we can say, therefore, that the genetic endowment of an organism sets certain constraints which channel creative activity and provides a framework offering scope, depending on its level of organisation, for intelligence and purpose; and the outcome is constrained also by a wide range of environmental factors all of which influence and constrain efforts for survival in, and development from, the present state of the organism.

Within the limits of a given structure, therefore, which in its nature is dynamic, there will be forces which tend to restore and increase the order of the system but these same forces can tend also to constrain or disrupt it. In man, as in higher animals, integrative tendencies which entail a certain build-up of tension, which then resolves itself by enhancing the order of a system, are associated with pleasurable emotions such as satisfaction, pleasure and joy. Such tendencies take specific and largely genetically determined form in behaviour and emotion associated with sex and reproduction but reveal themselves also in play, and, in man, in the entire range of creative activities on which we comment further later. But because openness and so a certain measure of uncertainty and tension are necessary to further growth of the personality, for those who cannot tolerate such a build-up of tension, satisfactions associated with the resolution of tension are typically sought too easily and cheaply and lead to the stultification of growth and to foreclosure. On the other hand, a situation that threatens the existing order of the system may demand a change in the situation or the removal of the system from the threat and may so lead either to aggression and attack, which in man and higher animals are associated with anger, or with retreat which is associated with fear: and if neither such resolution is available, there occurs anxiety.

The Demands of Faith

Almost inevitably, however, most men, even when inspired by the best intentions, tend to reduce the plenitude and unexpectedness of life in God to terms which fit their own limited and largely static understanding. Stable systems and patterns of thought are essential to all life but without a deep, rational and balanced faith, they fail to be seen as steps on the way to even deeper and more adequate systems and patterns of understanding. Their provisional nature has thus only too rarely been recognised and set in the context of the richness of the divine life whose very plenitude requires that each in turn has to be broken up so as to be replaced by something better. It is precisely this process that marks the progress of science in its own specialised fields and more centrally constitutes the pilgrimage of life towards wholeness and maturity and life in God. Yet, despite this, the Christian Churches have, throughout their long history, often offered fairly classic instances of the operation of closed systems which have perpetuated and even lauded immaturity.

It can be seen, therefore, that openness to ever new situations requires a deep orientating faith if it is not to be an openness to disaster; whereas, all too often, faith is seen in terms of a determination to adhere to existing situations and is often a rationalisation of that sense of insecurity associated with a lack of faith. In this profound sense, sin in terms of specific deviations including moral deviations from the will of God perpetrated by 'bad' men may be less heinous and destructive than that foreclosure against the creativity of God that, as Jesus found, is often found amongst the 'good', and is a sin against the Holy Spirit.

What is more, in so far as creative forces themselves require a breaking up of that premature order and its replacement by an openness to their further development, this entails also the threat of collapse of that order — a threat that can be met only by faith that allows full openness to the reason and love of God which may at that point be many leaps ahead. In so far, the joy of creation entails the risk of tragedy at many levels, notwithstanding that it is one of the marks of more highly developed systems, and in particular of human beings, that they have developed in such a way that their ability to learn allows for great resilience, flexibility and openness, at any rate at the early stages of life, despite the rigidities and warping that so often ensue as men get older. As Jesus said: suffer the little children to come onto me. As we shall see, it is that openness that Jesus found in children and in those near the bottom of society — the tax gatherers and prostitutes — and which he could not find, other than exceptionally, amongst those with a more settled, satisfying pattern of life who needed desperately to preserve it. It is precisely in this sense, as we shall see, that in overcoming sin, one needs to lose one's life in order to gain it.

CHAPTER NINETEEN

CHANCE AND PROVIDENCE

This is no sentimental picture that is emerging: how could it be, given the world we live in? The Jewish emphasis on God as a jealous God (Ex 20 5; 34 14; Deut 4 24; 5 9; 6 15; Josh 24 19) and their claim that his wrath is to be feared, is no less part of the Christian message than his ever present forgiveness and his mercy and his love. What is more, sin can occur without conscious intent and at all levels of creation, but however it occurs, sin incurs his wrath in the form of the self-destructiveness of deviation from his will. This, however, raises the question precisely how God can create, sustain and ultimately redeem a world where over large areas, chance is king.

In recent years there have been a number of studies of the relationship of chance to the providence of God. Perhaps the most comprehensive and important is D J Bartholomew's *God of Chance* (1984), but an earlier work, *Chance and Providence* (1959) by W G Pollard and the comments of Arthur Peacocke, notably in *Creation and the World of Science* (1979) and in *God and the New Biology* (1986) are very relevant. Much of the discussion subsequent to 1972 has had regard to Jacques Monod's *Chance and Necessity* (1972) which itself was the subject of an important commentary in *Beyond Chance and Necessity,* edited by J Lewis (1974). To those who have read the views of these authors, which are reviewed by Bartholomew, it will be obvious how substantial are their divergences within both science and theology and so in the implications of each subject for the other. To comment on these works in any detail would be beyond the scope of this study but the picture that has been emerging in these pages needs to be related to certain basic features of them. One specific point stands out: in the indexes of none of these works does the 'wrath' of God feature.

The first in time of these works was that of Pollard, whose *Chance and Providence* was published in 1959. He wrote as both physicist and theologian and sought to do justice to both fields. Pollard appreciated that much of the uncertainty in the world springs from our ignorance but he recognised an irreducible randomness at sub-atomic level which is not open to scientific explanation and there he saw the hand of God. He distinguished the uncertainties in science and notably in sub-atomic physics from the uncertainties arising from the interactions of seemingly unrelated chains of events in history. This important distinction features in the work of Eigen and Winkler, *The Laws of the Game* (1982), where, as we noted earlier, they compare the world to a vast game in which only the rules are laid down and it is the interplay of the rules and the events of chance that determine the game — which can itself be identified with neither separately.

Chance, however, as Pollard saw it, was not ultimately a blind process for he saw God in deliberate control of every event in the cosmos. For him, therefore, there emerged an unresolved paradox between the control of God over creation and the freedom of man: a paradox which he compared with complementarity of electrons as particles and waves in quantum physics.

In contrast, Monod, who saw the world as the product of blind chance, argued that this struck at the root of any idea of its being the product of a purposeful God. Peacocke, however, stressed the positive role of chance in allowing all possible potentialities to become actual. In other words, he broadly accepted Monod's science, though amplified and qualified by later work, notably by Prigogine and Eigen, but saw it as the way in which God, whom he saw as present in, as well as transcending, creation, realises his plans.

Bartholomew, also, accepted the view that God uses chance to ensure the variety, resilience and freedom necessary for creation but took a more external view of God as working from outside the world. He argued that the doctrine of creation was not only compatible with the role of chance but requires it if people are to 'grow into free responsible children of their heavenly father.'[1] This led him to conclude that most events are not planned by God for immediate and specific ends. While, therefore, he made God ultimately responsible for everything, he saw him as not intimately involved in all things and emphasised that we do not diminish God if the limitations on his power and knowledge are of his own choosing.

The position that has emerged in this study accepts the scientific picture presented by, for instance, Monod, that there is a genuine indeterminacy in the heart of matter. It accepts the views of Pollard and Peacocke that God is intimately and directly involved in and present in creation, but it does not accept that this requires God to be directly responsible for everything that happens in it, as distinct from its consequences. It therefore seeks a path between the view of Pollard that God's presence requires total control and responsibility and Bartholomew's view that God's giving freedom implies that God is not directly involved in all things. Though the view emerging here sees God as creating the world to share in his life, it sees that sharing as entailing a sharing in his freedom either to grow in accordance with his creative will or to deviate from it. In this way, God continuously seeks to sustain and guide creation into his life but does not seek to force it to remain within his life. He thus gives it freedom to deviate from it; and though it incurs a heavy cost in doing so, (his wrath), he unreservedly welcomes it back into his life at any point (his mercy).

---

[1] *God of Chance* (1984) p 145

The resulting picture can be summarised thus: at atomic level and seemingly at higher levels, too, genuinely random events occur, some of which lead to creative outcomes but most of which are destructive of the level of order from which they occur. As we have sought to show, however, God is present in every such event and it is his creative energy that gives rise to it. But each dynamic, creative event carries with it freedom to direct itself in accordance with the creative will of God towards higher levels of order or to deviate from it; and at lower levels of creation, God's reason and love, which would lead it to remain in accordance with God's creative will, are lacking. There are, therefore, deviations from the creative will of God which are seemingly random at all levels save the highest.

As we shall see, at the higher levels, man assumes some moral responsibility for his actions which are increasingly constrained by reason and by love, and the higher the levels of order attained, the more these operate. It is the love of God for his creation that sustains it but that love entails freedom in order that creation may make a loving response: and that freedom is also freedom to deviate from his love and from his order. Such deviation is destructive of that love and order and, being self-destructive, in so far invokes the wrath of God. God does not, therefore, relinquish control of creation in the sense of giving it existence apart from his existence. In deviating, however, it decreases its hold on the life of God and in some measure destroys its freedom to find fulfillment in his life: a fulfillment which has to be fully free and entails perfect service to his will. God therefore relinquishes control of his creation only in the sense that he allows the creation which he sustains to grow within his life or self-destructively to deviate from it. But this rather simple picture has to be elaborated by recognising that the order of creation exists at many levels and in systems which have varying degrees of autonomy from one another. The linkage and degrees of dependence and interdependence are such that some deviations are lethal not only to the unit directly involved but to larger systems of which it is part and with which it is linked. Many deviations, however, do not destroy but limit and cripple. And such is the plenitude of God that these limitations of the divine plenitude and the paths of growth into it are so various that creation takes the multiplicity of interacting forms which we find in the natural world, all cooperating and competing to participate more fully in the life of God in so far as the rigidities of their structures allow: rigidities that are themselves the result of foreclosures which deviate from the underlying need for openness to and faith in the creative will of God.

It follows that creation and destruction both occur within the life of God and are to be thought of in terms of creative, dynamic processes tending towards greater or lesser participation in his order. However, any deviation, whether by frustrating the creativity of God by foreclosing on further growth, or by dissipating or actively disordering an existing system, is parasitic on that system, which, in so far as it exists at all, can do so only when sustained by his dynamic will and act. Even the lowest levels of matter, where the state of near disorder prevails, are sustained by the creative will of God who is continually bringing energy into existence despite its constant frustration of his will by deviations. In this carefully qualified sense, therefore, we can say that there is no evil actually in the life of God itself though there is continuous interplay of the forces directed to the creation, restoring and sustaining of its order and those directed to its dissipation. In this sense, we can see sin as *privatio boni* for we have to see the waste, suffering and evil of the world as deviations from a dynamic and creative flow and in terms of the hindering of development of the standing patterns in it or of their dissipation and destruction.

CHAPTER TWENTY

PHYSICAL, MENTAL & SPIRITUAL

If God is thought of as 'outside' the world, creating it *ad extra*, it is natural to think of him as spiritual and of creation as a form of materialisation by some kind of 'outreach'. In that case, the sharp contrast drawn between God and the world by the Western Churches finds its counterpart in a contrast between spiritual and physical: though just how a spiritual God creates a physical world remains wrapped in obscurity save as one instance of his claimed ability to do anything whatever. When, however, we think of God creating the physical world within himself, and of its order structuring it and rendering it transparent to — as carrying — his attributes, there is implicit a picture of God — and so of the spiritual — as in some sense present in or underlying the physical processes and matter. In this case the need becomes more pressing to clarify the sense in which we are to understand the relationship of God who is spiritual to the physical world. But before it is possible to pursue the relationship of the spiritual to matter, we need to have some understanding of what is meant by matter.

That matter is reducible to energy and is to be thought of in highly dynamic terms, is now a truism of science. Yet, as Michael Lockwood says, most philosophers who have tackled the body-mind problem 'have tended to regard matter as having a conceptual solidity to match its supposed literal solidity;' and in so seeking to accomodate mind to the material world, 'all the "give" has had to be on the side of mind.'[1]

As he says, however, quantum mechanics has robbed matter of its conceptual quite as much as its literal solidity and both, philosophically speaking, are alike in being profoundly mysterious.[2] Similarly, Bohm notes that at present many physicists tend to adopt the attitude that our overall views concerning the nature of reality are of little or no importance, but in so doing, they are left with whatever (generally inadequate) world views happen to be at hand, such as of particles as the ultimate building blocks of reality.[3]

Bohm goes on to remark that such ideas are now highly confused, for quantum physics has shown that such 'particles' move discontinuously and are also waves.[4] He suggests that an atomic particle can perhaps best be regarded as a poorly defined cloud, dependent for its particular form on the whole environment, including the observing instrument.

---

[1] *Mind Brain and the Quantum* (1989) p ix

[2] *op cit* (1989) p x

[3] *Wholeness and the Implicate Order* (1980) p xiii

[4] *op cit* (1980) p xiii

On this understanding one can no longer maintain the division between observer and observed which is implicit in the atomistic view that regards each of these as separate aggregates of atoms.[5]   Indeed, as Michael Lockwood notes, 'The apparent "entanglement" within quantum mechanics, of observer with observed, is a far subtler and far more mysterious affair than the popular account would suggest.... What the quantum-mechanical measurement problem is really alerting us to, .. is a deep problem as to how consciousness (specifically, the consciousness of the observer) fits into, or maps on to, the physical world. And that, of course, is the question that lies at the heart of the traditional mind-body problem.'[6]

Quantum Mechanics is *the* theory of matter as currently conceived, but when we seek from physicists a picture of the nature of matter more appropriate than that of particles, we find, as we have already noted, that most seek to avoid commitment to any wider implications of quantum physics for the understanding of reality. Thus some physicists regard quantum theory as a calculus of knowledge and do not enquire further about how this knowledge is obtained. Some — the supporters of the Copenhagen interpretation — emphasise the role of the measuring apparatus which plays an objectifying role in determining the outcome of any quantum experiment. Yet it seems less than clear how at these levels the dependability of the instruments is to be reconciled with the uncertainty of the very constituents of the instruments, as well as the material that is being experimented on. Yet other physicists have sought to trace back the chains of events to the consciousness of the observer; while a fourth group imagine that every possible outcome of an act of quantum measurement is realised and that those that are not realised in this world are realised in others, so that other worlds are being created in continuous profusion. Differing from all these are the views of Bohm who argues that all events are causally determined but some of these causes — the so-called 'hidden variables' — are inaccessible to us.[7]

Only probably a small minority of physicists have supported Bohm's view but some of his related ideas are conceptually of relevance to the argument being developed here. In particular, Bohm claims that all matter is of the nature of a 'universal flux that cannot be defined explicitly, but which can be known only implicitly, as indicated by the explicitly definable forms and shapes, some stable and some unstable, that can be abstracted from the universal flux.'[8] He goes on to insist that not only is everything changing

---

[5] *op cit* (1980) p 9

[6] *op cit* (1989) p x

[7] see e g   J Polkinghorne *One World* (1986) pp 47-8 & p 10

[8] *op cit* (1980) p 6

but all is flux. This is to say, what is is the process of becoming itself, while all objects, events, entities, conditions, structures, and so on are forms that can be abstracted from this process.[9] And he comments that 'even the "elementary particles" can be created, annihilated and transformed, and this indicates that not even these can be ultimate substances, but rather, that they too are relatively constant forms, abstracted from some deeper level of movement.'[10]

Bohm describes this deeper level more explicitly when he says that what we call empty space contains an immense background of energy, and matter as we know it is a small, 'quantized' wavelike excitation on top of this background, rather like a tiny ripple on a vast sea. 'In current physical theories, one avoids the explicit consideration of this background by calculating only the difference between the energy of empty space and that of space with matter in it.'[11] As Paul Davies comments: 'What might appear to be empty space is, therefore, a seething ferment of virtual particles. A vacuum is not inert and featureless, but alive with throbbing energy and vitality. A "real" particle such as an electron must always be viewed against this background of frenetic activity.'[12] And Frijof Capra says: 'Modern physics thus pictures matter not at all as inert, but as being in a continuous dancing and vibrating motion whose rhythmic patterns are determined by the molecular, atomic and nuclear structures.'[13]

It seems, therefore, that for the purpose of this study, we should no longer think of the physical world in terms of a basically static structure of interacting particles. What is more, we should not think of them as located in empty space. 'There is no space outside the universe. ... Space came out of the big bang, and not the other way round. ... Many cosmologists believe that time did not exist before the big bang, i e that there was no "before". One of the lessons of the new physics is that space and time are not simply there, they form part of the physical universe.'[14] We may, therefore, think rather of a continuous energy dance with physical objects, processes and events as standing patterns or systems in it that develop and decay through 'internal' characteristics of the dance and which organise themselves spatially and temporally. Some of these systems are relatively stable over

---

[9] op cit   (1980) p 48

[10] op cit   (1980) p 49

[11] op cit   (1980) p 191

[12] Superforce   (1984) p 104

[13] The Tao of Physics in *Science and Consciousness*   ed M Cazenave (1984) p 25

[14] Superforce   (1984) p 16

long periods, some are highly transitory, and they interact throughout the entire flux in many complex ways.

Indeed, scientists have been seeking to carry their understanding back to something underlying space and time and to before the big bang in order to understand what might have brought it about. What seems tentatively to be emerging is that the vacuum energy can arrange itself in more than one way by adopting any of a number of states of very different energy levels. These involve leaps by huge amounts from one vacuum state to another, and at the highest levels there are seemingly equally enormous changes in pressure. What is more, these pressures are sufficiently strongly repulsive to have caused the vast explosion of the big bang. At a very early stage, however, these forces fade into insignificance, leaving the evolution of the universe to take place as normally understood. As Davies says, this cosmic bootstrap comes close to the theological concept of creation *ex nihilo* and he points to a group of distinguished American scientists who believe in one sense or another that 'nothing is unstable' and that the physical universe blossomed forth spontaneously out of nothing, driven by the laws of physics. He comments that 'matter, energy, space, time, forces, fields, order and structure: these are all items on the Creator's shopping list, the indispensable requirement for a universe. The new physics holds out a tantalising promise that we might explain from science how all of these things came to exist.'[15]

Now these ideas of a cosmic bootstrap have been described as 'speculation squared' and to try to relate them to theology compounds this. But although there is still a big gap, it may be clear that there is here a possible convergence between science and an understanding of God in the form being presented in this book; and the way in which their ultimate convergence may come about becomes conceivable. But if it is to become conceivable, it is clear that the deep conceptual separation of God and the world, of spiritual and matter, which enables scientists to disregard the spiritual as of no possible relevance to science and some theologians to disregard science as of no relevance to theology, will have to be discarded. In particular, we are suggesting, the form of the physical world may eventually be understood as deriving from the very nature of the inner dynamics of the life of God: for the plenitude of God requires his creativity to take the form of a potential hierarchy of microcosms of himself, incorporating within them and structured by the inherent order of his Word, the Son. The freedom inherent in that creativity requires that his creation should attain that order, step by step, as it develops into the full life of God; yet because creation cannot manifest and respond fully to his order and

---

[15] *Superforce* (1984) pp 199-200 & 204

reason and his love until it has entered fully into his life, at lower levels, it therefore deviates from and forecloses against the creative will of God, resulting in the proliferation of forms of this world, each of which explores and presents different facets of his plenitude. The evolutionary process has, therefore, to start in the emptying of the divine life to the point furthest removed from its ordered plenitude: a point where chaos operates. This chaos veils creation from his plenitude and protects it against reabsorption into his life; and the entire spatial and temporal process comes into existence at that point as the opening up of the timeless and spaceless eternity of the plenitude of God. This spiritual plenitude in which there is otherwise neither a 'beyond' nor a 'before', must, therefore, almost certainly be understood as in some way incorporating energy and order in a profound and subtle form that is glimpsed in quantum physics.

We can see this further when we enquire about the way in which the spiritual may take material form. It will be recalled that in theological terms we have found a direct attribution of the 'order' of the world to the Divine Christ and its directed creativity to the Holy Spirit and we have found sin — in the widest sense of the word — identified with deviation from that order and with frustration of its further development. Physics itself recognises disorder in terms of entropy which is directly related to temperature, the lower the temperature, the greater being the order. The question therefore arises whether this has any implications relevant to the picture being developed here.

In a lecture given in 1950, F E Simon said: 'In a somewhat abbreviated way one can say that all substances at absolute zero are in a state of perfect order — a state of affairs only possible in a quantum world.'[16] And Bohm says that according to the quantum theory, a crystal at absolute zero allows electrons to pass through it without scattering. They go through it as if the space were empty. If the temperature is raised, inhomogeneities appear, and these scatter electrons. 'If one were to use such electrons to observe the crystal ... what would appear would be just the inhomogeneities. It would then appear that the inhomogeneities exist independently and that the main body of the crystal was sheer nothingness.' And he goes on to say: 'It is being suggested here, then, that what we perceive through the senses as empty space is actually the plenum, which is the ground for the existence of everything, including ourselves. The things that appear to our senses are derivative forms and their true meaning can be seen only when we consider the plenum, in which they are generated and sustained, and into which they

---

[16] F E Simon et al *Low Temperature Physics* (1952) p 5

must ultimately vanish.'[17] The importance of this suggestion in the context of this book will be obvious.

Bohm is not alone amongst physicists in suggesting some deeper sub-stratum that underlies time and space. Thus John Wheeler has commented that if we are ever going to find an element of nature that explains space and time, we surely have to find something that is deeper than space and time — something that itself has no localization in space and time.[18] And John Bell is strongly sympathetic to going back to the idea of an aether.[19]

Even at absolute zero, however, some constant 'quivering' is still going on in the vacuum field. It would seem, therefore, that there are still features of the physical world present in the vacuum field even at this point and, if we regard the 'physical' as exclusive of the 'spiritual', this may be felt to be getting us no nearer to understanding the relationship of this activity to God. However, the idea that the plenum needs to be thought of as physical *or* spiritual derives from the Western contrast between God and creation. So, by implication, the idea of God including the world, as understood by the older tradition, should find its counterpart in the idea of the spiritual including the physical as one specific form which it can take in the special circumstances of creation which we have described.

Since, therefore, the plenum out of which all this energy emerges and into which it disappears is itself unobservable by physical systems, including the sense mechanisms and the physical processes that they necessarily use, and it is in that sense 'nothing'; since, secondly, as this energy organises itself to higher and higher levels of order — order which is ultimately in and of the plenum, it must be from the plenum itself that life, consciousness, understanding, love and holiness emerge: then it also seems reasonable to suggest that the plenum is not itself just physical in any ordinarily understood sense, and the energy which constitutes the physical is a feature of or form taken by the plenum: a form which is in certain circumstances observable by way of our physical instruments and the sense mechanisms. These circumstances appear to be when disorder occurs around the ordered systems in the plenum and reveals through our physical instruments and sensory systems the order underlying it. By implication, if the order were perfect there could be no such physical interaction and so there would be nothing observed. But creativity involves leaps to higher levels of order and for there to be creativity, a certain freedom and openness and so a certain openness to disorder and instability is required.

---

[17] *op cit* (1980) pp 191-2

[18] *The Ghost in the Atom* ed P Davies and J R Brown (1986) p 39

[19] *op cit* (1986) pp 48ff

If, then, the physical is a particular form taken by the spiritual in certain circumstances, perhaps the vacuum field with virtual particles continuously emerging from and falling back into the plenum may be the point of transition. It is the point at which God, by an act of abnegation, offers himself in a state bereft of the higher levels of order which allow his life, consciousness, reason, love and holiness to manifest themselves. But God at this originating stage only very exceptionally finds response from his creation in attaining higher levels of order within a universe that is still largely empty and unformed. When, therefore, Paul Davies comments: 'Empty space does not appear a very promising subject for study, yet it holds the key to the full understanding of the forces of nature',[20] it seems that this statement, made in the context of physics, may well prove to be equally true about natural theology.

This picture then has further implications for if we are to discard the Western understanding of the separation of God and the world, this must carry through into understandings of the body-mind relationship. In particular, it suggests that the spiritual must in some way itself have mental and physical attributes. More specifically, it suggests that life and consciousness in some sense underlie and are inherent in the ground from which the ordered systems of creation develop; but that they are manifested and experienced by the systems concerned only when they attain the relevant degree of order and flexibility of response to the chains of events which reach them from the surrounding world.

Findings of Michael Lockwood in *Mind Brain and the Quantum* are very relevant to this theme though only brief reference to them can be made here. Lockwood discusses at length various understandings of the relationship of our consciousness to the world around us and reaches the view that the phenomenal qualities presented in perception, and other so-called 'raw feels' are among the intrinsic attributes of certain physical states of the brain.[21] 'Why should one not think of awareness precisely as disclosing certain intrinsic attributes of states of, or events within, our brains — intrinsic attributes moreover, which do not, in general, depend for their existence on their being sensed.'[22] And he adds that if mental states are brain states, then introspection is already telling us that there is a lot more to the matter of the brain than there is currently room for in the physicist's philosophy. Lockwood then goes on to consider consciousness in terms of quantum physics and suggests tentatively that the relevant physical counterpart of consciousness in the brain may prove to be the quantum-mechanical state

---

[20] *Superforce* (1984) p 104

[21] *op cit* (1989) p 160

[22] *op cit* (1989) p 162

known as Bose condensation.[23] As he notes, there is a certain amount of indirect evidence that coherent states of this kind exist in biological systems and calculations suggest that they would be capable of carrying, within the space of a cubic centimetre or less, as many bits of information as are contained within the maximum range of consciousness at one time.[24]

Two further points are worth making here. Whereas the Western understanding sees natural and supernatural, physical, mental and spiritual, as separate and different features of the world, in the picture being presented here, this is not so. The oneness of the world is here emphasised: spiritual is seen as the ultimate ground or nature of the world in all its plenitude; mental can, perhaps, then be regarded as a lower level, differentiated form of the spiritual; and physical, as we shall see further, may be regarded as an aspect, mode or dimension of the spiritual. Indeed, as is already entailed in what has been said, it may prove that all mental events have some kind of minute physical aspect. It is worth noting that Roger Penrose says: 'Descriptions of quantum theory appear to apply sensibly (usefully?) only at the so-called quantum level — of molecules, atoms or subatomic particles, but also at larger dimensions, so long as alternative possibilities remain very small.'[25] And he envisages that when a correct theory of quantum gravity arrives, it may then become possible to elucidate the phenomena of consciousness in terms of it. He adds that, in that event, consciousness itself will fit only very uncomfortably into our present conventional space-time descriptions.[26]

We shall have to touch on these issues again later when we come to consider the problems associated with understandings of the physical world as transitory. But first we need to consider mind in its personal and social settings, and in particular, the support for the arguments being set out here that is to be found in the views of Thomas Nagel.

---

[23] *op cit* (1989) p 252ff

[24] *op cit* (1989) pp 257-8

[25] *The Emperor's New Mind* (1989) p 296

[26] *op cit* (1989) pp 446-7

CHAPTER TWENTY ONE

MIND IN ITS PERSONAL AND SOCIAL SETTINGS

Not surprisingly, the picture of the relationship of God to the world that is emerging in this study carries substantial implications for the understanding of mind; and relevant empirical evidence has the potential either to falsify or support it. We have already seen arguments suggesting that creation needs to be thought of in terms of the development of a hierarchy of potential microcosms of God within his life and we shall point to more empirical evidence for this claim. As we have seen, the underlying order of the world was understood by the early Church as manifesting the order and reason of the Divine Christ. We need now to see the way in which the mind and personality of man, which are to a large extent the product of learning, also come, however imperfectly, to incorporate this order and reason. As Iris Murdoch, speaking of Plato's Philebus, says: 'We should imitate only God and that by sorting out and emphasising and attending to harmonious patterns which are already latent in the universe.'[1] In coming to see how this 'imitation' comes about, light will be cast on certain deeply embedded dichotomies such as subjective and objective, mental and physical and mind and body.

The Structuring of Mind

We have already referred at several points to the work of Piaget. Though his work has been subject to a lot of criticism of emphasis and detail, it stands as a massive contribution to understanding in this field.[2] Piaget showed how from infancy we discriminate the uniformities, the consistencies, in the continuous flow of our experiences. Thereby the tendency is to eliminate the disorder in which these consistencies are embedded and to stabilise them, rendering them relatively static; a tendency which, if weight is to be put on ideas in the mind of God, points in this direction. We then classify and conceptualise these consistencies to which we normally give names; and in due course, after taking a conceptual leap, we repeat the process at a higher level, thereby forming hypotheses to explain these concepts and so on at many stages. These processes take place at most levels without conscious intent and as the process takes place from

---

[1] *The Fire and the Sun* (1977) p 12

[2] M Boden *Piaget* (1979) offers a brief and perceptive account of his work

infancy, we build up a very broad-based hierarchy of abstractions to higher and more embracing levels which give meaning to subsequent experiences.[3]

The idea that there are many levels of order embedded within the disorder of the world around us and in our experiences of it is of profound theological significance within the picture being presented here, both for our understanding of that order, of the Divine Christ, and of the way in which our personalities structure themselves and develop on the basis of that order, thereby coming to participate more fully in Christ. That process of discrimination of uniformities, of consistencies, and of learning to interpret each new experience in terms of them, is deeply rooted in the entire evolutionary process. Peter Munz points out that, without such regularities, there could be no adaptation by natural selection. 'Every organism which is adapted is adapted to the regularities in its environment. It makes no sense to say that it is adapted to the infinitely random vagaries of all possible details and particulars in its environment.'[4] As he notes, organisms 'learn' from the environment, but as species rather than individuals, for only those adapted to expecting the regularities survive and have offspring.[5] In this way, the regularities which exist in nature are transferred to the organisms which survive by natural selection: and as Munz says, the order of nature thus becomes the nature of order.[6] And he remarks that without the ability to abstract and disregard irrelevant details in the environment, the paramecium would not have survived. Progress thus consists in the formulation of theories which are more and more universal. As he says, therefore, progress in this sense is a matter of increasing depth, not an increase in reclaimed land.[7] Clearly, however, there is room for error in this process, for, as Munz remarks, both organisms and conscious knowledge are underdetermined by the environment[8] though the wider the scope of the evidence embraced, the more closely it may be expected to approach towards the truth.

This process of discriminating the order within the flux of our experiences and of forming higher level hypotheses to explain lower level uniformities or hypotheses, is, in practice, fallible at human level, not least because at least some of our learning takes place from our experiences of the disordered, irrational responses of other people. What is more, as we have

---

[3] see e g J Piaget *Biology and Knowledge* (1971) pp 84-5 and p 152; *The Principles of Genetic Epistemology* (1972) pp 46-7

[4] *Our Knowledge of the Growth of Knowledge* (1985)   p 29

[5] *op cit* (1985) p 34

[6] *op cit* (1985) p 35

[7] *op cit* (1985) p 38

[8] *op cit* (1985) p 214

already noted, the formation of new concepts and hypotheses cannot be forced, and, though at higher levels it is guided by reason, at each step to a new conceptual level, a conceptual leap is entailed and such leaps can be erroneous and lead to irrationalities being built-in to the structure of our minds. Such disruption of order and the consequent blocking of further development of that order are the marks of deviation from the creative will of God, of sin: and the wholeness and integrity of our personalities depends, therefore, on how far they can incorporate accurately that order at many levels, in so far making them microcosms of God. No general law can be said to depict or represent any given state of affairs in the world around us: yet the very process of selection in the course of evolution requires that our understanding of the world around us is not far removed from the truth and the wider the range of evidence that it covers, presumably the closer it is to the state of affairs to which it relates. As Munz noted, Konrad Lorenz held that Kant was too modest in his claim that we could never come to know the world as it is, for as Lorenz explains, it is inconceiveable that the world as it really is would have fashioned by chance mutations and selective retention, an instrument of knowledge which would grossly and consistently mislead us about the world in which we seek to survive.[9]

As a simple example which may help to illustrate the learning processes entailed at human level, we may think of a very young child watching clouds passing across the sky, distinguishing them from all the other features in his field of vision, learning their name, and then noting how clouds differ from smoke to which he applies the same procedure. At some point, he will then try to understand something about each and how they originate. This process of forming hypotheses is, of course, taken to extremely advanced levels in science but it is not special to science. It reaches back into the very nature of perception itself, though as Ulric Neisser says: 'Perception is hypothesis testing only in a very general sense.'[10]

M Donaldson, who acknowledges her debt to Piaget, takes this idea further when she comments that 'We approach the world wondering about it, entertaining hypotheses which we are eager to check. And we direct our questions not just to other people but to ourselves, giving ourselves the job of finding the answer by direct exploration of the world. In this way we build up what it is fashionable to call a model of the world — a kind of system of inner representations, the value of which is to help us to anticipate events and help us to deal with them.'[11] It is thus in the light of the formal structures which constitute this conceptual model that we interpret the

---

[9] *op cit* p 185, referring to K Lorenz *Behind the Mirror* (1977)

[10] U Neisser *Cognition and Reality* (1976) p 28

[11] M Donaldson *Children's Minds* (1978) p 68

continuous flow of experiences — primarily sense experiences — reaching us, and select and give meaning to those consistencies and patterns that are of particular relevance to us at any particular moment. Some, or as we shall have grounds to suggest, all of these experiences, then pass back into memory from which, as so enriched, some can be recalled. From time to time we then gain fresh insights into the interpretation and meaning of these experiences, past and present. These insights add to the meaningfulness of all relevant experiences, not just in the future but also in the past. In so far, we continually re-work our memories and add to the model and so to the very structure of our minds and personalities.

Notwithstanding that, as Barbel Inhelder and Jean Piaget note about the concept of personality, 'there is no more vaguely defined notion in psychological vocabulary',[12] the importance of that model and of its development in structuring our minds and personalities will thus be obvious. That importance is confirmed by them when, at the end of that work they say: 'To understand the role of formal structures of thought in the life of the adolescent, we found that in the last analysis we had to place them in his total personality. But, in return, we found that we could not completely understand the growth of his personality without including the transformations of his thinking; thus we had to come back to the development of formal structures.'[13]

When we look in more detail at the conceptual model that each of us establishes and which is made up of many levels of order, we find, as we have already noted, that we build up within it, from our experiences, sub-systems or sub-models. One such conceptual system or model is of that of the objective world; a model which largely but not entirely coincides with that of the physical world. These pictures or models are at many conceptual levels and, as we have noted, these different levels of meaning are brought to bear on all our experiences. These experiences are, therefore, theory-laden but some are more theory-laden than others. Thus when I look, from whatever angle, at a table, whatever form of table it is, I recognise it as a table: what reaches my eye is a very complex welter of forms and colours but what I see involves picking out the relevant form from that welter of shapes and colours in my visual field and giving it meaning. The recognition of it as a table therefore derives from the conceptual model which is built out of earlier experiences. And if a scientist looks at some simple streaks on a photographic plate and recognises them as the marks of some particular form of particle, what he sees may be even simpler but the conceptual contribution is even larger and more abstract. In each case, there

---

[12] *The Growth of Logical Thinking*   (1958)   p 349

[13] *op cit*   (1958)   p 350

is brought to and discriminated from a sense experience, or rather, a shifting sequence of sense experiences, a conceptual understanding of its meaning which has been built up from earlier experiences, including experiences of other people having the same kinds of experience. In this way, we come to recognise that each person's own conceptual system is a particular and limited version of a much larger, more comprehensive, conceptual system, much of which is common to us all, but parts of which are highly specialised so that none of us can grasp the system as a whole.

In other words, we, each of us, grow up as members of communities of language-users and in that sense, our own community plays a major role in structuring the way in which we see the world, contributing to our personal limitations and errors the collective limitations and warps that characterise all such models. These models, which form the very structures of our minds, are thus, as we have seen, potential microcosms of God — a potential that none of us realises fully. This feature of the human condition thus has bearing on the early Christian understanding of Christianity as the Way, the education of man — *paideia* — which offers to each person an understanding that can help to realise that potential in each person as a part of a community, a communion of souls, which itself develops as a larger microcosm of the richness of the divine life.

Our experiences are, however, not only of the world around us. There are also in our experiences uniformities relating to various subjective features. Consciousness, as distinct from unconsciousness, is itself a uniformity, and so are such features of our experiences as attention, emotions, values and even colours. By discriminating and classifying such features, we are able to build-up a conceptual sub-system which broadly we label as mental. Hence we form in some ways contrasting, in some ways complementary, concepts of subjective and objective, mental and physical, and we can build cross-correlations between them, including such correlations as can be discerned between our experiences and our brain states.

Materialism as 'Metaphysical' and a Science of God

This concept-building process brings to attention several points. First, the entire conceptual framework in terms of which we understand each further experience is built up from our earlier experiences, including our experiences of other people, though certainly on a genetic base. But, and following from this, though we can build up higher level and more all-embracing concepts or hypotheses, including hypotheses embracing concepts of ourselves as experiencers, there is no way in which we can get 'outside' or 'behind' our experiences to check on our experiences of physical objects and other people, save by inference from yet further experiences: we are, as it were, locked in an experiential world. Furthermore, in conceptualising not only the objective aspects of our experiences but also the subjective, we objectify both, as well as their correlations.

But if that is so and if we are locked in an experiential world, there is something odd about the materialist view of the world, for the materialists want to explain our experiences entirely in terms of physical events: yet all they know of physical events comes from their experiences, and every attempt that they make to test and falsify their claims can be only in terms of yet further experiences. Of course, the claim that the physical is in this sense prior to our experiences can be held as an article of faith but it has no cash value: it is an entirely 'metaphysical' claim in the sense that it has no empirical roots. This is not, of course, to imply that there are not objective aspects to our experiences or that, having built our objective conceptual understanding of the physical world, we cannot, both conceptually and physically, manipulate one part in relation to others. This is the basis of our normal lives and of science. But it is one thing to operate within and to make inferences about it on the basis of the world of experience: it is quite another to seek to get out of the world of experience — behind it. We are, therefore, in this study in the paradoxical position of seeking to present an understanding of God and the world which would normally be thought of as 'metaphysical', but to do so in a form which has clear empirical roots and is in that sense 'scientific'; yet in so doing, it emerges that the materialist view which is normally thought of as quintessentially scientific, is itself 'metaphysical'.

Within the scenario being presented here, however, order is implicit in the nature and life of God and the physical as we know it appears (following Bohm) as such as a result of disorder occurring around that underlying order. The various attributes of mind then manifest themselves cumulatively as ordered systems develop. These systems develop by drawing energy and order (and information is a form of order) from other parts of the system, and the mechanisms for doing so in the higher level organisms become highly specific and specialised. The consciousness of each human being is therefore at a deeper level one of the attributes of God manifesting itself through the order of the organism; but the form taken by that consciousness in sense experiences derives largely from the order and disorder relayed to the organism from the world about it and incorporated into its own order and disorder. In other words, and this is the point of specific relevance here, consciousness, awareness as such, derives directly from the participation of the organism in the higher levels of the life of God; but the form taken by that consciousness in everyday sense experiences derives mainly from lower levels in the life of God interpreted through its own system. We can, therefore, at any rate in principle, explain the form of our experiences, and particularly our sense experiences, in terms of the chains of physical events linking the order of the world outside us to the brain but we cannot explain consciousness as such in these terms, the explanation of which has to derive from a deeper level: hence the problems of trying to explain consciousness in terms of the physical which is itself only a formal aspect of reality (albeit disordered) and which we know of only through the forms taken by our consciousness.

Naturally, if we assume that our sense experiences are in some sense 'in' the mind and that physical objects and events are in some sense 'outside' it, then we are faced with the problem of providing a bridge between them. If we place total reliance on physical events 'outside' the mind, then we are led to metaphysical theories such as epiphenomenalism or materialism; if we place such reliance on experiences 'in' the mind, we are led to phenomenalism; and if we give equal weight to events 'inside' and 'outside' the mind, we are left with dualism. But these problems do not arise when it is realised that our specific experiences are specific forms taken by consciousness which is a general feature of mind. Such experiences have both subjective and objective aspects, and these two aspects provide the basis for our concepts of mental and physical which are built up from them. Individual minds then find their place as aspects of a common ground in the life of God.

The Relevance of Thomas Nagel's The View from Nowhere

Some of these wider issues have been approached from a very different angle, in an important and original work by Thomas Nagel, *The View from Nowhere* (1986). Nagel's approach is based on the tensions that arise between our subjective and objective views and our attempts to harmonise them. It is a rationalist approach but it not only accords with much has has been argued here but it evokes also echoes of Israelite Wisdom which was discussed earlier in this book. Nagel notes that the internal-external tension pervades human life but is particularly prominent in the generation of philosophical problems.[14] He claims that it is beliefs and attitudes that are objective in the primary sense and that only derivatively do we regard as objective the truths arrived at in this way. The pursuit of detachment is an indispensable method of advancing our understanding of the world and of ourselves, increasing our freedom in thought and action and 'becoming better.'[15]

Yet, he claims, the logical goal of these ambitions is incoherent, for to be really free we would have to act from a standpoint completely outside

---

[14] *op cit* (1986) p 6
[15] *op cit* (1986) p 6

ourselves, choosing everything about ourselves, including all our principles of choice — creating ourselves from nothing, so to speak.[16]   That incoherence resolves itself, we may suggest, in God in whom subjective and objective and, as Nagel recognises, full freedom and necessity, coincide.

To acquire a more objective understanding, Nagel contends, we need to step back from our initial view and form a new conception which has that view and its relation to the world as its object. We need to place ourselves in the world that is to be understood. The old view then comes to be regarded as an appearance, more subjective than the new view, and correctable or confirmable by reference to it. The process can be repeated, yielding a still more objective conception. He adds that only the supposition that we and our appearances are part of a larger reality make it reasonable to seek understanding by stepping back from appearances in this way.[17] And later he makes the important claim that 'each of us is a microcosm, and in detaching progressively from our point of view and forming a succession of higher views of ourselves in the world, we are occupying a territory that already exists; taking possession of a latent objective realm, so to speak.[18]

Nagel argues, therefore, that the distinction between more subjective and more objective views is really a matter of degree, and it covers a wide spectrum. We can add to our knowledge of the world by accumulating information at a given level — by extensive observation from one standpoint, but we can raise our understanding to a new level 'only if we examine that relation between the world and ourselves which is responsible for our prior understanding, and form a new conception that includes a more detached understanding of ourselves, of the world and of the interaction between them.'[19] Nagel is thus drawing a distinction between simply adding knowledge and the leap of insight to a new conceptual level which not only gives new knowledge but transforms what we already know: that leap of insight to a new, more objective level that was known as *gnosis*.

Such leaps, as we have seen, cannot be commanded but come to a person by insight or inspiration. As he says, 'objectivity allows us to transcend our particular viewpoint and develop an expanded consciousness that takes in the world more fully.' This applies, he shows, to values and attitudes as well as theories.[20] Like the Wisdom writers and in contrast to most churches, he emphasises the provisional nature of all our understandings. He suggests

---

[16] *op cit*   (1986)   p 118

[17] *op cit*   (1986)   p 4

[18] *op cit*   (1986)   pp 82-3

[19] *op cit*   (1986)   p 5

[20] *op cit*   (1986)   p 5

that the pursuit of truth requires more than imagination: it requires the generation and the decisive elimination of alternative possibilities until, as we have noted, ideally, only one remains: in other words, the supersession of choice by an utterly free necessity. And it requires also a habitual readiness to attack one's own convictions.[21]

All this, he claims, depends on our capacity to generate hypotheses which come not from experience but from within ourselves: and he notes the role played by the luck of particular experiences and the age in which we live in prompting questions and possibilities that we might not have originated ourselves.[22] This leads him to claim that the search for generality is one of the main impulses in the construction of an objective view, in normative as in theoretical matters.[23] And he comments that our ability to call up whole worlds out of our heads accounts for the extremely high ratio of rational to empirical grounds in theoretical advances like Newton's theory of gravitation or the special and general theories of relativity: for, as he says: 'even though the empirical predictions of these theories are enormous, they were arrived at on the basis of relatively limited observational data, from which they could not be deduced.'[24] But, as he argues, we can do this only if there are facts which we do not know which account for the possibility and he points to the role assigned by Descartes to God as an explanation. He himself does not entertain this possibility but he does remark that unless we suppose our beliefs 'have a basis in something global (rather than just human) of which we are not aware, they make no sense — and they do make sense.'[25] Without such a property of the natural order, human knowledge is unintelligible. He makes the fundamentally important claim that all this entails, not bringing the mind into correspondence with an external reality which acts causally upon it, but of reordering the mind itself in accordance with the demands of its own external view.[26]

Nagel points to some very radical implications of this quest for objectivity and generality. In particular, he points to the need to bring our understanding of mind within this process. The first requirement is to think of our own minds as mere instances of something general. 'By a general concept of mind, I don't mean an anthropocentric concept which conceives all minds on analogy with our own. I mean a concept under which we

---

[21] *op cit* (1986) p 9

[22] *op cit* (1986) p 83

[23] *op cit* (1986) p 152

[24] *op cit* (1986) p 84

[25] *op cit* (1986) p 85

[26] *op cit* (1986) p 148

ourselves fall as instances — without any implication that we are the central instances.'[27] He says he wants to think of mind, like matter, as a general feature of the world which can provide us with a way of thinking that we can apply to ourselves.[28]

This leads him to a view of mental and physical as aspects of something more fundamental. As he says: 'If both mental and physical aspects of a process are manifestations of something more fundamental, the mental need not entail the physical nor vice versa even if both are entailed by this something else.'[29] And he points to 'one unsettling consequence of such a theory': that 'it appears to lead to a form of panpsychism — since the mental properties of the complex organism must result from some properties of its basic components, suitably combined: and these cannot be merely physical properties, or else in combination they will yield nothing but other physical properties.' If, he says, any two hundred pound chunk of the universe contains the material needed to construct a person, and if we deny both psychophysical reductionism and a radical form of emergence, then everything, reduced to its elements, must have proto-mental properties.[30] As he says, 'The strange truth seems to be that certain complex, biologically generated physical systems, of which each of us is an example, have rich non-physical properties. An integrated theory of reality must account for this, and I believe that if and when it arrives, probably not for centuries, it will alter our conception of the universe as radically as anything has to date.'[31]

And he adds that the enormous development of mental capacity is antecedently so improbable that the only possible explanation must be that it is in some way necessary. 'It is not the kind of thing that could be either a brute fact or an accident. .. The universe must have fundamental properties that inevitably give rise through physical and biological evolution to complex organisms capable of generating theories about themselves and it.'[32] It is interesting to recall that some scientists, too, are arriving at just this conclusion having regard to the anthropic cosmological principle.

Nagel notes that we act on the basis of the most complete view of the circumstances of action we can attain, including ourselves. But, as we have recorded, we cannot take this to its logical conclusion, for we remain as

---

[27] op cit (1986) p 18
[28] op cit (1986) p 19
[29] op cit (1986) p 48
[30] op cit (1986) p 49
[31] op cit (1986) p 81
[32] op cit (1986) p 81

pursuers of knowledge, creatures inside the world who have not created ourselves, and some of whose processes of thought have simply been given to us.[33] As for values, he sees these as judgements from a standpoint external to ourselves about how to be and how to live.[34] Ethical thought he therefore sees as the process of bringing objectivity to bear on the will. Just as realism about facts leads us to seek a detached point of view from which reality can be discerned and appearances corrected, realism about values leads us to seek a detached point of view from which it will be possible to correct our inclinations and to discuss what we should really do. The subject matter of our investigations, he claims, is how to live, and the process of ethical thought is one of motivational discovery. 'The fact that people can to some extent reach agreement on answers which they regard as objective suggests that when they step outside of their particular individual perspectives, they call into operation a common evaluative faculty whose correct functioning provides the answers, even though it can also malfunction and be distorted by other influences.'[35]

J M Rist notes a similar thrust in the views of the Stoics: 'A wise man is not simply a man who acts freely from pure motives; he is also one who knows and does the right thing. There are types of behaviour that are objectively right, such behaviour being guaranteed to promote the divine order and rationality in the cosmos and to be in harmony with it. The divine order and rationality is itself to be discovered by the proper use of the mind in the study of nature.'[36] By implication, even when, as so often, we are faced with a choice of evils, the whole and rational person will discern what is objectively the most rational and so the best decision. To respond rationally, however, is not simply to take just account of the passing situation for such rational response requires appreciation in depth in which more superficial, transitory features are set in context. A rational response is, therefore, a matter of degree — of depth of penetration — and tends towards a view which embraces all levels from the most superficial to the deepest — which is precisely what is entailed in a view *sub specie aeternitatis*. And, of course, such a rational response in depth entails and implies a corresponding development of the personality in depth — a 'purification' of the personality. In other words, this suggests that there are implicit in the natural order of which we are part, and in our own personalities, in so far as we develop to reflect that order truly, values and meanings which can in principle be generalised and objectivised in ethics:

---

[33] *op cit* (1986) p 118

[34] *op cit* (1986) p 135

[35] *op cit* (1986) p 148

[36] *Human Value* (1982) p 66

a view which is strongly enshrined in the Israelite Wisdom teaching and its heirs, but which is equally strongly denied by much modern philosophy.

As Philip Hefner says: 'In some circles, it seems to be agreed that the dualism between *is* and *ought* is a dogma so firmly attested that it merits no further discussion. Efforts to reassess the relation between *is* and *ought* and to negotiate a transition from the one to the other are dismissed simply as the "naturalistic fallacy", with a ritualistic reference to David Hume's *Treatise of Human Nature* and G E Moore's *Principia Ethica*.' Matters are not so simple, however. 'There seems to be a basic human sense that human knowledge and existence should be in touch with and live in accord with "the way things really are".'[37] The reordering of the mind to see itself and the world around it clearly thus allows us to act well: a claim that makes sense within the picture being developed in this study, for to see clearly, one has to become an ordered, integrated, whole person: one has to develop within the order and reason of the Divine Christ and in so doing, one manifests, however incompletely, the other attributes of the Divine life, including love, which are aspects of it.

Nagel notes the conflict between the good life and the moral life but suggests that there is something deeply unsatisfying about it.[38] He points to two possible approaches towards a solution: the first being a leap of self-transcendence to change one's life so radically that service to one's morality becomes one's overwhelming concern and dominant good. Though this may seem a terrible sacrifice, if the leap is successful, it will seem different from the other side and harmony is restored. The other approach which he suggests is political for institutions can externalise the clash of standpoints and in principle reduce it. Behind all this, Nagel suggests that we can reduce the conflict between the subjective and objective points of view, not by denying either but by a humility which falls between nihilistic detachment and blind self-importance and he characterises this as an attitude of nonegocentric respect for the particular. This is conspicuous in the aesthetic response for, as he says 'particular things have a non-competitive completeness which is transparent to all aspects of the self. This also helps to explain why the experience of great beauty tends to unify the self: the object engages us immediately and totally in a way that makes distinctions among points of view irrelevant.'[39]

In other words, in so far as, through progressive leaps of insight, we become more whole persons and our vision of the world becomes more

---

[37] Is/Ought in *The Sciences and Theology in the Twentieth Century* ed A R Peacocke (1981) p 59

[38] *op cit* (1986) p 205

[39] *op cit* (1986) p 223

whole too, we bring to our experiences of each particular object, person or event, a richness of meaning that becomes increasingly more objective, that embraces both specific and general, and tends to unify the mind and helps it to see clearly. But obviously, as we say elsewhere in this study, some objects, persons and events are in themselves more meaningful than others, and the more whole persons we are, the more we are able to respond to and identify with them in their full richness, whereas the less whole we are, the more we tend to find satisfaction in less rich, impersonal, things or reduce richer things to fit our restricted vision.

CHAPTER TWENTY TWO

THE RELEVANCE OF F A HAYEK AND CLASSICAL LIBERALISM

At first sight, the concerns of this book may seem to be far-removed from the work of the influential and controversial thinker on economic and social issues, F A Hayek. However, there are some important affinities between his claims and those being made here and when some basic features of his thought are set in this context, their relevance should be apparent. John Gray, one of Hayek's most perceptive commentators, in his book *Hayek on Liberty*[1] has emphasised, not only the importance of his thought but the broad coherence of its many facets. In particular, Hayek's economic and social thought is rooted back into his work on epistemology and philosophical psychology, and notably into his important but neglected work, *The Sensory Order*[2]. On the other hand, Gray has also stressed Hayek's sceptical Kantian approach and his total rejection of any form of speculative metaphysics. Hayek therefore sees the work of philosophy as an investigation of the limits of reason. This, however, as will be appreciated, is not out of step with the arguments being developed here.

In *The Sensory Order*, Hayek seeks to show that the properties which we attribute to experienced objects are not, in fact, their own properties but are the outcome of classificatory processes in the brain and sensory mechanisms. These processes are rooted in the relationships of objects to one another and to ourselves. However this may be, these processes entail the discrimination of order at many different levels. What is more, they entail the selection of order and this discriminatory process extends from the most basic sense experiences to the highest levels of science. It is only at the higher levels of this classificatory system that there emerges consciousness. Our conscious experiences thus rest on a vastly more extensive sub-conscious basis, to some extent of genetic origin but largely learned, which provides conscious experiences with their significance and meaning. Hayek recognises many stages intermediate between fully conscious and fully unconscious events and thus recognises that consciousness is capable of many degrees of intensity. It follows, therefore, that underlying all our experiences is a vast reservoir of 'tacit' knowledge and of skills which guide and give meaning to our conscious experiences but which normally are not, and in large measure cannot, be made conscious.

---

[1] 2nd edn 1986

[2] *op cit* (1952)

This process of discrimination and selection is not, however, one which depends on a survey of all or even many instances of particular uniformities. Rather, as we have seen, it typically entails leaps of insight (*gnosis*) from a limited number of instances to form higher level concepts or hypotheses whose application is then far wider or even universal. The achievement of such leaps of insight is central to all learning. The pioneers, the geniuses, who achieve such insights initially are thus of fundamental importance. Their insights can, however, be achieved far more easily by others who follow, when they are explained and set in context; though each individual has to make these leaps for himself. The incorporation of such insights into the social system and so their conveyance to each individual as he develops and matures is, therefore, basic both to his assimilation to the culture in which he grows up and to his growth as an individual.

Several points of importance are relevant to this. The fundamental significance of order, of patterning, is brought out by Roger Penrose when he asks what it is that gives a person his individual identity. As he says, it is not the atoms that constitute his body for not only has virtually the entire material that constitutes our bodies been replaced many times since birth, but according to quantum physics, particles of particular kinds are identical. 'What distinguishes the person from his house is the pattern of how his constituents are arranged, not the individuality of the constituents themselves.'[3] Of course, this conclusion of science reflects the fact that in science, as in all perception, we are concerned with identifying order, patterns of behaviour. What is more, this process is an extension of the innate processes of the sensory mechanisms identified by Hayek and by Piaget. The patterns that we discriminate thus get built-in to our nervous systems at many conceptual levels and it is this that enables us to identify and render meaningful the relevant patterns of order that are embedded in the welter of sense stimuli that bombard us.

Clearly, however, more is entailed than just a process of discriminating and classifying the order in our experiences. We have to be able to unify them and bring them together within the range of our consciousness. Hayek is surely right to emphasise that this can be done only because of strong spontaneous organising and unifying tendencies which operate, not only in the world around us, but in the mind, and which build up in hierarchical form many levels of order, each of which can embrace ordered systems at lower levels. In this way we establish within our own minds at many conceptual levels, a spontaneously ordered hierarchical conceptual system which is potentially a microcosm of the order of the world around us and in which cybernetic forces operate.

---

[3] *The Emperor's New Mind* (1989) pp 24-5

The tendency for spontaneous ordering and unifying processes to occur is not, therefore, just in the mind but at all levels of reality, from crystals and galaxies to social systems. What is more, at all higher levels of order, given sufficient freedom, these systems are cybernetic, self-regulating. This insight was, of course, to be found also in the work of L von Bertalanffy and subsequently of Eigen and Prigogine, to which we referred earlier. For Hayek, one particularly clear and important instance of this tendency for spontaneous, self-regulating systems to form is to be seen at social level including in the operation of the free-market economy.

Because all such spontaneous social systems embrace and incorporate as sub-systems, human beings, each with their own vast reservoirs of genetic and learned skills and knowledge, these social systems are able to incorporate and utilise the vast amount of fragmented knowledge, most of it lying at a tacit level, spread amongst all the individuals comprising that society. Indeed, Gray claims that Hayek's conception of social institutions as vehicles for the generation and dissemination of knowledge known only to small numbers of individuals or groups, represents an important paradigm shift in social theory — 'a shift from the criticism and evaluation of social institutions by reference to preferred principles of morality to an assessment of them in terms of their ability to generate, transmit and use knowledge (including tacit knowledge).'[4] This has some radical implications for the role of the Churches in leading to the development towards wholeness and integrity of their members through deepening insights — *gnosis*.

Inevitably, therefore, as Hayek stresses, attempts to oust such spontaneous systems and instead to impose planned social and economic systems, are limited by the gross inadequacies of the knowledge of one or a few such planners. What is more, the very resilience of spontaneous systems means that they will not passively comply with such plans which tend to contain or cripple them and lead inexorably, if followed through, to restrictions on freedom and to ultimately self-defeating autocracies which normally continue to function only because of their inherent inefficiencies.

In no way, however, does Hayek deny that order and rules — notably, at a social level, rules of morality, law and economics — are necessary for freedom. We can see this need if we appreciate that without such rules, one man's freedom is almost bound to be exercised at the expense of the freedom of other men: hence the need to regulate that freedom at points of potential abuse. But these rules need to be formulated and applied pragmatically to meet situations as they arise or can clearly be foreseen: not to meet some preconceived ideology. Hayek further argues, I believe persuasively, that at a social level, the right to hold and transfer property is

---

[4] *op cit*   (1986) p 41

an important feature of that freedom for it offers each family or person something of its own, however small, on which that family or person can operate creatively and around which the personality can grow and develop.

Hayek argues that such creativity is essentially a process of discovery of the unknown; it entails the achievement of creative insights which in many ways provide their own satisfactions and reward. In practice, however, the very satisfactions and rewards that their attainment offers tend to involve also the satisfaction of the needs and desires of others — whether the satisfactions and rewards are marked by money or more intangible forms of recognition. If, therefore, some system of guiding and encouraging these creative processes to meet the desires and needs of others beyond one's immediate social group, is to be established, other than by the very limiting device of barter, one is driven towards some form of currency in terms of which the scarcity of materials and the work entailed can be broadly equated and measured, and which can tell people where their efforts are best directed and how their needs can best be met. Hayek shows that the market is such a dynamic and cybernetic mechanism which provides such information. It is a competitive system yet it is, in principle, remarkably sensitive, constantly adjusting itself in response to the specialised discoveries of countless enterprising individuals who are mostly unknown to each other and who are each pursuing their own creative interests. The market is, therefore, a higher level self-regulating system. It is a system which, as it develops, potentially offers enormously increased freedom to each individual to find creative satisfactions in new and creative ways involving contributing to meeting the desires and needs of others.

Though it is a system of persons, the extended social system at its own level is necessarily impersonal and this leads Hayek to make an important distinction. As he stresses, the rules by which the extended social system operate are moral only in so far as they are consistent and 'just'. The love and understanding which are crucial to the success of personal social relationships are necessarily of limited relevance when we are dealing with persons of whom we know little or cannot even identify. Altruism at this level is blind and so is arbitrary and can thus be counterproductive. Hayek goes so far as to suggest that at the extended social level, the substitution of cooperation for competition can be positively harmful to the system, entailing as it normally does, reduced creative striving and reduced responsiveness to the needs to which it is directed. Instances of this in our own society both in cartels and in cooperation between managment and unions at the expense of consumers are not far to seek.

Hayek distinguishes sharply, therefore, the community in the sense of those members who know each other and in whose relationships morality in its full sense is essential; and the extended social system where such personal relationships cannot apply and attempts to apply them impair the working of the wider system. Attempts at this level to exercise altruism and love without close personal knowledge are likely to be arbitrary, inconsistent and open to abuse. At this level, therefore, rules need to be consistent and fair, while leaving the greatest possible scope for freedom and morality to operate in the in-group to mitigate the harsh impact of rules in particular cases. But, of course, as circumstances change and new discoveries are made which alter the system, these rules need to be constantly scrutinised and developed to maintain justice and consistency and limit abuse. Hayek points to the great confusion of thought caused by failure to distinguish the concerns of the in-group from those of the extended order by indiscriminate use of words such as 'social', 'community' and 'altruism', and by attempts to apply the morality of the in-group to the extended order.

The extended order is not and cannot be the product of conscious thought or 'planning' by particular individuals. It is a spontaneous system of relationships which grows in response to discoveries or insights of large numbers of individuals each exercising knowledge and judgements in circumstances known only to a few, and not fully to them. But this activity by individuals leads none the less to the development of the extended order in ways which can offer greatly increased freedom of choice and other benefits to the many. It is a system that is as imperfect as the people who comprise it and needs constantly to be adjusted to ease points of friction and injustice. But whatever its failings, the system can never be redesigned root and branch without gravely limiting and ultimately catastrophic results. What is more, such fields as ethics, law and economics and the institutions which administer their findings, are yet higher level systems for regulating the operation of the extended system which itself regulates the activities of large numbers of overlapping groups of personally related individuals. This spontaneous growth of higher level systems as a cumulative result of insights attained by vast numbers of individuals is clearly a development of order that is rooted in genetic evolution. The creative growth of the order of the extended social system potentially allows the growth of the personality of the individuals that comprise it and the corresponding growth of diversity and of freedom of choice for individuals. As was said by von Humboldt and quoted by John Stuart Mill on the title page of his essay *On Liberty*, 'Civilisation is based on human development in its richest diversity.'

That such development is the natural product of deep evolutionary forces in the world which are realising themselves through men without their being conscious of it, seems obvious; it is a development which should depend on and encourage openness, discovery, creativity, an exploration of the plenitude of God and the realisation of as many aspects as possible of that enormous plenitude in our lives. Indeed, we may add that, in its very nature, an evolutionary system cannot be equal and in that extreme sense cannot be 'fair' or 'just'. God is an élitist, at least in the sense that though his kingdom is open to all, and all may ultimately attain it, only by growth into his life can entry be effected. As the parable of the talents shows, God is just in the sense that he rewards openness and responsiveness to his creative will; he is merciful to those who try but fail in that his doors remain always open; but those who lack humility, by trusting in themselves and man, face, sooner or later, catastrophe which reveals itself in the natural order as his wrath. It is in this way that evolution operates to channel creativity to yet higher social levels.

This said, however, it needs again to be emphasised that any such system, like any other, is bound to be imperfect and open to abuse; though the emphasis on the freedom of all its members tends to limit this. But secondly, and fundamentally, the strengths of such a system need to be seen in the context of a wider system where the understanding of it as a means of exploration and realisation of the attributes of God is all-pervasive; where the underlying objective is to seek growth and development towards wholeness and maturity (righteousness) which reveals itself in understanding, wisdom and in love; and where humility towards the wisdom of God which is gradually revealing itself in the world, is paramount. In such a society, however important material things, including money, may be in its functioning, they cannot be an end in themselves, nor can any other form of materialism. The Wisdom of Israel never disregarded personal wellbeing, material success or honour, though it saw them as evidence of a 'listening heart' or 'mind', and never as ends in themselves.

Yet despite the failings of the system, attacks by the Churches and others over the centuries on trade and property as such can be seen as deeply misconceived. Hayek traces these attitudes back to Aristotle who had little understanding of the extended group or of the importance of trade, and whose ideas became embedded in the thought of the Western Churches. And he shows how such ideas were given a powerful boost by Rousseau, who wanted to free men from the 'artificial' restraints of society.[5] In particular, none of these had any awareness of the role of evolution and natural selection, which, as we have seen, applies not only at the level of the natural and social worlds, but, in a profound sense, in the very life of God.

Not surprisingly, therefore, an emphasis on the role of natural selection is another basic feature of the thought of Hayek but it appears to have been much less adequately formulated. Hayek sees social and cultural evolution as continuous with evolution at a biological level and as embodying the same fundamental principles of natural selection. Gray notes, however, that natural selection as so understood 'is not of individuals, but of groups and populations, and it occurs via the impact of the practices and institutions, the

---

[5] *The Fatal Conceit* (1989) pp 45 et seq

rules of action and perception, of groups on the life chances of their members.'[6] The mechanism of continuous reproduction against which biological selection takes place does not, therefore, apply at a social level and, as Gray accepts, the role assigned by Hayek to emulation by others to ensure successful behaviour is hardly adequate. Nor is the other factor on which Hayek puts weight, migration. As for the test of success that Hayek offers — the capacity of the institution to allow for the increase in the numbers of human beings — this seems wholly inadequate and ultimately self-defeating. What is more, it is at least very questionable whether the identification of what is good with what survives at any one time is satisfactory. And, in any event, there seems no necessary link between the survival of social institutions, at any rate in the short run, and the liberty of the individual to which Hayek is dedicated. We need, therefore, to look again at these features of the thought of Hayek within the context of the picture that is emerging in this study.

As we have seen, Hayek claims a strong continuity between basic sensory processes and the highest reaches of science and between the spontaneous formation of systems at all levels of the natural and social worlds. Now these spontaneously formed systems normally incorporate within them systems at lower levels of order. At the level of molecules or cells, mutations allow for new, higher levels, of order to emerge which embrace the constituent units; and at the conceptual levels in the mind, similar reordering processes allow new insights to emerge: insights which normally enable us to see in the existing data deeper and more all-embracing levels of order. These insights 'come to' a person: as we have seen, most creative workers see themselves as the vehicles for something which comes to them from beyond and is not under their control.

If, therefore, we discard the idea of increase of population as an inadequate criterion of success in natural selection, one obvious alternative is the attainment of higher levels of order, in the sense discussed earlier, which are not only the source of deep creative satisfactions but which allow for a more flexible response to, and in man, control over himself and the environment. As we have seen, at the level of man, this developmental process takes place primarily at the level of mind and points straight towards *gnosis*, and so towards integration, wholeness or maturity of the individual and the development of higher level social systems, within which he can find fulfilment. What is more, in so far as higher levels of order are achieved, so far does man attain not only social freedom but inner freedom, which, as we saw, is necessary for *gnosis*. In so far also, man becomes spontaneously more rational, understanding, caring — more moral — and

---

[6] *op cit*   (1986)   p 33

so is able to sit lightly in relation to the letter of the law, whether moral, religious or civil — as Jesus showed: yet, because men are imperfect, that law remains an essential framework for freedom.

Of course, higher level social systems not only support but require more people to operate them because of the specialisations entailed. But the recognition of this does not make the multiplication of numbers of people of itself a criterion of success. We are already seeing how such multiplication can lead to destruction of the environment, can lead to social unrest and become disturbingly counter-productive.

However, if interpreted in terms of growth of order, Hayek's paradigm shift, on which we quoted Gray above, does provide a test of social institutions in terms of their ability to generate, transmit and use knowledge: but 'knowledge' in this context has to be understood, not just in terms of the acquisition of skills and facts but of insights which allow us to see the world at greater depth and become more whole, mature and so more open persons. On this basis, too, the test of institutions in terms of liberty and the development and maintenance of morality both stand but take their place within the wider picture. As for the important insight of Hayek about the self-destructive character of man's attempts to impose his own conceptions of order, which has been a major theme of all his work and particularly of *The Road to Serfdom* and *The Fatal Conceit*, this stands, and so does his concern for freedom. But competition, which can be for destructive, selfish, short-term ends, in this context takes the form of strong creative strivings for deeper insights and achievements which are informed by and enhanced by mutual support and mutual respect of individuals and social groups and of the world we live in.

This can be so for, though in the world we live in, resources are scarce and needs are many, yet it is the base for development into the plenitude of God where there are no scarce resources and each man's ability to draw on them depends on and is enhanced by the love of God and so of man's own fellows. These ideas of the role of wholeness, and its implications for the spontaneous development of harmonious social systems, point to the importance of the idea of freedom when thought of, not just as negative freedom — freedom from oppression — but as personal autonomy, self-determination and self-realisation in accordance with the will of God. As John Gray says: 'Both Spinoza and Kant deployed a positive view of freedom as autonomy and self-determination in defence of toleration and limited government. This is not a view of freedom as collective self-determination, but rather as rational self-government of the individual agent. It informs Mill's most liberal work *On Liberty* and it has roots in liberalism's pre-history in the Stoic writers. This version of the positive view seems entirely congenial to liberal concerns and to have an assured place within the liberal intellectual tradition.'[7]

Gray goes on to comment, however, that freedom as autonomy has been much criticised by contemporary liberals and he notes particularly criticisms by Sir Isaiah Berlin and Hayek of some understandings of such autonomy. As he says, however, 'the ideal of autonomy, as it figures in social psychology, connotes not the inner-directed man who is unmindful of his social environment, but rather of the critical and self-critical man whose allegiance to his society's norms is informed by the best exercise of his rational powers. Such an open conception of autonomy, which avoids the rationalist metaphysic of the self criticised by Berlin and which has an insight into the role of conventions and traditions as conditions of freedom that was denied to Mill, seems entirely congenial to liberalism.'[8]

Gray goes on to show how this links with private property as an institutional vehicle for decentralised decision taking and to the role of the market in producing harmony amongst men's activities. 'It is in this sense that the market may be considered the paradigm of *a spontaneous social order* and to illustrate Proudhon's dictum "Liberty is the mother of order".'[9] As Gray notes, however: 'Whereas the classical liberals of the Scottish school, like the great French liberals Constant and Tocqueville, had seen a primary argument for liberty in the incapacity of human intelligence to grasp the society that had produced it, the new liberals sought to submit the life of society to rational reconstruction. .. Once progress is conceived as the realisation of a rational plan of life rather than an unpredictable exfoliation of human energies, it is inevitable that liberty should eventually be subordinated to the claims of progress. This is a conflict which the classical liberals avoided with their wise admission that human intelligence cannot plot the course of the future.' And he comments that 'with the decline of the classical liberal system of thought, liberalism assumed its modern form, in which rationalistic intellectual hubris is fused with a sentimental religion of humanity.'[10] — words which, in the context of this book, stand as an indictment both of much modern politics and religion. It is in accord with the claims of classical liberalism and with the claims of Hayek, to emphasise the fundamental importance of the use of such liberty both as the product and enhancer of creativity.

All this finds interesting and important confirmation in the findings of Axelrod based on games theory, to which we referred earlier. These

---

[7] *Liberalism* (1986) pp 58-9

[8] *op cit* (1986) pp 59-60

[9] *op cit* (1986) p 70

[10] *op cit* (1986) p 92

findings are that the spontaneous formation of a cooperative social order actually requires a very strong teleology to be acting at the individual level. In the words of Barrow and Tipler, 'Such an order can form spontaneously only if the future expectations of the individuals in the society are dominant over their immediate expectations in determining their present actions'[11] The role of the understanding of religion that has been emerging in this study in providing such expectations will be clear. In particular, God guides men into his life if they have sufficient openness and faith and this adds a profound dimension to the first commandment. It also points to the way in which those within and without the Churches, have, in their efforts to honour the second commandment to love their neighbour, arrogated to man powers which bespeak a lack of insight and of faith about his limitations. This is a process which, as we have seen, is bound ultimately to be self-defeating and disastrous.

Once again, therefore, we find that morality cannot operate without insight and insight is directly linked with wholeness and maturity, the attainment of which requires individual freedom and striving yet demands also humility, love and understanding at all social levels. It is a field, perhaps the only field, where the striving for and attainment of success is not at the expense of others. A comment by Rist about the thought of Plotinus is relevant here: 'There is for Plotinus only a limited amount that we can do for other people. Ultimately each man must face reality for himself ...; he cannot find a substitute, any more than he can find someone to die for him. And what should be done for other people must depend on the possibilities open to them and the choices they have made about their own.[12] As Hayek shows, the higher the level of social order, the wider are those choices and, of course, the fact that each individual must make his own is no argument for the witholding of the caring concern that the whole person spontaneously gives to those he knows: nor for seeking to ensure the fairness and sensitivity of the rules of the extended group which provides a context for them.

The arguments being presented in this study find, therefore, strong support at crucial points in the claims of Hayek and of classical liberalism. In the most general terms, this argument is of God as the ground and plenitude of all being and of the processes within his life evolving spontaneously to share in different levels of order and so participate in his life. One implication of this emerging picture is, therefore, as we should expect on theological grounds, that the Divine Plenum, though it has within it the potential for taking physical form, is also mental and at a deeper level

---

[11] *The Anthropic Cosmological Principle* (1986) p 100

[12] Plotinus and Moral Obligation in *Platonism and its Christian Heritage* (1985) p 229

embracing both, is spiritual. As we have noted, the spiritual is therefore not to be regarded as a third class of phenomenon alongside the mental and physical but as carrying attributes that give rise to both.

Furthermore, within this picture, as we must now show, the physical is to be seen as a transitory phenomenon, a wave of energy emerging from and returning to the life of God as it traverses and organises it. This claim will, however, entail facing certain controversial issues relating to the nature of time, which will in turn raise the question how these transitory processes effect permanent changes in the life of God — for if they did not do so, the very purpose of the life of God as understood by Christian teaching, would be set at nought. We shall need, therefore, to explore the character of those changes, and for reasons that will become clearer, memory is their exemplar.

CHAPTER TWENTY THREE

THE TRANSIENCE OF THE PHYSICAL WORLD

We tend, in thinking of the everyday and physical worlds, to concentrate on their enduring features. We recognise, of course, that some features, such as a lightning flash are highly transitory; that other features such as stars and mountains are highly durable and that our bodies, with our hoped-for span of life of three score years and ten, fall somewhere between. Yet we are also well aware, though it does not normally feature largely in our thoughts, that there is a continuous and more basic transience of the entire physical world of which we are parts and of our experiences of it: that what is about to happen and does happen, then at once becomes part of the past. Indeed, on this basis, if the physical is all that there is, there is seemingly no such thing as the future or the past, but only our present guesses as to the future and our present memories and other present traces of what is past: the world needs to be seen, as it were, as existing on a moving knife-edge.

Some of the issues relating to the different ways of thinking about time were crystallised in a famous article by J M E McTaggart about the unreality of time.[1] It was originally published in 1908 and has underlain much subsequent discussion. For our purposes, however, it will suffice to point to two ways of conceiving and talking about time which he distinguished and which are described by Richard Gale thus: 'McTaggart's paradox is deeply rooted in two fundamentally different ways in which we conceive of and talk about time. On the one hand, we conceive of time in a dynamic or tensed way, as being the very quintessence of flux and transiency. According to this way of conceiving time, events are represented as being past, present and future, and as continually changing in respect to these tensed determinations. Thus what is now happening ceases to happen and becomes past as future events become present or come to pass, this requiring that past events become more past or future events less future. This temporal becoming is often referred to by various metaphors and aphorisms — the gnawing tooth of time, the river of time, time flies, here today and gone tomorrow, gather ye rosebuds while ye may, enjoy yourself it's later than you think. This dynamic concept of time lies at the basis of the temporalistic view of man and existence which is presented in certain religions, philosophies and works of art. This conception of time finds expression in our tensed way of talking.

'Yet time, in which all things come to be and pass away, necessarily involves a static structure or order. It is, to use T S Eliot's phrase, "a pattern of timeless moments". The very same events which are continually

---

[1] reprinted with additions in *The Philosophy of Time* ed R M Gale (1967)

changing in respect to their pastness, present and futurity are laid out in a permanent order whose generating relation is that of earlier than. This is the static or tenseless way of conceiving time, in which the totality of history is viewed in a God-like manner, all events being given at once in a *nunc stans*. Here is no gnawing tooth of time — no temporal becoming — but only a democratic equality of all times. This way of conceiving time finds expression in our tenseless way of talking, in which temporal relations of precedence and subsequence between events are described by timelessly true or false statements.'[2]

It is the first of these ways of thinking and speaking about time that matters for present purposes for it emphasises the sense in which the physical world is transient and it enables us to point to the seemingly very obvious fact that the physical world is in a sense a transient phenomenon of the present moment. Yet, according to relativity, there is no such thing as the present moment, 'now'. One reason is that the physical theories *per se* make no reference to this property; they are impartial in their treatment of all points in time and, in particular, provide no role for the concept of the 'present instant'. Modern physicists have therefore introduced the concept of the 'block universe' in which time is one dimension of a four dimensional static block, and this usually has the rider that it is in some sense being progressively explored by our individual consciousnesses.

This has led some physicists to regard the ordinary transitory world of experience, or at least its changing character, as 'subjective' in the sense of dependent on the consciousness of observers. Thus D F Lawden speaks of 'consciousness directed to successive sense-data arranged along a filament of consciousness, thus creating the sensation of the passage of time.'[3] And Paul Davies says he suspects that time does not flow at all; it is all in the mind; and he claims that if there is any meaning at all to these concepts such as flow of time, then it would seem that they belong to psychology rather than physics.[4]

Such claims deserve close scrutiny. Imagine a prominent tree standing in a garden. It could in principle be viewed from near and far from an infinity of perspectives by an infinity of observers, none of which was privileged. But because we all build a common conceptual framework into which all or any of these perspectives and observers, together with all the other knowledge which I or others could bring about the tree and anything related to it, find a coherent place, we think of the tree and our experiences

---

[2] R Gale *The Language of Time* (1968) p 7

[3] Some Thoughts on Birth and Death *Journal of the SPR* vol 52 no 817 October 1989 p 41

[4] *God and the New Physics* (1983) pp 127 & 133

of it as 'objective'. What is more, the tree has grown virtually continuously over many years; it constantly moves in the wind; it lost a branch at precisely 10.31 on 26 January 1990. That constant change, together with the constant change on the part of observers, all find a coherent place in that objective picture. On the other hand, if, one dark night, I saw the tree as a gaunt menacing figure, that anomalous experience could indeed be regarded as 'subjective', the product of my mind. It is difficult, however, to see how we can regard the changes in the world around us as subjective while the objects and events that change are in some sense objective: how the tree can be objective while its changing states are subjective: the world does not divide itself up that way; we derive our concept of the tree from those specific states. If, on the other hand, we seek to treat all our knowledge of the tree as subjective: its botanical features as well as our seeing it as a menacing figure, we would still need to distinguish the status of its botanical features from that subjective experience: so we would have to distinguish the 'objective-subjective' from the 'subjective-subjective' while giving the label 'objective' to high level theories: a change of labels that does nothing to advance understanding.

It is surely most implausible, simply on the basis of a disjunction with a very high level scientific theory which, as we shall note, is itself seemingly incomplete, to downgrade either the entire normal world or the transitory aspects of it, to being the product of individual minds. And the case for such a view becomes the more tenuous when it is appreciated that all high level scientific theories, including relativity, are necessarily built on the basis of, and presuppose, the objectivity of all the (transient) observations of science, as well as the calculations of the scientists. The ordinary events of life, including the observations of scientists, must surely be as objective as the higher level theories built on them, each at their own level. The fact that the transitoriness of the physical world at 'local' level does not find a place in higher level theory is not sufficient ground for taking such a fundamental and probably incoherent step as to treat the world at local level as subjective: when the alternative is to treat the disjunction as evidence of an incompleteness of theory.

Such considerations have led Roger Penrose to express grave misgivings about attempts so to sweep away this discrepancy in this manner. Having noted that the successful equations of physics are symmetrical in time, putting past and future on an equal footing and that according to relativity, there is not such a thing as 'now' at all, he says: 'it seems to me that there are severe discrepancies between what we consciously feel, concerning the flow of time, and what our (marvellously accurate) theories assert about the reality of the physical world. These discrepancies must surely be telling us something deep about the physics that presumably must actually underlie our conscious perceptions — assuming (as I believe) that what underlies these perceptions can indeed be understood in relation to some appropriate kind of physics. At least it seems to be clearly the case that whatever physics is operating, it must have an essentially time-asymmetrical ingredient, i e it must make a distinction between past and future.'[5]

Penrose goes on to note that though the very idea of the 'present' fits so uncomfortably with relativity, our physical understanding actually contains some important ingredients other than just these equations and some of these do involve time-asymmetries. The most important of these is the second law of thermo-dynamics which asserts, broadly, that the entropy of an isolated system increases with time. Penrose shows that for us the sun is the main low-entropy source.   He relates its low entropy back to the quite extraordinary precision entailed in the big-bang and this in turn leads him into the still deeply obscure realm of quantum gravity. His conclusion, with the problem of simultaneity in mind, is that our present picture of physical reality, particularly in relation to the nature of time, is due for a grand shake-up — 'even greater, perhaps, than that which has already been provided by present-day relativity and quantum mechanics.'[6] It suffices for me to say, therefore, that in this situation in physics, it is not unreasonable to retain a belief that in some sense, the transitoriness of the physical world is not just subjective or illusory and that it must have some eternal significance.

Indeed, this point needs to be pressed further, for it seems quite obvious that it cannot just be our experiences that are transitory. On this, J R Smythies, picking up a point made by C D Broad, says that 'what is very rarely recognised by physicists discussing the matter, is Broad's observation that if we posit a "static-looking fixed space-time in which the events of the universe are laid out" we get rid of not only the "now" and flow of time but all movement as well. In the geometrization of time .. all movements of physical objects are transformed into static complex four-dimensional geometry of which we perceive successive instantaneous cross-sections as objects extended in three-dimensional space and enduring in time.' He claims that the real shape of the earth on this basis is a four dimensional stationary hyperhelix wound round the world line of the sun. And he notes that the conclusion that all movement must be illusory would surely be most unwelcome to any physicist or biologist.[7]

If we seek to translate this into ordinary experience, in which, after all, science is ultimately rooted, it is difficult to make sense of the idea that my

---

[5] *The Emperor's New Mind* (1989) p 304

[6] *op cit* (1989) p 371

[7] J R Smythies 'Mind, Brain, Space, Time: an Essay Review of Roger Penrose's *The Emperor's New Mind'*   *Journal of the S P R*   vol 56 no 820 July 1990 p 231

body when I was a baby, in my present state, and in a possible future decrepit old age, and all the gradual and continuous stages in between, all exist concurrently; or that Europe in the Ice Age still co-exists with its present state and only consciousness changes. And even if the idea of the concurrent existence of the past, present and future states of the physical world could be given some cash value, it seems obvious that some highly privileged 'objective' status would have to be given to the moment 'now' that is continuously moving forward. Indeed, we shall find ground for thinking of the divine life in terms of some form of eternal superposition that opens up, not only in the one major system of the physical world, but also in lesser systems such as dreams and other states which we shall be discussing later, all of which have their own times and spaces.

It may be worth adding here that there are arguments within quantum physics itself for the abandonment of strict locality — of treating systems as physically separated — and this has implications for time also. As Davies and Brown note, if locality is abandoned, it is possible to recreate a description of the microworld closely similar to that of the everyday world, though non-local effects bring their own crop of difficulties: specifically, the ability of signals to travel back into the past.[8] What is more, mind has traditionally not been located in space, though in some sense it has in time.

The picture of the physical world as standing patterns which progressively organise themselves spatially and temporally in a transitory energy wave which is crossing the eternal mind of God, finds some support in the ideas of Bohm. He has developed the idea of a multi-dimensional implicate order that is continuously unfolding and then enfolding again, the moment of unfolding being 'now'. In the implicate order, time and space no longer determine the independence of different elements but from it time and space and separately existent material particles emerge as forms derived from a deeper order. He comments that 'What is essential to this new model is that the electron is ... to be understood through a total set of enfolded ensembles, which are generally not localised in space. At any given moment one of these may be unfolded and therefore localised, but in the next moment, this one enfolds to be replaced by the one that follows. The notion of continuity of existence is approximated by that of very rapid recurrence of similar forms....'[9] This picture of an explicate order constituting the moment 'now' and marking the taking of physical form of ideas or events that otherwise lie in the implicate order, the Plenum, which is for Bohm the source of all things, can seemingly broadly be equated with the idea of the the passage of an energy wave across mind of God as it is being presented here.

---

[8] *The Ghost in the Atom* (1986) p 39

[9] *Wholeness and the Implicate Order* (1980) p 183

At this point we need to face another issue that is profound and paradoxical. In the picture being presented here, all events lie within the life of God which is itself outside time and space. Some limited understanding of this may be glimpsed if we compare the unfolding vision of a traveller along a narrow winding rural road that lies between high banks, with the vision of an observer in a helicopter above who sees the entire stretch of road at one glance. It is not given to us to attain a vision outside time for we are inexorably locked within our own time perspective, though we can employ higher level theories to show us that for different observers there are countless alternative perspectives. The theory of relativity therefore shows that, whereas for one observer, an event may still be in the future, for another in a different time perspective, it may already have happened. And the implication of this seems to be that while for the first observer a decision about what should happen remains to be decided, for the other it has already been decided: and this may be felt to point to the illusoriness of our sense of the freedom of our wills.

The crucial word in this account is, however, the word 'already'; for implicit in that word is an observer who can in some way be aware of the decision and event from both perspectives and measure it against some absolute or common scale. But these different time perspectives or scales do not themselves occur within some greater, overarching time scale. In the real world there is no such observer or scale. Of course, as we have noted, the high level, abstract theory of relativity tells us <u>that</u> different observers can have different time perspectives and <u>that</u> this can in principle arise. But all actual observations are made within some particular perspective and whatever the perspective, the agent's freedom is determined only at the point of decision. Therefore neither the evidence of relativity nor the fact that God sees all events outside any or all particular perspectives provides support for determinism.

If, then, we can think of the physical world in terms of a transitory wave of energy crossing the mind of God, with developing standing patterns on it which, as we shall consider presently, pass back into his eternal mind; and if this is the way in which God has organised the creative process in order that his creation may evolve to share eternally in his life, then by implication, it is this transitory creative process that must be giving rise to creatures, and in particular, to human beings, who in some way survive within the mind of God to share in his life eternally. And in so far as such human beings are living, conscious, understanding, caring, even holy, and these attributes are ultimately his attributes in which they participate, God must know this eternally. By implication, therefore, what survives this transitory physical process must be, at least in part, of a personal mind character. Yet in our ordinary lives and so our minds, sense experiences play a dominant role, and it is difficult to envisage sense experiences in the absence of the physical world and, in particular, the physical organs that give rise to them. It seems, therefore, that it cannot be mind as a whole that survives.

We need, therefore, to ask just what aspect of mind could reflect or retain the personality as a whole and survive: and the obvious and only answer to this is memory: for memories do indeed retain the order and structure of our experiences of the physical world as well as of our emotional and other experiences. It will, however, also be necessary to show that what survives is not just a passive memory of past experiences but, on the basis of structured memory systems that constitute the personality, that there remains the ability to organise and reorganise these memories on a shared 'objective' basis, so as to be able to live, at any rate at the early stages, a life recognisably similar to that on earth within a memory world; and to be able to open the personality to yet deeper insights and so develop further.

In our current materialist understanding of memory such answers are ruled out from the start for memories are thought of as stored in the brain and clearly, the brain decays on death and, in some measure, earlier. We need, therefore, to look more closely at the evidence for this understanding and see how far it is supported by scientific findings or whether, perchance, it is the product of our current materialist paradigm in which mind has lost its roots within the eternal mind of God and has now, perforce, had to find a conceptual home entirely as a by-product of the physical. We need also to consider whether memory is restricted to experiences that have passed through the mind of man, and perhaps of some higher animals; or whether there is evidence to suggest that memories of all events pass back into the mind of God in some form of universal or akashic memory, of which the memories of human beings are specific and extremely specialised instances: in other words, that God forgets nothing. There is indeed support for such ideas, but first we need to consider memory in its normal sense.

CHAPTER TWENTY FOUR

MEMORY

It is virtually indisputable that the patterning of our sense experiences is relayed from the world around us to the brain by the sense mechanisms and that these experiences can, in turn, influence directly our responses, including guiding our attention and so the sense mechanisms themselves. In so far, consciousness can be seen as occurring at the highest levels of a many-level cybernetic system where inputs and outputs are regulated and controlled. Clearly, therefore, in this process, physical events in some way translate through into those mental events and vice versa. But whether those mental events are to be seen as identical with their physical counterparts; whether they are one aspect or component of these physical counterparts; or whether they are in some sense quite separate systems that somehow are able to interact, is much more disputable, for in current thought, each of these views has its supporters. Of these positions, the one that is most fully compatible with the theological picture being presented here is that the sense mechanisms at this level of organisation must have a mental component or vice versa. As we have already seen, this is the thrust of Thomas Nagel's claims and Michael Lockwood, in his important book, *Mind Brain and the Quantum*, after full consideration of the alternatives and other relevant issues, also argues for such a view. In particular, he suggests that the physical events in question may be a quantum phenomenon, Bose-Einstein condensations, which appear to have the necessary characteristics to be the physical counterpart of consciousness.

If there is survival of death, however, whatever form experiences may take after death, they cannot include sense experiences as such, in view of the clear dependence of these experiences on the sense mechanisms of the brain and body. Yet if the personality does survive, it would seem that it must continue to have some form of experiences in some way akin to sense experiences. In other words, if we are to take survival seriously, it seems that it cannot be mind as we ordinarily know it, in which sense experiences loom so large, but some other aspects or aspects of mind that survives. Yet survival of persons, to be meaningful or significant, would seem to require survival in a form that allows communication with their environment, including other people who similarly survive. This therefore raises the question whether there is any feature or aspect of mind other than the sense experiences, that is experientially distinguishable yet which, if it survived, would still allow the personality so to function as an intelligible and intelligent whole. This suggests, in other words, that the question of survival turns, not on the body-mind relationship as such, but on the survival of some such distinguishable feature or aspect of mind, though no doubt dependent on brain for its initial formation, that does not depend on the brain for its continued existence.

When we seek an aspect of mind that is subjectively distinguishable, that offers a sufficient basis for understanding survival, and whose survival is in any event clearly necessary if the survival of the personality in any recognisable form is to take place, the obvious, and probably the only candidate is memory; for there cannot be survival of the personality without survival of the memory in some form, and, as we shall see, of itself, memory may offer a sufficient basis for survival. Indeed, it is itself a specific instance of survival of earlier experiences.

To this suggestion, there will, of course, be an immediate response from many philosophers, psychologists and neurophysiologists that no aspect of mind can survive death, for all aspects of mind are identical with, or are components of, events in the brain: and so memories must be stored in the form of physical events in the brain and must dissolve with it. However, as we shall see, despite intensive search for some form of memory trace in the brain for more than a century, not only has evidence in support of this claim yet to be found, but the very extensive evidence that has been found appears to point clearly against any such form of memory trace. Of course, it seems that the brain itself must develop in response to experience in ways which enable it to process our ordinary experiences at increasing levels of sophistication, as we develop from childhood. In so far, it must carry with it some form of memory; but the idea of the brain as a processor of experiences that develops in response to experience, does not itself entail that the brain is a store of all such experiences.

We tend often, however, to think of memories in terms of individual, mainly passive, recollections and not as multi-level cybernetic systems of a kind needed to support the complex experiences and behaviour of human beings. Cybernetic forces do, of course, operate at the level of mind — being referred to in very general terms as the Life Instinct — and memory does, of course, play an integral role in virtually all aspects of mental life. Dreams themselves are complex and dynamic memory systems. There is, of course, great variation in the character of the dreams of different people, and indeed, of the same people at different times. Thus some dreams are vivid and in colour, and most dreams involve experience of many of the activities of the self and other people which are experienced in everyday life. There are also the so-called eidetic memories which appear to be experienced particularly by children and primitive peoples, which have a distinctive vividness and objectivity, and which can be controlled to a remarkable degree by the subject.[10] And, of course, there is no clear-cut line between memory and the imagination.

It might be claimed, of course, that dreams are, as it were, 'parasitic' upon and presuppose the physical systems that constitute human beings; but again we have to face the point that it is from our experiences that we start: all we know of our bodies derives from our experiences of ourselves and other persons, objects and events. And while dreams lack, in retrospect, the immediacy and consistency of normal everyday experiences, they seem real to the dreamer while he is experiencing them. In so far, our everyday and dream experiences are on a par, whilst the physical world is a construct from our experiences.

Even if such memory systems could survive the decay of the body, however, there would be those who would claim that such survival would leave each surviving person locked up in his own memories; for it is widely assumed, both in Western Christian thinking and in materialism, that minds, assuming they exist at all, are separate substances, communicating only through the senses. As we shall note later, Professor H H Price adduced strong grounds on which this assumption also should be questioned. We have already seen how, in the course of the development of Western thought, Aristotelian understandings of minds as separate cul-de-sacs open to the senses, became incorporated into Western thought; and how the polarisation of our concepts of God and the world and the development of the conceptual gap between them, left mind disconnected from a common ground in the mind of God. It is by this route, rather than any investigations of science itself, that mind has come to be seen as a by-product of the physical, isolated from other minds except by way of the body through the senses. Although the idea of individual minds as rooted back into — or as particular forms taken by — the mind of God has at intervals reappeared, notably in the works of Bergson and Jung, this concept has not taken root in scientific thinking. Memories are, therefore, almost necessarily thought of as stored in the brain, for there is no other conceptual home for them within the materialist conceptual framework that structures and dominates our minds. Yet, as we have indicated, this almost unquestioned understanding does not flow from the empirical evidence; and, bearing in mind the enormous effort and resources that have been employed and the enormous number of animals sacrificed in the quest for the memory trace over the last 150 years, it stands as a tribute to and warning of the power of our preconceptions. What is more, in the next two chapters we shall review

---

[10] see e g C R Gray & K Gummermann The Enigmatic Eidetic Image *Psychological Bulletin* vol 82 no 3 pp 383-407; C F Stromeyer iii & j Psotka The Detailed Texture of Eidetic Images *Nature* vol 225 Jan 24 1970

evidence that suggests that communication between minds can occur in certain circumstances other than by way of the senses.

Traditionally, memories were thought of as linked and recalled on the basis of associations, though the term 'association of ideas' has vanished from textbooks of psychology except as an historical footnote, notwithstanding its importance in the history of thought. Aristotle formulated the doctrine of association by contiguity, similarily and contrast; it was elaborated and commented on in classical and mediaeval times; and it played a major role in post-Cartesian philosophy, particularly in Britain where the British Empiricists used to be known as the British Associationists. Humphrey drew attention to the great vitality of the doctrine and noted that 'in every age it has risen superior to the psychological fashion of the moment, and has, in fact, been progressively reformulated to meet the fashion of the day.'[11] Donald Hebb explained the current situation succinctly when he noted that the term 'association of ideas' had disappeared from current psychology 'as a result of the house cleaning by Watson that had got rid of all mentalistic terms.' Hebb added, however, that it had regained its meaning 'now that we have found out how to deal with mental and cognitive terms behaviouristically.' 'Whether it is called "association of ideas" or "connections between mediating processes", that tendency of simultaneously active central processes to become capable to exciting one another appears fundamental to the existence of organised thought.'[12] As Lindsay and Norman say: 'The things we remember are organised into a complex structure that interconnects the events and concepts built up by past experience.'[13] Hebb defines the 'mediating process' as an 'activity of the brain which can hold the excitation delivered by a sensory event after this event has ceased, and this permits a stimulus to have its effect at some later time.' But he goes on to stress that 'We do not know, certainly, what a mediating process is, as a psychological mechanism. By definition, however, it can hold an excitation for some short period of time.'[14] Such short periods of excitation are, therefore, understood somehow to bring about physical changes in the brain which can give life-time permanence to memories. These long-term changes are normally assumed to be structural or chemical changes in the brain which allow for the storage of long-term memories.[15] The most usual assumption is that the counterparts of memories lie in the patterning of neuronal circuits in the brain. From

---

[11] G Humphrey *Thinking* (1951) p 2

[12] D O Hebb *A Textbook of Psychology* 2nd edn (1966) p 112

[13] P H Lindsay & D A Norman *Human Information Processing* 2nd edn (1977) p 366

[14] D O Hebb *op cit* pp 90-91

[15] P H Lindsay and A D Norman *op cit* p 421

these quotations, however, the weight put by Hebb, as by others, not on what is, but on what must be the case, will be obvious.

It was generally assumed until fairly recently that memories could be divided into two classes: the so-called short-term memories and the long-term memories. The short-term memories were though to have as their physical counterparts reverberating circuits which, unless they effected structural changes in the brain, were irretrievably lost once the reverberations ceased. Some such reverberations, however, were thought to effect such structural changes by synaptic growth, in which case, the memories were available from re-excitation throughout life; but not, of course, once the body died. This understanding was largely circular for if events were recalled, this was seen to have been the result of structural or other physical changes; if not, such changes could not have taken place.

In practice, however, the reverberating circuits in the brain remained active for far too short a time for the necessary changes in the brain to take place. Thus J C Eccles, writing in 1977, noted that 'we are confronted with the urgent problem of filling the temporal gap between the short-term memory of seconds and the hours required for the synaptic growth of long-term memory.[16] Hence an intermediate memory to bridge the gap was proposed and since them the number of memories with specialised roles has proliferated.

The resulting picture has proved to be so complex that it would be impracticable to attempt to chart a course through recent findings and attempts to interpret them. That there are structural or chemical changes in the brain as part of the process of learning seems difficult to doubt. Whether these changes in the brain include the counterparts of memories of individual events and sequences of events (episodic memories) or whether they simply provide the 'language' in terms of which individual memories are understood, (semantic memories) seems more questionable.[17] There seemingly must also be changes in the brain to take account of habit. In other words, that the brain develops as one facet of conceptual learning in order to be able to act as a processor of the data reaching it and as an activator of responses seems difficult to doubt: but whether it is also a store of individual memories is far more open to question.

In considering whether memories are stored in the brain, there is first the question whether every memory has some form of physical counterpart in the brain specific to it. Not only has intensive brain research over the past

---

[16] K R Popper & J C Eccles *The Self and its Brain* (1977) p 402

[17] For the distinction between episodic and semantic memories, see E Tulving Episodic and Semantic Memories in *The Organisation of Memory* eds S Tulving and W Donaldson (1972)

150 years failed to find evidence for such physical traces but those involved in the research have failed to formulate and agree about what is being sought. The position in 1976 was summarised by P Rozin thus: 'In a classical paper in this area, "In Search of the Engram", Karl Lashley (1950) after a long series of experimental attempts at excising the engram in animals, admitted that he had not been able to locate them. The story in humans is remarkably similar. Even massive lesions of the brain do not result in what can be defined as a loss of long-term memories. Though it is logically impossible to prove that a loss is not a loss of access, the actual phenomena do not suggest significant true losses. Most losses of past memories are impermenent. Pribram (1969) in summarising the literature on impaired memory consequent upon experimentally produced local brain damage in animals, concludes that "the impairment is apparently not so much a removal of localisable engrams as an interference with the mechanisms that code neural events so as to allow facile storage and retrieval." This holds good as well for humans. We are still in search of the engram.'[18] The reader may wish to bear in mind these conclusions in what follows.

Quite apart from the question whether the failure to find memory traces is to be explained by the fact that there are none, the problem of retrieval of memories itself entails serious conceptual difficulties. If (as Pribram and others assume) there is to be coding to allow for retrieval, either there must be some form of coding of the coding to allow for retrieval and so one is led into an infinite regress, or, at some point, the postulated mechanism must 'pick out' the memories or the relevant code; but if it can 'pick out' the code it could in principle 'pick out' the memory instead. Conceptually, the coding does not help. At some point, therefore, the postulated mechanism to 'pick out' the memory must 'know' and 'remember' what it is looking for and we simply find ourselves facing the original problem. We are, in effect, postulating a homunculus and so putting the problem back one step from the nature of brain processes to the nature of mind.

Thirdly, H A Bursen has sought to show in an argument too long and complex to summarise adequately here, that the idea of a memory trace is misconceived.[19] Basically, by showing how memories can be imaginatively altered, he seeks to show how one can eliminate any need for a memory trace and can show the very idea to be incoherent. Certainly, it seems true to say that the memories of at any rate some people, have a flexibility and a dynamic creativity that is difficult to reconcile with the inherent

---

[18] P Rozin The Psychobiological Approach to human memory in *Neural Mechanisms of Learning and Memory* eds M R Rosenzweig & E L Bennett (1976) pp 41-2

[19] *Dismantling the Memory Machine* (1978)

inflexibility presumably to be associated with a memory trace or other physical form of storage that may endure over a lifetime.

Of course, despite the failure over so long a period of intensive work to find the physical counterpart of long-term memories, or, indeed, given the emergence of so much evidence that seems incompatible with the forms that such counterparts might take, for agreement to be found about precisely what is being sought, this failure is normally explained by the widespread dispersal of these physical traces in the brain, and by its enormous complexity. The first point is seemingly less true than was once thought, but the latter must certainly carry weight. It would seem, however, that an explanation might come closer if the historical reasons for assuming that all mental events must have counterparts in the brain were to gain wider currency and if the role of the brain were to be seen primarily as a processor rather than a store: something that would be likely also to ease problems of understanding retrieval, which as we have seen, present problems within the current picture, hardly less intractable than that of finding the physical counterparts of memory itself. In other words, it seems that the confidence that memories must be stored in the brain stems not from reasonable projections from existing empirical evidence but from underlying assumptions about what must be the case in the light of the current materialist paradigm; and this in turn derives, not from empirical evidence but from ideas handed down by earlier generations, including particularly theologians.

The view that memories must be stored in the brain has not, however, gone unchallenged. Wittgenstein commented: 'I saw this man years ago: I see him again; I recognise him, I remember his name. Why does there have to be a cause of this remembering in my nervous system? Why must something or other, whatever it may be, be stored up there in any form? Why must a trace have been left behind? Why should there not be a psychological regularity to which no physiological regularity corresponds?'[20] The whole idea of a memory trace in the brain has been the subject of attacks in other works in recent years. Thus much more detailed and specific criticisms than can be deployed here have been put forward by Norman Malcolm in his book *Memory and Mind*[21], by Stephen Braude in *ESP and Psychokinesis*[22] and by R Sheldrake in *A New Science of Life*[23]as well as by H A Bursen whose work we have already referred to.

---

[20] L Wittgenstein *Zettel* (1967) pp 608-610

[21] *op cit* (1977)

[22] *op cit* (1979)

[23] *op cit* (1981)

We have already seen how the physical world can be pictured in terms of standing patterns in a transitory energy wave that is crossing the mind of God, so that events in the implicate order become thereby explicate and then fall back, enriched and structured by associations, into the implicate order again as the wave moves forward. What is more, within this picture, God is not just causally related to the world as in much Western theology. The world is created and sustained within his life and actually participates in his attributes. By implication, therefore, though systems that have attained a high level of order are, through the senses, conscious of what goes on around them, all events in the physical world must presumably have a mental or conscious component which is retained as they pass back into the eternal mind of God — for, *ex hypothesi*, God is omniscient; he knows everything, in what is for us past present and future, that occurs within his life; and God cannot forget. This suggests, therefore, that in the case of my personal memories, what makes some of God's memories also my memories as simply that, as a result of being rendered meaningful by my brain by their being brought together on the basis of associations with others of my memories, so forming intense and wide-ranging associations with them, they can be recalled on the basis of their associations by me; and they cannot normally be recalled by other people, for these memories have not passed through their brains and lack strong associations with them.

This picture carries a number of implications some of which are open to empirical verification or falsification. First, we might expect it to be an inherent feature of the mind of God that any two events brought into meaningful juxtaposition will tend to establish links or associations which will endure eternally: and we shall find evidence shortly pointing to a form of universal or Akashic memory. On this basis, our individual memories are specific and intensely specialised instances of a universal process. The purpose of the physical world as it rolls forward would appear to be the establishment of ordered memory-based systems, culminating in human beings, within the mind of God, to share in his life eternally; and the brain can then be seen as one particular and highly specialised processor to achieve this end. We shall find evidence to support these views presently.

It follows, therefore, that the more intensive associations are, the more we might expect personal memories to be easily recalled, and 'memories' which have weak associations, and which, in particular, have not passed through our brains, would then be difficult or impossible to recall in normal circumstances. But the brain, on this basis, would not be inherently different, save in degree, from the rest of the physical world which would be establishing associations with earlier events in the mind of God. We shall have to consider evidence of 'memories' that have not passed through the minds and brains of particular persons in the next chapters, and the role of associations in their recall.

Of course, even if 'memory' in this extended sense were such a universal phenomenon, there would still have to be some traces in the brain deriving from sense experiences; but these patternings would be of a semantic character: in other words, they would be forms that evoke a host of structured memories in the mind of God which in turn give meaning to each memory and to each new sense experience. What is more, these patternings would not need to be of an isomorphic character any more than a word is isomorphic of its meaning; their main role would be to evoke memories and give them meaning.

What this might entail would be that a given sense (or other) experience would evoke specific structured patternings in the brain largely established on the basis of earlier experiences. These sense experiences would themselves carry strong associations with earlier structured sense experiences that had passed back into the mind of God as memories. These earlier experiences would be recalled to near the threshold of memory. The new experience would thus be brought into association with the earlier structured clusters of memories that had been evoked; and, as the new experience itself passed back into the mind of God, it would take its place in these ordered structures. In other words, on this basis the brain would accept each new sense experience; it would discriminate a range of uniformities within it, each of which would tend to evoke its own brain traces; the awakened traces would evoke from the mind of God, the appropriately structured cluster of memories of earlier experiences. This would give meaning to the new experience; and as it in turn passed back into the mind of God it would join that structured cluster, the appropriate associations having been at that moment been established.

It would be inappropriate here to attempt to marshal empirical evidence of the working of the brain and in particular of memory that might fit within this picture, for the processes involved must be extremely complex and far more subtle than anything suggested here or perhaps even so far envisaged. But several implications should be drawn out and the main points made so far should be summarised. First, if evidence for individual physical memory traces were found, the kind of picture pointed to here could in principle allow for traces of some or all memories once established to remain in the brain throughout life: but they would concurrently be in the mind of God. Then as the brain decayed in senility and death, the structured memory system in the mind of God would endure. This account is thus not necessarily incompatible with the retention of memory traces during life; but in the absence of any clear evidence for them, it appears unnecessary to assume that there are or need be any such individual memory traces in the brain.

More specifically, it is to be assumed that a structured memory system that has passed back into the mind of God would retain the form or order attained in this world and so would continue to carry the attributes of God attributable to that human personality in incarnate form. The structured memory system constituting the personality would thus survive death and, by implication, would also occupy a structured memory environment already established by associations deriving from the structuring of events in the ordinary physical world.

Secondly, on the basis of earlier arguments suggesting that the ordinary physical world might be thought of in terms of standing patterns in an energy wave which crosses the mind of God, by implication, everything that happens in this world passes back enriched by associations in a continuous flow into the mind of God. There it retains the spatial, temporal and meaningful structure established in this world, as, of course, do our memories and dreams. Though many of our experiences pass beyond our normal recall, for the associations are too weak, and, *a fortiori*, so normally are events occurring in the world around us which we have not experienced, God does not forget and we shall find evidence suggesting that it may be possible exceptionally to evoke some of even these memories.

Thirdly, though the mind of man itself is to be seen on this basis as a structured memory system in the mind of God which is held in close association with the brain by associations, the mind is not to be thought of as located 'in' the brain, nor is it bounded by it: indeed, it is not located in space or time though it normally operates in association with the spatial and temporal system that is the brain. On this basis and fourthly, therefore, the human personality is to be seen as a dynamic system of memories ordered by intense associations which, in so far as it is ordered, is transparent to the attributes of God, just as it was in an incarnate personality. What is more, on this basis, one mind may in principle link with the memories constituting other minds or with memories of other events not experienced by it, if it is in a sufficiently receptive state and has strong enough associations with them: and we shall find evidence for this. And fifthly, although with increasing age the brain, and so the mechanisms that process new experiences, decay, within this picture earlier memories, once established, endure within the mind of God.

Although there have been questions raised about whether old people who lose their recent memories, really do have particularly clear memories of earlier years, many people who work with old people believe this to be true. The relevance of this is that the brain starts to decay from quite an early age and if memories were stored in the brain, one would expect earliest memories to fade first. But if the brain is just a processor that decays and earlier memories, once established in the mind of God, endure, then even if the brain is no longer capable of processing new experiences sufficiently intensively to allow for their ready recall, provided there are sufficient traces remaining in the brain to evoke earlier memories — which themselves retain a full quota of associations — a *prima facie* explanation is available both of the retention of earlier memories and the loss of later memories. In this context, it will be recalled that Rozin noted that even massive brain lesions do not result in the loss of long-term memories and that most losses of memories are impermanent.

The relevance of all this is that if the mind as so constituted lies in the mind of God, not only is it eternal and unbounded by space or time, but it suggests that the eternal life in God may have the character of a vast but dynamic memory system, presumably with many sub-systems: the many mansions referred to by Jesus. Evidence for this lies close at hand but it lies in events which are controversial, primarily because on a materialist basis, such events cannot occur and no explanation can be offered for them, save in terms of fraud or self-delusion. In fact, however, there is quite massive testimony from virtually all ages and peoples for such events and experiences, and a substantial proportion of the population of Great Britain appears to be satisfied that it has personal experience of them. This is the field of psychic phenomena, including evidence of survival of death, to which we must now turn.

CHAPTER TWENTY FIVE

THE MIND OF GOD: I

Until fairly recently, ideas of an after-life in some form, in Heaven or Hell or Limbo or Purgatory or Paradise, and of a world closely related to this one, populated by spirits, good and evil, were almost unquestioned by most Christians, and broadly similar beliefs have been held by supporters of most other faiths. Of course, all sorts of non-religious factors added strength to these beliefs. Today, however, many people, including many who believe in survival in some form, would be likely to dismiss what they understand to be the Christian formulations of such beliefs as superstition. Even theologians, while presumably retaining some sort of belief in an after-life, tend to avoid the subject as an obvious source of embarrassment: yet such beliefs lay at the very heart of the Gospel as understood by the Church of earlier days and still must lie at the heart of the Christian message.

The reasons for this embarrassment should now be fairly clear. First, in our current framework of thought the world is regarded primarily as physical and this is so even when God is seen as creating it *ad extra*. Mind and personality are therefore usually seen as by-products of the physical and since most present-day theologians, like most other people, seemingly accept that this is so, it would be natural for them to expect the destruction of the body to imply the destruction also of the mind and personality. But if, as they presumably believe, mind and personality survive, this must seemingly point to some kind of dualism; and the philosophical problems raised by dualism have been notorious at least since the time of Descartes.

The problems, however, are more deep-seated even than this for in current imagery, God is thought of as a person in some way outside the world and the idea of a person carries some sort of picture of a localised transcendent entity, complete in himself in the life of the Trinity. Because God and the world are thought of as utterly contrasted and there is, therefore, normally thought to be no question of degrees of participation in Christ and so in God, survival can hardly be thought of as within such a God; and if survival is to take place outside God, amongst the questions raised is where that survival can be conceived to be. Of course, the very formulation of these issues in these terms lays bare the crudity of the imagery that underlies the questions and they would be dismissed by most theologians and others on such grounds. But the fact that there is currently no alternative picture or model of God and the world that can offer a conceptual home for life after death points to the difficulty of any more adequate formulation even of the relevant questions, let alone the answers to them. What is more, for Christians the issues are further complicated by the traditional formulations of survival as involving the resurrection of the body: and this also is thought to link with the hardly less contentious issue of the bodily resurrection of Jesus Christ and the empty tomb.

Within the framework of thought of the New Testament and the early Church as it is being developed here, these questions take much more intelligible form. First, because creation is seen as a process within the life of God, with the Father as God transcendent and the world being created within his life by the Divine Son and Holy Spirit, not only is there no conceptual gap between God and the world, but we can envisage degrees of participation in the order and so the life of God, though always and necessarily falling short of complete absorption. What is more, because God, though seen as fully personal, is not seen as a person, there is greater conceptual scope for envisaging a 'depth' to the life of God which allows for the formulation of some understanding of entire realms between the world and the full transcendence of the Godhead. All this is implicit in the idea of growth and development 'in' the Divine Christ.

This conceptual scope is made much greater also if, instead of thinking of this world in relatively static terms, we think, as has been argued, of the physical world in terms of standing patterns in a transitory 'wave' of energy in some sense 'crossing' the mind of God, with the implication that there must be vast 'areas' in the eternal mind of God wherein lie 'memories' of the past and God's foresights about the future, as well as a vastly greater depth of meaning. And if we think of the physical world and more specifically the body in terms of dynamic energy patterns which manifest their form on the basis of disorder, the idea of some non-physical — spiritual — order which embraces both physical and non-physical becomes more intelligible. What is more, if the purpose of this transitory physical world is basically to create eternal ordered systems within the life of God that are in some way 'memory' systems, then after death, as we have already suggested, within the life of God, the body itself might be expected to take such a non-physical 'memory' form: and it will be recalled that Paul specifically says that the raised body will be 'spiritual' in contrast with a 'natural' body: 'It is sown a physical body; it is raised a spiritual body. If there is a physical body, there is also a spiritual body.' (1 Cor 15.44)

But if there is a non-physical realm where mind finds its home and where there is survival of the dead, then this raises a number of questions, notably questions concerning the relationship of mind to mind, of mind to its own body and mind to the physical generally. Our current framework of thought implies that any phenomena that cannot at least be paralleled by the physical and so be explicable in physical terms cannot occur and experiences that seemingly conflict with this must therefore be explained away in terms that are susceptible of more normal explanation. Indeed, any attempt to press the case for such phenomena to be taken seriously may be felt by some people as deeply threatening — threatening to the very structure of their minds, for it will be recalled that the way in which we view the world and the structure of our minds are closely correlated. Not surprisingly, therefore, though some of the evidence claimed for paranormal phenomena has been shown convincingly to be fradulent or erroneous, fraud and error has not been all one way for there is a lot of evidence for this on the part of those anxious to prove that the phenomena do not occur. The evidence for the occurrence of these experiences does, however, come in remarkably similar forms from many parts of the world and many ages and massive testimony to their occurrence has been accumulated over the last hundred years. What is more, it is now becoming clear that a large proportion of people have personal knowledge of such experiences though they normally will not discuss it for fear of ridicule or embarrassment.

For the purpose of this study, we need not attempt to prove that these phenomena occur. Many readers will accept that they do and, as we have seen, to try to do so would be a fruitless exercise in the face of determined disbelief, for all evidence, whether of spontaneous phenomena or experimental results, even in orthodox science, depends ultimately on personal experience and testimony and if sufficient assumptions of conspiracy to defraud and error are made, alternative explanations, even retrospectively of our own experiences, can always be, and often are, provided. It therefore suffices here to see whether, assuming they do occur in the forms claimed, a convincing explanation of them can be offered within the framework being developed: and if it can be, to point to some of the implications of these experiences. As we shall see, assuming these phenomena occur, they cast a flood of light on the nature of this world and, more widely, on the nature of survival and life in God. More specifically, as we have already noted, whereas in current thinking the concepts of God and the world are normally seen as exclusive, the alternative view being developed here of the world within the life of God, points to an entire conceptual zone within the life of God — the Mind of God — which has largely vanished from current thinking.

The systematic investigation of psychic phenomena can be dated as beginning in 1882 when a distinguished group of men and women associated mainly with Trinity College, Cambridge, founded the Society for Psychical Research. The American Society for Psychical Research was founded soon after. Whereas the earlier assumptions had been that these phenomena were manifestations of higher powers and, in particular, of those who had died, work of the SPR established the view that most of these experiences, whatever their nature, were essentially human and so open to psychological, scientific investigation. Since that time, not only has a vast amount of testimony to these experiences been collected but recently programmes of investigation in universities have been started in many parts of the world, particularly as developments of psychology and quantum physics. Of

course, much of the investigation undertaken earlier had been carried out by
university staff but the burgeoning of the work within universities
themselves has now become marked.

Primarily as a result of the efforts of J B Rhine to investigate these
phenomena scientifically, the emphasis moved in the 1930's from
investigation of the experiences themselves to the processes or the 'forces'
involved. But this entailed the assumption that there were such causal
processes or 'forces' to be studied. Whereas the experiences obviously
occur, whatever their explanation, it is much more difficult to demonstrate
the occurrence of psychic 'forces', for human beings are not precisely
predictable or controllable. S A Schouten, in a valuable discussion of these
issues,[1] notes that this is a problem in psychology as a whole and quotes
Gordon Westland as saying: 'Doubt is now unquestionably growing within
the ranks of professional psychologists over whether laws, prediction and
control, as conceived for traditional science make sense for psychology.'[2]
Notwithstanding this, however, a high proportion of the experimental work
undertaken has been to try to prove that the phenomena occur under
controlled laboratory conditions.

This work tends to be inhibiting, both because of the sceptical attitudes
of some experimenters and from sheer boredom. Also, because much of the
work has been designed to prove the occurrence of the phenomena and since
gifted psychics know full well that they do, they find long hours spent on
otherwise pointless tasks deeply uninspiring. In any event, because most
sceptics do not want to face such evidence, success and failure in
experiments has come often to be judged, less on what they reveal about the
experiences but on how far they are proof against even the remotest
possibility of fraud — an unattainable ideal, as we have seen, in the face of
determined disbelief.   And because experiments involving psychic
phenomena can rarely be repeated on demand, hostile critics have seized
upon this and have elevated it to the level of a criterion for scientific
credibility — conveniently forgetting not only sciences such as astronomy
and geology, but also that these phenomena depend on very sensitively
relaxed states of mind which cannot even be closely defined, let alone
measured, and for which the regularities of physical phenomena provide no
parallel.

This point needs to be stressed, for the idea of repetition of experiments
applies only in circumstances that are in relevant respects identical: no one
expects to ensure the same behaviour in different circumstances. But if we

---

[1] A Different Approach for studying Psi in *Current Trends in Psi Research*   eds B
Shapin and L Coly (1986)

[2] *Current Crises of Psychology* (1978) p 69

cannot identify sufficiently precisely, let alone measure, the relevant states of mind in which the phenomena occur, we cannot establish experimental conditions which ensure that the circumstances are in relevant respects identical. This is not a criticism of the experimenters or the phenomena but a fact about minds and our knowledge of them. Those who criticise the non-repeatability of experiments on psychic phenomena appear often to have very naïvely simplistic ideas of mind.

Criticisms designed to show that such phenomena do not occur and ignoring such basic factors have often been given hospitality in otherwise reputable journals, including the pages of *Nature*.[3] As Stephen Braude has shown, however, the claim that parapsychology has failed to produce a repeatable experiment 'rests on a naïve conception of what experimental repeatability is, in both parapsychology and science generally; second,.. it fails to take seriously the nature of parapsychology and the reasons why it should, in principle, be difficult to repeat experiments in this field; and third, .. once we see how loose a notion experimental repeatability is, the claim that there have been no repeatable experiments in parapsychology is at best highly questionable.'[4]

Perhaps the most basic reason why there has been no breakthrough in understanding these experiences has, however, been that, in a desire for 'scientific' respectability, the emphasis has been placed on experimental work which has been undertaken without the conceptual problems to which the phenomena give rise having first been adequately grappled with. Broadly, given that these phenomena have very wide-ranging implications which go to the very roots of our understanding of the world of which we are part, including the nature of mind, if there is no even tentative relevant conceptual framework within which adequate hypotheses can be formulated, there cannot be adequate or plausible hypotheses, and if adequate hypotheses set in an adequate context cannot be formulated, either experiments cannot be designed to test them or, when adequate experiments are designed — and this is increasingly being attempted,[5] their findings add little to the understanding of the phenomena.

This is a problem not confined to parapsychological research. The current state of research in a not unrelated part of psychology seemingly reveals a similar state of affairs. In *The Annual Review of Psychology* for 1983,[6] L G Rorer and T A Widiger reviewed work on 'Personality Structure and Assessment'. Their conclusion was that 'There has obviously been no

---

[3] see e g D F Marks Investigating the Paranormal *Nature* vol 320 (13 March 1986)

[4] S E Braude *ESP and Psycho-kinesis* (1979) p 41ff

[5] see eg R L Morris Psi and Human Factors in B Shapin and L Coly *op cit* (1986)

[6] pp 431-463

overreaching plan or theory, implicit or explicit, guiding the selection of topics for trait researchers.' The choice of fields of investigation over the last 25 years appears to have been 'determined by an author's reading of the *zeitgeist* in terms of frequency with which the names of fields of investigation have appeared in the titles of journal articles'. And they sum up by saying that 'our assessment is that this literature constitutes a negligible increment in our understanding of personality structure.'[7]

All this is not irrelevant to the theme of this book for it points to the conceptual cul-de-sac into which not merely religion but the non-physical sciences have been drifting: something which contrasts most strikingly with the excitement and even exuberance of conceptual thinking occurring in quantum physics and cosmology. This said, however, it would be wrong to suggest that no conceptual work of significance has taken place into psychic phenomena. Though in such work the names of C D Broad and Stephen Braude stand out, it is arguable that the most penetrating insights into the conceptual problems that are involved were shown by the distinguished Oxford philosopher, H H Price. As it would be beyond the scope of this work to survey the subject in any detail, it is primarily on his work that we shall draw to show how these phenomena find a place within the theological picture that is emerging here.

In an important essay, 'Psychical Research and Human Personality',[8] Price, having sought to show that there is no room for telepathy in a materialist universe, went on to say that telepathy did not altogether fit in with the traditional Western European religious conception of human personality, either. 'For the traditional religious conception of human nature is not only dualistic, regarding mind and body as two different and separable entities. It is also, if I may say so, an "isolationist" conception with regard to the individual mind. It holds that each individual mind is a separate and complete substance, whose only direct causal relations with the rest of the universe (apart from God) are relations with its own brain. The individual mind, it is supposed, can affect and be affected by other finite minds only in a very indirect and circuitous manner, by a long intervening chain of physical causes.' Price went on to say that the existence of telepathy showed this 'isolationism' to be false, even with regard to embodied minds; and *a fortiori* false to disembodied ones, if there are any.[9]

Price then pointed out that when the traditional religious theory of human personality maintains that the individual mind is a psychical substance, the notion of substance does not seem to fit the empirical facts. 'Here, as

---

[7] p 432

[8] reprinted in *Science and E S P*   ed J R Smythies (1967) pp 33-45

[9] H H Price *op cit* pp 38-9

elsewhere, Psychical Research joins hands with Abnormal Psychology. The phenomena of dissociated and alternating personality seem to show that the individual human mind does not have the internal unity which the notion of substance requires; and they certainly show that it is not a simple substance which the old dualistic philosophers thought it to be. On the other hand, the phenomena of telepathy show that one mind is not separated from another by any sharp and clear-cut boundary.' Price sums up his argument thus: 'It comes to this: both *ad intra* and *ad extra* (if I may so put it) the unitariness of the human mind seems to be a matter of degree, and not a matter of all or none. In relation to other minds, it is without clear boundaries; and its internal coherence is greater or less in different circumstances, and never perhaps complete.'[10]

Price went on to suggest that though there may be some factor in the personality which deserves the honourable title of *res cogitans*, we should go behind Descartes to an older tradition which divided human nature into three parts, body, mind (or soul) and spirit, instead of Descartes' two, body and mind. 'This tripartite division of human nature appears under various names in Neoplatonism, in some religious philosophies of the Far East, and in some Christian thinkers also. There are philosophical arguments in favour of it which have some weight; moreover certain forms of mystical experience seem to support it.'[11] The words of Sir Thomas Browne come to mind: 'There is surely a piece of divinity in us, something that was before the elements, and owes no homage unto the sun.'[12]

In his *Presidential Address to the Society for Psychical Research* given some ten years earlier,[13] Price had commented on the hypothesis of a Collective or Common Unconscious. 'The suggestion is that although our conscious personalities are isolated, yet in the deeper levels of the Unconscious the distinction between I and you no longer exists.' And he suggested that the hypothesis of a common unconscious is only another way of saying that at their deepest levels all personalities are in complete and continuous telepathic rapport.'[14] And earlier, he had suggested that mental images were 'dynamic', endowed with a kind of 'force' of their own and he had added a footnote: 'Is it possible that Associations by Resemblance might occur without unity of consciousness, so that an "idea" in my mind

---

[10] H H Price op cit p 39

[11] H H Price *op cit* p 41

[12] *Religio Medici* 12

[13] Haunting and the 'Psychic Ether' Hypothesis *Proc S P R* (Dec 1939) pt 160 vol 45 pp 307-343

[14] H H Price *op cit* (1939) p 320-1

could be associatively linked by resemblance with an "idea" in yours? Or
is this suggestion too non-sensical?"[15]

In his later writings Price appears not to have used the words 'association
of ideas' but he kept such a thought in mind. Thus in his *A S Eddington
Memorial Lecture on Some Aspects of the Conflict between Science and
Religion* given in Cambridge in 1953, he said: 'In fact, when we consider
the implications of super-normal cognition, something more like the old
Dualistic conception of human personality begins to be plausible again. ...
Only, as against some traditional forms of Dualism, and especially the
Cartesian version of it, we have to insist on the reality and crucial
importance of unconscious mental processes'. This, however, meant
abandoning the principle of 'one mind, one body' if, 'at the unconscious
level, or at any rate in the "deeper strata" of it, ... one common mind could
be associated with two or more human bodies.' And Price presses home the
point by noting that it does not even seem always to be true that there is just
one conscious mind to each body. 'The curious phenomena of divided
personality suggest that sometimes two distinct consciousnesses can be
associated with the same body, and some of the equally curious phenomena
of mediumship suggest it too.'[16]

Speaking earlier in the same lecture about extra-sensory perception, Price
noted that the word 'perception' did not seem at all a happy one. 'Whatever
these processes are, they must surely be extremely unlike what we ordinarily
call perception. If we try to consider how they work, the most promising
model to use is not perception, but something like the Freudian theory of
dreams.'[17] Price went on to distinguish two strata or levels of mind, the
conscious and the unconscious, and suggested that there may be some form
of barrier or censorship or repressive mechanism which tends to prevent
supernormally acquired information getting through to consciousness.

It may be, however, that no special barrier may need to be postulated:
if the associations are weak, and bearing in mind that such experiences
involve many levels of meaning, only some of which may be shared by the
supernormal message and the mind of the subject, one might expect one idea
to trigger another in a somewhat haphazard fashion, so that only
exceptionally would such ideas get through to consciousness, and then often
in unpredictable form and circumstances: though they would be much more
likely to get through if the mind were relaxed — as it were, 'idling' —
rather than if it were preoccupied with directed activity. There is a lot of
evidence that such a relaxed state of mind can be of critical significance for

---

[15] H H Price *op cit* (1939) p 320

[16] H H Price *Some Aspects of the Conflict between Science and Religion* (1953) p 46-7

[17] H H Price *op cit* (1953) pp 37-8

the occurrence of psychic phenomena. Indeed, it is this very problem of getting people into this relaxed state of mind that proves so difficult in experimental conditions. As we have already noted, the presence of someone who is sceptical or just a bit tense, particularly as an experimenter, may make the subject defensive or just unrelaxed and this of itself may preclude positive results. Indeed, so critical may this factor be, that when attempts are made to repeat experiments, the replacement of a state of mind of open enquiry by a concern to achieve the same outcome as before may itself preclude success. It is, I believe, this same factor that makes states of dissociation so important and, as we shall see, when these states of dissociation are taken to the extreme in the case of deeply disturbed minds, there can occur poltergeist and related phenomena. The relationship of this relaxed but alert state of mind to the openness advocated in the Wisdom literature of Israel will be obvious.

We saw earlier that Price, in commenting on the processes of extra sensory perception had suggested that 'the most promising model to use is not perception, but something like the Freudian theory of dreams.' As he notes: telepathy can take many forms. 'The impression may emerge in the form of a mental image; in the form of a dream; as a waking hallucination, whether visual or auditory; in the form of a unaccountable but veridical "hunch"; or, finally, in the form of non-voluntary bodily behaviour, such as automatic writing or automatic speech which occurs in mediumistic trance.'[18] And he remarked earlier that 'we have to envisage the possibility that telepathy is going on all the time in some people, or perhaps in everyone, though the results only show themselves in consciousness occasionally.'[19]

From a different angle, the importance of associations in the case of shared experiences gains support from work done by Ian Stevenson who has shown, in an analysis of 160 earlier recorded telepathic cases, that 62.5% were between members of the same immediate family, 35% were between members of the extended family or friends and acquaintances and only 2.5% of cases involved strangers.[20] Similar results were obtained from an analysis of 35 new cases.

It is relevant to our earlier discussion of memory to note that in practice, it is often difficult to distinguish memory from telepathy for subjectively they may be indistinguishable in character and can come together in the same sequence of experiences. What is more, telepathy is subjectively indistinguishable from clairvoyance — where a subject seemingly becomes aware of events which have not been experienced by anyone else.

---

[18] H H Price *op cit*   (1953) p 39

[19] H H Price *op cit*   (1953) pp 38-9

[20] I Stevenson *Telepathic Impressions* (1970) p 16

C W K Mundle, in an article on 'The Explanation of E S P'[21] noted that clairvoyance presented much more severe problems of explanation than telepathy, notwithstanding that the evidence was, he claimed, as strong as for telepathy. In particular, he noted the peculiar difficulty of explaining how a subject can obtain impressions relevant to the object when it may lie in the past — or future — and sometimes at a great distance from the subject. However, Mundle in his article did not survey the ideas of a common unconscious as put forward by Price, Tyrrell[22] and Carington[23] on the ground that they could apply only to telepathy. This is so, however, only if the unconscious, albeit common, is receptive only to the experiences of persons.

If, on the other hand, as we have suggested, not only is the role of the brain that of a processor, but it is a special case of the role of the physical world as a whole, this objection need not apply; for we are then thinking in terms of a form of world or Akashic memory. That role is to order and develop, on the basis of associations, an entire hierarchy of systems within systems in the mind of God which can come to share in his life, Indeed, it seems that, if we believe in God, we must have some such idea, for God is omniscient and omniscience must cover events as well as persons: as we have said, we can hardly think of his forgetting.

Such ideas are, of course, not new: William James, in his study of the medium, Mrs Piper,[24] proposed that memories may exist not only for human beings but for physical objects also. According to the ideas of James, who had developed ideas of Gustav Fechner, a person's memories may persist in the objects with which a person was connected when living. He sought to explain psychometry — the ESP method of getting information about events from objects associated with them — in these terms. And Bohm's implicate order assumes something like such a memory.[25]

What on this basis tends to distinguish clairvoyance from telepathy therefore must seemingly be the relative paucity of associations, for the physical events concerned, being far less complex than the events in the brain and less highly organised, might be expected normally to have associations far less intensive than would be effected by the brain. This is subject to several qualifications but in support of this view, it may be noted that, as far as spontaneous cases are concerned, clairvoyance would appear normally to be the prerogative of specially gifted psychics and if they are

[21] C W K Mundle The Explanation of E S P in *Science and E S P*   ed J R Smythies (1967)   pp 197-207

[22] G N M Tyrrell *Apparitions* rev edn (1953)

[23] W Carington *Telepathy* (1945) especially pp 118-120

[24] Report on Mrs Piper's Hodgson-Control *Proc SPR*   1909 23 2-121

[25] *Wholeness and the Implicate Order* (1980) pp 207-8

seeking clairvoyant experiences, for example to trace a missing person, they normally have to have some form of 'token' or 'K' object which itself has strong associations with the person concerned, if they are to establish the necessary chain of associations between themselves and the person or the object sought.

Price had thought deeply about the problems of clairvoyance and in 1943 allowed a personal communication to be quoted to members of the S P R. He started by saying: 'The more I consider clairvoyance, the less I seem to understand it.' He went on to distinguish different kinds of clairvoyance and continued: 'If there is any one theory to cover the whole lot, I think it will have to be on Bergsonian lines. We shall have to change the question and puzzle ourselves not about clairvoyance, but rather about normal sense perception, treating it not as "normal", but rather as a sub-normal and biologically explicable limitation imposed upon an inherent and aboriginal omniscience. We shall have to say (as Leibniz did) that in principle every mind is aware of what is going on everywhere; and then the puzzling thing will be that in most people at most times this awareness is repressed — which puzzle we then solve by invoking Bergson's *attention à la vie* with the brain and the physical sense organs as its instrument.'

'If this is indeed the right line to take, we ought not to expect to get light upon the *modus operandi* of clairvoyance (or indeed other supernormal cognition) from experiments. For it will not have any particular *modus operandi*; being so to speak the natural and inherent condition of the psyche. What we must seek light on is the manner or manners in which the ordinary processes of sense-perception and everyday consciousness are switched off — a question of *modus inhibendi* rather than of *modus operandi*.' And he adds: 'Philosophers sometimes say that it is wrong in principle to seek for a causal explanation of "rational" or "valid" thinking. What requires a causal explanation is erroneous or invalid thinking — which indeed is not really thinking at all, but the temporary cessation or inhibition of it.'[26] The way in which this line of thinking approaches the picture being presented here of creation in general and persons in particular as potential microcosms within the omniscient life of God, will be sufficiently clear in broad terms for it not to need to be developed further in this work.

The, in principle fairly simple, hypothesis being presented here has, therefore, very far reaching implications. First, it presents the brain primarily as a processor and as a system that is in principle not unique. Rather it is seen as an extremely specialised and highly developed processor but, in this respect, as playing precisely the same kind of role as the rest of the physical world in relation to the mind of God. This would explain the

---

[26] H H Price (Personal communication) *Journ SPR*   vol 33 no 592-3 (1943) pp 12-3

lack of success in identifying any physical trace of episodic memories in the brain, though, as has been noted, if these were in due course discovered, this would probably present no insuperable problem for understanding normal (or paranormal) experiences within the picture being developed here. But secondly, just as the processing capacities of the brain continuously feed back into memory, so do the processing capacities of the physical world as a whole. Memory is therefore to be seen, not as a by-product of the storage capacities of the brain but on a wider basis as an active, dynamic feature of the eternal life of God which is being structured by associations. In so far, minds as basically memory systems in the mind of God are not entirely separate systems but can in principle interact one with another and even merge in so far as associations are sufficiently strong and the receiving mind is sufficiently relaxed and receptive. Furthermore, even when a chain of associations is established, it is to be expected that there will be a certain lack of directivity in the chain which will often not be able to discriminate between the memories of the person receiving and the 'memories' reaching it from beyond his own system.[27] And, of course, as Price said, the events reaching the consciousness of the subject will therefore bear a much closer resemblance to dream work than to normal perception.

Perhaps one of the most significant products of this hypothesis, however, is the explanation that associations offer for the selectivity of telepathy and above all of clairvoyance, for it has always been a source of total puzzlement to those seeking to understand clairvoyance in terms of a physical model, how a clairvoyant can pick out (home-in on) relevant scenes associated with his quest, whose location is sometimes far distant and unknown to him and sometimes, when seeking, for instance, the location of the body of a drowned person, to anyone else. Indeed, an explanation also becomes available of the even more puzzling phenomenon of how clairvoyants (and dowsing appears to be a particular form of clairvoyance) can often achieve results by scanning maps: for obviously maps have close and widely spread associations with the terrain mapped. Such psychometry is thus not limited to things but can include persons alive and dead, and information about their locations.

There are a number of strands of evidence which offer support for these claims about the relationship of psi to memory, some of which we have noted already and some of which are referred to in an important article by W G Roll: 'A Systems Theoretical Approach'[28]. Thus he noted that Louisa Rhine, in a study of precognitive experiences, commented that those

---

[27] see e g Gilbert Murray Presidential Address S P R 1952 in J R Smythies *op cit* pp 27-8

[28] in *Current Trends in Psi Research* eds B Shapin and L Coly (1986) pp 47-91

concerned often 'marvelled at the fact that the precognitive experience was just like "remembering the future"'.[29] William James noticed that Mrs Piper had an unusually good memory in her trance states though her memory in the waking states was not unusual.[30] And Sara Feather found that subjects who did well in memory tests also scored well in ESP and those who did poorly in memory tests had low psi scores.[31] What is more, as we shall see, there is quite a lot of evidence that suggests, not only that persons survive death but that they do so in what is fundamentally a memory environment.

All such factors are, therefore, it seems, fully consonant with the idea of minds, both in this world and the next, being substantially constituted by ordered, intensely structured clusters of memories, held together by associations, and enshrining in various degrees the order and reason of the divine Logos. Insofar, they are sustained also by the cybernetic forces of the Holy Spirit, and manifest the other attributes of life, consciousness, understanding and reason, love and even holiness associated with the level of order that has been attained. In this life, while the body survives, these memory systems are normally firmly attached to the body with which each system has so many associations and through which it grows and develops to participate in the life of God. But exceptionally, particularly if attention is relaxed, this allows for some openness to other psychic messages and systems which are attracted on the basis of associations. Exceptionally, too, the mind may loosen its links with the body, especially in circumstances of low vitality, particularly after accidents and operations, and the mind finds itself able to move around in the memory world which flows back from the physical world where its body remains — in the so-called out-of-the-body experiences. And, for everyone, as we shall see, when the body dies and loses its attractive hold, the mind system that constitutes the person slips away into a deeper memory world.

This picture is developed in the next chapter but one further issue remains to be clarified here: how we can understand the not-infrequent experiences of precognition and premonitions, and their seeming implication that in some way the future is determined? Within the picture being established here, the answer to this problem does, I believe, become clearer, but it requires that we distinguish carefully the different levels involved. We need first to distinguish the unchanging timeless plenitude of the Godhead from the

---

[29] Frequency of Types of Experience in Spontaneous Precognition *Journ of Parapsychology* (1954) 18 p 121

[30] A Record of Observations of certain Phenomena of Trance *Proc SPR* (1889-90) 6 pp 555-7

[31] A Comparison of Performance in Memory and ESP Tests in *Parapsychology from Duke to FRNM* (1965)

changes taking place within his life. It is the failure to make this distinction that is the source of many difficulties with the Western concept of God. As we have seen, it is within the life of God that the developing sequence of events that constitute the physical world, as well as its memory counterpart that flows back from it, both lie. Changes that take place within and as part of both sequences have their own temporal and spatial character; but the sequences as a whole, lying within the Mind of God, are not themselves 'in' time or 'in' space. It is from the way in which the sequence of events that constitute the physical world organise themselves spatially and temporally, that we get our concepts of time and space. As these sequences change, insofar they necessarily change the life of God. But his life itself within which they develop, embraces and transcends that sequential process and insofar does not itself change. God therefore can see the entire process and all parts of it within his life, for his vision embraces the whole. What is more, these changing sequences within his life do not add anything to the life of God that does not derive from God himself, for he is organising the entire sequences within his life that is not itself sequential.

On this basis, therefore, persons, who exist within the evolving sequence of events that constitute this world, may, by some gift of insight, if associations are strong enough, be able so to 'home in' on the 'memory' of some particular event or sequence of events within a larger sequence that is itself evolving temporally within the mind of God. But this memory sequence, as a whole, lies outside time and space, in the mind of God. Therefore, though the events in question may be part of a sequence that is in the future or the past in relation to any particular person, and though, as he experiences them, they may retain their own local temporal and spatial character, as experienced precognitively, they 'break in' to the quite different sequence of events that constitute that person's normal life. They have been, as it were, 'pulled out' of their normal spatial and temporal place in a wider sequence of 'memories' in the mind of God that is not itself 'in' time or space, and have been drawn into the other sequence that that person is experiencing. Yet, as we shall see, not all such premonitions are wholly accurate for there can remain some scope for altering the events foreseen.

On the basis, therefore, that all events, and, therefore, all temporal and spatial processes and memories are formed within the life of God, he knows them eternally for they lie within his life sustained by his creative will. But entailed in his creative will is freedom to deviate from it, with consequences that either dissipate or destroy the order so far attained or frustrate its further development. In so far, he knows all events that (from our point of view), have occurred, are occurring or will occur; but he does not determine them. And the plenitude of his life is such that deviation from countless states can be restored in countless ways, so leading to the vast proliferation of forms within the plenitude of his life. Yet, the more fully creation comes to share in his life, the stronger are the forces of understanding and love which seek to draw creation into his life in which freedom and necessity coincide.

CHAPTER TWENTY SIX

THE MIND OF GOD: II

We have seen something of how extra-sensory experiences may come about. Often they are associated with some form of emergency which arouses concern in the subject and this may facilitate the coming into consciousness of the experience. This is, perhaps, particularly true of precognitive experiences which appear to be predominantly of a premonitory kind. Of course, many extra-sensory experiences must occur without being recognised as such, and only some of these will lead to any conscious change of action. An investigation carried out some years ago into the numbers of casualties in rail disasters, suggested that the numbers of people involved were markedly lower than might have been expected from normal usage of the trains, even when allowance was made for various factors that might have affected the figures. Yet presumably few of those involved or who might have been involved experienced any conscious premonition.[1]

Pre-cognitive experiences can be divided broadly into two groups, both of which raise important issues. The first group is of those experiences in which what is foreseen comes about; and the second is where what is foreseen happens broadly in that way but with some very significant change. The obvious cases of this are where the persons concerned were able to act to avert the foreseen outcome.

The general idea of precognition finds a basis of explanation if we appreciate first that our experiences of time and space derive from the ways in which physical events organise themselves in four dimensions and that, therefore, as cosmologists are now suggesting, time and space came into existence with the physical universe at the big bang — an idea foreshadowed by Augustine when he said that the world was created with time and not in time. On the basis that the physical universe lies within the life of God, it then becomes intelligible that the life of God itself lies outside time and space, but with various systems, each with their own temporal and spatial organisation, within it. Furthermore, though our sense experiences organise themselves temporally and spatially, it is questionable whether we can think of them as in space or time. This is even clearer when we think of memories and dreams which normally have a spatial and often a temporal, sequential, character, but are not themselves within the quite different temporal and spatial world of which our bodies and normal sense experiences are part.

If, then, as we have suggested, the flow of 'memories' of events in the physical world, including our own memories, passes back into the mind of

---

[1]   W Cox Precognition: an analysis *Journ Am SPR* (1956) vol 50 pp 99-109

God as the energy wave that constitutes the physical world moves forward, it becomes intelligible that that flow of 'memories' should retain, as a result of the associations established in the physical world, the general form and structure (including the spatial and temporal organisation) that it acquired in the physical world. But if, for some reason, in the mind of some person, there forms a complex of ideas and memories which has strong associations with some particular event or sequence of events that lies in the mind of God, that event or sequence may, as it were, be 'pulled out' of its context by these associations and can enter the consciousness of the person in quite the quite different spatial and temporal context of the normal physical world. What would be entailed would be not basically dissimilar from the situation when, in the normal course of sense experiences, I come upon some place or event that brings vividly to mind some earlier memory or memories; and within the picture being presented here, this can apply to past, present and future events, any of which can, in principle, be experienced telepathically or clairvoyantly.

This account allows us to understand also how it can come about that events 'foreseen' in a precognitive experience can be changed. To understand this we need to note that all our sense experiences entail both the sensory stimulus itself and the wide range of memories of earlier experiences that it evokes and which give it meaning. These associations structure the individual components of a memory sequence both temporally and spatially, so tending to ensure that the memory sequence retains the form in which it was initially established. What is more, each normal sense experience evokes memories that are already meaningful and which carry their own range of structured associations, which have their associations, and so on indefinitely. On this basis it becomes intelligible that a particular sequence of experiences may carry forward on its own temporal momentum which flows from earlier experiences and which will lead the sequence forward to a conclusion established on the basis of such earlier experiences. But a person who has or learns of such a precognitive experience remains free to take action in some different direction so that what actually happens is not what is precognised. A particular case may illustrate this. A mother had a vivid dream that her baby, asleep in a cot beneath a chandelier, was being killed by its falling. She clearly 'saw' the clock in the room and noted the time. She at once awoke and, despite the scepticism of her husband, brought the baby into their bed. At the time foreseen, the chandelier fell but the baby was not, of course, killed. Presumably the action of the mother did not establish associations strong enough to divert the sequence of experiences from its expected path. We shall refer to other such examples later. Similarly, a contemporary or retrospective telepathic or clairvoyant experience may deviate significantly from the truth for the same reason and may, indeed, wander off on the basis of associations to some quite different conclusion as in dreams and free association.

There are, however, many other forms of psychic phenomena besides extra-sensory perception and it is worth considering some of these briefly to indicate how they, too, find a place within the wider picture being developed here. We have suggested that the physical world is continuously establishing associative 'memory' systems in the mind of God and the most highly organised of these which thus manifest most fully the attributes of God, are human beings. Such systems normally adhere closely to the physical so long as the relevant physical form or sequence endures, but they are not themselves physical; and this suggests that if in some way we, as persons, could part temporarily from our bodies, we might have experiences relevant both to our current lives in the body and to life after death when that parting becomes permanent. That some people do have such experiences is now well recorded. A valuable collection of such cases was made in her book *Out of the Body Experiences*[2] by Celia Green and these were discussed briefly by H H Price in his Introduction to the book. Other such cases were recorded by Sir Alister Hardy in his book *The Spiritual Nature of Man*[3] in which he assembled cases collected by the Religious Experience Research Unit which he founded in Oxford. Two particularly suggestive collections of out-of-the-body experiences of one man, Sylvan Muldoon, were made by Muldoon himself and H Carrington.[4]

Suffice here to say that though these experiences seemingly occur to quite a lot of people, for most of whom they occur only once, there are a few people, like Muldoon, to whom they occur frequently and who gain a considerable measure of control over themselves in this state. For many people, it is simply a matter of finding themselves looking at their bodies lying on the ground or in bed and observing the actions of those around — for such experiences often occur after a serious accident or operation or in other states of low vitality. Some people, however, who have the experiences more frequently, achieve fuller control. In the light of their reports it appears that, though many of their experiences are of the normal world in the vicinity of their bodies, what they are observing is none the less a world of memory and thought, though having taken form in the ordinary world of sense experience possibly only a moment earlier. Thus events can sometimes be observed with an accuracy and in a detail that would not be open to the senses in those circumstances. Presumably this 'memory' world

---

[2] (1968)

[3] (1979)

[4] S Muldoon and H Carrington *The Projection of the Astral Body* 4th edn (1968) and *The Phenomena of Astral Projection* (1951)

normally comprises memories (in the widest sense) that have not necessarily passed through anyone's mind and which can be experienced virtually contemporaneously with their occurrence in the natural world. As memories and thoughts, they are subject to some measure of control by those experiencing them. As Muldoon says: '... every thing in the astral plane seems to be governed by thought — by the mind of the projector. As a man thinks, so he is. .. As one is in his mind he becomes in reality, when he is in the astral body.'[5]

If, for instance, one thinks of oneself travelling somewhere, one finds oneself so travelling; if one thinks oneself at that place, one finds oneself there. As Muldoon says: 'If you ever learn to project consciously, ... even before you complete a thought you have already attained what you are thinking about.'[6] And the suggestion that such experiences are structured by associations is supported by further cases where the experience seemingly develops on the basis of associations according to its own momentum. Thus Muldoon tells of an experience when he was visiting the home of an aunt. When he found himself out of the body, he found himself above his bed at home and it was the absence of his body on the bed and his desire to find it quickly which translated him back to his aunt's house. As he says: 'In any projection, the astral body will always "project" with much more ease to a familiar place than to a strange place; in fact, the astral body when exteriorised and unconscious, will be forced to meander about in the subject's familiar haunts very much of the time — going through activities which have become habitual to the subject. And this applies not only to temporary, projected phantoms but to permanently disembodied phantoms also (phantoms of the dead).'[7]   Again, we find confirmation of the suggestion that these experiences are based on 'memories' and systems of 'memories' with their associations.

Psychic phenomena do not classify themselves neatly but the next group that we may identify is of those entities that are not surviving persons yet which bear some of the attributes of persons. The now classic case of this kind is that of 'Philip'. The essential features of the case were that a group of psychic experimenters in Toronto under the guidance of Dr A R G Owen (formerly a don at Cambridge and then at Toronto University) and his wife, set out to 'create' their own ghost. They wrote a brief scenario and biography with anachronisms built in.   After a time, they established communication by means of raps with just such an entity. The case was widely observed and similar entities have since been brought into existence.

---

[5] *The Projection of the Astral Body*   (1968) p 286

[6] *op cit* (1968) p 287

[7] *op cit* (1968) pp 182-3

'Philip' was the product of their joint minds and he appears to have been dependent on their minds for such vitality as he had. He appears, in other words, to have been a kind of structured memory system which, when it attained sufficient ordered complexity, manifested a measure of life and consciousness and intelligence.[8]

Somewhat similar are the so-called 'false communicators'. A notable example occurred when R Hodgson was working with Mrs Piper, the famous trance medium, the day after he had been reading the *Life and Letters of Sir Walter Scott* and pondering on them. 'Sir Walter Scott' communicated through Mrs Piper, speaking fluently but totally implausibly and weakly excusing himself for failing lamentably under cross examination to know many of the things that the real Sir Walter Scott could certainly be expected to have known. He was seemingly a quasi-autonomous product of Hodgson's own mind communicating back through Mrs Piper, and which, having developed some sort of rudimentary personality of its own, was probably able to draw vitality from her and was able to communicate through her, given her very great sensitivity.[9]

Both 'Philip' and 'Sir Walter Scott' were essentially benign figures but it is probable that the troublesome and sometimes quite malign phenomena associated with poltergeists have the same kind of origin, seemingly often being deeply dissociated and repressed parts of the personality of the person or persons with whom the phenomena are identifiably associated and which form into a partially autonomous rudimentary personality. It seems not improbable that a somewhat similar explanation may apply to some communications purportedly from the dead, and to many hauntings and apparitions. If, as is possible, a similar explanation applies also to certain communications which came to another subject, purportedly from identifiable but   minor historical figures, but which were found to incorporate errors from printed books, this would suggest that such memory clusters may draw constituent 'memories' from further afield and even from printed sources — something which would find an explanation within the picture being developed here. It should, however, be added that the investigators in this case expressed doubts about the credibility of several of these communications, but this appears to have been based in part on the *a priori* grounds that no other explanation was available.[10]

---

[8] I M Owen and M Sparrow *Conjuring up Philip* (1976)

[9] E M Sidgwick A Contribution to the Study of Mrs Piper's Trance Phenomena *Proc S P R* (1915) vol 28 pp 85 *et seq* and p 297

[10] see e g I Stevenson and J Beloff   An Analysis of Some Suspect Drop-in Communications   *JSPR*   vol 50, no 785 (Sept 1980) pp 427-447 and subsequent correspondence in *JSPR* vol 51 no 792 (Oct 1982) pp 392-7

If, however, even some such cases are accepted as evidence of these phenomena, the implications are substantial. They are obviously incompatible with any idea that personality, and memories in particular, are by-products of or are inseparably linked to the brain. They are almost equally incompatible with the idea that God creates life or consciousness by a special act of intervention. On the other hand, they fit remarkably easily into the picture being presented here of creation as an evolutionary process within the life of God in which the attributes of God manifest themselves wherever order has developed sufficiently; but at lower levels of order those personal attributes are rudimentary, whereas his more fully personal attributes can manifest themselves only at the higher levels of order. We shall find further support for this view later.

Two further points deserve comment. First, whereas some of these phenomena are subjective in the sense that they are experienced by one person only and are thus thought of as 'in' the mind, others are objective in the sense that they can be observed by two or more people and are thus thought of as 'outside' the mind. Apparitions can notoriously fall into either category. The implication of the picture being developed here is that the classification of some events as 'in' the mind and others as 'outside' it is conceptually inadequate. The distinction seems to be that some such events lying in the mind of God are drawn into the mind of the subject by associations with his own experiences of, for example, the place where the events occur; others have such strong associations with, for example, the place itself that they get drawn into the wave of energy that constitutes the physical world, where, having taken physical form, they can influence the sense mechanisms of one or more people, sometimes altering the normal sequence of physical events in unusual ways. In any event, the implication, to which we shall return, is that apparitions can, perhaps, best be thought of as 'memory systems' in the extended sense of memory: that insofar as they have sufficient organisation to manifest even rudiments of life they have some autonomy, in some cases conscious, and can in some measure change and reorganise themselves on the basis of associations in the mind of God, so affecting the form in which they become explicit in the physical world. The activities of the poltergeist at Rosenheim which disrupted an office over a considerable period of time and entailed sustained investigation by the electricity and telephone authorities and the police is a case in point and is particularly well documented.[11] What is more, although this particular poltergeist may have been, in effect, a semi-autonomous sub-system of the mind of the girl who was at the centre of these disturbances and may have

---

[11] see e g H Bender Modern Poltergeist Research in *New Directions in Parapsychology* ed J Beloff (1974) pp 122-143

drawn energy from her, it seems that some such systems have greater autonomy and can attach themselves to, and draw energy from, more than one person.

As for psycho-kinesis, one essential point here is not just that such events can take an extremely wide variety of forms, but that they are often highly selective and directed seemingly in an intelligent manner. They thus can range from the movement of sometimes quite heavy objects to changes in the operation of complex equipment of whose inner workings the subject may have no conscious knowledge. Experiments into such phenomena are now often mounted with the use of sophisticated electronic and radio-active random event generators with automatic recording. Evidence of these investigations has been brought together by the American philosopher, Stephen Braude, in his book *E S P and Psycho-Kinesis*[12] where he has sought to bring up to date C D Broad's *Lectures on Psychical Research*[13] which were given as the Perrott Lectures at Cambridge in 1959 and 1960. As for the explanation of these phenomena, it must suffice to say that as mind phenomena, they are not limited by time and space; and, as mind phenomena, there can probably be a strong measure of identification of the subject with the object in the implicate order which allows for its thought form to be changed. If, then, in such changed form, the object is drawn from the mind of God (Bohm's implicate order) into the energy wave which constitutes the moment 'now', (Bohm's explicate order), the normal pattern of physical events may be changed to take unexpected form.

These and other kinds of psychic phenomena are often not of any deep significance in themselves: a few are troublesome, most are trivial and their pursuit can become near-addictive for a few people. But their significance for our understanding of the world is very great. The volume of testimony to such experiences is very large and, because people will often not willingly admit to these experiences, their frequency is rarely recognised, even by those who have them. When they are taken seriously, our current materialist view of the world can be seen to be deeply inadequate. Essentially, these phenomena provide striking evidence of an entire realm that has no conceptual home in current thinking and it points to an understanding of God who, though profoundly personal, reveals that personality through each and every aspect of creation; but only in so far as it is able to develop to a level at which his personal attributes can reveal themselves, albeit in warped form. This includes even the limited consciousness and life of spirit entities.

---

[12] (1979)

[13] (1962)

Christianity, in its deep and fully justified concern to emphasise the personal love and understanding of God, has failed to give sufficient weight to the entire realm within his life to which psychic phenomena point. This gives some credence to the reports of 'invisible companions' and 'evil spirits' that played such a large role in the life and thinking of the early Church. What is more, as we must now note, there is a possible explanation of why psychic phenomena, though much more frequent than normally recognised, may still be less prevalent today than in those times.

It seems plausible to assume that with more systematic education in many societies today, most men's minds are more highly developed and large areas of thought are more tightly integrated and organised (though not necessarily more whole and integrated overall) than were the minds of many people in the past, so that they might be expected to be less open and responsive to stray or casual associations. Indeed, this point is simply an application of Price's point, quoted earlier, that 'We shall have to say (as Leibniz did) that in principle every mind is aware of what is going on everywhere; and then the puzzling thing will be that in most people at most times this awareness is repressed — which puzzle we then solve by invoking Bergson's attention à la vie with the brain and the physical sense organs as its instrument.' It must be added, however, that though, overall, these experiences are very much more frequent than is generally appreciated, they probably occur most frequently to relatively simple people towards both ends of the spectrum of human development: those more primitive people whose minds are relatively undeveloped in terms of abstract thought (though not necessarily of wisdom) and those whose minds are very highly developed and integrated — in Wisdom terms, the sages. In both cases, such people may be able more easily to relax, to still their minds — an effect which may occur also where there is quite deep dissociation. Some support for such speculations is to be found in the work on religious experiences carried out by the Religious Experience Research Unit founded by Sir Alister Hardy which has itself found confirmation in surveys, including some carried out in several other countries.[14] On the other hand, people whose minds are quite highly developed yet suffer division and alienation, may well find it very difficult to relax and open their minds: and in so far as those with less developed minds succeed, they may make themselves vulnerable to forms of psychic invasion.

Obviously, within this picture, 'memories' in this extended sense include not only single units (like 'stills') but dynamic clusters and sequences organised temporally and spatially as complex systems. Indeed, since we

---

[14] see e g Alister Hardy *The Spiritual Nature of Man* (1979) and David Hay *Exploring Inner Space* rev edn (1987)

cannot on this basis think of mind as held together by the physical mechanisms and structure of the brain, we ought not to be thinking of the content of the mind as separable from its form and structure and can best think of it as itself an immensely complex, structured, dynamic 'memory' system. Normally it is 'glued' to the flow of incoming sense experiences by strong and complex chains of (meaningful) associations, but when we cease to pay attention to the world around us, our thoughts and memories can wander; when we are asleep, so can the content of our dreams; in states of dissociation it seems that 'parts' or sub-systems of some people's minds can join up with other 'memory' systems as in clairvoyance; and in more extreme cases, there can occur out-of-the-body experiences in which the mind can move freely in the organised and structured stream of 'memories' flowing from the physical world. And when the body ceases to function and begins to break down at death, the mind is freed from its links with the body and from the other standing patterns of the energy wave that constitute the physical world, and it can then move freely within the network of associations of which it is part: for, of course, the mind is constituted by and is embedded in a network of associations continuously flowing back into the collective unconscious. And, as we know from our ability to control our thoughts and memories, we have some control of our own relationships within this network of memories. We noted earlier the remarkable and little understood ability of some children and primitive peoples to visualise vividly and realistically and manipulate their memories and this may be relevant here. Of such 'eidetic' memories, Cynthia Gray and Kent Gummerman say: 'The eidetic image is, in fact, a dynamic, fluctuating image that usually can, like more commonplace images, be altered and manipulated voluntarily.'[15] This applies after death.

Survival of Death

All this has bearing on survival of death, for not only does it point to depths in which the survival of the dead and their spiritual progress towards the Godhead becomes intelligible, but survival can be seen to be continuous with and to share some features of ordinary experiences, including psychic phenomena. The amount of testimony bearing on survival is vast in quantity and, notwithstanding its very varied quality and sources, in the light of the picture being presented here, it can be seen to have a remarkable consistency and coherence. To illustrate this, we can again turn to the work of H H Price who set out his ideas in some detail in an important paper 'Survival

---

[15] The Enigmatic Eidetic Image *Psychological Bulletin* vol 82 pp 383-407

and the Idea of Another World'[16] and in *Essays in the Philosophy of Religion*.[17] based on the Sarum Lectures for 1971.

Price started his paper of 1953 by noting that ideas similar to his had been put forward by W Carington in his book *Telepathy*[18] and by C J Ducasse in *Nature, Mind and Death*.[19] He also noted the similarity of the Hindu conception of 'Kama Loka' (literally the world of desire); and that something very similar was to be found also in Mahayana Buddhism. In these two religions, there were not just one but several other worlds experienced in succession; but, as he said, this is also true of some theories of the Christian life after death where we may move from Purgatory to Paradise and then, perhaps, to Heaven: and in some theories there are no less than seven heavens.[20] Price, however, was content to concentrate on what for us is the next world and so, for the purpose of this chapter, we shall be.

Price first distinguished the possibility of survival as embodied from survival as disembodied. Embodied survival implied a world with spatial characteristics and secondary qualities though not necessarily the same as in this world. He noted that in many mediumistic communications the next world is described as if it was a kind of material world and that in the Pre-Reformation tradition, Paradise was described as a kind of garden or park.[21] As for disembodied survival, Price commented that in that state we would have no sense experiences but would, and indeed must, have memory in order to retain our personal identity and our characters and, he suggested, disembodied survival would involve a kind of dream world constructed out of its own memories and desires. As he noted, dreams can have spatial characteristics but they are not located in physical space. They can seem perfectly real, particularly if we have no real world to compare them with. Among the images remembered would be familiar places and images of our own bodies. But the laws governing movement in such a world would not be the laws of physics but much more like the laws of psychology.

There would on this basis doubtless be many worlds rather than one world shared by all, but they need not be entirely private. Given the possibility of telepathy, there might be a common image-world which was the product jointly of many interacting personalities who would probably be

[16] *Proc SPR*   vol 50 (1953)

[17] (1972)

[18] (1945)

[19] (1951)

[20] *Essays in the Philosophy of Religion*   (1972) pp 99-100

[21] H H Price *op cit*   (1972) pp 102-3

like-minded. And Price reminded us of 'the great gulf fixed' between the
next world of Dives in the Gospel parable (Luke 16 26) and that of Lazarus.
'The "great gulf", I suggest, was a consequence of the unlike-mindedness
between Dives and those like-minded with him, on the one hand, and
Lazarus and those like-minded with him, on the other. Between these two
groups of persons there could be no telepathic interaction.'[22]

Price went on to argue that though we need bodies to be social beings
and to express ourselves and be recognised, provided the body plays these
roles it need not have the body's functions. So Price suggested that on this
basis the pictures of embodied and disembodied survival converge, though
neither fits quite perfectly.

Price noted the many different descriptions of the after-life which we get
from different communicators but that they could be made consistent by
assuming each is describing a rather different world of his own experience.
As Price said: 'Religious traditions, both Western and Eastern, suggest a
similar view. They usually lay stress on the moral aspects of the next life,
and insist that after death each person gets the pleasant experiences that are
the consequences of his good deeds on earth, and the unpleasant experiences
which are the consequences of his misdeeds.' And he added that 'it is not
easy to see how this could be arranged, unless the after-death world
experienced by a particular person is correlated pretty closely with the
memories and moral character of that person.'[23] Though this world would
be a wish-fulfillment world, if the barrier between the conscious and
unconscious were removed, some people's Next World could be like a
nightmare from which one could not wake up.[24] We should, perhaps, here
add that such a wish-fulfillment world would, of course, like this physical
and all other worlds, be sustained by the creative and redeeming act and will
of God: and this therefore leaves the way open for redemption for the whole
of creation and for God to be all in all.

Much more could, of course, be said about all this. Since Price gave his
lectures, attention has focussed on the reports of the experiences of many
people who have, in effect, died and have been revived and of many people
for whom death is imminent.[25] These reports appear to be very much in line
with the picture presented by Price, which is itself in line with many reports

---

[22] H H Price *op cit* (1972) pp 108-9

[23] H H Price *op cit* (1972) p 115

[24] H H Price *op cit* (1972) p 117

[25] e g R A Moody *Life after Death* (1975) and *Reflections on Life After Death* (1977),
K Ring *Life at Death* (1980) and, more recently, a valuable survey having regard also to
evidence from Great Britain, by Margot Grey *Return from Death* (1985). See also the relevant
chapter of D Lorimer *Survival?* (1984) which surveys the field more widely.

through mediums. The volume of testimony in support of Price is impressive. It is broadly compatible with the earlier brief indications that we have seen about other paranormal phenomena, and this is itself compatible with the picture we have sketched of the ordinary world as understood in the light of empirical evidence from scientists. The whole picture then finds its place within the theological picture being developed here; and this in turn is in large measure based on the New Testament and the work of the Early Church Fathers whose ideas of survival and heaven make sense not only — perhaps even not primarily — in terms of individual survival but in terms of each individual finding fulfillment in a community of love.[26]

Two points need to be stressed about the picture presented in this and the previous chapters. The first point is that psychic phenomena give us valuable insights into the nature, not only of the next world but of this one. But while these phenomena may deepen our understanding, their experience also normally by-passes our senses through which our personalities become structured. As Price realised, this is presumably the reason why extra-sensory perception, which is seemingly the normal means of communication throughout the rest of the mind of God, is usually excluded from our lives in this world. Unless, therefore, the insights that these experiences offer are used to develop our personalities, they frustrate the very purpose of this life. Yet on the other side, if we ignore the implications of the picture that they give us, then we narrow the base of experience on which we develop our personalities in order to come to a full life in God and it becomes much more difficult to escape from the thraldom imposed upon us by our current materialist framework of thought — with results that can be seen around us.

On this basis, therefore, it becomes in some measure intelligible that some 'memory' workings and transformations may take place spontaneously on the basis of associations in the collective unconscious or mind of God. In particular, we may think of associated events tending to be drawn together in the collective unconscious 'before' they issue in the physical world, thus accounting for many instances of synchronicity or coincidence which, though extraordinary, are often quite trivial and without personal significance and probably far more frequent than noticed.

More important, an explanation may be glimpsed of how it comes about that, within the mind of God, events may come to organise themselves to meet the whole, mature or righteous man. The essential point here is that, the more fully man develops to participate in the order and life of God, the more fully he opens himself to the guidance of the Holy Spirit. But we

---

[26] e g C H Dodd The Immortality of Man *New Testament Studies* (1953)

must not think of that guidance as seeking just to draw each individual towards a distant God. The Holy Spirit is seeking all the time to organise the life of God in an entire hierarchy of groupings within which man grows and develops. Each of these at each level manifests collective, cybernetic forces. But whereas at lower levels, these are largely impersonal and blind, the higher the level of order and the fuller the participation of the individual and the group within the life of God, the more these forces are able to respond personally to the needs of each individual and group, tending to draw them more fully into the order of the life of God as manifested in this world and allowing each to manifest more fully the richness of the Plenum. It is precisely in this sense that we must understand the way in which, not just individuals but whole communities, may prosper. It is one of the ironies of much modern social and theological thought, that in emphasising the need for man to love his neighbour, the utter and complete dependence of the whole of creation on the plenitude of God and the wisdom enshrined in it has been forgotten, and man, in a profound blasphemy, has sought to plan and operate as if he was himself virtually omnipotent, omniscient and self-sufficient.

Obviously this account offers only a highly tentative sketch and seeks to do no more than be suggestive. But it does offer the potential for a more developed account which would embrace the evidence of the physical, biological and social sciences, the evidence of parapsychology and the essential insights of the early Christian Church, the New Testament, and Ancient Israel and, in large measure, too, of the Greeks — insights which, it should be plain, we have increasingly lost or diminished. At this point, therefore, we need to turn to the testimonies about Jesus who seemingly ran the entire gamut of human development and revealed many of its implications — the process described by Irenaeus as 'recapitulation'.

CHAPTER TWENTY SEVEN

JESUS CHRIST

The Jewish Background to the Reception of Jesus as Divine

It is hardly surprising that our current materialist framework of thought, with God, if he is recognised at all, being seen as a person outside the world, should be presenting serious problems for the understanding of Jesus Christ. Not, of course, that this is new in the history of the Church. In recent years, however, these problems appear to have become more severe as more and more evidence bearing upon the world into which Jesus was born, grew up and died, and within which the early Church developed, has become available. It raises many questions about how far, if at all, when read in the context of current Western thought, Christian doctrines can be credible. We have seen how theologians in the Western tradition have tried to bridge the gap by thinking in terms of God 'sending' Christ into the world as the greatest of all miracles. But increasingly this has seemed a not very adequate solution and many theologians have been driven to qualify the sense in which Jesus is seen as God. Thus Maurice Wiles says: 'Talk of his pre-existence ought probably in most, perhaps in all, cases to be understood, on the analogy of the pre-existence of the Torah, to indicate the eternal divine purpose being achieved through him, rather than pre-existence of a fully personal kind.'[1] We noted, at an early stage in this study, John Knox's much quoted statement that we can have the humanity of Jesus Christ without the pre-existence and we can have the pre-existence without the humanity: but there is absolutely no way in which we can have both. In the course of this study, we have seen the steps by which the question how we are to understand Jesus Christ has come to take this form as a result of the conceptual separation of God and the world that has taken place over the centuries. Wiles himself has noted that the basic difficulty in the statement of any doctrine of Christ is that it interacts at a very profound level with so many other fundamental doctrines. And he adds: 'It is not, in my judgement, possible even to understand what sort of thing a doctrine of Christ would be, let alone what specific form it should take, without some prior beliefs about God and the human situation.'[2] The aptness of this comment should by now have been amply illustrated in this study.

If the Incarnation is seen in terms of God sending his only Son into the world in a uniquely miraculous event, not only is the Old Testament

---

[1] M Wiles *The Remaking of Christian Doctrine* (1974) p 53

[2] M Wiles *Working Papers in Doctrine* (1976) p 39

relegated to a purely preparatory function: so is the entire evolutionary process. In effect evolution provides a kind of backcloth to this one all-important event. What is more, everything that follows looks back to that event and is seen at best as a somewhat indeterminate period of waiting, if not of anti-climax. If, on the other hand, Jesus is seen as the first-fruits of a process which started in the Big-Bang and still has to be brought to its full culmination, Jesus having shown, and indeed provided, the way, the emphasis moves to the process as a whole as the Divine cosmic plan: Christianity becomes less backward-looking and more forward-looking towards achieving the destiny of each person and the world, and indeed, the eschaton itself is no longer to be seen as incredibly remote.

Barr sets this in its New Testament context when he suggests that, within the Gospels themselves, Incarnation is a secondary concept. 'The first-line question in the Gospels about Jesus is whether he is the Messiah expected in Israel'[3] This observation is the more relevant because Barr had earlier argued that though the writers of the Gospels were moved by a desire to narrate history, they were primarily concerned to convey what they saw as significant about Jesus.[4]

The title of Messiah, however, for the Jews, did not carry any implication of divinity. A E Harvey has emphasised that the earliest Christians could hardly have occupied themselves with the question posed by later theologians: whether and in what sense Jesus was 'god', for the Jewish people were severely and passionately monotheist. But when Harvey goes on to say 'Nor would it have occurred to them to think of Jesus as a manifestation of God on earth', care is needed.[5] As we have seen, there was a profound sense in which for the Jews, the entire world manifested the presence of God who was seen as more intensively present at certain times and places and in certain persons.

The problem here is, of course, that in current thought not only are 'God' and 'the world' sharply contrasting concepts, but we have lost any sense of the normal presence of God in the world; the separation which we conceive of entails, not just a difference of physical and spiritual, but a sense, too, of the immediacy and autonomy of the physical world and of a corresponding remoteness of God. Despite the claims of many Christian commentators, this sharp contrast was not at all the same for the Jews of the time of Jesus. It needs constantly to be borne in mind, therefore, that for them, there was

---

[3] J Barr Some Thoughts on Narrative, Myth and Incarnation in *God Incarnate* ed A E Harvey (1981) p 22

[4] J Barr *op cit* (1981) p 17

[5] A E Harvey Christology and the Evidence of the New Testament in A E Harvey *op cit* (1981) pp 52-3

no sharp separation into natural and supernatural for they were constantly aware of the presence and accessibility of God in the world. G F Moore notes that the appearance of the Lord in the thornbush was seen as teaching that there is no place on earth void of the Presence; it was the Presence which, like the sea flooding the cave, filled the tabernacle with its radiance, while the world outside was no less full of it. When God sends lightnings, they go but do not need to return for they are constantly in his presence.[6]

The world was thus seen as created and sustained by the Word and Holy Spirit. God was therefore seen as present throughout the world and the world participated in God. He was met in the daily round and particularly in prayer and study. He had inspired the prophets. Also, man was in the image of God. The idea of the mutual indwelling was not, therefore, far to seek and so the sense that Jesus manifested the attributes of God so as to be clearly revealing of his character and will was not an idea alien to the near contemporaries of Jesus as it is to us. Through the miracles and in other ways Jesus is portrayed in the Gospels — and was believed by some of those who flocked to his presence — to be acting with the power and authority of God.

Although, therefore, the Jewish God was indeed understood in passionately monotheistic terms, as we have seen, this was in no way felt to preclude his presence in and dominion over the world generally and Israel in particular. R S Barbour notes that in a number of places in the literature of Judaism, God's Wisdom is his agent in creation, 'In Rabbinic Judaism, Wisdom surrendered her cosmic functions ... to the Torah, in Philo she surrendered them, for the most part, to the Logos, and in Christianity she surrendered them to Christ. But she stands behind all of these, in some sense at least.'[7] Barbour points, therefore, to the role of Wisdom in making specific the presence of God in the world and in Jesus in particular. As he says: 'It is obvious that the presence of Jesus is indeed a tabernacling of the Divine Wisdom or Logos with men' and he points to John 1 14, 'The Word became flesh and dwelt among us.'[8] These words find their context in the Prologue as a whole. It is difficult to see how the Prologue could be more explicit: The Word was with God and the Word was God; all things were made through him, and without him was not anything made that was made. In him was life and the life was the light of men. And the Word became flesh and dwelt among us.

---

[6] *Judaism*   vol I   (1927)   pp 370-1

[7] R S Barbour   Creation, Wisdom and Christ   in   *Creation, Christ and Culture*   ed R W A McKinney   (1976)   p 23

[8] R S Barbour   op cit   (1976)   p 33

In line with this Johannine understanding, Barbour notes how in Christ, the early Christians found the revelation of God's hidden Wisdom which had been active from the beginning in all things, and so found continuity between creation and redemption. And he quotes C H Dodd who, speaking of the realism of the parables of Jesus, says: 'It arises from a conviction that there is no mere analogy, but an inward affinity, between the natural order and the spiritual order. ... Since nature and supernature are one order, you can take any part of that order and find in it illumination for other parts. ..This sense of the divineness of the natural order is the major premiss of all the parables.'[9] This divineness of the natural order applies directly to the humanity of Christ.

Some Constraints on the Personal Development of Jesus

We have seen how all our experiences are laden with meaning — theory-laden — and that that conceptual loading is derived largely from learning which normally necessarily takes place within our own community. The conceptual framework within which we develop conditions the very way in which we see the world and think about it, as well as being a necessary condition of the language that we use. This learning is implicit in, and is a necessary condition of the growth and development of, every child to be a person and Jesus cannot have been an exception. This framework of thought both orders and constrains the development of the personality and this requires that Jesus, too, must have developed within his community, however much he grew to transcend it. In his important study, *Jesus and the Constraints of History*,[10] A E Harvey has gone some way along this line of thought for he has sought to illuminate the life of Jesus by reference to the constraints which his life in Palestine at that time placed on him, and place on our interpretation of him. Near the beginning of the book, he comments that his work represents a preliminary attempt to study some of the constraints which bore upon the activity of Jesus, and to define them with such precision as has been made possible by recent research. As he says, within these constraints, only a certain number of options, a relatively small number of styles of action, was open to Jesus, and it is possible to use the evidence of the Gospels to make a well-founded judgement on the question of which of these options was actually adopted by him.[11] Harvey goes on to examine some of these constraints but there is one constraint, or cluster of constraints, on which, understandably, he restricts his comments:

---

[9] C H Dodd *The Parables of the Kingdom* rev edn (1971) pp 20-1

[10] (1982)

[11] A E Harvey *Jesus and the Constraints of History* (1982) p 9

this is in his final chapter which is on 'The Son of God: The Constraint of Monotheism', where he seeks to show how, within that compelling Jewish constraint, Jesus must have been understood.

Harvey points out first that for the ancients what the son owes to his father is above all — obedience, and this was no empty exhortation: a clause still stood in the Law to the effect that a son's stubborn disobedience was punishable by death.[12]   Secondly, the basic instruction and apprenticeship offered by a father to his son served as a model, both for general education and for the transmission of esoteric knowledge.[13] And thirdly, the son was normally the preferred agent of the father, acting in his name and with his authority, and was therefore accorded the honour due to the father himself.[14] As Harvey says: 'To call Jesus Son of God was therefore to accept the claim implied in his words and actions that he was totally obedient to the divine will, that he could give authoritative teaching about God, and that he was empowered to act as God's authorised representative and agent'.[15] Harvey concludes that this understanding of the implications of Sonship, and of the overwhelming authority possessed by Jesus if he was indeed (in all the senses described) 'Son of God', enabled the first followers of Jesus to use the title as a way of stating his unique relationship with God, and his total authority over us which flows from that relationship.[16] This, Harvey says, did not imply that Jesus or his followers saw him as divine: he asserts that there is no evidence whatever that he spoke or acted as if he believed himself to be 'a god', or 'divine'.[17] Yet, as we have seen, this conclusion needs always to be read in a context in which the divine was seen as constantly present in the world and more fully in some places and persons.

The Heart of the Gospel

This then raises the question of Jesus' attitude to sin. It will be recalled that, as Moore stressed, sin was not for the Jews a moral concept. The term thus covered, for instance, those who lent money for interest (the usurers) and was not directed just to those who were 'immoral' in our sense. It was a question whether a man observed the Law. God had entered into a

---

[12] *op cit* (1982) p 159

[13] *op cit* (1982) p 160

[14] *op cit* (1982) p 161ff

[15] *op cit* (1982) 'p 164

[16] *op cit* (1982) pp 172-3

[17] *op cit* (1982) p 168

covenant with Israel and there was never any question that God would renounce or cancel it. But it was always open to man to withdraw: he could obey the commandments of God or disobey. What is more, in practice, men did constantly transgress the Law, often unwittingly. There were prescribed ways in which those who transgressed the Law could put themselves right with God: but the essential requirement was repentance.

The question of Jesus' own attitude to the Law has been a major preoccupation of New Testament scholars and E P Sanders has sought to show that it has been the subject of serious misunderstanding. Many scholars have seen a major conflict between Jesus and the Law but Sanders stresses that to be stricter than the Law was not against the Law. As he says: 'God gave the Torah to Israel by the hand of Moses; obedience to the Torah is a condition for retaining the covenant promises; intentional and unrepenting disobedience implies rejection of the law, rejection of the covenant for which it is the condition, and rejection of the God who gave the law and the covenant.'[18] It follows, therefore, that if Jesus had rejected the Torah, he would in a very clear sense have been for the Jews — and Jesus was himself a Jew — a sinner. Sanders' conclusion is clear. Jesus' mission was to Israel in the name of the God of Israel. He thus evidently accepted his people's special status, that is the election and the covenant and he accepted obedience to the law as the norm. And Sanders sums up by saying that if he had truly opposed the law, we would know it from early Christianity, but he did think that the Mosaic law was neither absolute nor final. In the new age that was about to dawn, God would go beyond the law: he would admit the wicked.[19] The 'wicked' here referred to are those who went against the Law wilfully and heinously and did not repent.[20]

This role of repentance needs to be clarified. 'Repentance' in English suggests being sorry for one's sins: the Greek word, however, means to think again, have second thoughts, change one's mind. As C H Dodd puts it: '"Repentance" as the gospels mean it, is a readjustment of ideas and emotions, from which a new pattern of life and behaviour will grow (as the "fruit of repentance")'[21] And on the basis that that new pattern was for the better, we are speaking here of a change towards greater wholeness of character.

It seems fair to assume that repentance in this thorough-going sense was in practice a good deal rarer than was the taking of the formal steps

---

[18] *Jesus and Judaism*   (1985)   p 56

[19] *op cit*   (1985)   p 336

[20] *op cit*   (1985)   p 177

[21] *The Founder of Christianity*   (1971)   p 58

associated with repentance. For the Jews, however, repentance at a minimum would have entailed not only those formal steps but also that those who broke the Law would have had seriously to attempt to change their ways. Indeed, it is normally only by such a change of behaviour that one can judge whether repentance in the full sense has taken place.

Jesus, however, appears to have turned the normal requirements associated with repentance around. For him, the formal observances were not a basic requirement provided repentance in the full sense of a change of character had taken place, notwithstanding that that change of character without the formal acts would not normally have been recognised as repentance by the Jews. It seems fair also to note here Jesus' uncanny insights into human character, on which we comment later. However that may be, as Dodd says: 'This constant and emphatic dwelling on the inward disposition rather than the overt act might well excite the suspicion of those who insisted on the deed as the sole visible test of obedience to the Law of God. It is clear that Jesus, too, attached importance to the concrete act; that is the reason why he cast so much of his ethical teaching in the form of vivid word pictures of action instead of abstract general maxims. But he did so with the proviso that the act is the sincere expression of an inward disposition. "A good man produces good from the store of good within himself, and an evil man from the evil within, produces evil. For the words the mouth utters come from an overflowing of the heart." (Matt 12.35; Luke 6.45). *It is a matter of wholness of character, consistency of word, thought and act.'* (my italics)[22] Dodd adds that for Jesus an act is a moral act only so far as it expresses the whole character of the man who acts.[23] And he emphasises that with the coming of the Kingdom of God, a new era of relations between God and man had set in. Morality might now draw directly from fresh springs. The whole apparatus of traditional regulations lost its importance.[24]

This, however, is not the whole picture, for Jesus did not just open the door of the Kingdom to all who sinned and failed to follow the normal procedures associated with repentance. As Sanders stresses, he substituted a different requirement, namely that they should believe in him. We need, therefore, to ask why and in what way belief in Jesus carried the keys to the Kingdom and the observance of the Law did not. The answer to this question should now be fairly clear. First, observance of some aspects of the Law were a valuable and even necessary prerequisite of salvation, for in some broad sense morality was seen as a precondition and consequence of

---

[22] *op cit*   (1971)   pp 72-3
[23] *op cit*   (1971)   p 74
[24] *op cit*   (1971)   pp 76-7

the growth and development of the personality in righteousness. But observance of the Law, or even of conventional morality, did not of itself offer the keys of the Kingdom: something much more positive was needed and Jesus offered this from many angles.

The fact that some people were able to see in Jesus as a person, and in his teachings and actions, including, of course, the miracles, the powers of God, must in itself have radically disrupted their normal views and have given them some deeper insight into the relationship of God to Jesus, a man who had grown up amongst them; it must, therefore, have given those who were receptive some deeper insight into God's relationship to the world and to them personally. This must have been in many ways a life-enhancing and liberating experience, but one producing complex reactions of awe, even fear, joy, thanksgiving, understanding and love. Above all, it must have opened their eyes to see the ordinary disorder and suffering of the world around them in a new, insightful light. And in so far as they came to see the world more insightfully, so far did they themselves become more whole, mature people who thereby shared more fully in the order and love of God. They lived more fully in what came to be seen as life in Christ. It was this extension of the entire evolutionary process by attaining fuller participation in the life of God that opened the doors of the Kingdom: it was this that the Gospel was all about: it was about growing and developing in the order and reason of the Word of God and so becoming more whole and mature people and, as a consequence of this, becoming more rational and moral: it was to grow in Christ.

Jesus was not, therefore, just a teacher of morality: he was not just a teacher: he was a living manifestation of the creativity of the powers of God to whom he was obedient: Jesus thereby showed the way to others to achieve salvation through the Word of God which was itself the Way. Of course, as we have seen, this carried strong moral implications: as 1 John 3 9 says: 'Whoever is born of God does not commit sin, because the seed (of God) remains in him; he cannot sin, because he is born of God. It is hereby that the children of God and the children of the devil are made manifest; he who does not carry out justice is not of God, nor he who does not love his brother.' But that morality was not, as such, the heart of the Gospel, the good news, though it was a consequence and often a pre-condition of its acceptance. The insights that came to those who had faith were the insights of *gnosis* with the reorientation of character that this entailed, and so the fuller participation in the life of God.

We can gain more insight into the relationship of the Gospel to morality by asking whether Jesus was 'sinless' in our normal moral sense. The records reaching us give us little information and there is obviously no reason to think that Jesus was 'immoral'. There is, however, a very large area between immorality on the one side and absolute moral perfection on the other. Indeed, the question arises whether in this sinful world it is possible to be morally perfect and what such an idea could mean: for every human being is often faced with the choice of evils. Two examples may suffice to put this in perspective. Sanders discusses at some length the impact of the saying 'Follow me, and leave the dead to bury the dead.' (Matt 8.21f and Luke 9.59f) He brings out the deep offence it must have caused for it conflicted with not only the Mosaic legislation as it was understood throughout Judaism, but also normal and common Graeco-Roman piety.[25] This, it may be added, was the subject of Sophocles' 'Antigone'.

Sanders discusses at length also the 'cleansing' of the Temple. This, again, he claims to have been the subject of deep misunderstandings. In particular, it has normally been seen as an act against the profanation by trading in and around the Temple precincts. But, as he shows, this must be a misunderstanding, for a supply of unblemished animals to meet the demand of those who had come, often long distances, to make sacrifices required by the law, was essential for the functioning of the Temple. Sanders sees it rather as a symbolic action pointing to the destruction of the Temple in the coming eschaton. But however it is seen, it again must have given deep offence and indeed is one of the factors that was to lead Jesus to the crucifixion. Many of the sayings of Jesus, too, if they accurately reflect his words and attitude, must have been deeply hurtful. 'If anyone comes to me and does not hate his father and mother, wife and children, brothers and sisters, even his own life, he cannot be a disciple of mine.' (Luke 14.26)

Whatever is made of such sayings, any unbiassed reading of the Gospels must convey a picture of someone far removed from 'Gentle Jesus, meek and mild'. Nor did he meet each situation pragmatically by seeking the least of evils. His saying 'You must not think that I have come to bring peace on earth; I have not come to bring peace but the sword' (Matt 10.34-9) has often been followed to the letter. What should be quite clear is that Jesus had too important priorities in opening closed minds to the insights which he offered in every aspect of his presence, to be just a 'nice' man. What is more, the accusation of his being a 'glutton and drinker', (Luke 7.34) however unjustified, would hardly have been made of an extreme ascetic — an approach which would have been largely irrelevant to his life and work, and probably counter-productive. Yet, as we have seen, this was later to be regarded as a virtual *sine qua non* of spiritual development seen in terms of moral purity.

---

[25] *op cit* (1985) p 252

As we have found, however, there is a third sense of 'sinless' and one which is basic to this study. This is sinlessness in the sense of following the creative will of God to grow and develop to participate more and more fully in and manifest the order and reason of God — which is the Divine Christ — and the love of the Holy Spirit. This sense need not coincide completely with the observance of the Torah nor with some normal facets of morality, though it is often compatible with both. It is this aspect that needs now to be considered. As Harvey shows, the very title 'Son of God' itself points to the total personal obedience of Jesus to the will of God which is itself creative: and it is this that is the salient feature of the New Testament record. But, as we have seen, sin, in the sense of deviation from the order and reason and will of God, has a wide base in the very nature of the physical world. No human being, and Jesus was human, leaps ready-made into a state which is fully in accord with the will of God: that state has to be attained freely, step by step, and this is precisely the character of the entire evolutionary process and which was implied in Irenaeus' concept of recapitulation.

The will of God operates throughout the world as a whole, and not just in situations where moral issues arise. Deviations from his will are found throughout the physical world and, indeed, following Bohm, it seems that they are intrinsic to its very constitution. Yet the physical world is the instrument by which, step by step, order is being created and creation is being led to participate more fully in the life of God: and in this process, the body plays an essential role. In other words, 'sin' in this wider sense is an ingredient of the human condition, and in being incarnate, Jesus must have carried these marks of this sinful world. What is more, Jesus had to learn from those around him simply in order to develop as a person. But if that is so, however perfect his mother Mary may have been, he must have had to learn also from other, imperfect, human beings. From both these points of view, Jesus, if he was human at all, must have had to grow and develop as a person and that, for him as for others, must have involved a process of overcoming disordering and foreclosing forces in his personality as well as further developing in accordance with the order and reason of God.

In other words, given the disorder and warping that is inherent in the world, obedience to the will of God is to be seen, not as a state of sinlessness but as a process entailing responsiveness to the creative and redeeming powers of God that lead to creative development and so to fuller participation in his life. It does far better justice to the humanity and steadfastness of Jesus if we recognise that he, like every human being, had to develop and order his personality against all sorts of disordering and foreclosing forces and temptations, than to make the totally implausible suggestion that he could be human yet (in some sense) sinless from birth: a suggestion that virtually denies his humanity.

The Personal Development of Jesus

It is an implication of the argument of this book that the whole of creation has to find its own way into the life of God entirely freely. This does not mean without divine help. Creativity is inherent in the powers of God and is the *sine qua non* of creation; but that help has to be freely assimilated into the attributes of creation before it can be utilised by creation: it cannot be thrust upon creation as an extra. But individual men and women do not start from scratch; they are part of the entire creative process and their genetic and social endowment ensures, first, that they start a long way down the track and secondly, because creation does not move forward as one solid block, some start far further down the track than others. Some have formidable genetic and social advantages, some have formidable genetic and social disadvantages. But wherever men start, there are still great obstacles ahead of them and most men have created as many as they have overcome before they die. That Jesus had great genetic and social advantages — though neither might be recognised as such if he were born into present day Western society — seems a fairly obvious assumption. But whatever his genetic and environmental advantages, it follows from the entire argument of this book that he cannot have had divinity thrust upon him, for the whole of creation has to find its way into the life of God entirely freely and Jesus as a man cannot have been an exception. His human qualities are made plain in a large number of passages in the Gospels and this should be obvious from the fact that so many Jews around him failed to recognise anything special about him. Indeed, Hebrews 5 7-8 speaks in terms of his learning obedience in the school of suffering, and once perfected, becoming the source of eternal salvation for all who obey him.

J V Taylor notes what are, in effect, stages in the development of Jesus. Thus he points out that one tradition clearly associated his special endowment by the Spirit with his birth (Luke 1 34); a second with his baptism (Mark 1 10-11); and a third with his resurrection (Rom 1 3-4); and he distinguishes various points at which his vision was enlarged, as when his encounter with the pagan woman of Syro-Phoenicia led him to see his mission as extending beyond the house of Israel. As Taylor says: 'Though we must think of all the powers exercised by Christ, not as superhuman, but as being inherent in manhood where manhood is whole and complete, yet to recognise this does not silence the exclamation, "What sort of man is this?", nor does it eliminate that mingled amazement and dread with which his disciples followed him.'[26]

Clearly, then, the powers of Jesus were, at a deeper level, the powers of God, not conferred on him *ad extra*, but freely assimilated by him into himself before he could use them. And these powers could come to him only insofar as he developed in accordance with the will of God which, as we have seen, carries with it God's understanding, love and other attributes. But as we shall see more fully later, the will of God must not be conceived as rigid nor in simple moralistic terms. It is, indeed, unchanging in its aim to develop creation to share fully in his life; but our situation changes constantly as we deviate in countless ways and, as we have noted, in many situations, not only is there a totally right answer but what is in the long run right can in the short run cause great trouble: as the life and death of Jesus itself showed. The very condition of the world does not permit our actions to be perfect and this must have applied also to Jesus. As he himself said: 'Why do you call me good? No one is good save God alone.' (Mark 10 18) Of course, this is not to say that Jesus was ever evil. It is simply to recognise that, even granted that he was continuously responsive to the will of God, he had to cleave his way through disruptive forces. In that he had to grow and develop as a person, and so respond to, and overcome disruptive and foreclosing forces constantly assailing him, he had to cause disruption. More generally, this entails recognising that the will of God, simply because it is creative and seeks to order creation so as to bring it into his life, often cannot do so without breaking up systems that are warped, disrupting the cosy, fragile stability of the imperfect and corrupt. The whole point of the openness to the will of the Father, which Jesus, following in the steps of Israel's Wisdom teachers, manifested, was to allow these necessarily interim stages of growth to be used as stepping stones to further creative development, rather than letting them become barriers to further growth.

On this basis, we should expect Jesus, as he grew up and developed as a person, not just to become more learned and loving, but to develop so as to see the world around him in greater and greater depth and with deeper and deeper insight into the divine activity in himself and others. We should thus expect him to become increasingly perceptive, caring, holy, from an early age, but as other men attain that state exceptionally, there is no need to comment on it further here. As, however, Jesus continued to develop in response to the creative will of God, we should expect the powers that God increasingly manifested in him to increase far beyond the normal and also his control of them.

---

[26] *The Go-Between God*   (1972)   pp 86 and 92

Taylor remarks on the superb restraint of the four canonical Gospels contrasted with the legendary extravaganzas of the same period; but he wonders whether our taste for common sense may not have blinded us to a strong element of the uncanny in the figure of Jesus as the Gospels portray him. He points to writers and artists who have sensed and captured this quality. He notes that Margaret Field, the anthropologist, sees a parallel between the Spirit driving Jesus into the wilderness after his baptism and the experience of the primitive prophets of Ghana, who almost invariably begin a career of divination by running off in a state of possession into the bush where they remain lost for weeks or even months. Taylor suggests that even after the start of his distinctive ministry, Jesus exhibited many strange and incalculable traits: 'When the crowds surge after him, seeking and threatening, he suddenly cannot be found. He reads men like a book and has an even more disturbing ease of communication with the deranged and devil-possessed.'[27] Taylor draws attention to the open awareness of Jesus towards the world around him, to his untroubled dependence on God and his sense of intimacy with him which gave him a confident authority which was not only recognised by the Roman centurion, but was seemingly endorsed by Jesus himself.[28] The exemplification in Jesus of the Wisdom teaching of Israel to which we earlier drew attention will be clear.

Taylor might have gone on to make more of the miracles. They are so prominent in the Gospels that we cannot fail to respond to them; but such responses vary from embarassment to a stressing of them as further evidence of the unparalleled uniqueness of Jesus. Generally, however, we do not know how to respond to them today. It is, therefore, important to make reference here to a work entitled *Jesus, the Magician*[29] by Morton Smith who is Professor of History at Columbia University. E P Sanders notes ironically that the guild of New Testament scholars has not paid Smith's work the attention it deserves, despite the fresh evidence in it that Smith offers from his unrivalled treasury of learning. Sanders notes that the title "magician" may be a hindrance, as may be Smith's habit of tweaking the noses of the pious, but he goes on to stress that we should not allow ourselves to be so easily deflected from considering the work for what it is: 'a serious effort to explain historically some of the principal puzzles about Jesus, and specifically why he attracted attention, why he was executed and why he was subsequently deified.'[30]

---

[27] *op cit* (1972) p 92

[28] *op cit* (1972) p 95

[29] (1978 and 1985)

[30] *Jesus and Judaism* (1985) p 7

Smith seeks to show that the first and surest fact about Jesus was that he was a miracle worker and why in his ministry, it was healing rather than teaching that attracted the crowds. There were a lot of teachers and some prophets known in Israel but there was no tendency to make them miracle workers. If Jesus was a miracle worker, however, that he should also have his prophetic and teaching roles becomes intelligible, and the tendency of the miracles and especially the healing to attract crowds would lead the authorities to fear him. As Smith says: 'the rest of the tradition about Jesus can be understood if we begin with the miracles, but the miracles cannot be understood if we begin with a purely didactic tradition.'[31] This approach is in sharp contrast with most studies of Jesus which focus on him as a teacher or preacher.[32] Sanders claims that Smith has struck a blow for redressing the balance in the study of Jesus, by moving us away from the almost exclusive concentration on him as a teacher; and that, building on the undoubted fact that Jesus was known as a miracle worker, he has brought forward evidence for showing that Jesus followed some of the standard practices of magicians.[33]

As we saw earlier, Sanders offers two reasons for favouring this alternative approach: first, that scholars do not agree on the authenticity of the sayings material, as a whole or in part; and secondly, when Jesus is seen as a teacher, he is seen either as a clear straightforward teacher or as a difficult, riddling teacher. Sanders stresses, however, that whatever sort of teacher he is held to have been, it is difficult to move from Jesus the teacher to Jesus, a Jew who was crucified, was the leader of a group which survived his death, which was persecuted and which formed a messianic sect which was finally successful.[34]

Smith adduces an impressive range of parallels between Jesus' miracles and those of pagan magicians, Apollonius of Tyrana in particular.[35] And he creates a context in which a lot of evidence finds a place. But after considering Smith's claim that Jesus should be seen primarily as a magician, Sanders concludes that, however illuminating this claim and the evidence brought forward may be, Smith's hypothesis as a whole is unsatisfactory because it leaves out of account the evidence which points to Jewish eschatology as defining the general contours of Jesus' career.[36]

---

[31] *Jesus the Magician*   (1978 & 1985) p 16

[32] *Jesus and Judaism*   (1985)   p 6

[33] *op cit* (1985) p 8

[34] *op cit* (1985) p 4

[35] *Jesus the Magician*   (1978 & 1985)   pp 84-93

[36] *Jesus and Judaism*   (1985)   p 169

Sanders sums up his conclusions by saying that in his book, he went in search of a thread which connects Jesus' own intention, his death and the rise of the movement. He found first a general context embracing both Jesus and the movement which succeeded him: hope for the restoration of Israel. Secondly, he found a specific chain of conceptions and events which offered an understanding of how, historically, things came about. As he says, Jesus claimed that the end was at hand, that God was about to establish his kingdom, that those who responded to him would be included, and (at least by implication) that he would reign. He suggests that, in pointing to that change of eras, he made a symbolic gesture by overturning tables in the temple area. He sees this as the crucial act which led to his execution, though there were contributing causes. He emphasises that Jesus' disciples, after the death and resurrection, continued to expect the restoration of Israel and the inauguration of the new age, and that they continued to see Jesus as occupying first place in the kingdom. Also, he claims, they continued to look for an otherworldly kingdom which would be established by an eschatological miracle. Jesus himself was also progressively interpreted, being no longer seen just as 'Messiah' or 'Viceroy', but as Lord. Some who were attracted to the movement began to win Gentiles to it. And he claims that the work of the early apostles, fits entirely into known expectations about the restoration of Israel.[37] But, of course, 'Israel' came to be understood in terms, not of those who upheld the traditional beliefs of Judaism, but of those, whether Jew or Gentile, who had faith in Jesus.

The Transition from Man to The Man

Within this context, we need here to concentrate the argument more specifically and so develop certain crucial points made earlier. Sanders claims that, whereas virtually everything which the early Church remembered about John the Baptist had to do with repentance and forgiveness[38], there is not a significant body of reliable sayings which explicitly attributes to Jesus a call for national repentance.[39] He stresses that the great themes of national repentance and God's forgiveness, shown in restoring his repentant people, are prominent in all the literature which looks towards Jewish restoration. Though Jesus fits somehow into that view of God, the world and his people, his message lacks emphasis on repentance

---

[37] op cit (1985) p 334

[38] op cit (1985) p 109

[39] op cit (1985) p 111

and forgiveness that are one of its most important themes.[40] More specifically, given that there would have been no problem for Judaism if Jesus had promised inclusion in the forthcoming kingdom of God to sinners who repented, what seems to have been special about his message was, as we have already seen, a promise of inclusion while they were still sinners — in the sense of disobeying the Law — without requiring repentance, *provided they accepted him as the one through whom God was speaking and acting in advance of the coming eschaton.* Having considered the passages about leaving the dead to bury the dead, Sanders concludes that here at least Jesus was willing to say that following him superseded the requirements of piety and the Law.[41]

Sanders comments that there is abundant evidence pointing to self-assertion, which was probably considered by others to be egoism and impiety.[42] But it seems clear that Jesus was not pointing to himself as self but as the vehicle for gifts and attributes which originated not with him but with the Father and, as we shall see further, whose manifestation depended crucially on a humility and abandonment of self which was the very antithesis of self-assertion. But obviously, as we have also seen, Jesus cannot have attained these insights and attitudes without a long period of growth and development: and that growth and development was itself rooted in the understandings of Judaism about the nature of the world and its place in relation to God. What is more, these same insights and their manifestations in his life must have conveyed themselves to those who gathered round him, attracted by his healing powers, his other miracles, his teaching and his personal charisma. One of the greatest problems experienced by later generations has been their inability to understand Jesus in that Judaistic context and their tendency, having abstracted what they knew of him from that context, to understand him in terms of their own vastly different preconceptions. If, however, we are to understand something of how Jesus saw himself and how he was seen by others who lived at the same time and shared that background, we need to develop further at least some of those shared preconceptions.

If, then, we grant that Jesus brought together in an integrated form the vast but ordered richness that goes to form the personality of a mature, integrated person and that this evoked the response of faith in his followers, we must note also that the resulting insights that impressed themselves on his followers did not do so for others. Whether it did so depended, as we saw earlier, on their openness to experience, to the constant surprises that

---

[40] *op cit* (1985) p 113

[41] *op cit* (1986) p 255

[42] *op cit* (1985) p 333

spring from the plenitude of God, perhaps the greatest of which was the emergence of Jesus from his humble beginnings in Galilee. In such circumstances, precisely as Sanders says, it would be amongst the pious, the leaders and the fickle populace that one would find those whose minds would be closed against him; and amongst 'the wicked' — those whose way of life as tax-gathers or prostitutes led to their rejection by the observing Jews — who perforce had little false pride or arrogance, that one would find those open to him. But, of course, there were exceptions — the rich Pharisee and the Centurion, for instance, especially when humbled by misfortune or grief. Not surprisingly, difficulty would be felt particularly by those who remembered Jesus' origins and up to that point could have felt superior.

But clearly, Jesus developed far further than even exceptionally mature people and it is appropriate, therefore, at least to form some view of whether there is a link here with his power to work miracles. It is ironic that Morton Smith, who casts much light upon the way in which Jesus was viewed as a 'magician' by analysing the Gospel and other traditions and comparing him with other magicians, is himself dogmatically sceptical about the occurrence of most such miracles. Thus he speaks of miracles involving control of purely physical bodies including resurrections from the dead as the most clearly impossible and the stories about them as the most surely false.[43] He notes the strong evidence for the use by Jesus of magical practices and comments that in view of this evidence it seems probable that he did use magical methods, 'which may have worked for psychological reasons.'[44] And he even ascribes Jesus' resurrection, ascension and post resurrection appearances to the psychopathic histories of his disciples.[45] Yet, as we have seen, well attested broad parallels to many of the miracles can be found in reports of paranormal phenomena.

What stands out about the miracles of Jesus is not, therefore, so much their character but the way in which they seem to have been under his full and conscious control. As the record makes clear, however, even for Jesus there was a need for an openness by others for these powers to work. Minds closed against them by scepticism, fear or other manifestations of lack of faith precluded the working of these powers: which is what we find today when sceptics try to put those with psychic gifts to the test, as we have already seen. As for the raisings from the dead, death occurs when the order of the body breaks down at certain critical levels, so leading to the collapse of the order of the physical system as a whole. The restoring of

---

[43] *op cit* (1978/85) p 118

[44] *op cit* (1978/85) p 152

[45] *op cit* (1978/85) p 139

order in a body that has died is arguably not different in principle from the restoring of order in healing, save that the body is not able to draw on its own healing resources: and both are instances of the healing and redeeming powers of the Holy Spirit — powers exercised through Christ and which, as Taylor says, we should think of not as superhuman, but as being inherent in manhood where manhood is whole and complete — and so transparent to the Spirit. The presence and exercise of these powers is thus fully consonant with the creative development of Jesus.

The Effect of the Crucifixion

In many ways, the crucifixion stands out in Western understanding as more important even than the resurrection and certainly than the ascension. It is not coincidence that, as the concepts of God and the world moved further apart and the presence of the Divine Christ in the whole of creation and thus in every man and woman dropped from sight, the relevance for ordinary people of the life, death, resurrection and ascension of Christ as illuminating the furthest implications of the way which each of them needed to follow to attain salvation, ceased to have strong relevance. The price that Jesus had paid in suffering in order to overcome the disorder of sin and its specific manifestation in death, in order to illuminate that way, and which had thus been spoken of in terms a ransom to death and to Satan, came instead to be seen as a price Jesus paid to the Father to free men from the penalties of sin. The emphasis moved from the need for men to participate more fully in the life of God to the need for them to escape the penalties of not doing so. Jesus ceased to be seen as the Redeemer in the sense of showing men the path of creative development —redemption — that they had to follow, and came to be seen as acting as their proxy, in their stead, in relieving them of punishment. But with so much emphasis on the suffering of Christ and on the freedom from punishment that it was claimed to offer man, the role of the crucifixion in the personal development of Jesus, as he came increasingly to manifest the powers of God through the ordering and development of his personality, has been neglected. Yet surely, it was of profound importance.

Death comes to men in different ways. When it comes in its due time it can be natural and peaceful. Or it may come with little or no warning in ways for which we are not prepared. But death came to Jesus in neither of these ways. He could have avoided it but, in full awareness of what he was doing, he chose to accept it. Such a decision must have a profound effect upon the personality. John MacQuarrie notes that the positive potentialities of death have long been recognised and he discusses them with particular reference to the work of Heidegger. Death, he suggests, brings into existence a responsibility and seriousness. In one sense destructive, death is in another sense creative of unified, responsible self-hood, the concerns of which become ordered in the face of the end. It exposes the superficiality and triviality of many of the ambitions and aspirations on which men spend their energies. MacQuarrie is thus led to suggest that selfhood is attained only in so far as the existent is prepared to look beyond the limits of his own self for the master concern that can create such a stable and unified self. This, he suggests, means in effect that by looking beyond himself or, as we may say, dying to himself, man becomes himself. As he says, this is a paradox well known to the religions, and expressed in such sayings as that one must 'die to live' and that 'whoever would save his life will lose it; and whoever loses his life for my sake and the gospel's will save it.' (Mark 8 35)[46]

Of course, in the case of Jesus, we need to qualify such an understanding. He had already opened his personality in obedience to the creative powers of God to a point at which the triviality of ordinary human ambitions and aspirations had no hold over him; and the form of death facing him was more protracted and agonising than almost any other; and he was seemingly free to avoid it. But none of these lessen the agonising decision that he faced — and which the Gospels recognise. In other words, this suggests that in facing death in this way, even Jesus faced some deep disruption of his personality which opened it to even more profound reordering. If that makes sense, then the cry of dereliction on the cross may have marked the same kind of process, though far greater in degree, as people undergo when they have to face the disruption of their personality in the course of therapy: the break-up of the existing order so that yet fuller order may be achieved — a theme that underlies much of this study.

This does not, of course, imply that Jesus was sinful in the ordinary sense but, as we have seen, by very virtue of his humanity, throughout his life he must be presumed to have been in process of developing and ordering his personality and this reached its culmination as he faced death. If this is so, then it follows that the creative powers of God in even greater strength must have flowed through him and conflicted with the disruptive powers of death in the crucifixion. It is precisely these powers of the Holy Spirit — powers of love and healing — that could restore and revivify even a dead body and bring about the resurrection. This is precisely what we should expect from the creative, sustaining, redeeming and healing powers of God when the personality has developed so highly. Given development to such a point, the powers of God working through and under the control of Jesus must have been such that the post-resurrection appearances might be thought to follow

---

[46] J Macquarrie *Principles of Christian Theology* 2nd edn (1977) pp 78-83

naturally: for again, as we have seen, these powers are not unprecedented in character but in the total and sustained power that Jesus had over them.

All this suggests, therefore, that given the creative, sustaining and redeeming power of God, given the total obedience of Jesus to the will of God, and given the development of his personality that might be expected to follow, nothing in the broad outline of events leading to the post-resurrection appearances appears to be anomalous. Even the fact that Jesus' expectation of the imminent eschaton did not prove correct is in keeping with this picture, for while it allows ample scope for his insights and his prescience, it recognises also his lack of omniscience and the fallibility inherent in the human condition. Given the overall picture being presented here, we can, therefore, with the benefit of hindsight, gain some understanding of its deep significance though there are questionable details. In particular, the recapitulation, summing up and fulfillment of the entire evolutionary process of the world and of each individual can be understood in terms of this broadly early Patristic picture. Even the empty tomb might find a place as a result of the ordering process, if we can so extend Bohm's understanding, for we have noted that at a point of total order, there is nothing that can be called physical.

On this basis, we need no longer get hung up on the seemingly extraordinary character of what happened save in the sense of what it reveals of the heroism of Jesus and the powers of God latent in each one of us. The witness to the powers of God borne by these events is deeply obscured if we think of Jesus as a kind of demi-God and of the events associated with his death and resurrection as the result of an intervention by God otherwise disconnected from the events of the natural world. He was as we are, save in his openness to the powers of God and his steadfast adherence to his will: yet, in so far, he was quite different from us. His life and death and resurrection bear witness to just how close God is to us and to the powers that are in principle available to us, yet it bears witness also to how far we are in practice from availing ourselves of them. But if we are to see in Jesus not just the recapitulation but the full climax of creation, then we have to face what is perhaps the most difficult issue in understanding Jesus: his ascension.

The Exalted Christ

As a man, Jesus was understood by his followers, to a far fuller extent than other men, as a manifestation of God, of his Wisdom, the Logos, the Word of God, the Divine Christ: but the Divine Christ was at the same time creating sustaining and redeeming — and was Incarnate in — the rest of creation. In pointing to Jesus as man, we would have been pointing also to the Divine Christ in him, to whom he was transparent. As God embraces the world, as the spiritual embraces the mental and the physical, so the Divine Christ embraces the Incarnate Jesus. But such a union — not of two entities, the divine and human, but of the all-embracing divine taking specific incarnate form — need not of itself imply or require that Jesus *became*, in the sense of being fully identical with, the Divine Christ. So we need now to ask whether, when we speak of Christ in the world and Christ in us, we are speaking of the Divine Christ or of Christ Incarnate who has risen and returned to the Father as other men may do when they die, or whether we can, and need to, conceive of the Incarnate Christ at the ascension as in some way breaking the bounds of finitude and becoming fully identical with the Divine Christ in his cosmic role.

In considering this issue, we need to bear in mind the conviction of many modern theologians that there is no way, or at least no way open to human comprehension, in which the Divine Christ can be the Incarnate Christ and the Incarnate Christ can be the Divine Christ. It is helpful, for this purpose, to turn to C F D Moule's study *The Origin of Christology*.[47] Moule there quotes from J D G Dunn's *Jesus and the Spirit*[48] in which Dunn says that, instead of being the charismatic exemplar, Jesus began to feature more or less from the beginning as a source and object of the first Christians' religious experience. Religious experiences of the earliest community, including experiences like those enjoyed by Jesus himself, were seen as dependent on him and as deriving from him. The religious experience of the Christian is not merely experience like that of Jesus, it is experience which at all characteristic and distinctive points is derived from Jesus as Lord, and which only makes sense when this derivative and dependent character is recognised.[49]

As Moule says, this testifies to an understanding of Jesus as present and alive in a sense quite different from that in which the inspiration of some great figures of the past lives on: and points to an understanding and experience of Christ as what Moule calls 'corporate'. He goes on to refer to the puzzlement of some other distinguished thinkers and then quotes C H Dodd who speaks of the phenomenon as illuminating, though without showing precisely how it might be handled or applied. Dodd says is that it is clear that this conception raises a new problem. He regards it as challenging the mind to discover a doctrine of personality, which will make conceivable this combination of the universal and the particular in a single person: and he claims that a naïve individualism regarding man, or a naïve

---

[47] (1977)

[48] (1975)

[49] C F D Moule *The Origin of Christology* (1977) (quoting J D G Dunn *Jesus and the Spirit* (1975) pp 194 ff, 342) p 48

anthropomorphism regarding God, makes nonsense of Johannine Christology.[50] This claim appears no less applicable to Pauline Christology and it stands as a commentary on the inadequacy of many current understandings of the Christian faith.

Moule comments that he is among the puzzled himself but reaffirms that what causes the puzzlement is a phenomenon that undoubtedly does present itself within the New Testament, explain it how one may.[51] It would be out of place to follow Moule's discussion of this issue beyond noting his comment that when all allowance is made for the wide range of the preposition *en* within the Pauline writings, there remain cases where it is difficult to escape the impression that Paul is using *en* with a name for Christ in a genuinely (though metaphorically) locative sense.[52]

As Sanders notes, what is particularly striking about Paul is that repentance and forgiveness, and indeed the whole expiatory system of Judaism, play virtually no role in his thought.[53] Paul does not characteristically think in terms of sin as transgression that incurs guilt which is removed by repentance and forgiveness.[54] It was not that Paul regarded them as valueless in absolute terms but that he had an entirely different conception of what was necessary for salvation. It was in comparison with this alternative that the categories of Judaism were virtually irrelevant and valueless.

Sanders goes on to stress that there should be no doubt as to where the heart of Paul's theology lies. It lies particularly in participatory categories. Paul thinks in terms of faith leading to 'Sonship', 'in Jesus Christ' and constantly uses phrases such as 'baptised into', 'put on', 'Christ living in me', and 'life in Christ'. There is 'a' righteousness based on works of law but it is not the kind that counts. *What is needed is righteousness by faith and that is equivalent to participation in Christ.* (My italics)[55]

Earlier in his book, Sanders had shown how the Rabbinic conception of the religious life took the threefold form of study of the Law, works of loving-kindness and prayer. The question whether studying or doing was the most important of the three was the subject of debate but study was often seen as the most important and particularly conducive to evoking a sense of the presence of God. Study as so understood was not, of course, primarily

---

[50] C H Dodd *The Interpretation of the Fourth Gospel* (1960) p 249

[51] C F D Moule *op cit* (1977) p 51

[52] *op cit* (1977) p 55

[53] *Paul and Palestinian Judaism* (1977) p 499

[54] *op cit* (1977) pp 502-3

[55] *op cit* (1977) p 502ff

an attempt to learn more facts about the Law but to gain deeper insights into it and its implications, for the keeping of the Law was itself rooted in the idea of *imitatio Dei*.[56] Judaism systematically cultivated, particularly by such study, an intense sense of the intimate presence of God. This intensity of Judaistic religious life carried over into the understanding of Paul and the early Church and assumed the intensity and vigour associated with life in Christ. This intense but deeply rational sense of growing into the fulfilling richness and joyousness of the plenitude of God which informed the whole of life, is to be compared with later anxious preoccupations with moral fervour and ascetic rigour which represent a deeply subjective narrowing of the entire approach to the religious life. While the peaks of this subjective approach can still attain a breakthrough into the life of God, over much of its course, it gives a deep sense of its impoverishment.

As the Divine Christ was that aspect of God that was his Word, the Logos, his order and reason, which, with the Holy Spirit was forming and ordering creation within the life of God, it should by now be clear how the idea of the development of creation as a whole and of the human personality by deepening insights which themselves make the personality more integrated and whole, could be seen in terms of development into the Divine Christ. Within this picture, the role of openness and responsiveness to new insights, and of creation itself changing to meet the righteous man, take their place. What remains obscure to us, however, is the precise sense in which the man, Jesus Christ, even granted that his teaching and life reveal this developmental process into the life of God, could have been seen as becoming fully identified with this aspect of God so as himself to become God.

If a key is to be found to this puzzle it seemingly must lie first in the understanding of creation as lying 'within' the Trinitarian life of God, as we have already seen. But secondly, it must lie in the ascension. The neglect of the doctrine of the ascension in Christian doctrine hardly needs stressing. Indeed, one might speak of the embarrassment that it causes to theologians which they meet largely by ignoring it. In particular, it is often treated as part of the resurrection. Yet the distinction between the resurrection and the ascension is vital. As Hermann Sasse said: 'As the risen one, Christ would be only the first fruit from the dead, the first-born among among the brethren. His resurrection would thus only be the beginning of the general resurrection of the dead. There would be no fundamental difference between his resurrection and ours. ...For this reason the New Testament draws a

---

[56] W D Davies *Christian Origins and Judaism* (1962) p 121

logical distinction between the resurrection and the exaltation.'[57] And later
he says: 'What is to be understood by the exaltation is clear. It signifies
that Jesus after his resurrection shares in the Eternity, Omnipresence and
Omnipotence of God.'[58] He stresses that Christ cannot be conceived apart
from the Spirit and adds that if the creation of the world cannot be
conceived apart from the Holy Spirit neither can it be conceived apart from
the eternal Christ. That is the central reason why Christ is described in the
New Testament as sharing in the creation of the world.[59] To this we need
add only that the process of creation cannot be separated from the processes
of sustaining and redeeming, either.

While here on earth, Jesus was one incarnation of the Divine Christ
whose creative activity continued to sustain the rest of creation. Even after
the ascension, if Jesus was simply an exalted person, that would not allow
us to speak of him in us or of us in him. Many modern theologians
seemingly would want at that point to rest their case. Yet, as Moule has
indicated, to stop at that point seems to omit an absolutely crucial step in the
understanding of the New Testament claims. The implications of the
passages to which Moule and Sanders draw attention appear to point
inevitably to the full identification of Jesus as the Risen Christ with the
Word, the Logos, the Cosmic, Divine Christ. Without this step Jesus
remains in the category of prophet. It is this step that seems to be necessary
to make him more than a great man, to make him God.

But in that case, how can we conceive that step? Jesus, we have
suggested, became man in the fullest possible sense. But how could he
become God? The first step to an answer must lie in the recognition of the
essential kinship of man and God. That we are in his image seems normally
to be taken to imply that the image is separate from God: but we are within
God: God is himself in the image *in parvo*. We are in God, created by him
to share in his life in an equal though utterly dependent status through which
the depths of the divine love are revealed. Jesus as man shared that status
with us, though realising the unrecognised potential that is in each man.
God is seeking to realise that potential by redeeming us as part of creation,
the whole of which has deviated from his will. His creative and redemptive
love was, therefore, at work in Jesus, too. But whereas Jesus was totally
responsive to the love and will of God, we are not. Jesus allowed the
creative power of the Holy Spirit to work through him to develop his
personality so as to become more responsive to and ultimately transparent

---

[57] H Sasse Jesus Christ, the Lord in *Mysterium Christi* eds G K A Bell & D A
Deissmann (1930) p 105

[58] H Sasse *op cit* p 106

[59] H Sasse *op cit* pp 116-7

to the powers of God. That led through the miracles, through the resurrection and the post-resurrection appearances to the ascension.

As we have seen, the implication of the Gospel is that the adherence by Jesus to the creative will of God, with the resulting assimilation into himself of the powers and attributes of God, subject to the limits of manhood, led to the overcoming of sin — in the widest sense of disorder within the life of God — and, following Bohm, we suggested, the disappearance of the physical body. It was this state that Jesus attained at the resurrection. But even when sin was overcome, there remained still the limits of self-contradiction, of finitude, which limited his participation in the divine life. It may be thought of as restoring Jesus to the potential pre-fall status of man within the spiritual hierarchy but, by implication, at that point he still remained man. The very logic of the divine life suggests that each level of the divine hierarchy is locked into its own dependent status. But the Christian claim implies that in some way even that can be overcome in these unique circumstances. The picture presented earlier was of God, through the Divine Christ, creating within his life, through the limits of self-contradiction, a hierarchy of microcosms of himself to share in his life. So if Jesus was to ascend to become wholly assimilated to the Divine Christ by breaking these bonds of finitude, then, by implication, he had to overcome the limits of self-contradiction, and in so doing he had to pass through the entire hierarchy of spiritual creation.

If, indeed, this is what we are to understand, it gives rise to two very difficult questions. The first is whether, if Jesus so broke the bounds of finitude to become totally identified with the Divine Christ, this would have effected in the divine economy any change that in some way makes it easier for the rest of creation to find its way into the life of God, in addition to following his example. On this it seems difficult to go further than Athanasius: 'But if now for us Christ is entered into heaven itself, though he was even before Lord and framer of the heavens, for us, therefore, is that present exaltation written ... that we may be exalted in him, and that we may enter the gates of heaven which he had opened for us .. '[60]

A second question is whether if Jesus passed through the spiritual hierarchy to become the Divine Christ, this is not an ability in principle necessarily inherent in all men. His total adherence to the will of God was a *sine qua non* of any further steps. Yet if it were of itself sufficient, that ability would in principle be shared by all men.

Perhaps, however, this issue can be approached from another angle, for Jesus was understood to have become the perfect man and so the universal man in the sense that if anyone else were to attain that perfect state of

---

[60] C A 1 41

personal development, he would be essentially the same person as Jesus —
another full incarnation of the Divine Christ. This appears to have been one
implication of the much discussed and disputed title 'Son of Man'. C H
Dodd summarises a discussion of that title as used in the Fourth Gospel by
noting that the term 'Son of Man' throughout this gospel retains the sense
of one who incorporates in himself the people of God, or humanity in its
ideal aspect. Dodd notes the parallel with the Platonic Idea (or Form) of
man but goes on to say that in the Fourth Gospel there is never any doubt
that the evangelist is speaking of a real person, that is, of a concrete,
historical individual of the human race, 'Jesus of Nazareth, the Son of
Joseph' (1 45) And yet, Dodd comments of the evangelist, in all this he
was much more than one individual among many. He was the true self of
the human race, standing in that perfect union with God to which others can
attain only as they are incorporate in Him.[61] Dodd somewhat changed his
views about the expression 'Son of Man' in the light of later work, notably
by Geza Vermes,[62] but his emphasis on the corporate role of Jesus including
also as Servant Messiah remained.[63] By implication, any other man who trod
that same path would attain that same personal and corporate status: in so
far, this would have entailed the return of Jesus.

But even if Jesus did grow and develop to the point of total identification
with the Divine Christ, there still remains the question how it came about
that the early Christians ceased to see Jesus as a man, albeit the Messiah,
and came to see him as Divine. To see him as Messiah was itself a gigantic
step: to see him as divine was even greater. If we are to understand this
even dimly, we need constantly to bear in mind that for those who came in
contact with him on earth, and responded to him, there must have been a
whole series of experiences which came about progressively and each of
which must have been profoundly disturbing, exciting and revealing. There
were the miracles and in particular the healings; there was Jesus' teaching
which appears to have made light of the fundamental features of Jewish life
and faith — the Law, repentance, the Temple, and the associated sacrifices
— and which substituted in some ways more exacting requirements but
above all, belief in him as revealer of the Father. This was supported by the
exceptionally intimate term for God, *Abba*. It was supported also by the
applicability of certain highly meaningful Jewish terms: Son of Man, Son
of God, and, above all, Messiah or Christ, a title which appears to have
played a major role in bringing about the crucifixion. All this must have led
those who responded to his charisma to a progressively heightened sense of

---

[61] *The Interpretation of the Fourth Gospel*   (1960)   pp 248-9

[62] see *The Founder of Christianity*   (1971)   pp 110 et seq and 178

[63] see *op cit*   p 106

awe, wonder and excitement. But all of this appeared to be utterly dashed by the crucifixion which evoked also strong feelings of guilt. This was then followed by the evidence of the resurrection and the post-resurrection appearances which appear to have evoked first bewilderment and then a yet more profound sense of awe, wonder and excitement and the conviction that in this man, and in this astonishing but deeply meaningful sequence of events, a full and complete revelation of God was emerging which would lead shortly to the culmination of the process in the establishment of the Kingdom of God and the restoration of Israel to him.

We have seen how the Old Testament can be read in terms of a series of new starts for Israel, each of which entailed reorientation of preconceptions and the attainment of new and deeper insights as Israel was led forward into the life of God. It is precisely in this sense that the disciples were led forward. Martin Hengel notes how after the resurrection what the disciples experienced ought to be compared with 'the violent force of an explosion which broke up all traditional conventions and burgeois assurances. Here something new and unheard of emerged, a new experience which radically transcended the everyday life of Palestinian fishermen, peasants, and craftsmen. To some degree people lived with an enthusiastic assurance that the heavens would open and the kingdom of God would dawn. It was no accident that the appearances of the risen Christ were connected with the eschatological experience of the Spirit which was compared with the force of heavenly fire.'[64] It was no coincidence because what was entailed was a profound re-ordering of outlook and the opening of their minds to God.

Each of these factors referred to so summarily here, but experienced as a whole sequence of particular 'mind-blowing' events, must at each point have led to profound reorientations of each receptive person's way of seeing the world and a substitution of new and deeper insights, of *gnosis*, and to the growing sense of joy, of wholeness and integrity associated with them — which was precisely what was entailed in 'salvation', so far as applicable in this world.

Viewed in this way, the culmination of this process can have left little choice of interpretation. Martin Hengel sums it up. He stresses that the general apocalyptic framework of earliest Christianity, in which the revelation of the saving power of God through Jesus was expressed, from the beginning irresistibly forced the development of christological thought in the direction of a unique, 'eschatological' saving event. 'With strictly consistent christological thought, the early communities were concerned with the *whole revelation of God*, the *whole of salvation* in his Jesus Christ,

---

[64] *The Cross of the Son of God*   (1986)   p 254

which could not remain one episode in salvation history amongst others'[65]

In other words, the more the early Christians were impressed by these revelations as the full revelation of God on earth, the less room there was to recognise as also important, or equally important, the fundamental features of Jewish faith — the Law, repentance for failures to observe it, the Temple and its sacrifices, and, particularly controversial in the early Church, circumcision, let alone any revelations of other faiths. These were at best inadequate and were in part misleading. But in that case, this revelation of God in Jesus Christ had to be the full revelation on earth not only for those still alive but for all men at all times in all places. And since God was constantly present in and revealing himself in some measure in the world through the 'Shekinah' and above all in his Wisdom, it was then only a small step to seeing Jesus as himself the incarnation of Wisdom and so, after the ascension, as himself the Wisdom and the Word of God.

---

[65] *op cit*   (1986) p 87

CHAPTER TWENTY EIGHT

CODA

This has been a long journey which has taken us through many academic disciplines and beyond. We started with some reflections on the power of our preconceptions — frameworks of thought — to channel our understanding and to make virtually unthinkable all that lies outside them. We then saw something of the understandings of the Old and New Testaments and the early Christian Church, and how they were gradually transformed or lost; and new, more limited, more fragmented, and in some ways less rational and less coherent, views were substituted, radically altering and diminishing the significance of the Christian message. Thus men's concepts of God and the world were separated; God came to be sought, not in and through the world as it unfolded, but by a retreat into and beyond the self. And it came to be thought that the concern of God was with men's moral behaviour as such, rather than with growth towards wholeness and maturity, growth 'in Christ'. As a result, religion ceased to embrace and inform our understanding of the whole of creation and became one activity amongst others. And it became largely separated from reason and from science. The fundamental significance of the evolution of the entire universe and the need for life-long growth and development of each person into Christ, was thus displaced by the need for constant vigilance to prevent immoral thoughts and acts: and the entire understanding of the profound subtlety and richness of the world was radically reduced.

More generally, we noted that the order of the God which sustains the world at many levels as it unfolds and develops, can be perceived only by the growth and development of the personality. This growth and development takes place by a long series of leaps of insight (*gnosis*) that come to men: something that lies at the very heart of science. The early understanding was, therefore, that men needed not just to maintain a constant moral vigilance but to have a 'listening heart', a 'listening mind'. It was this that enabled men to grow in virtue and righteousness, and to respond rationally and caringly as God, acting through the world as it unfolded, organised events to maintain and develop the world into his life and to meet the needs of each such person in it.

As we saw, therefore, creation can grow to share in the life of God only by growing, step by step, entirely freely. The creative and life-enhancing activity of God is thus constantly frustrated and diverted by the blindness, not only of the lower reaches of creation, but of men and women, too; for, the understanding and love which guide creation, come late in that developmental process. Sin, therefore, needs to be understood as not so much as a moral as a religious concept where religion is not separated from the world but informs our understanding of it; a world where, perforce, creatures have had to use those attributes of God that they have so far attained, to develop further into the life of God; for God cannot force his attributes upon them. Within this picture, we saw how the findings of modern science found a natural place and we saw, too, how the transitoriness of the world was continuously creating systems in the Mind of God to share in his eternal life. Finally, we sought to show how the life, death, resurrection and ascension of Jesus Christ summed up that development in what the early Fathers saw as a recapitulation of the entire developmental process.

It may be felt by some to be surprising that after such a long journey in which fundamental beliefs of Christianity have been reassessed and presented in a different, often scientific, perspective, we should find that they still offer an unfashionably traditional picture. Yet that is how it is. What is more, this return to traditional beliefs, within the perspective in which they have been presented, has the potential to affect every aspect of our lives. Thus the grounds for belief in a triune God are strongly reasserted but his relationship to the world is not that of the Western Churches. Grounds for belief in the life, death, resurrection and ascension of Christ have similarly been reasserted but their significance is not that normally claimed. Instead, Jesus Christ has been presented as the Way, the One who has shown us not just the proximity but the presence of God and the road which we must follow to carry on and ultimately complete the evolution of creation into his life.

On this basis, the dialogue with those of other faiths who worship the same God in different forms is able to proceed; though the Christian formulation of his character and his relationship to us, does, I claim, fit the evidence more precisely and constructively. Similarly, we can point to the relevance and significance of Jesus to our understanding of this approach to God, without disparaging the ways of others. Yet this does not entail saying that Christians have one faith and others have their faiths which are just as good. The claim is that the Christian formulation of the concept of God and of the role of Jesus Christ are of significance to every man, whatever his faith, and ultimately has the potential to fit the facts as no other does. In so far, Christianity is in its essence a universal faith. Yet though the life, death, resurrection and ascension of Jesus have changed and can change further the course of history by changing the attitudes of men, so leading them further into the life of God, the claim that Christ has in some sense altered the attitude of God to us, does not feature in this picture.

Finally, we have seen how at every stage in the evolutionary history of this world, a balance has had to be struck between too great openness to change which offers no firm foundation for growth, and too great rigidity which allows no room for growth. Though many stages in Christianity have been marred by too great rigidity, in recent years the pendulum has swung the other way and many churches have sought, usually unsuccessfully, to be all things to all men.

At the same time, Christianity has been invoked by pressure groups seeking to promote specifically secular, and particularly political concerns, some more worthy than others. Thus the profound deprivation and suffering of the poor all over the world has led not only to proper claims for Christian concern and support but to attacks on the very instruments by which the necessary resources to help them are generated: and the idea that the poor have also spiritual needs and responsibilities has become virtually unmentionable. Yet, as we have seen, striving in some form is an essential feature of all levels of this evolutionary world and the fact that, both in the Old and New Testaments, humility and openness to God and faith in Christ, which are far from equally manifested, are promised to lead to prosperity in this life, as well as life in God, has been forgotten. The idea that all men should be able to walk abreast into the life of God, regardless of effort or merit, is surely novel.

This, however, is only one of many controversial issues in many fields of scholarship through which we have threaded our way on this journey: and in charting this path there have certainly been inadequacies and errors. If the need to avoid these had been of critical importance, it would have been wiser to restrict the argument to one or other feature of it. However, no one part of the argument, however carefully presented, could illuminate the whole: and ultimately, it is in the realism and coherence — or potential coherence — of the whole, that any value of this work may lie. Its aim is summed up in the great Jewish word 'shalom' which is usually translated 'peace' but which speaks of balanced, integrated and harmonious relationships of man with God, with his fellow men and with the rest of the natural world: relationships held together by the idea of creation as the gift of God in which he is himself present, revealing himself particularly in the creativity of wonder, beauty, goodness, love and joy: gifts which are for man actively to enjoy but which demand from him a totally objective and humble realism illuminated by goodness, all of which he holds in trust from God.

In so far as the need for development into the life of God is seen as what is really important in his eyes and so to every part of creation, the common need for such development, and the reason and love it carries with it, can then assume a unifying role: a role which is in the fullest sense oecumenical, a word whose Greek roots refer to the whole inhabited world. The Christian message is thus not just altruistic: it is, in the profoundest sense, in everyman's self-interest.

Meanwhile, however, Western civilisation in its present form offers no integrated understanding of the world that can be reflected in the mind of man; it offers no adequate guidance to him as to the purpose of this life; it does not do justice to the wonder of the world; nor does it recognise the creative plenitude of God and man's potential.

We are today faced with the gradual disintegration of the social and moral fabric of our lives: a disintegration which is manifested not least in the loss of integrity and wisdom as ideals, including amongst the leaders of the world. There is, it seems a growing sense that whatever end is sought, whether good or bad, that end justifies the means used to attain it, whatever the cost may be to others. It is the vitality of youth, not the wisdom that can come with age, that is lauded. We may not succeed in destroying the world for it lies within the life of God who continues to sustain it. But deviations from his will are in their nature destructive and invoke his wrath, and in the nature of cybernetic processes, even the restoring of the damage that we do, seems likely to be on such a scale as itself to bring about vast unforeseen catastrophes. Perhaps this book may help to focus attention on largely forgotten paths that lead back towards its redemption and salvation.

SELECT BIBLIOGRAPHY

Anderson, B W *Creation versus Chaos* New York 1967

Armstrong, A H & Markus, R A *Christian Faith and Greek Philosophy* London 1960

Armstrong, A H *The Architecture of the Intelligible Universe in the Philosophy of Plotinus* Cambridge 1940

Askenazi, Leon The Relationship between the Soul and Creation according to Kabbalistic Thought in *Science and Consciousness* ed. M Cazenave Oxford 1984

Ayer, A J *Language Truth and Logic* rev edn London 1946

Barbour, R S Creation, Wisdom and Christ in *Creation Christ and Culture* ed R W A McKinney Edinburgh 1976

Baelz, P R *Christian Theology and Metaphysics* London 1968

Barr, J *Escaping from Fundamentalism* London 1984

———— *Old and New in Interpretation* London 1982

———— *Holy Scripture* Oxford 1983

———— Some Thoughts on Narrative Myth and Incarnation in *God Incarnate* ed A E Harvey London 1981

Barrett, W *Death of the Soul* Oxford 1986

Barrow, J D & Tipler, F J *The Anthropic Cosmological Principle* Oxford 1986

Bartholomew, D J *God of Chance* London 1984

Beloff, J *New Directions in Parapsychology* London 1974

Berlin, I *Four Essays on Liberty* Oxford 1969

Bigg, Charles *The Origins of Christianity* Oxford 1909

———— *The Christian Platonists of Alexandria* rev ed Oxford 1913

Bloom, Allan *The Closing of the American Mind* London 1988

Boden, M *Piaget* London 1979

Bohm, David *Wholeness and the Implicate Order* London 1980

Bouyer, Louis *A History of Christian Spirituality* vol 1 London 1968

Braude, S E *ESP and Psychokinesis* Philadelphia 1979

———— *The Limits of Influence* London 1986

Broad, C D *Lectures on Psychical Research* London 1962

Bursen, H A *Dismantling the Memory Machine* Dordrecht 1978

Capra, Frijof The Tao of Physics in *Science and Consciousness* ed M Cazenave Oxford 1984

Carington, Whately *Telepathy* London 1945

Chadwick, H *Early Christian Thought and the Classical Tradition* Oxford 1966

———— Freedom and Necessity in Early Christian Thought about God in *Cosmology and Theology* eds D Tracey & N Lash Edinburgh 1983

———— *Augustine* Oxford 1986

Collins, J New Testament Cosmology in *Cosmology and Theology* eds D Tracey & N Lash Edinburgh 1983

Craig, E *The Mind of God and the Works of Man* Oxford 1987

Crenshaw, J L *Old Testament Wisdom* London 1982

Daniélou, J *A History of Early Christian Doctrine* vol 2 London 1973

Davies, P *Space and Time in the Modern Universe* Cambridge 1979

———— *God and the New Physics* London 1983

———— *Superforce* London 1984

———— *The Cosmic Blueprint* London 1987

Davies, P C W & Brown, J R *The Ghost in the Atom* Cambridge 1986

Denbigh, K G *An Inventive Universe* London 1975

Dihle, A *The Theory of the Will in Classical Antiquity* Berkeley 1982
Dodd, C H *The Bible and the Greeks* London 1935
————   *The Interpretation of the Fourth Gospel* Cambridge 1953
————   Eternal Life in *New Testament Studies* Manchester 1953
————   *The Parables of the Kingdom* London 1961
————   *The Founder of Christianity* London 1971
Dodds, E R *The Greeks and the Irrational* Berkeley 1971
Donaldson, M *Children's Minds* London 1978
Ducasse, C J *The Belief in a Life after Death* Springfield 1961
Dunn, J D G *Jesus and the Spirit* London 1975
————   *Christology in the Making* London 1980
Eccles, J C Part 2 of *The Self and its Brian* K R Popper and J C Eccles Berlin 1977
Eigen, M & Winkler, R *The Laws of the Game* London 1983
Evans, G R *Augustine on Evil* Cambridge 1982
Evans-Pritchard, E E *Witchcraft Oracles and Magic among the Azande* Oxford 1937
Gale, R *The Language of Time* London 1968
———— *The Philosophy of Time* London 1968
Galloway, A D *The Cosmic Christ* London 1951
Gilson, E *God and Philosophy* New Haven 1941
———— *The Philosophy of St Bonaventure* Paterson 1965
———— *History of Christian Philosophy in the Middle Ages* London 1955
———— *The Christian Philosophy of St Augustine* London 1961
Gray, J *Hayek on Liberty* 2nd edn Oxford 1986
———— *Liberalism* Milton Keynes 1986
Grey, M *Return from Death* London 1985
Green, Celia *Out-of-the-Body Experiences* London 1968
Hardy, Sir Alister *The Spiritual Nature of Man* Oxford 1979
Harvey, A E *Jesus and the Constraints of History* London 1982
Hay, D *Exploring Inner Space* rev edn London 1987
———— *Religious Experience Today* 1990
Hayek, F A *The Road to Serfdom* London 1944
————   *The Sensory Order* London 1952
————   *The Fatal Conceit* London 1988
Hebb, D O *The Organisation of Behaviour* London 1949
————   *Psychology* Philadelphia 1966
Hefner, P Is/Ought in *The Sciences and Theology in the Twentieth Century* ed A R Peacocke
            Stocksfield 1981
Hengel, Martin *The Cross of the Son of God* London 1976/81
Hick, J *Evil and the God of Love* London 1966
Humphrey, G *Thinking* London 1951
Inhelder, Barbel & Piaget, J *The Growth of Logical Thinking* London 1958
Jaeger, Werner *Early Christianity and Greek Paideia* Oxford 1961
————   *Two Rediscovered Works of Ancient Christian literature: Gregory of Nyssadn
Macarius* Leiden 1965
Kantorowicz, E H *The King's Two Bodies* Princeton 1957
Kelly, J N D *Early Christian Doctrines* 5th edn London 1977
————   *Early Christian Creeds* 3rd edn Harlow 1972
Kenny, A *Action Emotion and Will* London 1963
————   *Will Freedom and Power* Oxford 1975
————   *Freewill and Responsibility* London 1978
————   *The God of the Philosophers* Oxford 1979

Kuhn, Thomas *The Structure of Scientific Revolutions* 2nd edn Chicago 1970
Lampert, E *The Divine Realm* London 1944
Leff, G A *Medieval Thought* London 1958
Lewis, C S *The Problem of Pain* London 1940
Lewis, J (ed) *Beyond Chance and Necessity* London 1974
Lilla, S R C *Clement of Alexandria* Oxford 1971
Lindsay, P H & Norman D A *An Introduction to Psychology* 2nd edn New York 1977
Lockwood, Michael *Mind Brain and the Quantum* Oxford 1989
Lorimer, D *Survival?* London 1984
Louth, Andrew *The Origins of the Christian Mystical Tradition* Oxford 1981
Lovejoy, A O *The Great Chain of Being* Cambridge, Mass. 1936
Lovelock, J *Gaia* Oxford 1979
———— *The Ages of Gaia* Oxford 1988
MacQuarrie, J *Principles of Christian Theology* rev edn London 1977
Malcolm, N *Memory and Mind* Ithaca 1977
Mascall, E L *He Who is* London 1943
———— *Existence and Analogy* London 1944
———— *Christian Theology and Natural Science* London 1956
———— *Words and Images* London 1957
———— *The Triune God* Worthing 1986
Medawar, Sir Peter *Induction and Intuition in Scientific Thought* London 1969
Meijering, E J *Orthodoxy and Platonism in Athanasius* Leiden 1974
Mitchell, Basil *The Philosophy of Religion* Oxford 1971
———— *The Justification of Religious Belief* London 1973
———— *Morality: Religious and Secular* Oxford 1980
Moeller, C & Philips, G *The Theology of Grace* London 1961
Moltmann, Jurgen *God in Creation* London 1985
Monod, Jacques *Chance and Necessity* London 1971
Moody, R A *Life after Life* Covington 1975
———— *Reflections on Life after Life* London 1977
Moore, G F *Judaism in the First Centuries of the Christian Era* Cambridge, Mass. 1927-3
Moule, C F D *The Origin of Christology* Cambridge 1977
Muldoon, S & Carrington H *The Projection of the Astral Body* London 1929
———— *The Phenomena of Astral Projection* London 1951
Munitz, M K *Cosmic Understanding* Princeton 1986
Munz P *Our Knowledge of the Growth of Knowledge* London 1985
Murdoch, Iris *The Sovereignty of the Good* London 1970
———— *The Fire and the Sun* Oxford 1977
Nagel, Thomas *The View from Nowhere* Oxford 1986
Neisser, Ulric *Cognition and Reality* San Francisco 1976
E Neumann *The Origins and History of Consciousness* London 1954
Nielsen, K *Contemporary Critiques of Religion* London 1971
O'Connor, D & Oakley, F *Creation: The Impact of an Idea* New York 1969
Oakley, F *The Crucial Centuries* London 1979
———— *Omnipotence Covenant and Order* Ithaca 1984
Oberman, H A *The Dawn of the Reformation* Edinburgh 1986
Owen, I M with Sparrow, M *Conjuring up Philip* Toronto 1976
Ozment, S *The Age of Reform 1250-1550* New Haven 1980
Pannenberg, W The Philosophical Concept of God in *Basic Questions in Theology* London
        1972
Peacocke, A R *Creation and the World of Science* Oxford 1979

Peacocke, A R *God and the New Biology* London 1986
———   *Theology for a Scientific Age* Oxford 1990
Pelikan, J *The Christian Tradition* vol 1 Chicago 1971
———   *Jesus through the Centuries* New Haven 1985
Penrose, R *The Emperor's New Clothes* Oxford 1989
Piaget, J *Biology and Knowledge* Edinburgh 1971
——— *The Principles of Genetic Epistemology* London 1972
Piault, B *What is the Trinity?* London 1959
Pollard, W G *Chance and Providence* London 1959
Polkinghorne, J *One World* London 1986
———   *Science and Providence* London 1989
Popper, K R *The Logic of Scientific Discovery* London 1959 and later edns
Portalié, Eugène *A Guide to the Thought of St Augustine* London 1960
Prestige, G L *God in Patristic Thought* London 1956
Price, H H *Some Aspects of the Conflict between Science and Religion* Cambridge 1953
———   *Essays in the Philosophy of Religion* Oxford 1972
———   Psychical Research and Human Personality in *Science and ESP* ed J R Smythies
            London 1967
Prigogine, I & Stengers, I *Order out of Chaos* London 1984
Quick, O C *Doctrines of the Creed* London 1938
Rahner, K *The Trinity* London 1970
Ramsey, M *From Gore to Temple* London 1960
Ring, K Life at Death New York 1980
Rist, J M *Plotinus: the Road to Reality* Cambridge 1967
———   *Human Value* Leiden 1982
———   *Platonism and its Christian Heritage* London 1985
Roll, W G A Systems Theoretical Approach to Psi in *Current Trends in Psi Research* eds
            Shapin, B & Coly, L New York 1986
Sanders, E P *Paul and Palestinian Judaism* London 1977
———   *Jesus and Judaism* London 1985
Scholem G G *Major Trends in Jewish Mysticism* New York 1946
Schouten, S A A Different Approach for Studying Psi in *Current Trends in Psi Research*
            eds Shapin, B & Coly, L New York 1986
Sertillanges, A D *Foundations of Thomistic Philosophy* Springfield n d
Sheldrake, R A *New Science of Life* London 1981
Sherrard, P *The Greek East and the Latin West* Oxford 1959
———   *Church Papacy and Schism* London 1978
Smith, Morton *Jesus the Magician* London 1978
Stanesby, D *Science Reason and Religion* London 1988
Stead, G C *Divine Substance* Oxford 1977
———   *Substance and Illusion in the Christian Fathers* London 1985
Stevenson, Ian *Telepathic Impressions* Charlottesville 1970
Storr, Anthony *The Integrity of the Personality* London 1960
———   *Jung* London 1973
Taylor, Charles *Hegel* Cambridge 1975
Taylor, J V *The Go-Between God* London 1972
Tillich, Paul *Systematic Theology* London 1953/1957/1964
———   *A History of Christian Thought* London 1968
Trethowan, Illtyd *An Essay in Christian Philosophy* London 1954
———   *Absolute Value* London 1970

Tshishiku, T Eschatology and Cosmology in *Cosmology and Theology* eds Tracy, D &
        Lash, N Edinburgh 1983
Tyrrell, G N M *Apparitions* rev edn London 1953
Ullmann, W *Medieval Foundations of Renaissance Humanism* London 1977
Vermes, Geza *Jesus the Jew* London 1973
————   *Jesus and the World of Judaism* London 1983
von Rad, G *Old Testament Theology* London 1965/75
————   *Wisdom in Israel* London 1972
————   *The Problem of the Hexateuch and other Essays* London 1984
Westermann, Claus *Creation* Philadelphia 1974
————   *What Does the Old Testament Say about God?* London 1979
Wiles, M Does Christology Rest on a Mistake? in *Christ Faith and History* eds Sykes, S
        W & Clayton J P Cambridge 1972
Wiles, M   *The Christian Fathers* London 1966
————   *The Remaking of Christian Doctrine* London 1974
————   *Working Papers in Doctrine* London 1976
Wingren, Gustaf *Man and Incarnation: a Study in the Biblical Theology of Irenaeus*
        Edinburgh 1959
Wolfson, H A *The Philosophy of the Church Fathers* 3rd edn rev Cambridge Mass 1970

INDEX

4 *The Sacral Kingship/La Regalità Sacra.* Contributions to the Central Theme of the VIIIth International Congress for the History of Religions, Rome 1955. 1959. ISBN 90 04 01609 0

8 K. W. Bolle. *The Persistence of Religion.* An Essay on Tantrism and Sri Aurobindo's Philosophy. Repr. 1971. ISBN 90 04 03307 6

11 E. O. James. *The Tree of Life.* An Archaeological Study. 1966. ISBN 90 04 01612 0

12 U. Bianchi (ed.). *The Origins of Gnosticism.* Colloquium Messina 13-18 April 1966. Texts and Discussions. Reprint of the first (1967) ed. 1970. ISBN 90 04 01613 9

14 J. Neusner (ed.). *Religions in Antiquity.* Essays in Memory of Erwin Ramsdell Goodenough. Reprint of the first (1968) ed. 1970. ISBN 90 04 01615 5

16 E. O. James. *Creation and Cosmology.* A Historical and Comparative Inquiry. 1969. ISBN 90 04 01617 1

17 *Liber Amicorum.* Studies in honour of Professor Dr. C. J. Bleeker. Published on the occasion of his retirement from the Chair of the History of Religions and the Phenomenology of Religion at the University of Amsterdam. 1969. ISBN 90 04 03092 1

18 R. J. Z. Werblowsky & C. J. Bleeker (eds.). *Types of Redemption.* Contributions to the Theme of the Study-Conference held at Jerusalem, 14th to 19th July 1968. 1970. ISBN 90 04 01619 8

19 U. Bianchi, C. J. Bleeker & A. Bausani (eds.). *Problems and Methods of the History of Religions.* Proceedings of the Study Conference organized by the Italian Society for the History of Religions on the Occasion of the Tenth Anniversary of the Death of Raffaele Pettazzoni, Rome 6th to 8th December 1969. Papers and discussions. 1972. ISBN 90 04 02640 1

20 K. Kerényi. *Zeus und Hera.* Urbild des Vaters, des Gatten und der Frau. 1972. ISBN 90 04 03428 5

21 *Ex Orbe Religionum.* Studia G. Widengren. Pars prior. 1972. ISBN 90 04 03498 6

22 *Ex Orbe Religionum.* Studia G. Widengren. Pars altera. 1972. ISBN 90 04 03499 4

23 J. A. Ramsaran. *English and Hindi Religious Poetry.* An Analogical Study. 1973. ISBN 90 04 03648 2

25 L. Sabourin. *Priesthood.* A Comparative Study. 1973. ISBN 90 04 03656 3

26 C.J.Bleeker. *Hathor and Thoth.* Two Key Figures of the Ancient Egyptian Religion. 1973. ISBN 90 04 03734 9

27 J.W.Boyd. *Satan and Māra.* Christian and Buddhist Symbols of Evil. 1975. ISBN 90 04 04173 7

28 R.A.Johnson. *The Origins of Demythologizing.* Philosophy and Historiography in the Theology of R.Bultmann. 1974. ISBN 90 04 03903 1

29 E.Berggren. *The Psychology of Confession.* 1975. ISBN 90 04 04212 1

30 C.J.Bleeker. *The Rainbow.* A Collection of Studies in the Science of Religion. 1975. ISBN 90 04 04222 9

31 C.J.Bleeker, G.Widengren & E.J.Sharpe (eds.). *Proceedings of the 12th International Congress, Stockholm 1970.* 1975. ISBN 90 04 04318 7

32 A.-Th.Khoury (ed.), M.Wiegels. *Weg in die Zukunft.* Festschrift für Prof.Dr. Anton Antweiler zu seinem 75. Geburtstag. 1975. ISBN 90 04 05069 8

33 B.L.Smith (ed.). *Hinduism.* New Essays in the History of Religions. Repr. 1982. ISBN 90 04 06788 4

34 V.L.Oliver, *Caodai Spiritism.* A Study of Religion in Vietnamese Society. With a preface by P.Rondot. 1976. ISBN 90 04 04547 3

35 G.R.Thursby. *Hindu-Muslim Relations in British India.* A Study of Controversy, Conflict and Communal Movements in Northern India, 1923-1928. 1975. ISBN 90 04 04380 2

36 A.Schimmel. *Pain and Grace.* A Study of Two Mystical Writers of Eighteenth-century Muslim India. 1976. ISBN 90 04 04771 9

37 J.T.Ergardt. *Faith and Knowledge in Early Buddhism.* An Analysis of the Contextual Structures of an Arahant-formula in the Majjhima-Nikāya. 1977. ISBN 90 04 04841 3

38 U.Bianchi. *Selected Essays on Gnosticism, Dualism, and Mysteriosophy.* 1978. ISBN 90 04 05432 4

39 F.E.Reynolds & Th.M.Ludwig (eds.). *Transitions and Transformations in the History of Religions.* Essays in Honor of Joseph M.Kitagawa. 1980. ISBN 90 04 06112 6

40 J.G.Griffiths. *The Origins of Osiris and his Cult.* 1980. ISBN 90 04 06096 0

41 B.Layton (ed.). *The Rediscovery of Gnosticism.* Proceedings of the International Conference on Gnosticism at Yale, New Haven, Conn., March 28-31, 1978. Two vols.
   1. *The School of Valentinus.* 1980. ISBN 90 04 06177 0
   2. *Sethian Gnosticism.* 1981. ISBN 90 04 06178 9

42 H.Lazarus-Yafeh. *Some Religious Aspects of Islam.* A Collection of Articles. 1980. ISBN 90 04 06329 3

43 M.Heerma van Voss, D.J.Hoens, G.Mussies, D. van der Plas & H. te Velde (eds.). *Studies in Egyptian Religion, dedicated to Professor Jan Zandee.* 1982. ISBN 90 04 06728 0

44 P.J.Awn. *Satan's Tragedy and Redemption.* Iblīs in Sufi Psychology. With a foreword by A.Schimmel. 1983. ISBN 90 04 06906 2

45 R. Kloppenborg (ed.). *Selected Studies on Ritual in the Indian Religions*. Essays to D. J. Hoens. 1983. ISBN 90 04 07129 6

46 D. J. Davies. *Meaning and Salvation in Religious Studies*. 1984. ISBN 90 04 07053 2

47 J. H. Grayson. *Early Buddhism and Christianity in Korea*. A Study in the Implantation of Religion. 1985. ISBN 90 04 07482 1

48 J. M. S. Baljon. *Religion and Thought of Shāh Walī Allāh Dihlawī, 1703-1762*. 1986. ISBN 90 04 07684 0

50 S. Shaked, D. Shulman & G. G. Stroumsa (eds.). *Gilgul*. Essays on Transformation, Revolution and Permanence in the History of Religions, dedicated to R. J. Zwi Werblowsky. 1987. ISBN 90 04 08509 2

51 D. van der Plas (ed.). *Effigies Dei*. Essays on the History of Religions. 1987. ISBN 90 04 08655 2

52 J. G. Griffiths. *The Divine Verdict*. A Study of Divine Judgement in the Ancient Religions. 1991. ISBN 90 04 09231 5

53 K. Rudolph. *Geschichte und Probleme der Religionswissenschaft*. 1991. ISBN 90 04 09503 9

54 A. N. Balslev & J. N. Mohanty (eds.). *Religion and Time*. 1993. ISBN 90 04 09583 7

55 E. Jacobson. *The Deer Goddess of Ancient Siberia*. A Study in the Ecology of Belief. 1993. ISBN 90 04 09628 0

56 B. Saler. *Conceptualizing Religion*. Immanent Anthropologists, Transcendent Natives, and Unbounded Categories. 1993. ISBN 90 04 09585 3

57 C. Knox. *Changing Christian Paradigms*. And their Implications for Modern Thought. 1993. ISBN 90 04 09670 1

58 J. Cohen. *The Origins and Evolution of the Moses Nativity Story*. 1993. ISBN 90 04 09652 3

59 S. Benko. *The Virgin Goddess*. Studies in the Pagan and Christian Roots of Mariology. 1993. ISBN 90 04 09747 3

60 Z. P. Thundy. *Buddha and Christ*. Nativity Stories and Indian Traditions. 1993. ISBN 90 04 09741 4

ISSN 0169-8834

DATE DUE